Asian American Spies

Asian American Spies

*How Asian Americans Helped Win the
Allied Victory*

Brian Masaru Hayashi

OXFORD
UNIVERSITY PRESS

Oxford University Press is a department of the University of Oxford. It furthers
the University's objective of excellence in research, scholarship, and education
by publishing worldwide. Oxford is a registered trade mark of Oxford University
Press in the UK and certain other countries.

Published in the United States of America by Oxford University Press
198 Madison Avenue, New York, NY 10016, United States of America.

Library of Congress Cataloging-in-Publication Data
Names: Hayashi, Brian Masaru, 1955– author.
Title: Asian American spies : how Asian Americans helped win
the Allied victory / Brian Masaru Hayashi.
Other titles: How Asian Americans helped win the Allied victory
Description: New York, NY : Oxford University Press, [2021] |
Includes bibliographical references and index.
Identifiers: LCCN 2021001784 (print) | LCCN 2021001785 (ebook) |
ISBN 9780195338850 (hardback) | ISBN 9780190092863 (epub) |
ISBN 9780190092856
Subjects: LCSH: World War, 1939–1945—Secret service—United States. |
World War, 1939-1945—Participation, Asian American. | Asian American
spies—United States—History—20th century. | United States. Office of
Strategic Services—History. | World War, 1939–1945—Propaganda. |
Propaganda, American—Asia—History—20th century.
Classification: LCC D810.S7 H38 2021 (print) | LCC D810.S7 (ebook) |
DDC 940.54867308995—dc23
LC record available at https://lccn.loc.gov/2021001784
LC ebook record available at https://lccn.loc.gov/2021001785

DOI: 10.1093/oso/9780195338850.001.0001

1 3 5 7 9 8 6 4 2
Printed by Sheridan Books, Inc., United States of America

For Yumei Song and Esther Yumi Hayashi

CONTENTS

ACKNOWLEDGMENTS

This book began years ago as part of a chapter for another book. However, finding a wealth of primary sources and a dearth of secondary materials, I expanded this project and, in the process, multiplied the number of people who helped make this book possible. At the early stages of the book, certain knowledgeable individuals encouraged me along the way, providing information, leads, and tips in the form of interviews that proved invaluable for this project. The Japanese American Veterans Association members, and Terry Shima and Grant Ichikawa in particular, provided a contact list of potential interviewees, some of whom appear in this book. Father Richard Kim and his brother Arthur, too, supplied me with many stories and insights about their family and life in prewar Shanghai that intersected with my work on the OSS. Dick Hamada, Maggie Ikeda, Shirley Chun-Ming, and Howard Furumoto opened their homes to me and allowed themselves to be interviewed about their involvement or their family members' role in the OSS. Debra Thurston, Hai and Tramh Le, and Ty and Loan Nguyen, all friends of mine, helped by putting this vagabond researcher up overnight as he explored the archives of key libraries in their area.

As the search for Asian Americans in the OSS expanded, my dependence on archivists and librarians enlarged to include a considerable number of specialists. At the National Archives and Records Administration II in College Park, Maryland, I received guidance from Larry MacDonald regarding the OSS records that he and a host of volunteers processed and organized after the CIA released them. The late John Taylor was especially helpful in pointing out the largely untapped Shanghai Municipal Police records the CIA pulled out of China before 1949. Nathan Patch, William Cunliffe, and Eric van Slander devoted an enormous amount of their time to track down personnel records of various individuals within the office. Jennifer Cole and Tad Bennicoff of the Seeley-Mudd Library at Princeton University, and Peggy Dillard of the George Marshall Library in Lexington, Virginia, went above and beyond the call of duty by locating and copying documents related to William Lockwood and Peter Kim. Naoki Kanno, senior fellow at the Military Archives Center for Military History at the National Institute for Defense Studies in Tokyo, was quite helpful in my search through various materials. Susan Hammond, director of the War Legacies Project and John McAuliffe, founder and director of the Fund for Reconciliation and Development, searched through their transcripts related to Mac Shin and Frank Tan's activities in Vietnam.

Other archivists and librarians who were generous with their time included Robert Tam of the Chinese Historical Society Archives in Honolulu, Marjorie Lee of the UCLA Asian American Studies Reading Room, and Sherman Seki of University of Hawai'i, Manoa. In tracking down the social scientists who worked with Asian Americans in the OSS, Timothy Driscoll of the Pusey Library at Harvard University, Susan Irving of the Rockefeller Archives Center, Susan Jania of the Bentley Historical Library at the University of Michigan, David Sun and Carole Leadenham of the Hoover Institution of War and Peace at Stanford University, and Anne Watanabe, Octavio Olvera, Simon Elliott, and Jeffrey Rankin of Special Collections at the UCLA Library were all extremely accommodating during my long perusals of their materials.

The extensive research behind this book would not have been possible without financial assistance or independent wealth. Lacking the latter, I was able to complete this project with the former. The Mitsubishi Foundation generously provided me with funds that allowed me to cross-check OSS materials against the Special Operations Executive records held at the National Archives in London and the Guomingdang records at the National Archives in Xindian City, Taiwan. The Japanese Ministry of Culture, Education, and Sports amply supplied me with research grants over portions of this project that paid for much of the high cost of traveling and lodging in so many different locations where the documents were deposited. In addition, my previous academic home, the Graduate School of Human and Environmental Studies, Kyoto University, supplied general financial assistance with the high cost of copying and equipment during the writing of this book. Henry Choi, Sonia Kim, and Aki Yamamoto helped me locate certain documents in Japanese and Korean languages. Anran Wei assisted with some of the translation of the Chinese-language materials, as did Jinhee Kwon, who ably assisted me when I went to inspect the Syngman Rhee Presidential Papers at Yonsei University in Seoul, Korea. Shōtarō Shindo and Shinichi Itagaki, as usual, provided valuable hints and insights from their own research which immeasurably help improve this manuscript. Funding from the Department of History, Kent State University, where I now have settled, was also helpful.

Special thanks goes to individuals who helped make the manuscript better. Susan Ferber, editor, provided many insightful comments, suggestions, and corrections, making this manuscript far more readable than it had been before. Lon Kurashige, Valerie Matsumoto, Yasuko Takezawa, and Rumi Yasutake gave invaluable advice along with opportunities to present portions of the research at their conferences.

And finally, my family deserves mention. My wife, Yumei, helped me as I struggled with some of the Chinese-language documents, digitally photographed other materials, and took care of our daughter Esther, whose help occasionally made the research and writing that much more difficult to do. This book is dedicated to them.

ABBREVIATIONS

AGFRTS	Air Ground Forces Resources & Technical Staff
AUS	Army of the United States
CBI	China-Burma-India Theater
CN	Chinese Nationalist (dollars)
CNO	Chief of Naval Operations, United States Navy
COMINTERN	Communist International
CPUSA	Communist Party of the United States of America
CT	China Theater
COI	Coordinator of Information
DOJ	Department of Justice
FE	Far East section
FBI	Federal Bureau of Investigation
GBT	Gordon-Bernard-Tan spy team
IBT	India-Burma Theater
ICP	Indochinese Communist Party
JACL	Japanese American Citizens League
JCS	Joint Chiefs of Staff
MID	Military Intelligence Division
MO	Morale Operations Division, Office of Strategic Services
NKVD	Narodnyy Komissariat Vnutrennikh Dei or People's Commissariat for Internal Affairs
ONI	Office of Naval Intelligence
OSS	Office of Strategic Services
OWI	Office of War Information
R&A	Research and Analysis Division, Office of Strategic Services
ROTC	Reserve Officer Training Corps
SACO	Sino-American Special Technical Cooperative Organization
SI	Secret Intelligence, Office of Strategic Services

SIS   Secret Intelligence Service (British)
SO   Special Operations Division, Office of Strategic Services
SOE   Special Operations Executive (British)
SSU   Strategic Services Unit
USN   United States Navy
WRA   War Relocation Authority
X-2   Counterintelligence Division, Office of Strategic Services

NOTE ON TRANSLITERATION

Personal Names
Chiang Kai-shek (Jiang Jieshi)
Chou Enlai (Zhou Enlai)
Ho Chi Minh (Nguyễn Sinh Cung)
Ilhan New (Yu Il Han)
Key H. Chang (Chang Ki Hyung)
Kilsoo Hahn (Kilsu Hahn)
Mao Tse-tung (Mao Zedong)
Pak Hoy Wong (Congxakhai)
Sisavang Vong (Sisavang Phoulivong)
Soong, T.V. (Sòng Zǐwén)
Syngman Rhee (Yi Sŭng-man)
Tai Li (Dai Li)

Geographic location names
Amoy (Xiamen)
Annam (central Vietnam)
Bias Bay (Daya Bay)
Burma (Myanmar)
Canton (Guangzhou)
Ceylon (Sri Lanka)
Chengtu (Chengdu),
Chinnanpo (Chinnampo)
Chungking (Chongqing)
Djakarta (Jakarta)
Dutch East Indies (Republic of Indonesia)
Foochow (Fuzhou)
Fo Shan (Foshan or Fatshen)
Foochow (Fuzhou)
Formosa (Taiwan)
Fort Bayard (Zhanjiang)

Genzan (Wonsan)
Hankow (Hankou)
Hoifung (Haifeng)
Hsian (Xian)
Icheng (Yichang)
Kangwŏn-do (Gangwon)
Karafuto (South Sakhalin)
Keijo (Seoul)
Kiukiang (Jiujiang)
Kongmoon (Jiangmen)
Kukong (Shaoguan)
Kwangtung (Guangdong)
Kweilin (Guilin)
Kweiyang (Guiyang)
Kweiyang (Guiyang)
Kweilin (Guilin)
Liuchow (Liuzhou)
Malacca (Malaysia)
Malaya (Malaysia)
Manchukuo (Manchuria)
Maoming (Mowming)
Mengtze (Mengzi)
Moneta (Gardena, California)
Mukden (Shenyang)
Nanking (Nanjing)
Pakhoi (Beihai)
Saigon (Ho Chi Minh City)
Seishin (Chongjin)
Shameen (Shamian)
Sheklung (Shih-lung)
Shensi (Shaanxi)
Soochow (Suzhou)
Suiho (Sup'ung)
Sunwai (Sun Wui, Xhinhui)
Swatow (Shantou)
Tientsin (Tianjin)
Tsinan (Jinan)
Tientsin (Tianjin)
Toishan (Taishan)
Waichow (Huizhou)
Yangtze River (Yangzi)
Yenan (Yan'an)

Asian American Spies

Prologue

A Trojan Horse?

On a cold day after Christmas 1944, Joe Teiji Koide stepped forward and placed his hand over the Bible as others looked on. He pledged his solemn oath of office, as had so many others as part of their induction into the United States' first centralized intelligence agency, the Office of Strategic Services (OSS). His words echoed through the room in more ways than one:

> I do further solemnly swear (or affirm) that I will support and defend the Constitution and laws of the United States of America against all enemies, foreign and domestic; that I will bear true faith and allegiance to the same; that I take this obligation freely, without any mental reservation or purpose of evasion; and that I will well and faithfully discharge the duties of the office on which I am about to enter. So help me God.[1]

After the ceremony was over, Koide went to Catalina Island, some twenty-two miles southwest of Los Angeles, California, for his training. Koide worked for the Morale Operations section of the Office on Project Green, a radio propaganda unit designing materials for broadcast direct to Japan from the recently-captured Saipan in the Marianas Island. The project was based in San Francisco, a city from which thousands of Koide's coethnics were forcibly removed only three years earlier. He enjoyed a $3,000 annual salary, which was more than ten times higher than his previous one in the War Relocation Authority camp at Heart Mountain, Wyoming. Koide directed and produced radio scripts designed to undermine the support the Imperial Japanese forces received from that nation's civilian populace. Before San Francisco, when Koide was in the "Collingwood" group at a secret location outside of Washington, DC, he had proven himself a capable leader deserving of his high salary and leadership status. Koide's recruiter Thomas McFadden wrote:

> He and three other members of the staff have demonstrated outstanding ability and have been designated as the chief creative workers of the group. Their work is of a highly skilled and technical nature requiring a broad educational background combined with a natural aptitude for the creation of subversive propaganda. Subject and the three other individuals in question direct the other Japanese personnel in their work and have been given positions involving a great deal of responsibility.[2]

Yet Joe Koide's behavior prior to working for the OSS raises questions about his loyalty, despite his obvious skills and production. One might excuse his invoking of God's help as simply verbalizing the standard wording of the oath, but his pledge made "without mental reservation" to support the Constitution "against all enemies" raised questions after the war, given his membership in the Communist Party in Moscow and New York City during the 1930s. Worse, his behavior prior to joining the OSS made some Communist Party members doubt his commitment to the Allied war effort, though they kept silent during the war. During the 1970s and 1980s, Koide came under attack from Communist Party members Karl Yoneda and James Oda, both of whom accused him of undermining the Party while serving as its underground agent. He violated basic security procedures regarding membership lists, even though he received training at the Lenin International School in Moscow during the 1930s, where he learned from the Communist International (COMINTERN) about the art of espionage, sabotage, and propaganda. In particular, Koide compiled a list of forty-seven Japanese communists in 1938, a copy of which surfaced in February 1972 in the Imperial Japanese (Police) Security Bureau's files, raising suspicions that he was, in fact, an agent of Imperial Japan.

Koide was also known to have stirred up draft resistance among Japanese Americans interned at the War Relocation Authority's camp at Heart Mountain, actions deemed by Party and non-Party members alike to be detrimental to the Allied war cause. Hence, Koide's life appeared "like that of a double or triple agent," as James Oda declared.[3]

AN AGENT FOR HIRE?

Kunsung Rie crept through the underbrush as stealthily as possible. His aim in the exercise was to place a "bomb" next to an "enemy" gasoline tank to destroy it. Rie's three-man sabotage team included Jimmy Pyen and Diamond Kimm, all Korean Americans, who had successfully rowed into Johnson's Landing in nylon row boats. They stealthily crept up to the gasoline tank and set their charges, after which the three quietly withdrew to a secluded spot to set up their portable radio set. Rie, the fastest of the three at twenty words a minute, tapped out coded messages and received a reply. The Korean Americans then returned to base where they listened to a critique of their performance on their sabotage practice run at night on Catalina Island in late March 1945.[4]

"Napko" was the name of the sabotage mission that Rie was a part of. Led by Colonel Carl Eifler of the OSS, its departure was scheduled for mid-August 1945. This Special Operations' mission, code-named "Einec," was to land the three Korean Americans in the Chemulpo Bay area, near present-day Incheon, and another three-man Korean American team called "Charo" close to Chinnampo, near Songnam. Both Einec and Charo aimed to establish a base inside Korea from which to report on the Imperial Japanese forces and make contact with the Korean underground. Once completed, they would launch sabotage operations, action that Kunsung Rie preferred to intelligence-gathering. To successfully carry out their mission, however, the OSS required Napko members to complete the necessary training. It also needed them to form social connections with locals to shield them and their collaborators from Imperial Japanese forces and political connections to win the cooperation of the Korean underground. Above all, Napko required loyalty to the Allied cause.[5]

Kunsung Rie met most of Napko's requirements. His social connections were strong—the team was to be based initially at Rie's own house in Korea, which made it necessary for him to undergo plastic surgery to disguise his appearance. Before their mission's mid-August 1945 departure, he had excelled in the OSS training in Special Operations. He was rated "exceptionally well" in sending and receiving coded messages and quite adept at weapons training. His trainer wrote: "Very good with carbine because he likes the weapon." He earned only a "satisfactory" mark in map work, partly because he was inattentive in his military intelligence class. As Lieutenant Robert Carter Jr. wrote, Rie "would rather fire weapons than learn what makes them operate."[6]

But a critical requirement was in doubt. Who or what cause was Rie loyal to? The Office of War Information (OWI) determined that this young

Korean American held "questionable loyalty" after a special hearing on Rie's suitability for federal government service. It withdrew Rie's contract after fifty-eight witnesses, including Korean Americans such as Woon Su Chung, Secretary to the Chairman of the Korean Committee, and Korean independence lobbyist Kilsoo Haan, accused Rie of giving propaganda speeches for the Japanese while employed at the New York Japanese Consulate. They believed Rie had distanced himself· from other "loyal Koreans," fearing actions taken against Japan might trigger "reprisal after the war." OSS Chief of Security Archbold van Beuren informed Carl Eifler that Rie was not trusted by other federal government agencies either: "The Subject is regarded with suspicion by all government departments which have had contact with him, and these suspicions range from allegations that he is a Japanese agent to statements that he is loyal to the Allied cause but very unreliable." Upon further investigation, van Beuren found that Rie could not be trusted with confidential information since he was mercenary: "There is much evidence to indicate that the Subject will always be willing to sell out to the highest bidder and that he cannot be trusted with any type of confidential information."[7]

Evidence notwithstanding, Carl Eifler retained Rie. The colonel believed dropping Rie would in effect abort the mission before it began: "This entire plan of his particular group is built about him and if I lose him I lose the entire striking force of the plan, and I doubt seriously if the entire project could be carried on without this original striking force." Moreover, Eifler believed Rie's motive for serving on Napko involved Korean nationalism. He saw firsthand Rie's ruthlessness in wanting to assassinate a fellow countryman for actions deemed detrimental to the cause of Korean independence. When asked if he had any misgivings, the colonel responded: "Definitely not, because the man, in going back, is going back to a hard life of starvation, while carrying on the work which he is to do, where on the other hand he could live in the United States in comparative peace and comfort."[8]

AN AGENT TURNED?

"Where is Lincoln Kan?" Wilfred Smith, his superior, asked aloud in February 1945 after the suave Chinese American had not been heard from for about six months. Kan was dispatched on a spy mission into Japanese-occupied Guangdong Province of southern China. As a leader of one of four spy teams sent to this region, Kan was assigned to Sector Two (Macao) to gather intelligence on Imperial Japanese forces stationed there. His mission preceded a ground assault by Chinese Nationalist troops seeking to capture southern China and open up a port for the safe arrival of American "Liberty" supply ships that year. Kan's "Akron" team gathered information critical for planning this campaign, code-named "Carbonado." He needed to uncover the deployment, numbers, weaponry, and morale—information known as Order of Battle—of the Imperial Japanese forces the Chinese Nationalist troops would likely face, as well as the attitudes of the Pearl River Delta region's local population toward support, resistance, or neutrality in the event of such an assault. All of this, Wilfred Smith of the Fourteenth Air Force, Charles Dewey, and Charles D. Ambelang Jr.—Kan's superiors— expected Kan and the Akron team to deliver by March 26, 1945.[9]

Lincoln Sat Hing Kan, also known as Kan Yuen Fook, was well-qualified for the mission. Code-named "Karlin," Kan understood the importance of Order of Battle information since he was a lieutenant in the army and was experienced at collecting such data. He had once served in the famed "Flying Tigers" of the Fourteenth Air Force's Air and Ground Forces Resources Technical Staff (AGFRTS). He was also socially well-connected to Guangdong region, which provided him a measure of protection. His grandfather, father, and uncles were all owners of a cigarette and tobacco enterprise known as Nanyang Brothers Company, with an estimated value in 1924 of twelve million dollars. His loyalty was to the United States. After all, he had been born an American citizen, in New York City on February 12, 1919, and named after the sixteenth president of the United States, whose birthdate he shared. Kan himself was fluent in both Chinese and English. His language skills came easily to him as he was raised in Shanghai, and his English language skills were well-honed at the American School there. He had socialized freely with other American students, as evidenced by his founding of the Photographic Society. His college education began at the University of North Carolina as a political science major in 1938. He took a leave of absence to enlist in 1940, undergoing army training at Fort Bragg, North Carolina. Due to his training and qualifications, Kan understood the risk he was taking and, prior to departure behind enemy lines, he left a letter with Charles Fenn to deliver to his family, "just in case anything happens," he told Major Harold C. Faxon. With the requisite linguistic skills, cultural and social connections to the targeted region, military training, social science background, and correct "racial uniform," Kan was prepared for the challenging assignment facing him.[10]

Kan's assignment was fraught with danger. He faced the uncertain loyalties of many guerrillas—the Guangdong and Guangxi provincial areas alone had some 10,000 who could suddenly turn against the Chinese American and reveal his identity to the Imperial Japanese forces. Or he could be assassinated by one of the thousands of agents serving Tai Li, head of a Chinese Nationalist government's intelligence agency, who swore to kill any OSS operatives operating inside China without Chinese Nationalist government approval. Transiting by water was equally dangerous. The area was known for centuries for its piratical activities and the notorious pirate Kit Kung Wong preyed upon the boat traffic in the region. He was reputedly in the pay of Imperial Japanese intelligence. Compounding these dangers, Kan faced a formidable opponent—a well-trained Imperial Japanese intelligence unit. Headquartered at the Japanese Consulate office in Macao, they had recruited a large number of Chinese locals as informants who kept them well apprised about the local population. Under the capable leadership of Colonel Toyo Sawa, Vice-Consul Kan faced a formidable opponent and thus had to move around the region with considerable caution.[11]

The message from Karlin received on February 20, 1945, provided little comfort to Kan's superior. After such a long absence of contact, Wilfred Smith and Charles Dewey sent a test message to authenticate Kan's identity. "Every possible precaution in being taken," Smith assured the Akron mission planners. He planned "to ascertain the authenticity of his messages and a test message is being given Lt. Kan during the schedule on the night of 23 February." Karlin, however, gave an unsatisfactory response to the test message, raising suspicions that Kan had been captured, tortured, and "turned" by their nemesis Colonel Toyo Sawa.[12]

A TROJAN HORSE?

Both immediate supervisors and top-level OSS officers responsible for the spy and saboteur operations showed no apparent concern for the risks involved with two of the three Asian American agents. Herbert Little, chief of Morale Operations and the main recruiter for the "Green Japanese" American team, admitted that he and his staff gave only "carefully worded suggestions," not orders regarding the black radio propaganda materials they were creating. "It was rule by indirection," Little confessed, despite the obvious distrust by some European American staff members who scrutinized the materials submitted by Koide and other Japanese Americans for covert messages. Henson Robinson, chief of the Schools and Training, instructed Philip Allen at the Catalina Island training center to ignore Security's red flags on Kunsung Rie and proceed with Napko. After observing firsthand Rie and Napko members' training, the director, William Donovan, too showed no concern and took the plan directly to the War Department's Planning Group for approval.[13]

Following Donovan's lead, other high-ranking OSS leaders pressed forward with their plans, ignoring the possibility of an Asian American Trojan Horse in the midst. Instead, they saw opportunities for including experienced agents like Lincoln Kan with his wide commercial, social, and political connections in China into their postwar spy network for East Asia. In early May 1945, Paul Helliwell and Duncan Lee, legal advisor to the office and a colleague of Director William Donovan prior to the war, determined the best espionage system for East Asia would involve bringing into their fold experienced agents and American expatriates residing in the target area. Duncan Lee, whom Helliwell wanted to direct the entire postwar spy network for East Asia, further advised William Donovan: "An efficient intelligence system must have many roots among the masses of the population. In this respect, I believe we can well learn from the British and other Europeans in Asia who certainly make full use of their commercial people."[14]

Only those near the bottom of the chain of command continued to doubt the loyalty of the Asian American agents working directly under them. The European American personnel in the San Francisco Green office constantly checked the translations and content of the materials produced by the Japanese American staff, searching for hidden messages to the enemy. The Security Investigation office of the OSS continued protesting Rie's inclusion in Napko. Kan's superiors harbored doubts about the authenticity of his radio messages as well. Suspecting capture, Wilfred Smith decided to continue communications with Karlin for the purpose of feeding Sawa disinformation:

> Our agent [Karlin] in Macao is maintaining a daily radio schedule with us but . . . is at present suspicious as to his security and knowing something of Colonel SAWA (Chief Special Affairs Bureau in Macao) and his methods give increasing reason for misgiving. Our agent has been given test questions and has not entirely given satisfaction in his answers. However, in any case, . . . he will be useful, if not for our intelligence perhaps we can give [disinformation] . . . through him to the Japanese.[15]

The action and behavior of the three Asian American agents raises a question about their role within the OSS. Which of these OSS agents worked, voluntarily or involuntarily, for the enemy? To find this answer, one must understand how the OSS and Asian Americans understood each other, and their respective roles within that organization and the larger American war effort of World War II.

Introduction

"Race" was changing in the years immediately prior to and during World War II. For many European Americans in the Office of Strategic Services (OSS), it was no longer an idea that ascribed a fixed set of social or cultural characteristics to a given ethnic or racial group. Instead, William Donovan, the founding director of America's first wartime centralized intelligence agency, took pride in his organization's ethnic and racial inclusiveness by requiring loyalty, along with cultural and linguistic skills, as the basis for employment. On September 28, 1945, he characterized the OSS in his final speech to his employees terminating the five-year-old spy agency as "a group of Americans constituting a cross section of racial origins" that successfully collected, analyzed, and disseminated strategic and tactical intelligence necessary for America's decision-makers during the war. In the audience were African Americans, Latino Americans, and Asian Americans.[1]

Donovan's claim appears accurate as it applies to Asian Americans. Within this hybrid federal government agency of civilian and military personnel, Asian Americans numbered over 400 or under 2 percent of 23,978 names in the OSS personnel records. These numbers suggest racial discrimination at the entry level, since Asian Americans comprised roughly 3 percent of the total American population for the continental United States and its territories of Alaska, Guam, Hawai'i, and the Philippines. Yet these Asian Americans served in roles that affirm the agency's racial inclusiveness. Those with the necessary linguistic skills translated the mass of collected materials and documents for the Research and Analysis (R&A) section's reports on East Asia, earning high marks among military officers and federal government officials. Others slipped behind enemy lines, gathering covertly intelligence on the enemy forces and local conditions for Secret Intelligence (SI), having the requisite linguistic and cultural skills, local social connections, and the correct racial uniform. Still others served in Special Operations (SO), conducting raids against the Imperial Japanese forces in Burma, while those in Morale Operations (MO) cranked out propaganda pamphlets and radio broadcasts to stiffen Chinese resistance to Imperial Japanese occupiers and weaken the Japanese resolve in fighting against the Allied forces. Nearly all held the rank of "technical" personnel: noncommissioned or commissioned officers to whom European American enlisted men serving under them were required to salute and obey orders. In nearly all cases, Asian American civilian personnel handled classified materials without restrictions on their security clearance. Their salaries, too, were commensurate with other OSS employees of similar qualifications instead of relegation to the secretarial pool and janitorial service.[2]

Yet writers on the OSS differ in their assessment of the spy agency's racial inclusiveness. Bradley Smith suggests that racial segregation was commonplace, pointing to an instance of a Japanese American R&A employee unable to obtain security clearance to the Library of Congress due to race. However, Douglas Waller disagrees. He portrays the OSS as the opposite—very racially inclusive—after consulting a much a wider range of documents than what had been available to Smith thirty years prior. He portrays Donovan as staunchly defending one of his African American employees against racial discrimination and taking exception to the mass removal and internment of West Coast Japanese Americans.[3]

In addition to race, loyalty is another important issue when considering Asian Americans in World War II. The OSS placed a premium on loyalty, requiring it of all their employees to ensure that the intelligence they collected, analyzed, and disseminated to other federal government agencies was not disinformation originating with the enemy. Even today, the Central Intelligence Agency (CIA)'s employment ads list patriotism or loyalty to the United States as one of their requirements. But here too, one simply cannot borrow from previous studies on the subject matter. Past studies of Asian Americans in general portray them as exclusively loyal to the United States when loyalty is often not singular, nor directed solely toward one country such as the United States. Such depictions of Asian Americans as political "model minorities" presents only one side of a multilayered, fluid phenomenon known as loyalty.

Moving beyond oversimplification, this book widens the coverage of the OSS. Along with MO, it explores the SI, SO, and R&A sections to provide a wider and more complete picture of Japanese Americans in the OSS. It also examines Chinese Americans and Korean Americans, as their historical experiences in the OSS were intertwined with one another in the agency. The book does not cover Filipino Americans, however, since the OSS was banned from operating in the Philippines by General Douglas MacArthur, eliminating the need for such ethnic heritage speakers. In terms of time periodization, the book covers closely Asian Americans and their prewar backgrounds, as those experiences influenced their wartime participation in the OSS, a dimension often overlooked in studies on Asian American intelligence agents. The book also covers some months after the Japanese formally surrendered on September 2, 1945, as some of these Asian Americans were detailed to conduct war crimes investigations allegedly committed by other Asian Americans in collaboration with the Imperial Japanese forces.[4]

In this book, therefore, both race and loyalty are understood as fluid social constructions. They are not seen as a fixed, essentialized phenomenon, nor are they restricted to a single country, but can be multiple and changing. This study utilizes the social constructivist approach of Simon Keller to understand loyalty and its antithesis, treason and collaboration. Loyalty is not a stable identity in which, for example, one is born in the United States, therefore one is loyal to that country to the exclusion of others. Keller defines loyalty as "the attitude and associated pattern of conduct that is constituted by an individual's taking something's side" and once taken, makes "essential reference to a special relationship" between the individual and the object of that individual's loyalty. Patriotism is one type of loyalty that expresses itself in belief, and requires the creation of an imagined special relationship. It does not originate from where one is born, raised, or educated; it is not *sui generis* nor a product of the "historical self." Similarly, treason requires betrayal of that imaginary special relationship by the adoption of another object of loyalty at war with the United States. Article III of the Constitution defines treason as "levying war" on the United States and "adhering to the nation's enemies, giving aid and comfort." Treason and loyalty are therefore social constructions whose meaning change over time, especially after 1945. Collaboration is understood to mean "the continuing exercise of power under the pressure produced by the presence of an occupying power," a definition that removes the negative association with treason imposed by those on the winning side of a war.[5]

Other terms used in this book related to espionage should be mentioned here. Intelligence is, as John Ferris aptly puts it, "the collection and analysis of information by a power, to enable it to make maximum use of its resources against rivals and potential enemies." Such kind of information may be *tactical* in nature, designed to answer the question, "What is the enemy composed of?" This includes the targeted groups' military capabilities, such as the number of troops, the specifications of their weaponry, and general state of readiness for combat. Other information gathered and analyzed include *operational* intelligence aimed at determining where the enemy forces are deployed. To collect this type of intelligence, sometimes it is done overtly, as when military attaches of the army or navy are assigned to work in foreign countries. At other times, the information is gathered covertly or in secret. In the latter, an *agent* or an individual capable of gathering such information covertly is used. Occasionally used is a *double agent*, or one who has switched sides while in the service of one intelligence agency. Communication from the agent to his or her supervisor or case officer is usually done in writing or by radio in a language disguised so as to render the message meaningless to the casual reader. A *code* is where words, phrases, letters, or syllables are used to replace a plaintext element. A *cipher* is where a letter (or two at most) is represented by another letter or number. *Strategic intelligence* concerns what the enemy or ally is likely to do within the limits of their military capabilities. To determine intent, such agencies must pull together a wide range of information including the personalities and their tendencies in decision-making, and the political, economic, social, and cultural factors that come into play in the decision-making process. Agencies usually gather such information from *open sources* or those materials such as newspapers, magazines, technical and academic journals, radio broadcasts, and other sources deemed accessible to the public. Intelligence groups sometimes engage in propaganda work as well. The OSS conducted such operations, spreading disinformation to undermine morale and sow confusion among enemy military and civilian populations. Their distribution of leaflets and transmission of radio broadcasts for that end was known as "black" propaganda, as opposed to "white" propaganda, which is a straightforward and generally verifiable information. The latter was handled by the Office of War Information (OWI), an agency that also employed Asian Americans and is the subject of another book.[6]

In addition, some terms in Japanese are worth noting. Japanese Americans after World War II often use generational terms. *Issei* refers to the first generation that immigrated from Japan to the United States. *Nisei* refers to the second-generation or those born in the United States and its territories. Other terms, such as *kibei*, refer to American-born Japanese who spent some time in Japan before returning to the United States. *Yobiyose* refers to those Japanese who were born in Japan but came at an early age to the United States. *Inu* refers to "spy" in the singular or plural.[7]

Primary sources used in this study are another reason why *Asian American Spies* stands apart from other books. Unlike previous studies, this book takes advantage of a much wider set of documents related to the subject. The CIA released to the National Archives and Records Administration nearly 4,000 cubic feet of OSS documents in the 1990s and, after 2000, made available the personnel records and other recently declassified materials that are rich in detail and shed considerable light on OSS operations. To verify the essential integrity of the OSS documents, OSS records were checked against materials from their rival organizations—the SOE and the OWI—as well as former disgruntled employees such as J. Arthur Duff. The study also utilizes personal papers of various individuals who served in the OSS and were well-positioned to observe these Asian Americans. A few Asian American spies left their personal papers, which are also used here. To further sketch their backgrounds, materials in Chinese, Korean, and Japanese languages from around the world are also used for this study, the former two with considerable assistance of native speakers. Together, these sources provide a new look at the OSS, Asian Americans, and how they understood and constructed loyalty during their service in World War II.[8]

However, memoirs and oral interviews by former OSS personnel are used selectively. They are understood as being "between memory and history," to borrow a phrase from Pierre Nora, because their recollections of historical events are shaped by additional factors beyond individual abilities in recall and proximity, temporal and spatial. In the first place, former members of the OSS were legally obligated *not* to reveal publicly their wartime activities in accordance with their oath of office. Only a small handful were given permission to write or talk about their experiences. A half-century after the war ended they were released from their obligation of silence, though many members continued to conceal important details of operations and methods used in carrying out their duties for the OSS. Additionally, memoirs and interviews are subject to "schematic reconstruction," or the reframing of memory over time. When individuals recall their personal experience—or what cognitive psychologists call "episodic memory"—they apply a "schema" to facilitate recall. Those schemas are mental concepts that inform individuals about what to expect from a given situation. The schema or "lessons learned" change the details recalled with the passage of time and are shaped, even invented to fit the "semantic memory." The latter is a memory of knowledge, such as remembering how to speak a foreign language, and begins to shape the episodic memory when former participants gathered together to write accounts of their personal experiences. Hence, they are used only with corroboration from other materials generated at the time of the events under analysis.[9]

The few who received permission to write their memoirs consulted their colleagues prior to publication and avoided subject matters that might reveal ongoing operations. Elizabeth McIntosh, in *Sisterhood of Spies* and her previous book, *Undercover Girl*, penned her memoirs only after consulting with the top officials inside the OSS and the CIA. Carl Eifler wrote his autobiography with Thomas Moon, another SO agent, in *The Deadliest Colonel* and fictionalized names and details to cover his wartime activities thirty years prior. Joe Koide did the same, disguising the names of the personnel in MO he worked with. His two-volume autobiography, initially intended as a work of fiction, was based on unrevealed sources he collected and was written after consulting with colleagues. Unlike reports generated at the time or immediately after an observed event, memoirs and oral interviews are thus shaped by not only the individual author but by other unrevealed sources whose accuracy and proximity cannot be determined without other corroborating sources.[10]

Beyond sources upon which it stands, this book's unusual arrangement and findings require an explanation. The prologue opens with the question of which of the three OSS Asian American personnel in 1945 might have been a double agent or a mole. The first chapter considers the internal structure of the OSS—how it was put together and how its recruitment of agents was handled with respect to race and ethnicity. It finds that the intelligence organization founded by William Donovan was, for the most part, quite liberal with respect to both categories, though with such a large organization instances of discrimination were entirely possible. The second chapter examines Chinese Americans, Japanese Americans, and Korean Americans to assess the risk factors involved in recruiting agents from these ethnic groups. It reveals that there were a handful of Asian Americans recruited to serve foreign intelligence agencies and the risk, while low, nevertheless existed. Chapters 3 to 5 examine three sections of the Asian American agents introduced in the prologue. Joe Koide's MO, whose aim was primarily black propaganda, is examined to better understand how a possible foreign agent could transmit intelligence to another intelligence agency. It finds that this section had a higher risk than others, because MO recruited individuals with loyalty to the Allied cause of defeating the Axis powers rather than to the American Constitution, as had other sections. And it allowed its Asian American personnel considerable latitude in the creation of propaganda materials, both in print and over the radio. In contrast, SO posed the lowest risk of infiltration, in large part because field operations undertaken by this section were well behind enemy lines where the dangers were greatest and where mutual reliance among team members the strongest for survival. Except for their office in Istanbul, Turkey, Secret Intelligence avoided foreign agent penetration, since they carefully recruited agents from groups known for their loyalty to the United States. Counterintelligence and R&A sections were also free from foreign agent penetration, perhaps in part because the former was too small numerically while the latter, the largest section of the OSS, shielded itself from foreign interference by restricting its recruitment to their "old boy network," which kept out foreign agents but also excluded a number of qualified and talented female recruits of all racial and ethnic groups. Chapter 6 delves into the months immediately after Japan's surrender, when OSS Asian Americans were tasked to rescue Allied prisoners of war (POWs) and to investigate war crimes, which included alleged Asian American collaborators. It unveils a small but significant number of Asian Americans who served Imperial Japanese interests voluntarily and involuntarily. The last chapter ends with an examination of loyalty and treason, since these issues were crucial not only for the employment of Asian American agents, but also because many readers today have a particularly strong image of Japanese Americans having a singular loyal to the United States based on the stellar combat record of the 442nd Regimental Combat Team. While true for many Japanese Americans, historical truth is rarely so simple and in this case, both so-called loyal and disloyal Asian Americans are presented here in the belief that the telling of only the former reinforces the model minority image that many scholars today find detrimental. Hopefully, the last chapter will help remove that simplistic image of Japanese Americans as it reconsiders the meaning of loyalty and treason. The epilogue closes the book with a revelation of which OSS member was the agent for a foreign power.[11]

Given these findings, this study offers a new look in three different areas of scholarly examination. For studies on the OSS, *Asian American Spies* provides a valuable corrective to the Europe-centric view of the agency. It also brings to light Asian American agents and their activities for the OSS in ways not possible until 1996, when Congress released all former OSS members from their legal obligation of silence. For Asian American studies, it provides a rare comparative look at three Asian American communities historically, and how social, economic, and cultural tensions within and between these communities created a dynamic mix from which these agents for the OSS were recruited. It also points to how some Asian Americans were able to play a large but behind-the-scene role in postwar American intelligence. And finally, for studies on race and loyalty, this book shows that racial antipathy was far from pervasive in the OSS. *Asian American Spies* demonstrates how the OSS, notably SO and SI, were racially inclusive in part because Asian Americans had the correct racial and cultural uniforms that had greater value in close proximity to the enemy in Asia. This finding contradicts the broad generalizations made by John Dower in *War Without Mercy* and more recently by Peter Schrijvers in *The GI War against Japan*, that antipathetic racial stereotypes against all Japanese was pervasive and deep. Instead, this book finds that race as it applies to Asian Americans in World War II was a social construction whose definitional boundaries of categories of races changed over time, as articulated by Michael Omi and Howard Winant in *Racial Formation in the United States*. Its findings also match those of Lon Kurashige, who demonstrates in *Two Faces of Exclusion* that racialist exclusion was beginning to give way to inclusion of Asian Americans prior to World War II.[12]

A final comment on the spelling used for this study is in order. To the extent possible, the original spelling as it appears in the documents is used. However, for clarity's sake I have added a list of personal names and geographic locations with their *pinyin* pronunciation for the Chinese language and the same for the McCune-Reischauer system for the Korean language. For Japanese names, I have inserted long vowel marks to help those interested and able to read Japanese to better find the documents I have used. Given names followed by surnames appear here, except for those whose names are widely recognized by last name first, such as key leaders and royalty. I have also shortened some of the citations, since the OSS attached long labels to their folders and files. I left off the middle initial for most names, and omitted the military ranks and marital status of the personnel. I alone bear responsibility alone for any errors that may appear here.

CHAPTER 1

Creating an Inclusive, Centralized Intelligence Agency

The federal government agency Joe Koide, Kunsung Rie, and Lincoln Kan joined was an ethnically and racially inclusive organization. This was not common inside the Washington governmental bureaucracy in the early 1940s, as racial segregation was widespread. The State Department routinely practiced racial discrimination, restricting African Americans to the lowest positions within their organization. However, other newer agencies, such as the Office of Price Administration, provided higher-level employment opportunities for minorities while the Civilian Aeronautics Administration integrated National Airport's restaurants. How and why the Office of Strategic Services became the part of the newer group of federal government agencies turning away from Jim Crow and employing Asian Americans is the subject of this chapter.[1]

When the Office of the Coordinator of Information (COI) was established on July 11, 1941, its director, William Donovan, was not concerned with recruiting Asian Americans. Instead, he recruited individuals with European language skills as he sought information on the capabilities and intentions of potential enemies and allies in Europe. Donovan gathered from them information on weaponry, strength and size of combat troops, training and state of readiness, and supply delivery systems, all of which is known as "tactical intelligence." He pulled together "operational intelligence," or data on where those forces were deployed and in what strength. Furthermore, he required details on the infrastructure supporting those forces, such as the factories producing the weapons, raw materials necessary for such production, food supplies, and other necessities for deployment, all of which affects the capabilities of the enemy or ally. Yet to evaluate the enemy or ally's intent, Donovan further required an in-depth understanding of the enemy's people and its leaders, together with careful mapping of its topography— information referred to as "strategic intelligence." Prior to the COI, Donovan's job was handled separately and information compartmentalized: the Office of Naval Intelligence (ONI) and the Military Intelligence Division (MID) collected tactical intelligence; the State Department and the Treasury Department gathered strategic intelligence; and the FBI confined its agent to counterintelligence work. But once established, COI became indispensable for assembling both tactical and strategic intelligence after American embassies in enemy territories were closed and all State, Justice, and Treasury officials and army and navy military attaches were called home following the declaration of war against the Axis powers in December.[2]

The Joint Chiefs of Staff (JCS) of the War Department adopted the general outlines of Donovan's vision. They took Donovan's organization under their wing in the summer of 1942 when President Roosevelt renamed the group the Office of Strategic Services. Recognizing the need for an agency "distinct from the [army and navy] service intelligence agencies," the staff charged it with gathering "military, economic and political information" on enemy, neutral, and allied countries to shed light on "the conditions and

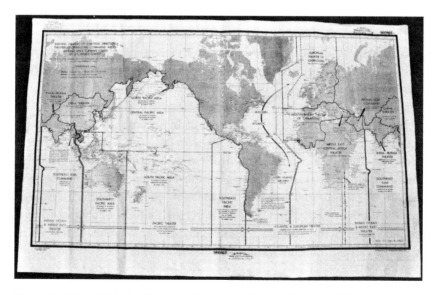

Figure 1.1 Map of Existing Theaters of Strategic Direction-Theaters of Operation, 1944. Courtesy of National Archives and Records Administration II.

intentions of opposing governments," as well as to conduct counterintelligence against foreign agents. To carry out these tasks, the JCS granted the OSS the right of access to intelligence reports and secret intercepts, to transmit and receive messages confidentially with its own codes and ciphers or through diplomatic pouches, and to have passports issued to its agents without "the usual formalities of proof of identity." In addition, the War Department's top brass granted the OSS the privilege of securing officers' commissions for its personnel, "adequate" priority in travel and supplies, and official recognition of "the military necessity of issuing simulated or facsimile documents such as identity cards, ration cards, travel documents and currency." In short, the Joint Chiefs of Staff assigned Donovan's group the task of centralizing American intelligence through various means and to conduct "irregular warfare" as they deemed appropriate.[3]

To assist in operations against Japan, William Donovan gathered intelligence outside of the main islands of Japan. He realized getting information out of Japanese-occupied territories was easier than inside Japan where Japanese authorities' tight control over their society made communication with agents difficult. But he also hoped to eventually slip agents into Japan before his rival MacArthur's anticipated invasion of those islands, so OSS agents could deliver his sarcastic welcome: "Japan is being delivered to you, General MacArthur, courtesy of Wild Bill Donovan." Donovan also planned to conduct guerrilla warfare in Japanese-occupied China and Korea, where locals were likely to cooperate with Allied forces. For his organization to function smoothly, Donovan divided his personnel into two categories—field agents and rear area personnel. For the former, he required people with the linguistic skills, cultural knowledge, and the correct racial uniforms to successfully secure local cooperation or passive acceptance of his agents operating in northeast Asia. For the latter, he needed individuals with knowledge and experience in the region acquired through academic study and through personal, social, or commercial experience to recruit and supervise locals tasked with collecting intelligence. For Donovan, then, the top positions of the office would demand recruits with high social, commercial, or academic connections and, equally important, people he could trust and rely on with security matters. He then had them recruit others who, utilizing their old boy network of social and professional peers, brought in European American males and overlooked females, but excluded nearly all racial minorities, including Asian Americans.[4]

Donovan gathered his resources to wage war against Imperial Japan amidst limitations imposed from outside. He tried to enter the China-Burma-India (CBI) Theater of Operation where the US Navy and Army were militarily weak, knowing the former sought updated weather reports on the region since climate patterns over northern China were useful for central Pacific Ocean forecasts. Donovan was aware that the navy placed observers in China known as coast watchers to identify Imperial Japanese Navy vessels and merchant marine ships for bombing. Instead of turning to the OSS, however, he watched in dismay as the navy dispatched Commander Marion "Mary" Miles to Chungking in 1942 to gather tactical intelligence and begin covert operations by creating a Chinese Nationalist government-led guerrilla force capable of tying down Imperial Japanese forces in China. Worse, his OSS was rendered irrelevant in China as Miles successfully founded with army approval the Sino-American Special Technical Cooperative Organization (SACO) in April 1943 and linked up with Tai Li, head of the Bureau of Investigation and Statistics and a top spymaster. Even the army, the director found, had locked his OSS out of strategic intelligence and covert operations in the region once the Theater Commander General Joseph Stilwell appointed his own son as head of the army's intelligence section in China and Burma to analyze the intentions of Chinese leadership and to mobilize the ethnically diverse local population in Burma against Imperial Japanese forces.[5]

Fortunately for Donovan, the British needed OSS assistance in East Asia. Their forces performed poorly in battles with the Imperial Japanese military during December 1941. Fixated on suppressing nationalist movements within their empire, their Secret Intelligence Service (SIS) inadequately assessed Imperial Japanese forces' capabilities and intentions, thereby contributing to the defeat and surrender of a numerically superior British force in Singapore and the Royal Army's retreat from Burma to India after their failure to stem the rapid advance of the Imperial Japanese forces. The Special Operations Executive (SOE) too was in disarray, since Chiang Kai-shek banned them from all guerrilla activities inside China in early 1942. Both the SIS and SOE were hampered by their inability to recruit within the diverse ethnic populations in East Asia, since the British policy of "imperial recovery" meant continuation of their unpopular colonial rule. They scoured the empire but acquired only a handful of Chinese Canadians to join the British forces in East Asia. Those few Japanese Canadians who were available for service refused to join the British forces until their demands for full citizenship rights were met. Worse, they came up with only a single Korean Canadian who, after her interview, was assessed as "a mental case" with "pro-Japanese sympathies." The British depended on the Americans to provide them with translators and had to make important concessions to the OSS in East Asia out of necessity. Thus, they agreed to operational boundaries that permitted the OSS to plant its headquarters and other bases inside India, share joint jurisdiction over Southeast Asia, and place all of China under American operational jurisdiction.[6]

The OSS's success in carving out a niche in East Asia, however, was undermined by others inside the Washington Beltway. Donovan divided his office into three major sections—administrative, intelligence, and strategic services—with a deputy director to oversee each. The Administrative Department, directed by Louis Ream, handled the day-to-day operation involving budgeting, supplies, and personnel matters. With over $12 million in 1942 and access to the president's $100 million annual emergency fund, the OSS entered the playing field of federal government agencies amply endowed to carry out its assignment.

It lacked, however, the independent means to provide supplies while operating in the Indian Ocean Rim region, even though they were promised priorities "within reasonable limits." Hence, they relied on British assistance for transport of their personnel and materials from the United States, across the Atlantic Ocean, through Cairo, to India. Additionally, their personnel section acquired military officers' commissions from army and navy without revealing the nature of their mission, but were stymied by Bureau of Budget officials demanding information on the OSS's table of organization and rationales for officer assignments. Thereafter, the OSS could

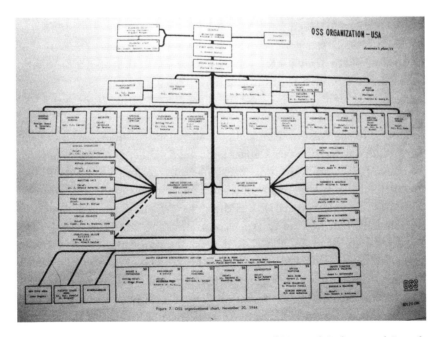

Figure 1.2 OSS organization—USA, 1944. Courtesy of National Archives and Records Administration II.

only give noncommissioned officer and technical representative status to their entry-level Asian American recruits. They also could offer American citizenship—an enticing incentive for some noncitizen recruits, since naturalization was virtually impossible for Asian immigrants defined by law as "aliens ineligible for citizenship." But for the most part, the OSS recruited among the American-born and, even then, was tardy in recruitment. Once training began, the Administrative Department's Schools and Training section was slow to build "schools." It did not train Carl Eifler's Detachment 101, which together with 500 of the earliest OSS recruits went to Camp X, an SOE training camp located in a small Canadian town of 45,000 near Oshawa, Ontario, on the north shore of Lake Ontario. Only when the last set of Asian Americans like Koide and Rie came in did Schools and Training teach them the fieldcraft at isolated training camp sites on Catalina Island, the national parks in Catoctin Mountain Park, north of Frederick, Maryland, or Prince William Forest Park, near Quantico, Virginia.[7]

Donovan's Intelligence Department also stumbled into trouble. Even though the Joint Chiefs of Staff recognized the need for OSS intelligence-gathering and centralizing the data, the War Department was undermined by others who saw the OSS as encroaching on their territory. Deputy Director John Magruder had his department organized into different subsections—Secret Intelligence (SI), Counterintelligence (X-2), Research and Analysis (R&A), Foreign Nationalities Branch, and Censorship & Documents—all but the last two of which conflicted with other organizations. The Office of Naval Intelligence was good with SI, which offered to merge personnel. But SI ran afoul of the army's intelligence director, General George Strong, who opposed the coordinator of information's transfer to the Joint Chiefs of Staff, fearing civilian control over intelligence. X-2 raised fears in the FBI, which saw the OSS as a threat to its own plan to expand counterintelligence operations in the Western Hemisphere and beyond. Even Donovan's prized R&A collided with the State Department. R&A's collection and analysis of large quantities of newspapers, magazines, directories, *Who's Who*, industrial manuals, and other open-source materials to develop strategic intelligence was not controversial. It was their recruitment of some of America's top scholars that drew away expert personnel the State Department habitually depended upon that caused tensions. Worse, its director James Baxter III, president of Williams College, lured some of the top talent from Harvard University, such as German historian William Langer, economist Edward Mason, and French historian Donald McKay, with high salaries. These scholars in turn brought in Edward Earle of Princeton University's Institute for Advanced Study; Joseph Hayden, chair of the Department of Government at the University of Michigan; and Calvin Hoover, a Duke

University economist, who formed the R&A's first board of analysts to evaluate the long-term, strategic intelligence reports. Board members used their own "eastern academic grapevine" to collect from thirty-five universities and colleges a group of a hundred intellectuals competent in thirty-six different languages, draining the pool of academics the State Department sought to tap.[8]

The Strategic Services Department also ran into trouble. It was tasked with undermining the enemies' capabilities and intentions through guerrilla warfare, commando-type operations on the enemy's flanks and rear, and with black propaganda to undercut the enemy's will, both civilian and military, to fight. Led by Deputy Director Strategic Services Operations Edward L. Bigelow, the department had six sections—Special Operations, Operational Groups, Maritime Unit, Special Projects, and the Field Experimental Unit (or Detachment 101)—all to conduct warfare against Japan utilizing the former methods, while Morale Operations (MO) adopted the latter. But MO under Karl Mann lost a sizeable segment of his staff to the Office of War Information (OWI), formed in June 1942. OSS guerrilla/commando warfare operations were halted by both army and navy theater commanders in the Pacific Theater of Operation, despite Donovan's friendship with Secretary of the Navy Frank Knox and his enviable Medal of Honor status within the army. The only concession he could wring from them was deployment of his Field Experimental Unit in the China-Burma-India (CBI) Theater of Operation, where supply priorities were the lowest and commanded by a general who was indifferent to guerrilla warfare. When Eifler and his executive officer John Coughlin reported to General Joseph Stilwell, Coughlin recalled that the cantankerous general warned them as they departed for behind-enemy-lines operations: "Just remember when your nuisance value exceeds your credit value you are out."[9]

Donovan's office circumvented these obstacles by strategically placing branch offices in key port cities. Although both the army and the navy did not permit OSS entry into the Pacific Theater per se, Donovan secured the approval of Lieutenant General Delos Emmons, commander of the Hawaiian Department for the army, and Admiral Chester Nimitz, navy commander in chief, Pacific Ocean Area, to establish an R&A branch in Honolulu on April 25, 1942. In return, Donovan's group supplied Emmons with 1,300 radio sets and provided his troops with morale-boosting materials and radio programs. He then turned to Alfred Tozzer, a Harvard University anthropologist specializing in Mayan civilization, to serve as the branch office head. Tozzer's wife, Margaret Tenney Castle, was the daughter of George Castle of the Castle & Cook Company, one of the territory's largest corporations whose holdings included Dole Pineapple and nearly all of the island of Lanai. Donovan knew the professor made frequent trips to Hawai'i to study local Okinawans and counted on Tozzer using his high social connections there for the OSS. Not long after Tozzer arrived on February 1, 1943, he hired Willowdean Handy, an anthropologist and the only female member of the Board of Regents of the University of Hawai'i, together with Marjorie Sinclair, novelist and wife of the president of the University of Hawai'i, and head of the Office of Postal Censor in Honolulu. Donovan did not anticipate the success Tozzer would have in eliciting greater cooperation from the navy through the distribution of the Honolulu office's strategic intelligence reports with data culled from the Federal Communications Commission's transcripts of Radio Tokyo broadcasts. That political, economic, and social information, Donovan learned, was judged by Admiral Chester Nimitz to be vital for his own war plans. Donovan, however, took satisfaction in Tozzer's initial report: "The personal experience of this R&A outpost," Tozzer said, "with the Army and Navy in this theatre in all echelons have been most pleasant."[10]

Donovan also succeeded in planting one of his agents inside MacArthur's Southwest Pacific Area Headquarters. He assigned Joseph Hayden to MacArthur's office, knowing the man's stellar military service and expertise on the Philippines would prove beneficial to the general. Hayden had earned a Silver Star for service in the navy during World War I as a gun train commander in France; spoke French, German, and Spanish; and had about five years of experience living in the Philippines on four different occasions—as an exchange professor at the University of Philippines, 1922 to 1923, and as a Carnegie Visiting Professor from 1930 to 1931. As if to further whet the general's appetite, Donovan knew Hayden's academic credentials were strong since, as a member of the political science department at the University of Michigan, he had authored *The Philippines: A Study in National Development* and *Pacific Politics*. Donovan may have told the general that Hayden was also on the board of analysts for the R&A and would be responsible for "a complete picture" of any given topic of importance with the information derived from private sources, government agencies, foreign periodicals, and shortwave broadcasts. All this information, the director promised, would become available to MacArthur even though Hayden and the board were to "integrate this information of a confidential and secret nature in such manner that it may be presented . . . to the President." The OSS director also gave Hayden "exceptionally wide latitude for unreviewed action and independent judgment" on projects similar to "secret intelligence." By early fall of 1943, Hayden had transferred intelligence materials on the Philippines from the R&A to the Southwest Pacific Area Headquarters, along with special SI and SO equipment. Donovan obviously succeeded, despite the personal rivalry with MacArthur, as evident by the visit of one of MacArthur's intelligence officer, Captain A. M. Russell, to "open the way to some form of collaboration between the OSS and the Allied Geographical Section." His agent Hayden joined the Southwest Pacific Headquarters later that year.[11]

In addition, Donovan established two important branch offices to run operations against Japan. He tasked the San Francisco office, also known as the Pacific Area office, with coordination of all departmental operations—secret intelligence, strategic services, and administration—as it related to the war against Japan. Donovan then got Robert Hall, professor of geography at the University of Michigan, to oversee this branch office, given Hall's expertise in dealing with the Japanese in Latin America, where he was conducting a detailed study of their settlements when the war broke out. Donovan viewed Hall's geographic expeditions to Japan from the late 1920s through the 1930s as important qualifications, in addition to the professor's experience as a decorated intelligence officer with the American Expeditionary Forces in France during World War I. Donovan appointed Hall as director of the Pacific Area office with orders to report only to himself, not William Langer, the head of R&A under whom Hall was initially assigned when he joined the OSS on November 17, 1942.[12]

The other branch office in New York was directed by businessmen, not scholars. From midtown Manhattan, businessman-philanthropist Vincent Astor led the group to take advantage of two important sources of information. His Oral Intelligence Unit, chaired by Colonel "Ned" Buxton, was set up in mid-August 1941 to collect information from refugees and Americans returning from foreign countries after receiving passenger lists from the Immigration and Naturalization Service. Such information useful for understanding a variety of subjects, from the mechanisms of governance in enemy territories to the condition of the local economy. The other group was the Insurance Unit, tasked with gleaning intelligence from records of insurance agencies. This group of a half-dozen businessmen examined standard insurance records for blueprints of bomb plants, timetables of tide changes, and thousands of other details about targets from a brewery in Bangkok, Thailand to a candy company in Bergedorf, Germany. Under the leadership of Cornelius van der Starr, better known as C. V. Starr, they compiled extensive files on the lives and property of their policyholders, information useful for determining influential leaders inside Germany.[13]

Choosing Starr as the head of the Insurance Unit of the New York office was logical. Starr understood how to build an organization from the ground up, a necessary qualification for the nascent OSS. Starr grew up in a working-class neighborhood near Fort Bragg, California, where he worked many odd jobs before matriculating at the University of California, Berkeley. But he dropped out to study on his own and passed the state bar exam. Although uninterested in military life after joining the US Army during World War I, Starr demonstrated a real flair for the insurance business after leaving his Pacific Mail Steamship Company job in Yokohama, Japan, for Shanghai. There he established his large insurance business in 1918 by teaming up with Frank Raven to form the American Asiatic Underwriters. Starr also hired two Chinese clerks upon whom he depended to bring in clients. His company was a success and accumulated large real-estate holdings, owned by the Metropolitan Land Company of Shanghai, opened up an automobile retail outlet for Studebaker and Buick-Vauxhall agencies, and began spreading his business across China's coastal region and into the interior. By 1940 Starr's Asia Life, known as "Yu Pang" or "friendly country," had offices across China in Tientsin, Hankow, Foochow, Canton, Chungking, Amoy, Mukden, Harbin, and Hong Kong. After establishing the American International Underwriters Corporation in New York in 1926, he established offices in Saigon and Haiphong of French Indochina; Djakarta and Surabaya of the Dutch East Indies, Kuala Lumpur and Malacca, Singapore; and the Philippines. His rapid expansion was in no small part due to Starr's disposition to select trusted Chinese personnel for positions of high rank within his company. His insurance company provided Donovan with a ready-made intelligence-gathering unit with trusted Chinese personnel.[14]

Esson McDowell Gale was chosen as Donovan's personal representative to China to independently verify intelligence reports received from SACO. Gale was highly qualified for this task. He was fluent in French and German, competent in Japanese, and his Mandarin Chinese language skills were so well-honed that he translated ancient Chinese documents. He acquired these skills as a result of his many years spent in China, initially as a government language student interpreter after graduating from the University of Michigan in 1907. His knowledge of China was evident in his book, much of it based on his experiences as director of the Salt Revenue Administration in major Chinese provinces and Manchuria, service for which he was awarded medals by the Chinese government.[15] Gale was equally suited to liaise with factions within the Korean Provisional government, a necessary qualification to ensure smooth operation of the Korean guerrilla operations Donovan envisioned. He had connections with key figures like Syngman Rhee through his uncle James Gale, who had assisted the leader's entry into the United States. Esson Gale's wife, born in Seoul and raised in Wonsan, was socially tied to many within Korean leadership circles. Gale also developed other connections from his Salt

Revenue Administration work in Hankow and Changchun (Manchuria) from 1914 to 1927 as its chief auditor, then as its officiating director general in the Chinese Ministry of Finance, Salt Revenue Administration, from 1932 to 1939. He came into the position recommended by Dr. T. V. Soong, minister of finance and brother-in-law of Chiang Kai-shek. Being a former neighbor and friend of Admiral Chester Nimitz also made him a logical choice.[16]

The OSS then secured for Gale the necessary credentials for work in East Asia. In September 1941, Joseph Hayden met with John Wiley, Calvin Hoover, and Stanley Hornbeck of the State Department to establish Gale's cover. They agreed that Gale should create an undercover organization that would report to Manila in case Americans were forced to leave Shanghai under Japanese pressure. Hayden then secured a letter of recommendation from Soong, who delivered the letter addressed to Chiang Kai-shek in a secret code. Two months later, Hayden completed Gale's official cover, making him a Foreign Service Technical Advisor to the US Ambassador to China. He then scheduled for Gale to leave for Shanghai on December 12, 1941.[17]

Gale's plan for his mission team was ambitious. He aimed to recruit highly qualified personnel and divide them into three sections— administrative, intelligence, and special operations. For his administrative positions, he pulled in talented individuals like Paul Linebarger to handle political observation and public relations role; Hunter Mann for transportation; I. G. Riddick for propaganda; and O. J. Todd for the engineering and conservation aspects of his work. For his intelligence work, he sought individuals with knowledge of specific regions in East Asia including Tibet, Indochina, Calcutta, Australia, Chungking, and Shanghai. Gale then placed Colonel Morris DePass to head the guerrilla operations section but brought in others to supplement trained military directives and to handle specific regions of East Asia. He searched for additional personnel to cover South China, North China, North Manchuria, Siberia, Korea, and Singapore.[18]

Gale's cautious approach should have endeared him to the Chinese and Korean leadership. He believed in moving slowly but deliberately in intelligence work inside China, fearing overlapping jurisdiction would spark jealousies and resistance. "Whatever misgivings there may be in some quarters as to possible functional overlappings," Gale reminded Donovan, they "could be allayed by this more gradual approach. I recall that your own opinion held that deliberate spade work would be desirable in a successful build-up of the project." Furthermore, Gale was open about his work for the COI and sought permission from the Chinese government before proceeding with intelligence-gathering, believing in being diplomatic "with a large D." As he said to Donovan,

> All my contacts here, both British and American, stress that any fact gathering activities must be with the cognizance of the national authorities. In this friendly but alert governments domain, obscurantist methods are not feasible. The situation here is entirely dissimilar to the earlier proposed undercover assignment to occupied areas. Therefore, I urge that in the assignment of any person to this office, the Ambassador should be previously advised of his status and duties through the State Department, for clarification to Chinese authorities.[19]

Gale's attitude toward Korean independence, however, was unequivocal and immediate. He denied that Koreans were unprepared to govern themselves, which won him the approval of many within the Korean independence movement. Gale reasoned:

> Certainly, no overseas Asiatic representation has a more experienced personnel, familiar with most governments of the world, good and bad. . . . The Koreans could indeed assume administrative control in their own country with less friction and greater effectiveness than either the French in Algiers or the Italians in Sicily . . . have demonstrated.[20]

Despite his willingness to work on Chinese and Korean terms, Gale's mission ground to halt soon after his arrival in Chungking. Gale encountered Gauss's "acute displeasure," which the US Ambassador registered right after Gale reported in on March 8, 1942, and for the next three months. He smeared his scholarly special assistant with vicious rumors and placed him under operational restrictions that clearly violated the presidential directive for the OSS. As one observer noted,

> Subsequently, Mr. Gauss spoke disparagingly of any attempt of the C.O.I. to conduct "secret" operations in China, asserting that any activities in China should be carried on through him and through him only. He also sought to discredit Dr. Gale on the basis of his previous record in China, and created the impression that he would do everything in his power to force Dr. Gale out of China.

Gauss's opposition was so deep that Joseph Hayden decided to halt the Gale mission less than a half a year after it begun "on account of Chinese feeling" and to protect another ongoing project. "It is also desired," said Hayden to Gale, "that the success of the microfilm project be carried on by [John] Fairbank for the Research and Analysis Branch not be jeopardized by suspicion however unfounded that he is engaged in or connected with any sort of secret operations." Gale then turned over the reins to R&A's Clyde Sargent, and the Korean Project was shelved.[21]

Cancellation of the Gale mission forced the OSS to work under the restrictive SACO terms of agreement. On the one hand, SACO prohibited all special operations, such as those contemplated by Carl Eifler, and all independent SI network plans. It also left the OSS vulnerable to compromised intelligence data and leaks because Japanese, British, and Chinese Communist moles were placed inside of Tai Li's bureau. On the other hand, the OSS was able to exploit the agreement's vagueness in the command structure to covertly establish their own SI operations inside the China Theater. Under SACO, they were able to send in their own R&A and MO personnel to quietly gather intelligence, an approach that allowed Lincoln Kan and other OSS agents to enter the field.[22]

To ensure a smooth flow of strategic intelligence out of China, R&A director William Langer appointed the China-friendly University of Michigan Professor Charles Frederick Remer to run its Far Eastern section. Remer in turn brought in Charles Stelle, Joseph Spencer, and Charles Fahs—all East Asia specialists—as his subsection chiefs. Remer himself was an experienced "China Hand," having taught for several years at St. John's University in Shanghai prior to and after World War I before receiving his doctorate in economics from Harvard University in 1923. As a professor at Williams College and University of Michigan, he authored or coauthored several books on the Chinese economy, including, *A Study of Chinese Boycotts*, and *Foreign Investments in China*.[23] Remer was already prepared for the possibility of war in East Asia once the Soviet Union and Japan signed a neutrality agreement in 1939, believing that just as Germany signed a nonaggression pact with the Soviet Union and went to war against Britain and France, Japan would also wage war against the Allied powers. Thus, he called for strengthening China militarily to resist Japan, even though the United States was neutral:

> The policy of the United States has been determined in broad outline by Japanese adherence to the Axis. This was an open alliance against the United States. No other interpretation is safe. In carrying out American policy certain steps seem imperative. Assistance must be given to China. A divided China is a victory for Japan and a defeat for the United States. Chinese military success will turn the tide against Japan.[24]

Remer's other assistants, too, were very knowledgeable about China. Charles Stelle, Remer's right-hand man, wrote "Americans and the China

Opium Trade in the Nineteenth Century."[25] Joseph Spencer, head of the China section, was a geography professor at University of California, Los Angeles, whose specialty was also China. Spencer had published numerous articles in the 1930s on China while working as the assistant district inspector for the Salt Revenue Administration, Ministry of Finance, under which he covered seven different districts stretching across thousands of square miles in central, western, and southwestern China over an eight-year period. Spencer and his wife were fluent in Chinese, having resided in Icheng on the banks of the Yangtze River and in Chungking. He was posted further inland to Kweiyang after the Japanese invasion in 1937 and moved to Yunnan before returning to the United States in 1940 to teach at UCLA. Spencer joined the OSS in April 1942 and was commissioned a captain in the army in September 1943. Thereupon he was sent to the China-Burma-India Theater Headquarters in New Delhi to take charge of the group assigned to gather information covering New Delhi to Kandy and Ceylon to Sian in western central China. But in the summer of 1944 he was assigned to China and was content with the appointment, even though he declared himself "busier than a dog with two kinds of fleas."[26]

Harvard University historian John Fairbank was also recruited to assist the R&A/Far East section until the end of 1943. Fairbank was tapped by James Baxter III in August 1941 as an expert on Chinese maritime customs, the subject of his doctoral dissertation at Oxford University in 1936. He was assigned to be a liaison contact to Lauchlin Currie, then an administrative assistant to the president on the White House staff. Before the war began, Fairbank began working in Washington, DC for American aid to Free China, whose aim was to "show the paucity of aid really given to Nationalist China and the urgent need for further aid." In this role, he was sent to Chungking to gather reference materials on Japan as a representative of the Library of Congress. He also served as representative of the American Publications Service of the American Embassy, which made American publications on microfilm available to Chinese universities.[27]

Charles Fahs was the lone Japan expert. Breaking loose of his family's close association with Christian missions in China, the Brooklyn-born scholar studied the House of Peers—the upper house of the Japanese Parliament—for his doctoral dissertation at Northwestern University, published in 1933. He then went to the Sorbonne in Paris, where he and Edwin Reischauer studied Japanese grammar under Serge Elisséeff before arriving at Kyoto Imperial University in 1934. Dressed like a native, Fahs studied the Japanese language further while taking up calligraphy, judo, and archery. In 1936, he accepted an academic appointment at Claremont College, where he taught Far Eastern history, Japanese and Chinese government, Japanese and Chinese literature in translation, and Japanese language while writing *Government in Japan: Recent Trends in Its Scope and Operation*. Like his peers, Fahs rejected racialist views of Japan, choosing instead to view his subject empathetically. Defending that country's expansion on the Asian continent, Fahs claimed that "Japan must obviously either have territory into which her excess population can migrate or which she can exploit economically so as to support the increased population at home." He countered scholarly and media condemnation of Japan by asserting the country was "more democratic than Germany, Italy or the USSR" and declared that its leaders were moved by domestic political and economic considerations, not unlike their counterparts in Europe and America.[28]

Fahs' defense notwithstanding, SI believed the Imperial Japanese government's rigid political control over the main islands of Japan effectively closed it off from intelligence-gathering. SI director Joseph Hayden therefore focused on Japanese-occupied territories and thus saw C. V. Starr's business enterprises as one of SI's most important sources of intelligence, especially the *Shanghai Evening Post and Mercury*, an English-language media that gave voice to the liberal American outlook on China. Its editor Randall Gould, former news reporter for *Time*, United Press, and *Christian Science Monitor*, was allowed to express his views in the editorial section and it was sharply antagonistic toward the Japanese military and their bombing of Chungking while full of praise for the Chinese public's "stoic fortitude" and their display of "an inexhaustible stock of courage." Gould was highly optimistic about Chiang Kai-shek's leadership of Free China, believing he had "mellowed and developed within the years into a figure of greatness for the democratic pattern." Gould's outlook on China's leadership won over Chiang Kai-shek and other top Chinese military leaders. Starr's other newspaper published in the Chinese-language, *Ta Mei Wan Pao* (Great American Evening Newspaper), was equally opposed Japan's Greater East Asia Co-Prosperity Sphere and insistently predicted the eventual demise of all treaty ports. This stance infuriated many European residents of Shanghai to the point that his offices were bombed; one of his editors, Samuel Chang, was fatally gunned down in a café; and Starr himself had to ride in a bullet-proof limousine for his own protection. But his newspaper in 1939 enjoyed a circulation of 100,000, the largest in the city, even after Gould was imprisoned by the Japanese and his offices in Occupied China closed. However, Starr's two newspapers still had offices operating in other parts of China and Asia in December 1942. Starr then offered SI his *Shanghai Evening Post and Mercury* to be used as a cover for gathering biographical information on over 5,000 individuals, including collaborators, in a project known as "Twinkle." Hence, Starr sent Randall Gould and F. B.

"Fritz" Opper, correspondents for the *Christian Science Monitor* and *Chicago Daily News*, to Chungking to re-establish his newspaper office and gather intelligence for the OSS.[29]

J. Arthur Duff was Starr's most appealing asset for SI. Duff's escape from Occupied China in 1942 proved that SI usage of Old China Hands, contrary to SACO policy, could effectively gather intelligence behind Imperial Japanese lines without having the correct racial uniform. Duff was fluent in Mandarin, Cantonese, and other dialects, having been born in 1899 to a Canadian missionary couple in a small village near Kiukiang on the Yangtze River. He had lived all but five years of his prewar life in the region and, though a Canadian citizen, was considered reliable, having a mission school education and married to an American citizen named Jeannie Woodbridge, who hailed from a family of thirteen generations of Christian ministers. Through his service with the Shanghai Volunteer Corps in the late 1920s and early 1930s, Duff cultivated relationships with a number of important foreign expatriates in Shanghai including C. V. Starr, whose Reliance Motors Company he managed. He was on a business trip to Hong Kong when the Imperial Japanese forces invaded the treaty port in early December 1941 and interned all citizens of the Allied powers. Despite his obvious foreign appearance, Duff eluded capture by the Imperial Japanese forces. He hid until January 9, 1942 before departing by speedboat to Bias Bay about forty miles east of Hong Kong, where he again went into hiding for nearly three weeks. While there, Duff agreed to carry letters by locals addressed to their relatives and friends in the Taipun Benevolent Association of New York. After arriving in Kukong, he made arrangements with Starr for his passage to New York through India and North Africa. He also got John Keswick of the SOE to transport the Taipun letters past Customs officials in a diplomatic pouch. After delivering the letters to their relatives and friends in New York, Duff met with Donovan to plan another mission to the same region without SACO permission.[30]

Donovan was clearly impressed with Duff's exploits and Starr's organization. Donovan heard from others that Starr had a comprehensive network of highly experienced Chinese and foreign personnel, owned the *Shanghai Evening Post,* and was quite familiar with China. He knew Starr's organization was badly off financially, having had all of its assets seized in China by the Japanese occupiers. He therefore gave Starr a temporary loan of two million dollars, believing Starr's employees were as skilled in intelligence work as Duff, who commented on the director:

Donovan was convinced that he had found the answer, assuming that all Starr's China staff were like me!!! He went ahead and concluded a deal with

Starr—involving large sums of money—in effect he took over Starr's Far Eastern obligations "for the duration,"with Starr in charge, details were never announced, of course. All were [sic] a closely-held secret between Donovan and Starr.[31]

Duff took up a new mission whose purpose he changed to better suit the SOE than the OSS. Duff switched the aim from conventional to economic warfare, in part of his own business background. He undertook field training at a school outside of Washington, DC to learn the art of codes and ciphers, recognition of warships by silhouette, and usage of various weapons and explosives. He did not perform well though, treating training as "a necessary evil" and remaining "stand-offish," much to the chagrin of his trainers. Duff then started Operation "Salt" in coordination with two young advisers to General Yu Hon Mow of the Canton government in exile at Kukong. Duff offered them 20 percent of the salt revenue collected by Yu's trucks in exchange for a military passport that would ensure his passage through the area. He planned to transport torpedoes and other supplies for US Navy submarines operating within range of Taipun Bay area.

Before his departure in mid-December 1942, Salt was scrubbed. Under the cover of a survey mission for the United China Relief, Duff was instead assigned to gather secret intelligence while establishing a system for rescuing downed aviators from General Claire Chennault's Fourteenth Air Force. Duff, however, created a new trucking company intended to deny the Imperial Japanese forces the Pearl River Delta region's supply of wolfram or tungsten, a metal used in aircraft manufacturing. He recruited Lewis Carson, an American, and Rudy Yung, head of the Overseas Chinese Affairs Bureau, and established the commercial venture with funds from Starr's account in India. Duff justified the change by citing the potential damage the new group could do to the Imperial Japanese forces—cutoff of wolfram supply to the Japanese and the creation of a network that could be used for either secret intelligence-gathering or sabotage operations. "The transportation company," Duff explained, "is principally a front and a means for providing our connections with machinery through which to operate and for giving them remuneration. The organisation can be used in any way desired."[32]

Duff's covert re-entry into the Pearl River Delta region in the winter of 1942–43 proved a fatal blow for OSS and the Starr organization. Although Duff's intelligence on the region was good and Donovan's faith in the Canadian's ability to slip past the Japanese and Tai Li's agents well-founded, his cover was blown by Miles, who sent out letters to various

Allied leaders in the China Theater regarding Duff's true identity. Worse, Duff himself, without OSS knowledge, had arranged to scout the area for ways the British SIS and the SOE could gain admission into the region after being banished by Chiang Kai-shek. Duff even promised Colonel Lindsay Ride of the British Air Aid Group (BAAG) that he would gather intelligence for them and joined his group while on the OSS payroll. His dual role came to light only after Duff walked out of the OSS and into the British Embassy in Chungking in December 1943, ostensibly to free himself from the obligation of remaining silent. Duff was incensed over an alleged plot by the American forces to prevent a British reassertion of its authority over Hong Kong after the war by immediately flying in Chinese troops to have them rather the British accept the Japanese surrender: "I considered it a particularly dirty trick, and therefore quit the OSS in order to expose it to the British."[33]

Despite the Starr fiasco, SI operations in the China Theater moved forward organizationally under Norwood Allman. Like Duff, Allman was an Old China Hand. Born in Union Hall, Virginia, he graduated from the University of Virginia in 1915. A year later he joined the American Embassy in Beijing as a student interpreter, where he worked with a young assistant librarian named Mao Tse-tung at the University of Beijing. In 1921 he became the US consul in Shanghai but retired from the consular corps three years later to manage his burgeoning business ventures, which included a paper mill and a cinema chain as well as his law practice in Shanghai. He published a couple of books on Chinese patents and copyrights, was the commander of the American company of the Shanghai Volunteer Corps, and was a member of the Municipal Council. In part because he was the editor of *Shun Pao*, a Chinese-language paper critical of the Japanese, Allman was arrested the day after Japan attacked Pearl Harbor and interned in a prison camp for six months until being repatriated to the United States in June 1942.[34]

Allman took over as chief of SI, Far East section. After interviewing "all the worthwhile passengers" on board the civilian exchange ship the *Gripsholm* to gather intelligence on Japan, Allman landed in New York with various tidbits of information useful to the military. He was scheduled to return to China as part of the Starr spy network, but shortly after he arrived at the end of October 1942, he was assigned to replace Gale and Price, both of whom resigned from the OSS, and Hayden, who was moved up to the planing board. Allman got W. M. Drummond and Major Austin O. Glass to run the China/Philippines/Indochina desk, while Daniel Buchanan and George McCune managed the Japan desk and Korea desk, respectively. He also brought in E. D. Pawley, who previously recruited and sent to China the American Volunteer Group of fighter pilots for General Claire Chennault's famed Flying Tigers. Although he found several hundred individuals among the *Grispholm* passengers well-suited for SI his Far East Section depended heavily on Chinese interpreters rather than linguistically-competent American personnel. He then directed Alghan Lusey to be the section's field commander over SI's field agents and included within his ranks John Fairbank and Clyde Sargent, the former using the Inter-departmental Committee for the Acquisition of Foreign Publications as his cover to do, "in his spare time," intelligence-gathering.[35]

While Allman did little to recruit Asian Americans into the OSS, he employed Daniel Buchanan, who did. Buchanan was well-qualified for his assigned task. Born in Kobe, Japan to a missionary couple in 1894, he grew up speaking both English and Japanese. He left Japan to attend college in the United States, receiving his undergraduate degree at Fredericksburg College in 1912, then his Master's degree at Washington and Lee University two years later. He returned to Japan to teach the English language and American culture in Tokyo, but decided to pursue his Bachelor of Divinity degree at McCormick Theological Seminary. He received his degree and his ordination into the Presbyterian Church in 1921. He served the Presbyterian Church Mission, Japan as its information officer and newspaper evangelism specialist, but left to study for his doctorate at Hartford Seminary. He became an expert on Japanese religion, publishing a portion of his doctoral dissertation on the Japanese Fox God *Inari* in 1935. Buchanan was well-versed in Japanese literature as well, collecting and translating Japanese proverbs and sayings that he would later publish after the war. The Presbyterian minister was also competent in German and French, a bonus to Allman, who made him chief of the Japan-Korea desk after recruiting him away from the OWI. With his fluent Japanese, he became a primary recruiter of Japanese Americans.[36]

Ernest Price was another key figure in pushing SI toward hiring Asian Americans. As Joseph Hayden's second in command, he drafted a plan in 1942 for the establishment of a bomber base inside Manchuria, supplied with Lend-Lease materials designated for both the Soviet Union and China. Price envisioned a Manchurian expeditionary force composed of Manchurians, Chinese students, and linguistically-qualified Chinese Americans, the latter to teach the former two groups how to maintain, supply, and defend the air bases for American bombers tasked with bombing the main islands of Japan. Price wanted to lead the advance survey force, to select the site and to lay the groundwork for the base despite the proximity of the Imperial Japanese Northern China Army. His confidence stemmed from extensive knowledge of China. Although born in Henzada, Burma, to Baptist missionary parents and educated in the US Midwest, Price had been in the US Foreign Service since his student interpreter days with the American Legation in Beijing in 1914. He had served in one capacity or another in Foochow, Canton, Nanking, Tientsin, and Tsinan before resigning in 1929. Frustrated at not being promoted to full consul-general, despite his demonstrated competence in his work and his fluency in Mandarin, Cantonese, and other Chinese dialects, Price quit and became president of China Airways before pursuing his doctorate at Johns Hopkins University. He demonstrated his sophisticated understanding of northeast China in his published dissertation, "The Russo-Japanese Treaties of 1907–1916 Concerning Manchuria and Mongolia" (1933), using documents written in French, Russian, and Chinese. While Price maintained a detached outlook on the Manchurian question, he asserted guerrilla operations were viable in this region because of the likelihood of continued "political banditry" (guerrilla warfare) by Manchurians against Japanese rule in Manchukuo.[37]

But Price's plan of using Chinese Americans for operations in northeast China was dropped by late 1942. William Langer saw flaws in the plan: supplying air bases in Manchuria was problematic; defending such air bases against a large and well-trained Japanese army nearby was difficult; and establishing the bases in secrecy was not possible, given Japanese control over Manchuria. William Donovan was even more emphatic: he had Price fired from the job. As Price confessed, "the Colonel [Donovan] is of the opinion that I have opposed his policies with respect to operations in China. Even though, as I have said, I have had little opportunity to express an opinion and my advice has never once been requested by the Colonel, this allegation is essentially true, and we can let it go at that."[38]

With Allied guerrilla operations prohibited inside northeast China, Special Operations turned to Burma. Due to that change in location, Special Operations under Carl Eifler, commander of the Field Experimental Unit or Detachment 101, opened its door to Asian Americans in the China-Burma-India Theater. Eifler demonstrated little affection for Japanese Americans when he was in charge of the Enemy Alien Internment Camp at Sand Island in Hawai'i. He showed, according to Yasutarō Soga, editor/publisher of the *Nippu Jiji* and a resident of Hawai'i for forty-five years, "a defiant attitude" toward the internees and tormented them with strip-searches, roll calls, and other harsh disciplinary measures. Eifler, in fact, shared in common with Stilwell a decidedly anti-Japanese prejudice. In early 1940, Stilwell told Eifler privately, "I have always claimed that Jap stock cannot be assimilated, and the more I see of it, the more convinced I am that the only reasonable solution is to throw them all out." While Eifler did not recruit

Japanese Americans, he was enthusiastic about other Asian Americans, especially getting a Chinese American doctor as his medical officer. He filled out the rest of his team of twenty-one with two more Chinese Americans and a Korean American, under the assumption that his guerrilla operations would cover all of East Asia.[39]

More than SO, MO carved out a large niche for Asian Americans inside the OSS. Unlike SI, MO's top leadership had no experience with East Asia. Its director, Colonel K. D. Mann, was the former vice president of an Ohio steel corporation and had had no previous dealings with China or Japan when he first reported to Deputy Director Strategic Services, Edward Bigelow. His Far East section head, Herbert Little, the individual who opened the door to Asian Americans including Joe Koide, had only some limited knowledge of the region. Little was born in Manchester, England, but immigrated to New York with his family as a five-year-old. They settled in Seattle, where in 1920 his whole family became naturalized American citizens. His father was self-employed in the insurance industry but also a minister. Herbert received his primary and secondary education in the Seattle area pursued a doctorate at the University of Washington, but completed only half before quitting in 1927. He joined a local law firm, where as a senior partner he earned from $12,000 to $24,000 annually, specializing in international law and estates. He was not known as a Japan expert despite the fact that he spoke some Japanese and had traveled to Japan, China, and Manchuria in 1931. When war broke out, Little joined the army as a major and then in July 1943, switched to the OSS as a lieutenant colonel. He was immediately sent to General Stilwell's headquarters in New Delhi and then to Chungking to plan for operations against Japan.[40]

Yet Herbert Little initially assembled his Far East administrative staff out of an odd collection of individuals, none of whom were Asian Americans. Tasked with producing and distributing effective black propaganda, Little required personnel with expertise in producing printed materials, such as pamphlets and newspapers, or with radio broadcasting experience. His circle of acquaintances from which he drew his first recruits was limited and thus provided him with less than ideal candidates. Little recruited Maxwell Kleiman, a lawyer and income tax consultant who was in the US Army Air Corps for thirteen months prior to joining the OSS. Kleiman was born in Russia, but became a naturalized citizen; some time after he received his education at New York University, he became involved in business dealings with the Japanese prior to the bombing of Pearl Harbor. These activities earned him the label "questionable" in terms of loyalty. OSS investigators believed Kleiman's entry into the army as an officer spared him from prosecution for failing to register himself as "an agent for a foreign principal."[41]

Fortunately, other recruits were more appropriate for the task. In particular, Little recruited two highly competent women for his office. One was Jane Smith-Hutton to manage the Washington, DC office. She was fluent in Japanese, having spent twelve years in Japan. Interned in a Japanese camp, she returned aboard the *Gripsholm* and was recruited by CBS newsman Edmund Taylor, who convinced her of the importance of morale operations in the German success in overrunning French and British forces on the European continent. The other was Betty MacDonald, a journalist from Honolulu. Her father William Peet was at the sports desk of the *Honolulu Advertiser* and her mother, a former Washington, DC columnist, was a schoolteacher in Honolulu. Betty graduated from the University of Washington with a degree in journalism and returned to Honolulu to work for the same newspaper as her father. There she met and married Alexander MacDonald, reporter and author of *Revolt in Paradise,* an expose of the moneyed establishment that controlled Hawai'i. After working for Scripps-Howard news service and the *Star-Bulletin*'s society section editor, Betty and her husband studied Japanese by living for a year with Dr. Saburō Watanabe, principal of a Japanese language school in Honolulu. After the Pearl Harbor attack, Betty promptly volunteered for the OSS and also got her husband, a naval officer, to join.[42]

Yet MO required more than European American personnel familiar with East Asia to wage an effective propaganda campaign. Since their primary audience was Japanese and Chinese—Koreans were assumed supporters of the Allied cause—MO sought individuals with native-level ability in Japanese or Chinese languages, knowledge of local conditions based on their recent residency in those targeted regions, and work experience in the print or radio broadcasting media. In return, MO could offer only a civilian status, having few officers' commissions to give. MO pay was not as high as other recruiting federal government agencies, as Morton Bodfish, deputy chief of MO admitted: "We find ourselves facing some very real obstacles which cannot be met by ordinary means. Not the least of these obstacles is the open competition of the OWI for skilled men at salaries generally in excess of those paid by OSS." By early February 1945, the chief of MO Kenneth Mann estimated their work in East Asia required 120 for the India-Burma Theater and an additional 146 for the China Theater. Given their expansion, where would these personnel come from?[43]

To fill their personnel requirements for MO and other sections, the OSS recruited Asian Americans. Throughout its existence, Donovan defined the office as a multiracial organization, as evident in his speech for the OSS' termination ceremony in fall 1945: "This experiment was to determine whether a group of Americans constituting a cross section of racial origins, of abilities, temperaments and talents could meet and risk an encounter with the long-established and well-trained enemy organizations." The director's behavior was consistent with his liberal outlook, as he refused the French government's Croix de Guerre medal to protest its anti-Semitism against his Jewish sergeant during World War I. He broke racial protocol again by hiring African Americans, such as James Freeman, as his chauffeur, and Chinese American sergeants Yueh C. Tsai and H. Kuei Chang as his personal cooks.[44]

Donovan's liberal racial outlook extended toward Japanese Americans as well. He suspected Ukrainian Americans, not Japanese Americans, of Axis support for German saboteurs plotting to strike the United States. Although he thought the German and Japanese navies were operating submarine bases inside Chile and in Baja, Mexico, he placed Japanese Americans in the safe zone of the OSS ethnic/racial security map. Donovan believed them loyal in sufficient numbers to be trusted. In mid-December 1941, he expressed to President Roosevelt his strong opposition to the mass removal and confinement of West Coast Japanese Americans, agreeing with Ralph Van Deman's view that the plan was "an entirely unbaked and illy [sic] considered proposition." Donovan called attention to the flaws of the mass removal and internment proposition—ignoring the findings of three federal government agencies tasked with such an investigation prior to the war; stirring up unnecessarily a relatively hysteria-free West Coast; creating confusion in the surrounding communities where Japanese Americans resided; disrupting defense, especially aircraft production; and pushing Japanese Americans to support Japan after providing inadequate care for their possessions which thieves and arsonists would despoil. Instead, Donovan recommended John Steinbeck's proposal for using the pro-USA Japanese Americans to keep watch over potential troublemakers within the ethnic group.[45]

The Pacific office's chief of morale operations shared Donovan's faith in Asian Americans by employing them. Herbert Little was responsible for pulling into MO many Japanese Americans, both US citizens and aliens, for black propaganda work. His willingness to hire them can be only be surmised, but it seems reasonable that his own immigrant status made him a willing employer of Asian immigrants. His legal practice in international law involving Japan gave him some measure of familiarity with the Japanese language and provided him with some knowledge of Japanese Americans, as did his long residency in Seattle. Little's close friendship with journalist Chester Rowell may have led him to also oppose the mass removal and internment of Japanese Americans. His trustee status in the American Council of the Institute of Pacific Relations, an organization that conceptually separated Japanese Americans from Imperial Japanese government foreign policy in the 1930s, also influenced his outlook.[46]

Daniel Buchanan also favored Japanese American recruits. Buchanan joined SI in April 1943 after leaving "a relatively minor position" in OWI to make better use of his near-native ability in the Japanese language, his solid expertise in Japanese culture and religion, and strong familiarity with the Japanese educational system due to his long residency in that country. He therefore saw a similar waste of talent as Japanese Americans were being isolated in the War Relocation Authority camps. Buchanan never believed a lack of citizenship should bar one from serving the United States during war. He was born in Kobe City, Japan in 1892 and, even though he received his entire collegiate and graduate education in the United States, was a British citizen until October 1918, when he enlisted in US Army and became a naturalized American citizen. For him, loyalty was a matter of the heart rather than citizenship:

> In my early youth though technically a British subject, I was always at heart and by training an American. During World War I my sympathies were with the Allies long before America entered. Although I was then teaching in a government school in Japan where I was not subject to any military draft, I rejected an offer of a commission in the British army, and resigning my position in July 1918, I returned to the United States at my own expense to volunteer as a private. I was attending an officers training camp when the war ended. While in the army I took the oath of naturalization before the Supreme Court of the District of Columbia.[47]

As Buchanan had with Japanese Americans, the OSS "mapped" Korean Americans in the secure zone. They saw certain Korean Americans as posing no security risk even before the federal government's change of the status of Korean immigrants in the United States from "enemy" to "nonenemy" alien status in October 1942. Yet they also shared some of the same stereotypes the American public embraced about Koreans and Korean Americans. In Hawai'i, for example, Koreans were seen as the opposite of Japanese. Coastal Carolina University history professor Brandon Palmer finds similar constructions, identifying eight particular images of Koreans in Hawai'i's mass media prior to 1925—shiftless, ignorant of American customs and practices, revengeful and bent on vigilantism, barbaric and childish, criminal, Christian, nationalistic, and incompetent at self-governance. International University of the East professor Craig

Coleman uncovered continuity of those stereotypes which juxtaposed Koreans as untidy, ungovernable, and rude while the Japanese were the opposite—neat, polite, clean, and highly governed.[48]

Under the influence of such negative stereotypes, Donovan limited Korean Americans' roles within the OSS. He followed the State Department's policy of nonrecognition of expatriate independence movements by issuing a directive: "Until Koreans in the United States have achieved some kind of unity, do not quote any individuals." He and others saw Koreans and Korean Americans as "childish," "revengeful and bent of vigilantism." He feared they might quickly mount their own offensive against the Imperial Japanese forces without adequate support which, he thought, was the same as "doing something suicidal." At the same time, Donovan and others thought strategically, withholding Korean and Korean American attacks on Imperial Japanese forces to scare the Japanese into thinking something big was in the works for Korea. "If adroitly handled," Donovan's order said, "this propaganda should have the effect of keeping the Japanese on the alert in Korea and possibly immobilizing troops in that area." Donovan allowed a dozen Korean Americans to enter the OSS out of deference to Syngman Rhee, but believed it best to bar all other applicants.[49]

Negative racial stereotypes played far less a role in the OSS' decision not to recruit many Chinese Americans. Edwin Martin of the R&A/China Theater admitted the main reason was fear of a security breach. Martin stated that contact with all "persons of Chinese race" was kept to a minimum in the Far East section of R&A because of the perception that the Chinese Nationalist government was "very assiduous in seeking to learn about OSS and what it is doing." The R&A/China Theater therefore kept out all Chinese citizens from their building:

> As you probably know, we have even been extremely reluctant to employ American citizens of Chinese origin with full security privileges, and at present have only one, Corporal Robert Chin. Because of the political problems involved in such actions, I should think it might be desirable before granting full security approval for anyone of [the] Chinese race to secure an opinion from this office. It has been informally reported to me, for example, that the Map Division now has on its staff with full security clearance a Chinese with Chinese citizenship, something which offhand we would consider quite questionable.[50]

Yet SI had no such qualms, perhaps in part because its leadership firmly rejected such negative racial imaginations of the Chinese. SI's Far East section head Norwood Allman, for example, deplored the "treaty port" mentality of foreign expatriates in China who disdained social contact with the Chinese. As he once explained to a group of readers:

> My wife, who had been born of American missionary parents in Tsinan, and I both deplored the usual lack in the Chinese treaty ports of social intercourse between Chinese and foreigners, and we ignored it. When we returned to Shanghai in 1922 the American University Club was the only common meeting ground other than religious circles. However, we continued our earlier custom of entertaining Chinese in our home, and in return were entertained by them. We both spoke Chinese, and that, along with the insatiable curiosity about all facets of Chinese life that I had developed in the diplomatic service, helped us greatly in our friendships with Chinese people.[51]

Despite the contrasting positions of the R&A with SI, the OSS was prepared to employ Asian Americans in many of their middling positions of responsibility and others as commissioned officers. With few exceptions, they were not to be assigned to the Services Division and were conspicuously absent from the less glamorous jobs as cooks, trash disposers, or barracks cleaners, as was common for Filipinos in the navy or African Americans in the army. Instead, the OSS determined most would serve as "technical representatives," or a rank equivalent to that of a noncommissioned officer, as Donovan ordered:

> In the conduct of certain secret operations to be carried on by this office, it will be necessary to utilize individuals who speak certain foreign languages with native ability. The trained personnel should be enlisted or drafted into the United States Army. The proposed work will be most effective if the willing cooperation and assistance of citizens and residents of the foreign country against which a mission is directed can be secured and properly directed. These leaders should be commissioned officers of the United States Army, even though they may be citizens of foreign countries. It is believed that many instances will occur whereby the effective cooperation and assistance of the foreign nationals can only be secured if a citizen of that nation, or a resident of the particular vicinity, is given a position of leadership and responsibility in the work to be performed.[52]

However, Donovan imposed three qualifications. He refused to assist immigrants in obtaining American citizenship beyond his general encouragement of Congressional members to grant such privileges, a position that some of his underlings ignored. All also limited their highest rank to that of Captain, also circumvented in a couple instances as it applied to Asian Americans. "The merits of each particular case," the director stated, "will be carefully studied before recommendations for appointment are made, but it is believed that it will be unnecessary to appoint such individuals to commissioned ranks higher than that of Captain."[53]

But the third qualification—the demand of loyalty—was potentially a sticking point for some bent on recruiting Asian Americans. Where did their loyalty lie?

Admittedly, Asian Americans like Joe Koide had the necessary linguistic skills and cultural knowledge of the targeted region. Some even possessed the desired high social contacts from which to extract intelligence, as was true of Kunsung Rie. Although possessing knowledge and contacts, Asian Americans like Lincoln Kan might be viewed as having a hidden agenda, as was the case with the SOE and SIS, whose their leadership was made of owners and managers of large British firms in East Asia interested in rescuing their own private economic investments. But for all, as some within the OSS saw it, children of immigrants might harbor divided loyalties, as a recruiter warned:

> Considerable difficulties over the question of divided loyalties may arise, particularly in the case of potential agents who have been some time out of their country. . . . A man will very often say "I am quite prepared to go back to Rurutania to do all I can against the Enemy, but I will do nothing which will hurt my country or her people." . . . It may be possible during the training period in this country to agree on a programme which he is prepared to carry out, but once he arrives in Rurutania, circumstances may arise to cause him to change his mind.[54]

The problem of divided loyalties plagued the OSS. Officials high in the agency circumvented the problem by using their personal and social connections to ensure loyalty of their employees. Their approach limited the number of talented, highly skilled females and failed to net more than a handful of individuals with different ethnic and racial backgrounds. Denied entry into the European and Pacific Theaters of Operation, the OSS entered the China-Burma-India Theater with hopes of proving its worth to the Joint Chiefs of Staff. But operating there required appropriate linguistic and cultural resources, not to mention the correct racial uniform. They found Asian Americans fit the bill, but nevertheless worried that they hailed from ethnic and racial communities with divided loyalties.

CHAPTER 2

༜

Recruiting Asian Americans with the Right Stuff

OSS fears of divided loyalties extended beyond their concerns over Joe Koide, Kunsung Rie, and Lincoln Kan. Despite this reservation, the agency's recruitment of Asian Americans was largely successful. They were able to find at least 378 Asian Americans with the requisite language proficiency and cultural knowledge of East Asia to join their ranks of an estimated 21,000-strong agency, comprising less than 2 percent of its employees. On the surface, this small figure alone suggests the OSS did not practice racial inclusiveness at the entry level, since Asian Americans in 1940 numbered over a half-million and comprised well over 3 percent of the entire American population in the continental United States and its territories, including Alaska, Hawai'i, Guam, Samoa, and the Philippines. Nevertheless, concerns for divided loyalties notwithstanding, they exhibited at least a qualified measure of racial inclusiveness. How the OSS was able to recruit highly qualified Asian Americans who met the intelligence agency's loyalty requirements in sufficient numbers is the subject of this chapter.[1]

At the outset, however, one must consider who the OSS enlisted into their ranks. Believing most of their recruits were headed for service in forward areas, the OSS focused on enlisting males rather than females. Nearly 90 percent of the Asian Americans who joined were men (344), and women became a distinct underrepresented minority whose talents were too often overlooked. This oversight, however, was typical of the organization that hired only about 4,500 females, which amounted to a fifth of all OSS

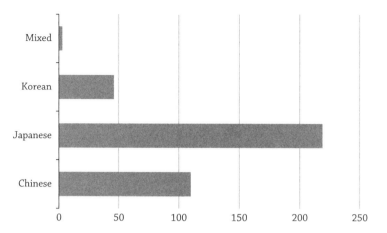

Figure 2.1 OSS Asian Americans, by ethnic group, 1943–1945. Entry 224, RG 226 Records of the OSS, Personnel Files, National Archives and Records Administration II.

employees. The OSS also hired many European American experts on "every single country in Europe," and turned to Asian Americans for expertise and experience in Asia. For the most part, Japanese (219) or Chinese (110) made up close to 90 percent of the group who were brought in, followed by Koreans (46) and those of mixed ancestry (3). Of the 105 whose nationality was known, half of them were American-born citizens, and another quarter (15) were naturalized citizens. As expected, nearly all were proficient in Asian languages.[2]

OSS Asian Americans' proficiency in the East Asian languages was matched by their high level of educational achievement. Some of them were recruited from graduate school, while others were plucked out of other federal government agencies after passing the civil service exams. Only a fifth of them (26) had the equivalent of a high school education; the majority were well beyond that. Half of them had college or trade school training, and another fifth (25) had professional or graduate training. Nearly a tenth (12) had advanced training at the doctoral level, reflecting the overall high educational level of the OSS Asian American recruit that was well beyond the average for the American and Asian American population.

Asian American civilians (221) formed the bulk of those entering the OSS. They were lured away from other government agencies such as the Office of War Information or the Bureau of Economic Warfare with offers of competitive salaries for their linguistic competency. Yet over a third of the Asian Americans in the agency (154) wore the military uniform of the Armed Forces of the United States, nine of whom were Women's Auxiliary Corps members. A tenth of these (18) were commissioned officers, and

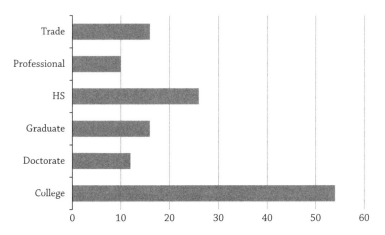

Figure 2.2 OSS Asian Americans, by education, 1943–1945. Entry 224, RG 226 Records of the OSS, Personnel Files, National Archives and Records Administration II.

about half (85) were noncommissioned officers or attained the higher enlisted men's status of technician. The latter were considered enlisted men but referred to as technical representatives—a special designation comparable to a noncommissioned officer. Only a third (51) of the OSS Asian Americans in military service held the lowest ranks of the army or navy. Hence, the Asian Americans in the OSS were two-thirds civilian and one-third military servicemen and women, with the two-thirds of the latter group commissioned or noncommissioned officers and technical representatives, not bottom-rung privates.

Moreover, the sections of the OSS the Asian Americans were assigned to reveals the importance the organization placed on these recruits. Most (279) were in sections that sent their personnel to forward areas close to the battlefront, reflecting a belief widespread among OSS leaders that Asian Americans were to take the same risk of death or harm as other Americans. Those sections that went behind enemy lines where the risks were highest included Secret Intelligence (SI), Special Operations (SO), and Maritime Unit (MU). But Communications (COMMO) and Medical Services (MED) also sent some of their personnel behind enemy lines or to the battlefront. While not at the battlefront, Morale Operations (MO) and Counterintelligence (X-2) also sent some of their personnel to China, Southeast Asia, or India where additionally, having the right racial uniform was necessary for performance and even survival in the field. Only sixty-four Asian Americans were placed in rear-area sections, the bulk of them in Research and Analysis (44) where they labored in Washington, DC, or some of the local branch offices cities in the continental United States and

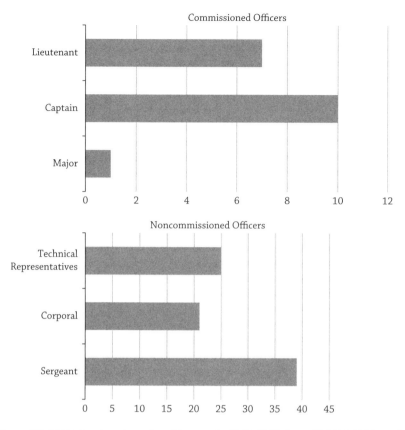

Figure 2.3 OSS Asian Americans, by military rank, 1943–1945. Entry 224, RG 226 Records of the OSS, Personnel Files, National Archives and Records Administration II.

in Honolulu. Only a small handful of individuals (8) were detailed to the less glamorous, manual-laborer type sections (Administration, Services), suggesting that the OSS was in fact racially inclusive when it came to assignments.

Enough Asian Americans had the "right stuff" for the OSS, in other words, they had the right racial uniform to move about in East Asia without attracting attention; they had the requisite educational background to know what information they needed to gather; they had the linguistic skills and cultural knowledge to engage locals to gain the desired intelligence; and two-thirds of them were civilians and not subject to military discipline, while the other third held military ranks that exempt them from nonintelligence related tasks that bottom-ranked soldiers performed. In short, they had the qualifications and the necessary status to gather, analyze, and interpret strategic and tactical intelligence. But where did their loyalties lie?

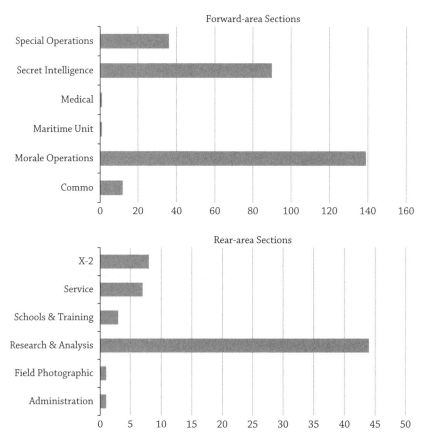

Figure 2.4 OSS Asian Americans, by sections, 1943–1945. Entry 224, RG 226 Records of the OSS, Personnel Files, Entry 224, National Archives and Records Administration II.

Divided loyalties were not an imaginary problem for OSS recruiters. The Chinese Nationalist Government attracted Chinese American support by offering them important concessions. As early as 1917 that government's National Assembly granted representational rights to over 700 Chinese residing abroad. The government further tasked each of its consul-generals with the responsibility of overseeing Chinese-language education in the countries where Chinese lived. From 1918 to 1922, Nationalist China created and placed its Department of Overseas Chinese Affairs within the Ministry of Commerce so that its officials could work with overseas Chinese businessmen to bring capital investment into the country. In Canton, which many Chinese Americans thought of as home, the local government officials established an Overseas Chinese Affairs bureau in 1921, which they turned into a full-fledged Commission in 1926 under the direct control of the Central Executive Committee of the Party. Finally, in 1929 the Nationalist Government adopted the *jus sanguinis* principle of nationality of the Manchu Dynasty—bestowing anyone born to a Chinese father, or in cases where the father was unknown, the mother, with Chinese citizenship regardless of place of birth. Thus, American-born individuals born to Chinese nationals became Chinese citizens and, at least until 1914, presumably owed allegiance to China.[3]

Furthermore, the Chinese Nationalist Government employed Chinese Americans to act as their agents inside the United States. Some were overt agents, such as Alfred Kip Lum, born in Honolulu a year after the American annexation of the Islands. After receiving his undergraduate degree from the University of Hawai'i in 1922, Lum enrolled at Columbia University and earned his PhD at New York University in government and international law. He became a professor at Hawai'i and in 1931 represented the Chinese of Hawai'i when the provisional constitution for Nationalist China was drafted. Two years later, he was commissioned by the Nationalist government to serve as its special envoy "to inspect Kuomintang and overseas Chinese affairs in Hawai'i, the United States, Canada, Mexico, Cuba, Central and South American countries." Lum then got Yen Goon Wong, leader of one of the largest clan (Wong) and district (Ning Yeung) associations, to become an adviser to the Chinese consulate in San Francisco. Others, however, operated covertly, keeping their presence secret until an American radio monitoring station detected radio broadcasts from Nationalist government-controlled China with coded instruction beamed to its agents in the United States. The district intelligence officer in Honolulu observed: "In this connection, it is interesting to note that the Central Executive Committee of the Kuomintang (Overseas Department) is currently using regular short-wave broadcasts from China for the transmission of instructions in code to Kuomintang representatives in the United States."[4]

Not all Chinese Americans allied themselves with the Nationalist Government. There was a language barrier between most Chinese Americans and the Nationalist Government, since they were Cantonese-speaking and the language of the government was Mandarin. Further dividing their loyalties were the competing visions offered by different political factions inside China—Nationalist, Constitutionalist, Collaborationist, and Communist. By 1940 Chinese Americans, numbering 77,504 in the continental United States and another 28,774 in Hawai'i, were divided over where their loyalty and support should be directed and the ways to expel the Japanese invaders. Those supporting Chiang Kai-shek's Nationalist Government advocated national unity through suppression of dissent especially by communists, prior to an all-out drive against invading Imperial Japanese forces, lest the Nationalist Government forces alone bear the losses incurred in battle. Others, however, prioritized expelling the Japanese regardless of the cost, since their goal was to restore the Chinese monarchy. Still others believed the only realistic political solution was to find a compromise with the Japanese occupiers until China gains sufficient economic, political, and military strength to drive them out. A small handful at most, primarily students, aimed at weakening the Nationalist Government and strengthening the Chinese Communist forces through a forced merger of the two and other factions into a multiparty coalition. Finally, some American-born Chinese Americans insisted that their generation should focus solely on the interests of the land of their birth or their adopted land, the United States.[5]

In Hawai'i, many Chinese Americans favored the "Americans only" approach, if military service is any indication. Chinese American males in 1940 between the ages of twenty to thirty-four years (approximately 3,762 men) were already serving in the Territory of Hawai'i's 298th and 299th Infantry Regiments, the Army Air Force, or the US Navy. They had a positive outlook on their future in the Islands, which led them to imagine themselves as part of America. Their parents immigrated to the Islands for the most part between 1876 and 1898 as sugar plantation laborers or as rice growers, and they had climbed out of the ranks of unskilled laborers within a few years to dominate wholesale marketing of fish, vegetables, and canned goods, as well as tailoring and shoemaking. Their relatively rapid success by the early 1930s further reinforced loyalty toward the United States and informed how they understood their ethnic community's history. They found University of Hawai'i sociologist Romanzo Adams's ethnic succession theory applicable to their situation. Kum Pui Lai, the English-language editor of the second volume of *Chinese in Hawaii*, repeated Adams's argument that immigrant groups such as the Filipinos, Japanese, Koreans, and Portuguese followed the same path taken by the Chinese, who had graduated from rural sugar and pineapple plantations to business houses, and finally to professional occupations in Honolulu and Hilo. By 1930, as Lai observed, there was an emerging Chinese white-collar group of 444 teachers, thirty-two engineers, thirty-one dentists, and twenty physicians and surgeons. The Overseas Penman Club in 1934 found further evidence of Chinese Hawaiians' upward mobility in the expanding number of white-collar Chinese Americans who were college-educated. Their success led some, such as lawyer Ernest Ing, to extol the benefits of American residency and citizenship and downplay the blatantly discriminatory 1882 Chinese Exclusion Act:

Living under these advantages and restrictions, the civil status of the alien Chinese cannot be said to be oppressive, though far from being enviable . . . If our Chinese American citizens suffer any hardships through restrictions imposed upon their alien relatives, this is on account of the disadvantages growing out of the operation of the immigration and naturalization laws of the United States and does not denigrate from the value of their citizenship.[6]

Hawai'i Chinese valued their American citizenship. They registered and voted in the 1936 elections at a rate comparable to other Hawai'ians. They followed in the tradition of nearly 800 of their elders who, although immigrants, had acquired American citizenship after annexation and participated in elections. And they were aware that by assisting the American war effort they were helping China, particularly the Pearl River Delta region, since Admiral Chester Nimitz talked openly of the US Navy's intention to establish a beachhead on the eastern coast of China.[7]

Despite a convergence of interests, few Chinese American men from Hawai'i joined the OSS. Of the 117 Chinese American recruits, only seven were from the Islands. Most probably lacked fluency in the Chinese languages required by the OSS, since less than a quarter of the students enrolled in public or private schools in the early 1920s in Hawai'i attended Chinese language schools. Some may have toned down their anti-Imperial Japanese stance out of deference to their numerous Japanese American customers. Most lacked a defining moment when they were labeled "Chinese," unlike the Japanese had experienced with the 1920 strike and later with the bombing of Pearl Harbor. Instead, they retained a strong regional attachment that competed with a national identification, further reinforced by the fact that most Chinese in Hawai'i had their roots in a single region in southern China.[8]

Archie Chun-Ming became the first of only two Chinese Americans from Hawai'i initially recruited by the OSS. He was one of the four Carl Eifler requested at the start to form the inner core of his SO team. Chun-Ming was brought to the Washington, DC headquarters in April 1942 and asked to serve as the unit's chief medical officer. He was part of the Reserve Officers' Association in Hawai'i prior to the bombing of Pearl Harbor as a First Lieutenant in 1930, and then as Captain in 1937. In 1940, he served the association as its president. The youngest of nine children, he had grown up in the Palama District, a working-class neighborhood of Honolulu, where he learned to speak, read, and write Cantonese. He graduated from the prestigious Punahou Academy, where less than 10 percent of the student body was Asian, and went to Columbia University, where he received his AB degree in 1928. Chun-Ming earned his medical degree from the Rush Medical College in 1932, when it was affiliated with the University of Chicago. He primarily socialized with elites of the Chinese Hawai'ian community as president of the large Hawai'i Chinese Civic Association. He also served as the project chairman for the China Emergency Medical Relief Committee, was on the World Outreach Committee of the YMCA in 1940, and was president of the 250-member Council Club. He was gifted at languages and, contrary to British intelligence's denigration of his language skills, picked up Mandarin and Hindi. Chun-Ming became one of eight officers to join Detachment 101's training at Camp X.[9]

John Francis (Yok San) Kwock was the other Hawai'ian Chinese to join the OSS. John was born in Hilo to two Chinese immigrant laborers in 1912 who acquired American citizenship through prior acquisition of Hawai'ian nativity rights. John grew up in Hilo and, after graduating from St. Louis College (Chaminade), became a shipping clerk for an art and jewelry dealer, where he learned about the importance of security. After World War II broke out, he entered the Office of the Provost Marshal General's Training School at Fort Custer, Michigan, where OSS recruiters interviewed and requisitioned him for X-2 (counterintelligence). Kwock was then sent to Washington, DC in late November 1943 to undergo training. He joined the Branch's Far East section as an assistant security officer and was tasked with personnel background investigations and internal security work. "Our investigation reveals," Lester Baylis of the OSS Security Office noted about Kwock, "that Subject is 100% loyal, intelligent, industrious, sober and thoroughly trustworthy. His personal habits are beyond reproach."[10]

Unlike Chun Ming and Kwock, most OSS Chinese Americans came from the continental United States. A quarter of them (28) came from the West Coast, especially California, but a comparable number also hailed from the mid-Atlantic region, particularly New York (16). A dozen of them were Chinese citizens studying in the United States, who therefore met the requisite language skills and residential requirement. Defined by law as "aliens ineligible for citizenship," these immigrants could not participate in local, state, and national politics and had no incentives for long-term capital and social investment in the United States. In contrast, their participation in the local and national politics of China was encouraged, and their remitted funds were welcomed as they were heavily invested in much-needed infrastructure such as railroads, schools, watchtowers, water development projects, and agriculture. Their monetary donations to political factions vying for control at the national level were also welcomed. Unlike American politics, Chinese immigrant support or opposition had a noticeable impact on Chinese politics, from the Qing Dynasty of nineteenth-century China, through the dictatorial rule of Yuan Shih-kai in the decade after the 1911 Revolution, to the Chinese Nationalist government's war with Imperial Japan following its outbreak in 1937.[11]

Questions of loyalty remained open for these Chinese Americans, given their coethnics' greater political interest in China than the United States. With only some 20,000 Chinese Americans having voting rights by 1940, they did not constitute a significant voting bloc for American politicians. But in China they drew considerable attention because of their financial contributions, occupational knowledge considered essential for the nation's modernization, and the fact that their American-born children were deemed Chinese citizens by the Nationalist Chinese Government.[12]

Chinese American political participation in China involved a variety of motives. Of course, many of them, especially the merchants, sought to protect their own capital investments inside China. But for many average Chinese Americans, their motives involved a dual conception of loyalty that became evident after the Imperial Japanese forces widened their offensive following the Marco Polo Bridge incident in 1937. In 1940, the left-leaning *China Daily News* newspaper in New York City, for example, conveyed this sense of dual loyalty to China and the United States. In its editorial, the author declared Chinese Americans' concern for China as "natural": "So we regard overseas Chinese concern about their motherland as a natural expression of normal human feelings, and their efforts to permanently develop their settlement [in the United States] as a rational development." As for the American-born Chinese, the author also believed that their loyalty should be dual as well: "Among the overseas Chinese in this country, many have acquired U.S. citizenship. To them, to love and defend [their] motherland is a bound duty, and to be loyal to the United States is an obligation." Hence, Chinese American monetary donations for China's national defense exceeded their normal remittances by several million dollars. In 1937, for example, the total amount of remittances the homeland region of Toishan received from Chinese in other regions of the world totaled some nine million dollars. After the war broke out in 1937 to 1945, a single organization in San Francisco known as the Association to Save China sent a staggering five million dollars in addition to smaller donations to aviation funds, medical supplies, and other items sent in support of China's defense. Others organized boycotts of Japanese consumer goods by rallying American public opinion to China through the dissemination of their pamphlets and other literature. Still others participated in China's Congressional elections, with so many of them participating in the July 1937 elections held in San Francisco that historian Yong Chen writes: "It is clear that many more

Chinese Americans cast their votes in this [Chinese Congressional] election than in American elections."[13]

The American-born Chinese also had an interest in politics in China. Their awareness of conditions in China was partly fueled by their own limited upward economic mobility in the United States. Despite having college degrees from elite American universities, they had to depend on family, clan, and regional place ties for employment in California at restaurants, art curio shops, hand laundries, and flower and vegetable marketing operations during the Great Depression. If they sought higher-paying or higher-status jobs, their options were limited to what they could carve out for themselves in China rather than the United States. By 1930, some 40 percent of the 19,470 Chinese American males over the age of ten years counted in the US Census were stuck in domestic and personal service. About a fifth of the same age group had gone to China to secure better employment a few years later. Their stated motives indicated that many American-born Chinese in the continental United States imagined their loyalty to China as greater than to the United States. As Kaye Hong of San Francisco wrote:

> I merely intend to become a good citizen of the great Republic, I shall support the nationalist government which is now gaining strength with each succeeding day. I shall accept the national policies as being the best moves for China. As a whole, I shall place the welfare of the nation [China] above my own.[14]

Others, such as New York Chinatown journalist Ernest Moy, pointed to the mutual, intertwining interests of the United States and China in that serving one meant serving the other. He spoke of meeting Sun Yat-sen, founder of the Chinese Nationalist Party, as a young boy. His response to Sun's query about why Moy wanted to join the Revolutionary Party or *Tongmenhui* illustrates his dual loyalty. "My answer," Moy recalled in 1955, "was that I wanted to bring freedom and independence to the country of my parents just as the American patriots won liberty for my native land." As a young man, Moy pursued this vision and trained in Massachusetts to become a bomber pilot for the Chinese Nationalist Air Force. Though the Revolution succeeded before Moy could drop bombs on the Manchus, he never lost his passion or interest in China politics:

> Our President Theodore Roosevelt . . . said that "the interests of China and the United States, along all lines . . . are identical." This meant to me that what benefits one, benefits the other, and what injures one, correspondingly injures the other. Where else, then, could an American-born Chinese render a more useful service to his country and to humanity than to serve in the land of his

forebears, to bring both countries together in an indissoluble partnership to promote world peace and prosperity? . . . My devoted interest in the Chinese people is basically a dedicated interest in the welfare of my own country, the United States of America—not in a Chauvinistic sense, but in the larger one of our country's importance in the community of nations.[15]

Active political participation, by voting or serving in China's military services, was not an option for many American-born Chinese. The 1940 Nationality Act made forfeiture of their American citizenship possible if they voted in a foreign government's election, held an official position in a foreign government, or joined a foreign military service. Hence the American-born Chinese, for the most part, limited their participation to raising funds for China's defense by granting certain privileges in return for donations received, such as a benefit dance, fashion shows, dramatic plays, exhibits, bazaars, movies, concerts, competitive games, skating, and button sales. Their button sales proved especially popular and profitable, with sales of these markers for monetary contributions denoted by color: red (under $100), yellow ($100–250), blue ($250–500), silver ($500–$1,000), and gold ($1,000+). American-born Chinese did not participate in the election of China's National Assembly; in 1946 only 9,533 of a possible 80,000 Chinese Americans of voting age cast their ballots. They were also understandably reluctant to serve in China's military service; only a small handful of Chinese American males served in China's air force, whose personnel was almost three-quarters overseas Chinese. Nevertheless, a few distinguished themselves as "aces," notably San Francisco-born Ban-yang Huang, who shot down fourteen Imperial Japanese bombers. One Chinese American even served in the nascent Chinese Navy in 1936, although only on US Navy-approved, temporarily assigned duty at the invitation of the Chinese Nationalist Government.[16]

With such strong dualistic loyalty, only a small number of continental Chinese Americans were recruited from the West Coast. Lincoln Mei was brought into counterintelligence while on assignment far from his home in San Francisco. Born and raised in Shanghai, his family moved to San Francisco, where he attended school and learned English. Lincoln then spent a year at a small college in Ohio, then another at Pomona College. He left college to manage his father's investment accounts while attending a business college. But in July 1941, he was inducted into the army before being recruited by the OSS and sent to Officer Candidate School at Fort Benning, Georgia, for what appeared to be a promising career as a primary investigator in the China Theater. Mei's language skills, officer training, and upbringing in China made him a desirable recruit.[17]

Harry Jung (Chung Kay Quong) was another talented Chinese American recruited by Secret Intelligence. He was born in Los Angeles to immigrant parents from Kwantung Province who ran a restaurant. Harry graduated Polytechnic High School, Santa Monica Junior College, and Pomona College a Phi Beta Kappa before earning a master's degree in international relations at Columbia University. Jung also received part of his education in Hong Kong, after which he was employed at the Universal Trading Corporation, the official Chinese Nationalist Government's trading company inside the United States. Given his language proficiency in Chinese, English, and Japanese, the latter learned from local Japanese classmates, Jung believed himself capable of providing important expertise advice to the OSS:

> I believe that I possess the unique combination of both American and Chinese viewpoints from education and racial background which may be of some use. My experience from working for the Chinese government in contact with Chinese government officials may also be of value in relation to possible postwar intergovernmental relations as well as trade possibilities.

In April 1943, he was one of a few Chinese Americans inducted into the US Navy. But he joined Secret Intelligence (SI) after OSS recruiters received definitive clearance for him: "Confidential informants recommend the Subject as to loyalty, ability, and personal character."[18]

Not all OSS Chinese Americans from the continental United States had the requisite language skills. Don Eng of Seattle was brought into Detachment 101 by Carl Eifler because of his expertise in radio technology, and not his Chinese language skills. He joined SO, leaving behind his wife Dorothy, his five daughters, and one son in Seattle. He immediately enlisted in the army, even though he was exempt from military conscription. By May 1942, he had been sworn into the OSS and departed with Detachment 101 for East Asia. Eng was to play a critical role in providing Eifler with radio communication sets that allowed for their deep penetration behind enemy lines.[19]

Most OSS Chinese Americans were from the American northeast. Some turned down the OSS, such as David Kai Foo Loo, a doctoral candidate at Clark University in Worcester, Massachusetts, who Norwood Allman tried to recruit for his expertise in climatography. Loo was working on the Kuriles using Japanese language materials for his dissertation and submitted his materials to SI. Frank Tan of Boston was another who turned down the OSS's invitation. Born and raised in Boston, Tan moved with his family to China in the early 1930s when Frank, through his father's connections with high officials in the Nationalist Government, worked as a minesweeper. Experiencing danger firsthand, he switched over to the Communication and Trade Company in Haiphong, which from 1939 to 1941 smuggled aviation fuel, gun barrels, and other supplies aboard Norwegian-flagged merchant ships headed for the Chinese Nationalist-controlled areas. Tan barely escaped the clutches of Japanese authorities in French Indochina by fleeing to Hong Kong. There, he joined J. Laurence Gordon and Harry Bernard to form the Gordon-Bernard-Tan spy team that smuggled information out of French Indochina to British, Chinese, and American intelligence agencies. Tan's group remained independent, turning down the OSS's merger offer in early 1945. Tan continued working with Ho Chi Minh, with whom he developed a close relationship, and spent his time training Viet Minh personnel for intelligence work when the OSS tried again to recruit him.[20]

Chinese Americans from New York became the primary recruits for the OSS and turned into agents for SI and SO. Richard Hong Chan was one of the first Chinese Americans chosen, was among the oldest, and was certainly the most mysterious. He listed himself as having no education, spoke the Chinese language, and worked in a New York restaurant. Despite his seemingly skimpy qualifications, he was recruited by Carl Eifler, who had him enlist in the army and then the OSS on April 14, 1942, after which he was immediately promoted to sergeant and assigned to SO's Detachment 101. "I was recruited by Colonel Eifler," Richard stated in his debriefing interview in 1945, "and was assigned under him in India from October 1942 to 1944. My duty was to get information from Chinese smugglers and Japanese spies." After presumably three months of training to elicit such information, Richard was sent by submarine to India ahead of the others in Detachment 101, who traveled by surface vessel over the Atlantic Ocean through the Middle East to India.[21]

Robert Chin was the other key Chinese American from New York. Born there in 1918 to an immigrant father and an American-born Chinese mother, Chin was educated at Columbia University, where he earned his undergraduate, graduate, and doctorate degrees in psychology. In 1943, he was hired by the Foreign Broadcast Intelligence Service to analyze propaganda radio broadcasts. Before the end of that year, however, he enlisted in the army and joined the OSS in the first week of January 1944. He was assigned to the Far Eastern Division of the R&A China Section Political Subdivision with special focus on Occupied China. His boss, C. Martin Wilbur, was an enthusiastic supporter of Chin's promotion to the officer rank and assignment to the China Theater and confidently placed him on the OSS's psychological assessment team:

We intend to send this man to China on an OSS assignment covering psychological testing of native Chinese. The particular details of the assignment for which the Chinese are to be secured cannot be divulged for security reasons. The assessment group which is being sent to China to carry out this task will be composed of two white and four Chinese Psychologists and Psychiatrists.

But Joseph Spencer, head of R&A China Theater, requested Chin's presence in China in mid-August 1945, knowing that he had a sterling character, high academic qualifications, and proficiency in Chinese, with a fair knowledge of French and German. As stated by C. Martin Wilbur, chief of the Political Subdivision, Far East Division of R&A in Washington, DC, Chin was the ideal person for the OSS:

I believe him to be entirely loyal to the United States. He has good qualities of group leadership, which he achieves in a quiet and gentlemanly way. He is well-bred, courteous, and discreet. He is very intelligent, well-disciplined in his thinking and possesses keen insight into individual and group psychology.[22]

Recruited out of Officer Candidate School at Fort Bragg, North Carolina, Lincoln Siu Hing Kan had strong qualifications. He was an American citizen by virtue of his New York birth during his father's student days. He was fluent in both Cantonese and Mandarin, the former picked up from his Cantonese-speaking parents and the latter in his surrounding environment growing up in Shanghai. Lincoln had high social connections sought by the OSS, since he was the grandson of the founder of the Nanyang Brothers Tobacco Company, Chiu-nam Kan of the Fo Shan district, Kwantung Province, and the son of Lydia Chen, whose family banking interests dominated much of the economic life on The Bund in Shanghai. He also retained and sharpened his English-language skills, as evidenced by his performance at the Shanghai American School. Although he was the lone Asian in his class of 1937, he excelled and subsequently matriculated at the University of North Carolina, Chapel Hill, where he enjoyed a luxurious college lifestyle. Lincoln was "a big man on campus and he made a big noise," his wife recalled; he changed his automobile's make and color to match his most current girlfriend, of which there were many. His patrician lifestyle and playboy outlook, reminiscent of the fictional spy James Bond, nevertheless provided him with political connections that reached as high as the Soong family that governed Nationalist China itself.[23]

The major issue with Kan was loyalty. On the one hand, his father's company had a history of compromising with Imperial Japanese authorities. To establish the company his grandfather became a naturalized Japanese citizen, adopted the name "Shonanshi Matsumoto," and received a Japanese passport, a status he retained for almost two decades. He used Japanese capital and was initially based in Kobe, not southern China as the company name suggested, and utilized all Japanese products— trademarks, packaging materials, tinfoil, cigarette papers, bamboo mouthpieces, blending spices, vats, and advertising picture cards. On the other hand, Kan's father's company—and, by logical extension, Lincoln himself—ran contrary to British, American, and Japanese economic interests. The Nanyang Brothers competed with the British-American Tobacco Company, a conglomerate founded by James Duke that in 1937 sold fifty-five billion cigarettes in China. His company also aimed to out-sell Imperial Tobacco, a Japanese government-owned corporation whose sales grew as Japanese forces gained more control over Chinese territory. Further complicating Kan's loyalty ties, the company allied itself with the Nationalist Government in the late 1920s and was taken over by the Soong family, the ruling family dynasty of China, a decade later. With Japanese military control extending further south in China, however, Lincoln's family fortunes were threatened, prompting him to action. After separating from his Japanese American wife, Jean Koizumi, Kan enlisted in the US Army. He was recruited for the OSS and then, after training, was sent to the Air Ground Forces Resources & Technical Staff of the Fourteenth Air Force under General Claire Chennault in China, who in turn sent him on the Akron mission to Macao.[24]

For the OSS, Korean Americans presented a different recruiting problem than Chinese Americans. On the one hand, most of them were viewed as allies with the United States in its war against Imperial Japan. Koreans in Hawai'i and California—where the majority of Korean Americans resided in 1940—illustrate this. In the early 1940s, they numbered about 7,000 in Hawai'i and another thousand in the continental United States, prima-rily in California. Koreans had achieved a modicum of upwardly mobility from their rural farming background after immigrating to the Islands in 1903–1905. Just a couple of years before the OSS started recruiting Asian Americans, many had left the ranks of sugar plantation field laborers and moved into pineapple cannery jobs and stevedore work. Perhaps over half of them resided in Honolulu, in the Palama or Liliha districts, or outside the state capital in Waihiawa, employed as carpenters and barbers at the Schofield Barracks. Influenced in part by their occupational ties to the American military, Koreans in Hawai'i readily supported the American war effort against Japan despite showing little interest in returning to a Japanese-occupied homeland and being staunchly committed to perma-nent settlement in the United States.[25]

Nevertheless, some of the young leaders among Koreans in Hawai'i displayed considerable enthusiasm for military operations against the Japanese. They thought such an approach would hasten Korean independence and were especially attracted to the OSS SO's emphasis on "irregular" warfare—espionage and sabotage activities—as a viable avenue for Korean American participation in the war. Korean National Association leader Jacob Dunn declared Korean Americans as ideally suited for covert warfare against Imperial Japan. In 1943 he wrote an essay shortly after Stalin, Roosevelt, Churchill, and Chiang Kai-shek met in Cairo to work out an agreement, among other things, on Korea's future as an independent nation "in due course." To hasten independence, Dunn called on Korean Americans to pull together and move "beyond the narrow scope of outworn partisan and individual will and ambition. Korea is bigger than parties or their dictators." He also discouraged Korean Americans from forming Korean combat units to fight alongside with Chinese troops in East Asia:

> Actually, the Koreans have no standing army of their own. Under Japanese rule the Koreans within Korea have had no opportunity for military training. The desire to create a large and independent Korean army on Chinese soil can be at this juncture only wishful thinking.

Dunn believed that "the obvious and reasonable phase of Korean war participation will be found in guerrilla, espionage, and sabotage activities" for Koreans and Korean Americans. He saw Koreans as a logical choice for this task due to their knowledge of the land, the enemy, and prior experience:

> Espionage is a vital form of Korean war participation. It combines the inherent hate for the Japanese with Korean familiarity of the Asiatic terrain. The Koreans have fluency of Chinese, Korean and Japanese languages, spoken and written. They have, undoubtedly, the best knowledge of any people of Japanese customs and habits. In fact, they have already demonstrated their espionage ability by bringing valuable military information to the Chinese intelligence.

Although appreciative of Chinese support for the Korean Provisional Government, he asserted that the United States was the best means for effecting this kind of warfare with Korean participation, given the country's "reservoir of armaments." Its leadership "in championing the cause of the oppressed and subjected," and its disinterest "in any territorial expansion or political hegemony," made the United States the best option for Koreans.[26]

Dunn's idea of supporting America's war effort in general was well-received by Koreans. Of those Koreans polled in Hawai'i public opinion surveys, close to 90 percent supported President Roosevelt's handling of the war, a significantly higher percentage than others in the same poll. The First Korean Methodist Church of Honolulu alone had fifty-eight members serving in the armed forces of the United States. On September 1, 1943, the Koreans of Hawai'i presented to General Robert Richardson Jr., commander of Pacific Ocean Area, a check for $26,265.35—a generous donation for the war effort from a community that numbered less than 8,000.[27]

While willing to join, few Korean Americans had the necessary language skills for the OSS. They could not send their children to Korea for language education, since Japanese Occupation authorities carefully controlled transit in and out of the country, with less than 14 percent of Korean immigrants migrating from Hawai'i to Korea. They had not established many language schools in Hawai'i, because the ethnic population was initially scattered throughout the Islands. Only after the 1920 strike were Koreans able to take advantage of high wages and move into Honolulu, where they lived in densely concentrated areas that allowed for the rise of Korean language schools. Despite nearly half of all Koreans in Hawai'i being under age fifteen by 1930, parents still did not send them to Korean language schools at a rate comparable to the Japanese or the Chinese; only a fifth of them received Korean language education. Moreover, Korean language schools had no suitable printing type available for production of textbooks in *han'gul*, the Korean alphabet. Nor could they point to large numbers of Korean American youth studying in Korea. By the early 1930s, less than a tenth (520 of the 6,461) of school-age children attended one of ten Korean language schools, which prompted Bernice Kim, a Hawai'i-born Korean, to observe, "The second generation knows some Korean but very little of it."[28]

In addition, many Korean American youth were lukewarm about Korean independence. They grew increasingly apathetic when they observed how many among their parents' generation heatedly debated the best means to effect independence. They saw some, such as Yongman Park, advocate immediate guerrilla warfare against Imperial Japanese forces, using Manchuria as their base of operations. Others, especially those who studied under Syngman Rhee, viewed the Imperial Japanese military forces as too powerful to be dislodged and opted instead for exerting diplomatic pressure on Japan until her grip on Korea was sufficiently weakened. Both made Oahu Island their base of operations outside of East Asia prior to 1930, as did Kilsoo Haan, leader of the Sino-Korean People's League, a leftist-leaning organization that demanded immediate independence for the country.

But many Hawai'i-born and bred Koreans took only a mild interest in the struggle their parents and older relatives deemed so important. Even after the outbreak of war, the majority of American-born Koreans in Hawai'i were not swept up in the renewed movement to free Korea. Donald Kang, the editor and publisher of the *American-Korean News*, the only publication in English for young Korean readers before 1943, admitted in *The New Pacific* that the Hawai'i-born Koreans were "not as keen in [Korean independence] politics . . . although they all long and hope for Korean independence." Another wrote in *The New Korea* during the summer of 1942, declaring, "We as Americans have one and only [one] duty at the present time, and that is a united effort in helping our American government in winning this war." An army intelligence officer reported a similar finding:

> The bulk of the younger generation of American-born Koreans in Hawaii are notably cool to the political activities of their parents. Their attitude is that, if the old folks get any enjoyment out of it, all right; but that they are Americans, interested in things American, including getting ahead, and they have no desire to pay salaries to [*sic*] swivel-chair Korean politicians. They very likely would be considered as foreigners should they return to a liberated Korea.[29]

A small number of Korean Americans found collaboration with Imperial Japanese authorities a viable alternative. Those few with capital to invest were at least outwardly accommodating toward Japanese rule over their country. They took advantage of the Japanese Governor-General's policy in the 1920s of slowly incorporating Korea into the Japanese empire by turning the land into an advance military supply base for Imperial Japanese forces on the Asian continent. Their investments in mining, textiles, pharmaceuticals, and other industries required cooperation with the Japanese rulers for business necessities such as travel permits to move both within Korea and abroad. Students seeking to go to the United States also had to register for Japanese passports, unlike the early Korean student immigrants who disavowed all connections with the Japanese government, fled the country, and openly participated in independence movement activities. Young Korean Americans moving to Korea were not subject to conscription until August 1, 1943, when some 190,000 young Korean males received their draft notices. Among them were at least one and, more likely, others who joined the Imperial Japanese armed forces. A Hawai'i-born Korean named "Okamoto" stood guard over British prisoners in Thailand, joining nearly 20,000 Korean volunteers in the Imperial Japanese armed forces in 1943. A handful of other young Korean Americans, native in Korean and fluent in the Japanese language due to their schooling in Occupied Korea, were also employed in the Japanese consulate offices.[30]

Some collaborated with Japanese consulate officials in the United States. Their numbers are unknown, though their actions prior to the Pearl Harbor attack in 1941 show that they reported irregularly to Japanese Consulate officials in Honolulu, who in turn reported to Tokyo on Korean Americans and the independence movement. Korean American cooperation with the Japanese Consulate made discerning their loyalty a difficult matter. The ONI discovered at least seven such Korean Americans working with the Honolulu Japanese Consulate. With exit and entry visa and passport control, the consulate was able to extract cooperation from Korean Americans, however reluctantly on the latter's part. These officials hired some Korean Americans part-time to report on their ethnic community. Seven Korean Americans received one-time monetary payments from Japanese officials for as little as $3.40 and as much as $100. Among the highest paid was Kwang Won Cho, better known as "Father Cho," an Anglican priest at St. Luke's (Korean) church. He once confessed to an informant for the OSS that he had worked for the Japanese Consulate from 1932 until April 1941 translating Korean-language materials: "He admits having performed work for the Consulate relating to Korean activities; further, that during the latter period approximately $200 was paid him by the Consulate for his services which included obtaining a translation of two Korean newspapers." Kilsoo Haan and Doo Ok Chung, Hawai'i members of the Sino-Korean People's League, were also among the seven. Father Cho was not a collaborator, at least not in the eyes of Admiral Chester Nimitz, who made him one of only three Koreans allowed into the navy. Cho joined the Second and Fourth Marine Corps that took Saipan. He went ashore, braving artillery and mortar fire, to ferret out Japanese soldiers posing as Korean civilians to infiltrate American lines. Haan, too, was not a collaborator, though the ONI interpreted his activities as beneficial to the Japanese war effort: "His espionage activities for the Consulate apparently were confined to spying on his own people. Ever since, his activities have fallen strictly within the pattern of normal Fifth Column tactics."[31]

The OSS had an additional reason for treading carefully with Korean American recruitment. Director William Donovan shelved a proposal to finance a half-million-dollar project to arm and train 500 to a thousand Korean Americans, Korean Chinese, and Korean prisoners of war captured from the Imperial Japanese Army. Although pressured by the Korean Provisional Government in late 1942 and by Syngman Rhee in early 1943, Donovan refused the advice of Carl Hoffman, who had attended the meeting convened by the navy to discuss the role of Korean Americans.

Those in attendance learned that Lieutenant Donald Davies, Robert Kinney, Lawrence Salisbury, and George McCune of the State Department had already determined that a united Korean front was unlikely and that there were multiple problems involving Korean Americans in an all-Korean combat unit assigned to China:

> First, because the Chinese suspect them and would limit their operations and secondly, because there are Koreans in good supply in China, some of whom are trusted by the Chinese and could be expertly trained by Americans in China. I further stated we had great difficulty in preventing Korean representatives from proposing all kinds of "deals" for training enormous numbers of "American Koreans," and secondly, the Koreans we have trained always insisted on special privileges and were generally somewhat difficult to handle.

Hoffman then advised Donovan that

> for the time being a "hands off" policy is advisable. When Korean leadership takes form it might be advisable to cooperate with such leadership if it is successful in getting unity among its following.[32]

Thereafter, the OSS moved slowly toward gathering and training a small group of Korean Americans from the mainland rather than from Hawai'i.

Despite their limited numbers, Korean Americans in the continental United States provided the OSS with qualified recruits. Initially they were difficult to find, since most Koreans lived in rural areas instead of in California's cities. None were members of skilled labor trade unions. A few potential agents had achieved considerable wealth in agriculture, such as the Kim brothers, whose cultivation of nectarines and other fruits earned them fame and fortune. But most California Korean Americans— some 80 percent—were less fortunate, making only modest incomes in agricultural-related occupations in farming communities like Upland, Riverside, and Redlands. The remaining 20 percent resided in San Francisco and Los Angeles, primarily working in groceries, hotels, and restaurants, with only a small handful in professional or semiprofessional jobs. The latter group, however, grew to over a third of the Korean American population in the continental United States by 1940, as college students congregated in those two cities where they could land the few white-collar jobs available to Koreans. With Japanese, English, and Korean language skills, these students became the main targets for OSS recruiters.[33]

As a result, Korean American students became the first Asian Americans recruits for the OSS, despite its policy. Soon Kyo Hahn was the first. He entered the United States on a student visa in 1925 and briefly attended college in Illinois before entering into the world of commerce. He was immensely successful, becoming the proprietor of the Oriental Importing Company, specializing in the importation and sale of incense, perfume, and other articles. Hahn also became the sole owner of the Sanithriad Products Company in Chicago before establishing a restaurant called the Korean Village in Lake Geneva, Wisconsin, known for its Asian cuisine. He had accumulated so much wealth that he purchased the Otto Young Mansion and its 247-acre estate on the east shore. Viewed by Syngman Rhee as a neutral and potential unifier of the various Korean and Korean American independence movement factions, Hahn was a logical choice to direct the Korean espionage and sabotage operations for the OSS under Esson Gale, as long as his loyalty was assured. He was vouched for by FBI Director J. Edgar Hoover, who met Hahn after local law enforcement officers erroneously arrested him for being a wealthy businessman with ties to the Japanese government, not realizing that he was "violently anti-Japanese." Before any determination of his loyalty could be made, however, the Korean Project was terminated and Esson Gale left the OSS. Hahn thereafter worked informally for the State Department's Stanley Hornbeck, for whom he penned a couple of reports, one of them titled "The History of the Korean Revolutionary Movements."[34]

Sukyoon Chang was another early recruit. Like Hahn, Chang was a student from Kangwŏn-do Province who arrived at San Francisco in December 1923 en route to the elite boarding school Mt. Hermon School for Boys, in Massachusetts. He went on to Oberlin College and then Vanderbilt University, where he graduated in 1936 with a degree in geology. Chang then moved to a small town just outside of Butte, Montana, to gain practical experience in mining before going to operate his family's undeveloped gold mine in Korea. It was not Chang's mining experience but his fluency in Japanese and Korean, as well as his ability to read and write Chinese, however, that made him an attractive OSS candidate. Also, Syngman Rhee's letter, recommending Chang as the OSS liaison officer to the Korean Provisional Government and the Chinese Nationalist Government while in the field, is probably what appealed most to Carl Eifler, head of the OSS Field Experimental Unit in his April 1942 interview. Although Chang's primary loyalty was to the Korean Provisional Government, his willingness to enlist as a private in the American Army and provide only indirect assistance to Korea persuaded Eifler to bring Chang into the unit.[35]

Others were carefully chosen after close screening in 1944. Once the Korean Project was revived, elite Korean Americans were sought to form a special team under the new project, code-named "Napko." Ilhan New was the lead on this project. Like Soon Kyo Hahn, New was a firm advocate of immediate Korean independence. Although he never adopted an Anglicized name, Ilhan was different from his peers in the Korean independence movement. His father was not *yangban* or an elite, but a successful silk trader who traveled to China and Manchuria while residing in Pyongyang. Ilhan received his entire education in the United States, having been sent by his father to Kearney, Nebraska, for his primary and secondary education. He initially attended Michigan State College but transferred to the University of Michigan, where he earned his bachelor's degree in business administration in 1919. Although he worked for the Michigan Central Railroad and General Electric in Schenectady, New York, New demonstrated his business acumen when he cofounded, with Charles "Wally" Smith, the La Choy Foods Product Company in 1921. In 1925 he married Mary Woo, a Chinese American who earned her medical degree from the University of Colorado, and they went to Korea in the following year ostensibly to take over his retiring father's business. His education, upbringing, and Christian faith made Ilhan New seem more "American" in "habits of thought" than Korean, and thus attractive to OSS recruiters.[36]

New had other traits the OSS found equally desirable. His YuHan Corporation, a pharmaceutical company established in 1926, had an extensive network of sales outlets in Japanese-occupied Korea, Manchuria, and Southeast Asia. YuHan became one of the largest companies in Korea, probably with the cooperation of the Imperial Japanese Governor-General's office, as had so many of Korea's prewar *chaebols* or conglomerates. Moreover, New was accused by some Korean Americans as having made his wealth by defrauding some investors and selling narcotics in China with the cooperation of the colonial Japanese administration. Despite these allegations, New was recognized widely as a successful Korean American businessman. After he settled in Boulder, Colorado at the end of the 1930s, Nobel Prize-winning writer Pearl S. Buck hosted a luncheon in his honor at the Roosevelt Hotel in New York.[37]

New saw joining the OSS an attractive vehicle for his own plans for Korean independence. Without access to his private papers, one can only speculate, but it seems reasonable to assume that New could have remained neutral and continued to accumulate wealth through his corporation. Yet he risked it all for the sake of Korean independence, even though he was hemmed in. He found the older leadership of the United Korean Committee, especially Ho Kim, Jong Ik Song, and Si Tai Han, unreceptive to his strident demands for a strong, independent Korea immediately after the war, causing him to deliberately sit out "in dignified isolation" the second session of the 1943 annual meeting. New also found the younger generation of Korean American supporters—while receptive to his ideas—veering to the political left in favor of the Korean National Revolutionary Party, a group advocating the nationalization of corporate giants like YuHan. To convey his own ideas of what postwar Korea should look like, in December 1943 New established the Korea Economic Society in New York and published the *Korea Economic Digest* with Chung Kew Won, K. Bernard Kim, Pai Min Soo, John Starr Kim, and some members of the Korean Student Federation. New's group assumed that once the war ended Koreans would have little time to prepare for nationhood, and the current Korean independence movement leaders in the United States were not ready to govern. Even though the United Korean Committee appointed him head of the commission on postwar Korea, New learned that winning over others was not easy. To do so, he researched and wrote "Korea: The Other Ally of the Orient" for Colonel Carroll Harris of the San Francisco Military Intelligence Service office, who in turn passed the report along to the OSS in May 1943.[38]

Unlike New, Kang "Diamond" Kim (sometimes spelled "Kimm") was part of the Korean American political left. Born in Korea in Long Chyun, North Pung On, Kim was educated at the Bynsung Academy in Bunchyun. He furthered his education at the Union Seminary in Seoul before arriving in Los Angeles to attend a religious conference in 1928. Kim got a student visa and began graduate work at the University of Southern California, where he earned a master's degree in geology in 1933. He returned to Korea, but quickly came back to the United States after war broke out in 1937. Returning to Los Angeles, Kim became active in Korean politics while attending the Los Angeles Korean Methodist Church. Opposed to Syngman Rhee's leadership but supporting a united front within the Korean Provisional Government, Kim's political activities reached an impasse. Facing deportation, Kim accepted Carl Eifler's invitation to join the OSS.[39]

Kunsung Rie demonstrated little previous commitment to the Allied war cause. At first glance Rie appeared similar to other Korean categorized as students in the United States. Born in Pyongyang, he grew up under the Japanese Occupation and learned the Japanese language well enough to enter Waseda University in April 1930 and graduate with a degree in English and Japanese literature. He planned to study in the United States for two or three years before moving to London, but with the outbreak of war in 1937, Rie changed his plans and went to the George Peabody College (Vanderbilt University) in Nashville. Rie struggled academically and soon drifted, moving to Boston University and taking up various jobs in the northeast. Once the United States entered the war Rie secured translation jobs, first for the Army-New York Public Library's joint dictionary project in the spring and summer of 1942. Thereafter, Rie was appointed as Associate Language Editor for the Office of War Information (OWI) in New York in December 1942.[40]

The other OSS infiltration project Korean Americans were recruited for was code-named "Eagle." Ryongi Hahm (or Ryongi Chyun Hahm, or Yong Chun Ham, as his name appears in various federal government documents) was the OSS' first choice as Eagle's leader due to his qualifications and willingness to fight the Imperial Japanese forces. Born and educated in Seoul, Korea, Hahm earned his LLB degree at the University of Korea and his ThB degree at the Union College of Theology. He then boarded the *Tatsuta-Maru* and entered the United States in April 1931 to matriculate at Vanderbilt University, where he earned his bachelor's degree. Hahm then went to Yale University for his PhD. Doctorate in hand, he became an instructor at the Harvard-Yenching Institute in 1941, as well as a researcher and translator for the ONI after 1943. As a result of his extensive education, Hahm acquired "native fluency in speaking, reading, writing Korean and Japanese" and was competent in Chinese and English languages. Moreover, he was not affiliated with any faction within the Korean Provisional Government or the independence movement. "I was [once] a member of the Korean Independence Society," Hahm declared in 1944, "but withdrew some time ago." Hahm was also eager to fight the Japanese. He did not have to volunteer for such a dangerous mission as Eagle. He was a foreign national, over forty years old, married, and was raising a son, all of which exempted him from the draft. He had no visa problems; as he stated, "I expect to remain in the United States permanently." Yet Hahm despised the Japanese because they had executed his father, a royal court member; they had also banned Hahm's own return to Korea and forced his two brothers and two sisters to scatter abroad, causing him to lose contact with them. Hahm's interview left OSS recruiter Edgar Salinger with the strong impression he was joining Eagle to fight: "Hahm is most anxious for real military service," Edgar Salinger reported. Hahm readily joined the OSS, enlisting as a private in the army.[41]

SI also recruited other students, like Peter Namkoong in January 1945. Namkoong was born in 1904 in San Francisco but later moved to Wahiawa in Hawai'i and had an accounting office in downtown Honolulu. Namkoong was well-qualified for the mission Daniel Buchanan had envisioned for him: "recruiting and training oriental personnel who will be engaged in an important secret mission" inside Korea. Fluent in Chinese and Japanese as well as Korean and English, Namkoong was "familiar with various Korean political movements and with Koreans both in this country and abroad."

He had also resided in Korea and travelled through Japan. Buchanan made him "head agent" of the spy ring scheduled to operate from July to December 1945.[42]

Hahm's Eagle team leadership core was filled with nine other Korean Americans. Five of them—David C. Kim, Carl Chun-Pok Sunoo, Frank Lee, Sang Pok Suh, and Shoon Kul Kim—were recruited in New York in December 1944. David Kim and presumably the others were selected because of language and cultural proficiency: "native fluency-speaks and writes Korean and Japanese, also reads and writes Chinese . . . familiarity with Korean leadership inside and outside that country; and a history of long residency in Korea." The other four—Harry Lee, Kyunsung Sun Lee, Peter Namkoong, and Chester Hoon Kim—were recruited from California for similar reasons. Chester Hoon Kim and likely the other students also received OSS backing for their respective applications for American citizenship in exchange for serving on Eagle.[43]

Like Korean Americans, Japanese Americans were also recruited for the OSS. Many of them were found in Hawai'i, where the largest number of Japanese, aged eighteen to sixty-four, registered for the draft and where the largest Japanese civilian population in the United States resided. While those in Hawai'i formed a large pool of candidates with Japanese- and English-language skills for entry into the OSS, their willingness to serve and their loyalty were important considerations.

Many Hawai'i-born Japanese imagined themselves as part of an America worth defending against foreign enemies. Their world, as compared with the life they could imagine in Japan, was far better in the Islands. They knew their parents and others of a similar age and background advanced economically in ways not possible in Japan. The Japanese in Hawai'i were moving rapidly into semiskilled positions on plantations, becoming the second most common ethnic group doing the *luna* or supervisory work on the plantations even as their numbers there declined. By 1930 so many had gone into independent farming that they comprised 70 percent of all small farmers, and the 1,300 Japanese families in Kona were growing most of Hawai'i's coffee beans. Others were moving into cities and towns, where in 1900 they had been less than 16 percent of Honolulu's population but a decade later had climbed to 30 percent. They crowded into such areas as the Palama District and the outlying areas of Kalihi, Pawaa, and Moiliili, opening nearly eight times as many retail shops as they had three decades earlier. Japanese shopkeepers became so common that by 1930 they were running almost half of all retail stores in Hawai'i, while their mothers and sisters made up more than half of the Islands' domestic servants. The Hawai'i-born themselves were already altering the occupational landscape of Hawai'i, comprising a third of the aspiring secondary school teachers enrolled at the University of Hawai'i in 1927–28. Other local-born Japanese went into professions such as medicine, dentistry, and to a lesser extent, engineering.[44]

Greater political and social resource accumulation coincided with upward economic mobility and demographic growth. By 1940 the Japanese alone comprised nearly 40 percent of the territory's population, three-quarters of whom were US citizens. They became the largest ethnic community in Hawai'i, with a rapidly growing Hawai'i-born voting sector that was making steady inroads into the political arena of the Islands. In 1930 World War I veteran Noboru Miyake was elected to the Kauai County Board of Supervisors, while Tasaku Oka of the island of Hawai'i and Andy Yamashiro of Honolulu won seats in the Territorial House of Representatives. Wilfred Tsukiyama became deputy tttorney for the City and County of Honolulu in 1929 and four years later attorney, an office he held until 1940. All of these individuals' visible presence in the politics, coupled with the growing number of registered Hawai'i-born Japanese voters, indicated that the Japanese of Hawai'i would soon exert political influence in the Islands in a manner that was not possible in Japan, where only a small percentage of the adult males could vote.[45]

Visions of a multiracial democracy provided an additional reason for some Hawai'i-born Japanese to imagine themselves as part of the American empire. They saw a brighter future, even though as late as 1935 family members of the original European American missionaries controlled much of the Island economy. Admittedly, the Big Five—Alexander & Baldwin, American Factors, C. Brewer & Company, Castle & Cooke, and Theo. H. Davies & Company, the largest corporations in the Islands—dominated the economy through their control over the sugar industry's financing, transportation, and shipping, together with the wholesale supplies, depended upon by 90 percent of all small retail stores in the Islands. Yet many Japanese in Hawai'i found comfort in the words and deeds of Charles Hemenway, former general counsel to Alexander & Baldwin, attorney general of the territory, and Board of Regents member for the University of Hawai'i. Hemenway was a known liberal among Hawai'i's elites who publicly supported unpopular causes and personally supported needy students of all backgrounds financially, whether native Hawai'ians or students whose parents were immigrants. After the United States unilaterally abrogated its commercial treaty with Japan in 1939, Hemenway formed a special advisory group made up of University of Hawai'i students, Professor Shunzō Sakamaki, school administrator Shigeo Yoshida, businessman Clifton Yamamoto, and city employee Tommy Kurihara that met weekly to find solutions to the "problem" of Japanese American loyalty as it pertained to possible espionage and sabotage. Under Hemenway's direction, they formed the Hawai'ian-Japanese Civic Association to launch a campaign to reduce the number of dual citizens among Japanese Americans by obtaining a simplified expatriation procedure through State Department negotiations with Japan. Hemenway's belief in a multiracial democracy was evident in his letter to Ralph Yempuku, the University's Athletic Department manager, a few months after the outbreak of war:

> This war can only be won by those who are fighting for liberty and justice to all—and all means everyone of every race. The old notion of superior and inferior races has been proved wrong and must be discarded in the thinking of all of us. No individual and no race has any monopoly of these traits of character which in combination make good citizens. Understanding, tolerance, integrity, justice and friendliness always win in the end, as they always have and will again.[46]

Allying themselves with the American military was an attractive option for many Hawai'i-born Japanese. Some recalled World War I, when volunteering for the armed forces of the United States was popular. Back then, as 11,000 Japanese immigrants and 596 local-borns, aged twenty-one to thirty-eight, registered for military conscription in Hawai'i on the first day. Their numbers swelled to 29,000 out of a total of 71,000 when the draft was expanded to include males from the age of eighteen to forty-five. Even though the selection and induction process reduced their numbers, 838 Hawai'i Japanese were inducted, enough to form an all-Japanese unit out of Company D of the First Regiment of the National Guard of Hawai'i. Their actions led to American citizenship for 454 Japanese immigrants, which provided many with the hope of continued benefits derived from their service to the American military. They also could see that joining the Hawai'ian Territorial Guard, for example, was important for the ethnic community's present and future. Thus, many of them refused to lose heart even after the War Department demobilized and reorganized them as a volunteer labor battalion under the name Varsity Victory Volunteers (VVV). They knew that the growing presence of the American military in the Islands after 1920 provided an important source of employment in construction, transportation, and consumer services. With defense spending accounting for nearly a fifth of Hawai'i's employment by 1939, Japanese Americans could finally leave the manual labor of the sugar plantations.[47]

Other factors contributed to Hawai'i-born Japanese imagining themselves as part of the American empire. Intraethnic tensions among the Japanese pushed some away from identifying with Japan and toward the

United States. Okinawans were the second most numerous of all Japanese immigrants in Hawai'i identified by prefectural origins, behind only those from Hiroshima prefecture. From 1899 to 1937, they comprised about a seventh of the Hawai'i Japanese population and formed a minority group among the Japanese with their distinctive family names and language. Other Japanese were called *naichi* ("mainland") because they came from the main island of Honshu, especially Hiroshima and Yamaguchi prefectures, where half of all Japanese immigrants hailed from. Okinawans, by contrast, came from a set of islands to the south of Kyūshū and were incorporated into Japan only in the late nineteenth century. Moreover, Okinawans were concentrated in certain occupations disdained by *naichi* Japanese, such as raising pigs, and they sported tattoos, which many *naichi* Japanese associated with the criminal element. Their sense of history was not shared; Okinawans had their own monarch until 1879, when he was deposed by Imperial Japanese officials and their country was forcibly annexed to Japan. Okinawans formed social groups based on common homeland city, ward, or even village section. Such differences contributed in part to mutual animosity between many *naichi* Japanese and Okinawans, in addition to the latter's distaste for the Imperial Japanese government. The groups exchanged insults with one another, with the former calling the latter "Ōkii nawa" ("big rope") and the Okinawans retorting "nai chi" ("no blood" or not human).[48]

Spying on the Hawai'i Japanese community ensured support for the American war effort. The army, navy, and the FBI began surveillance of the Hawai'i Japanese after World War I and their efforts, sometimes done openly, kept in check overt expressions of identification with Japan. As early as January 1919, the Military Intelligence Division of the army and the Office of Naval Intelligence maintained a postal censorship station in Honolulu, where they kept watch over correspondence between Hawai'i and Japan, searching for the disclosure of sensitive information regarding the military buildup in the Islands. The FBI began its own investigation into the Hawai'i Japanese after these immigrants launched their island-wide labor strike against the sugar plantation owners in the 1920 strike and sent in Special Agent Ralph Colvin to set up a Honolulu office the following year. Colvin developed a list of potential security risks among Japanese Americans and, as the bureau expanded its surveillance, hired a number of Hawai'i Japanese, among them University of Hawai'i Professor Shunzō Sakamaki. Japanese Americans themselves joined in the surveillance effort just months prior to the outbreak of war with the establishment of the Oahu Citizens for Home Defense, a group of prominent citizens whose aim was "to plan for and carry out the task of bringing out more positively the inherent loyalty of the Americans of Japanese ancestry to the United States." The Home Defense's approach was to convince Hawai'i Japanese of their responsibilities toward the United States in the event of war, reminding them of the "difficult position they will be put in" and admonishing them to "work with" authorities on "the task of evaluating what went on in the Japanese community."[49]

Enthusiastic support of the American military and spying for them was only part of the Hawai'i Japanese community's activities. With nearly four million Japanese living outside of Japan, support for the homeland over the host country was not unusual. In places distant from the homeland and the United States, such as the Dutch East Indies, local Japanese residents, including well-known Seattle-born Japanese American journalist Bill Hosokawa, actively cooperated with the Foreign Ministry and the Imperial Japanese armed forces in conducting their propaganda campaign and gathering topographical and oceanographic information in preparation for future military operations in the region. In Malaysia, local-born Yutaka Tani paved the way for the Imperial Japanese Army's invasion of the Malay Peninsula in 1942 by compensating for his deficiency in the Japanese language with effective leadership and prowess in guerrilla warfare. In the distant American territories of the Philippines and Guam, the local Japanese population also cooperated with invading Imperial Japanese forces. In the former, they utilized the knowledge of local conditions to assist the Japanese amphibious landing near Davao. In the latter, individuals such as Guam-born Juan Onodera became trusted assistants of the Imperial Japanese occupiers; in Onodera's case, when the Americans returned he was captured wearing the uniform and carrying the rifle of an Imperial Japanese soldier.[50]

In Hawai'i, therefore, backers of Japan were not uncommon. In 1940, 188 Hawai'i Japanese delegates attended the 2,600th anniversary of the mythical founding of the emperor's lineage, with some Hawai'i-born Japanese joining the celebration in Tokyo. Others who remained in Hawai'i had established a tradition of welcoming the Imperial Japanese Navy vessels that had visited Hawai'ian shores periodically since 1876. Large numbers of Hawai'i-born Japanese also participated in the community-wide collection of scrap metal, including tinfoil wrappers for chewing gum, to be shipped to Japan for its war industries, as well as assisting in the packaging and shipping of *imonbukuro* or packages stuffed with cigarettes, toiletries, and other personal items to comfort or encourage Imperial Japanese Army soldiers fighting at the front. With 14,000 Hawai'i Japanese in Japan in 1938, it is little wonder that some of them became involved in Japanese plans for a takeover of Hawai'i.[51]

Identification with the homeland was also reinforced by the issues of citizenship and education. Until the eve of the Pearl Harbor attack, most of Hawai'i-born Japanese had dual citizenship. They had American citizenship from being born on American soil, but also acquired Japanese nationality because their fathers had Japanese citizenship. In 1940 nearly two-thirds of the 119,361 Hawai'i-born Japanese retained dual citizenship, even though the 1924 Japanese citizenship law made it more difficult to acquire Japanese nationality at birth. Nevertheless, with dual citizenship they could easily travel to Japan, where many of them received part of their education. In 1933, over two-thirds of the Hawai'i-born Japanese had dual citizenship and two years later, Japanese consulate officials counted about 40,000 of them in Japan. By 1940 they numbered 50,000, or about a quarter of all American-born Japanese who went to Japan for part of their education. In Hiroshima prefecture alone there were over 5,000 Hawai'i-born Japanese in the latter half of the 1930s. But having dual citizenship, the Hawai'i-born Japanese between the ages of seventeen and thirty-seven in 1940 were also subject to military conscription by the Imperial Japanese Armed Forces upon return to Japan. While the exact numbers are not known, a small number of Hawai'i-born males were inducted into the Imperial Japanese Army, particularly those who grew up in the coffee-growing Japanese community of Kona on the Big Island.[52]

The Imperial Japanese Consulate was the other contributing factor. After the US government unilaterally abrogated the US-Japan Commercial Treaty in 1939, Japanese intelligence operations in the United States shifted away from propaganda to gathering tactical intelligence on the US Armed Forces necessary for war planning. The consulate provided cover and assistance for the Imperial Japanese Navy's Ensign Takeo Yoshikawa, who arrived in August 1940 to collect intelligence. The consul-general assigned him the title of "Chancellor" as his cover and allowed Yoshikawa to move about the Islands freely, observing the numbers and positions of US Navy vessels at Pearl Harbor and aerial defense systems, all of which Yoshikawa communicated to the navy headquarters using consulate communications. The consulate further assisted Yoshikawa in his work by assigning to him its Hawai'i-born employee of over five years, Richard Kotoshirodo, and another Hawai'i Japanese named John Mikami as his driver. Yoshikawa scouted the American fleet, often accompanied by Kotoshirodo and driven by Mikami. Yoshikawa expressly told Kotoshirodo he was engaged in espionage during these scouting trips, and his actions left no room for doubt about his assignments—they went to locations where Yoshikawa could observe the American fleet, such as Pearl City or Lahaina Roads, as well as the airfields and military installations near Kaneohe and Wahiawa. Their intelligence reports made their way to other Japanese officers aboard Japanese merchant ships visiting Hawai'i, such as the *Tatsuta Maru* and the *Taiyō Maru*. While aboard docked vessels, those officers directed data collection by local Japanese or European Americans. In one instance, Suguru Suzuki entertained some Hawai'i Japanese returning to Japan in November 1941 and learned from them a crucial detail that altered the Imperial Japanese Navy's plans for attacking Pearl Harbor: "He found that recently no ships had been anchored in the Lahaina anchorage and so the Japanese forces could all be concentrated on Pearl Harbor. The original plan had called for a split of the Japanese bombing fleet with half going to Lahaina and the other half going to Pearl Harbor."[53]

Once Pearl Harbor was bombed, military, federal government, and territorial government officials took swift action. They immediately arrested those deemed a high security risk, classified as "1-A," while maintaining surveillance on others deemed a lesser security risk and classified as "1-B." They interrogated and processed nearly 5,000 *kibei*, or those educated in Japan but returned to America, together with Buddhist and Shintō priests, language school officials, commercial fishermen, and consular agents, all identified through prior surveillance. They interned a total of 816, eighty-three of whom were subsequently released, but included among them a handful of Germans, Italians, Austrians, Finns, and Norwegians at Sand Island from the day after the Pearl Harbor attack to the end of March 1942. Although Carl Eifler and his wife allowed the internees to govern themselves, the threat of arrest and confinement was enough to deter many Hawai'i Japanese from overtly expressing their support for Japan.[54]

Dual loyalties notwithstanding, military officials moved quickly to mobilize Japanese American support for the war effort. Although the War Department initially discharged all Japanese Americans from the Hawai'ian Territorial Guard, it allowed 169 of them to form the VVV to support the Thirty-Fourth Combat Engineers at the Schofield Barracks in Oahu in February 1942. Led by Ralph Yempuku, the VVV performed rock quarrying, barbed wire fencing, building construction, and road work for about a year. While some joined with patriotic motives, or for upholding the loyal Japanese American image, half of them, as John Young, cofounder of the group, observed firsthand, did not know why they joined but "they were so glad to be accepted somewhere." VVV members then spearheaded the enlistment drive for the all-Japanese American unit known as the 442nd Regimental Combat Team. Although over 9,000 volunteered, the army inducted only 2,686 of them. The local community gathered at Iolani Palace on March 28, 1943 for their send-off to basic training at Camp Shelby in Mississippi, where the OSS recruited fourteen of them.[55]

"Now I am asking for volunteers," Daniel Buchanan of SI's Washington, DC office and recruiter for the OSS bellowed out before Japanese American soldiers undergoing basic training at Camp Shelby in July 1943. "This will be a Far East mission and it will be more dangerous than combat," he warned. Although many trainees balked at the mention of the Far East, since it meant fighting against Imperial Japanese forces, Buchanan still managed to secure about a hundred volunteers. He also reiterated his warning: "This mission can be a one-way street and you may not come back. Do you still want to go?" Buchanan then pared down the group to four officers and twenty enlisted men and ordered security checks on each before sending them off to Camp McDowell in Naperville, Illinois for special training in radio communications in January 1944.[56]

Richard Kiyoji Betsui was the leader of the Hawai'i Japanese men selected by Buchanan to secretly slip out to Camp McDowell. Not much is known about him except that he probably hailed from a large family on the island of Kauai and was a married math teacher who served as a commissioned officer in the Officer Reserve Corp from 1931. He made first lieutenant three years later and, while undergoing training for this OSS assignment, was promoted to captain in 1944.[57]

A second officer recruited by Buchanan was Junichi Butō. Like Betsui, Butō was a graduate of the University of Hawai'i. In 1940 Butō earned his degree in economics and business, but spent a good part of his college days mixing with members of the various clubs, from sports to the annual school album, the *Ka Palapala*. He also retained his interest in the military, joining the ROTC group Saber and Chain in his junior year. Butō was a cadet captain in charge of Company K, which, having an equal number of freshmen and sophomores, meant he was used to giving orders to all, including European Americans. On top of all this, Butō was rated an expert marksman, placing second by scoring 192 of a possible 225 points in the ROTC's Warrior of the Pacific competition held in June 1939.[58]

The third officer recruited by Buchanan was Chiyoki Ikeda. Born to emigrants from Kumamoto prefecture, he grew up in Honolulu surrounded largely by other Japanese Americans and attended public schools, including McKinley High School, before matriculating the University of Hawai'i in 1938. During his university education, Chiyoki proved himself physically fit for hazardous duty in the OSS by his participation in intramural sports, while majoring in engineering. He excelled at track (particularly the low hurdles), played football, and became a member of the exclusive athletic "H Club," whose adviser was Ralph Yempuku.[59]

Once the war began, Ikeda followed his personal convictions and his university friends into the armed forces. He put his college education on hold and joined the Hawai'ian Territorial Guard Headquarters Detachment, First Battalion, as a second lieutenant shortly after the bombing of Pearl Harbor. After the unit disbanded a month later, he followed Ralph Yempuku's lead into the VVV and served with this unit for almost a year as part of a fifteen-man Mechanic B group. Once Japanese Americans were accepted into the army, Ikeda quickly enlisted, along with his supervisor Ralph Yempuku and his new friends Junichi Butō and Calvin Tottori. He headed to Camp Shelby, where he and his Hawai'i friends met SI's recruiter Daniel Buchanan and joined the OSS.[60]

Ralph Tsuneto Yempuku was an unlikely choice as one of four officers for the OSS group headed for Camp McDowell. Originally classified by the draft board as "4-F," or physically unfit for military service because of a bad knee, Yempuku managed to slip past the physical exams. His small stature—he stood only five feet three inches tall—and Japanese features marked him a possible target for Allied soldiers' bullets. Worse, his family background made him an unlikely candidate to pass the stringent security background check. Yempuku's father was a Buddhist priest from Atatajima who, together with his mother, immigrated to Hawai'i in 1904. Ralph was born at a plantation in Papa'ikou on the Big Island before the family moved to Honolulu. His father opposed the Japanese participation in the 1920 strike and was labeled an *inu* or "spy" for the plantation owners and the Big Five. His entire family had moved back to Hiroshima in 1932, and his father left Ralph with a thousand dollars to pursue his graduate education. His three younger brothers were already in their early twenties and thus likely to be conscripted by the Imperial Japanese forces that Ralph would face. Leaving behind his new wife and well-paid job at the University of Hawai'i, Yempuku had little reason to serve on what was seen as a suicide mission. Before completing his training, Yempuku expressed regrets for volunteering: "If I knew it was going to be like this I would have never volunteered because it looks like I am going to be assigned to Tula [*sic*] Lake spying on Japs there, or be carrying a radio on my back through the jungles and be shot at by both Japanese and Americans."

However, Yempuku had other qualities that made Buchanan willing to take the risk. He was fluent in Japanese, especially in the Hiroshima dialect, having grown up around the temple where his father not only ministered to Japanese immigrants in their native language but also taught the language to Hawai'i-born Japanese. Ralph spoke some French, which might prove useful in French Indochina. He was a 1936 graduate of the University of Hawai'i and had proven his ability to analyze, correlate, and interpret new information rapidly, a skill necessary for someone working in SI. As a physical education instructor, he was in excellent physical shape and excelled at sports. On top of this, he was the adviser to the "H" Club, an exclusive group of sports lettermen of the University of Hawai'i that among other things, supervised the hazing of the freshmen. With Charles Hemenway recommending him, Yempuku had no trouble clearing OSS security.[61]

Unlike Yempuku, Fumio Kido had no University of Hawai'i connections or higher education. He did not have any ROTC training either, because Franklin High School, from which he graduated in 1942, offered no such course. Nor did he have a prestigious family background with important social connections. He was born in Hilo, one of seven children, to Japanese immigrants from Kumamoto prefecture but moved to a small cottage in front of the cannery district in Kalihi, Honolulu. His father peddled *saimin* noodles from his wagon to cannery workers for a living. Kido's main—and perhaps only—qualification for SI work in East Asia was his Japanese language ability. Though he was never educated in Japan, Fumio learned Japanese at Tōyō Gakuin in the Kalikai district of Honolulu. He had learned enough to pass Buchanan's initial screening test and expressed a strong dis-like for the Japanese nationalism that tinged much of Hawai'i's Japanese language school education. Years later, Kido recalled his disagreement with the school principal who exhorted the students in their allegiance to Japan. "The only thing I didn't buy was his telling me I am Japanese," Kido stated, "and that I owe my allegiance to Japan. I didn't think that was correct." What he did not gain from Tōyō Gakuin was sufficient confidence in his own linguistic abilities. When Buchanan's call for volunteers for the OSS came, Kido went because interviewees were exempt from the hated long marches, one of which was planned for that day. Much to his surprise, he was selected. "The right place at the right time," Kido would recall decades later when explaining how he came to serve in East Asia with the OSS rather than the 442nd Regimental Combat Team in Europe.[62]

Dick Hamada, however, was not a surprise selection by Buchanan. He was brought up outside of the Japanese American community, and yet his language skills were sufficiently strong enough to qualify for the OSS. Hamada's parents emigrated from Hiroshima and arrived in Hawai'i after the turn of the century. His father worked as a carpenter and his mother as a clothes seamstress, cleaner, and cook for the plantation workers of the Honokaa plantation, fifty miles north of Hilo. Hamada and his four siblings grew up in a neighborhood with Filipinos, Chinese, and Hawai'ians. Not until 1936, when he went to McKinley High School in Honolulu while living at his uncle's house, did he come into greater contact with other Japanese. When the Imperial Japanese bombed Pearl Harbor, Hamada renounced his Japanese citizenship and changed his first name from "Shigemi" to "Dick." He was ready to fight the Imperial forces after becoming a full-fledged carpenter's assistant at the Pacific Naval Air Base in Honolulu, making buildings and warehouses. Although his wages were fair—he was making close to $3,000 dollars a year in 1943—Hamada tired of this work and wanted to prove his loyalty after his older sister Ayako could not cope with internment and committed suicide on May 3, 1942 in a Wartime Civilian Control Administration (WCCA) Assembly Center. When the call for volunteers for the US Army came, Hamada got permission from his mother to enlist in the army. Selected by Buchanan, Hamada recited his oath of allegiance on January 16, 1944.[63]

Calvin Atsushi Tottori was also a logical selection by Buchanan. Like Hamada, he was born in 1921 into a working-class neighborhood in Honolulu. His father was a self-employed poultry farmer from Okayama prefecture and his mother, a self-employed cook from Yamaguchi prefecture. Tottori graduated from McKinley High School but had no ROTC training and was not destined for an officer's slot, even though he had some college course credits at the University of Hawai'i. Though standing only five feet six inches tall, he was a ruggedly-built football player and had a special talent for mathematics, which he readily applied to artillery firing in the 552nd Field Artillery Battalion at Camp Shelby. Quiet but easygoing, an excellent poker player, and nonchalant with security regulations—he smuggled a camera into the OSS training camp against regulations and took a photo of one of his trainers—Tottori hardly seemed the type to volunteer for a potential "one-way ticket" mission.[64]

Not much is known about other Hawai'i Japanese recruited by the OSS. Thomas Baba, William Kishinami, and Shōichi Kurahashi were all recruited by Buchanan while at Camp Shelby and passed the security checks, unlike the nine others who were eventually dropped. MO picked up on temporary assignment Howard Furumoto, a Hilo-born veterinary medicine student at Kansas State University when Pearl Harbor was bombed. He volunteered for a mission more dangerous than combat, became an interpreter for American forces fighting in Burma, and then was temporarily assigned in January 1945 to work with Japanese prisoners of war on propaganda materials in China for the OSS. Research and Analysis (R&A) hired Chitoshi Yanaga part-time rather than full-time in 1944, even though Yanaga was considered one of the top three young experts on Japan. A native of Kona, Yanaga was educated in Japan during his early youth and returned to the United States for his undergraduate education at the University of Hawai'i and the University of California, Berkeley, where he earned his doctorate in political science in 1934. He worked for the latter university and shared an office with police systems expert August Vollmer, for whom he translated a couple of books. Yanaga stayed at the university until he secured a translation position, first with the Office of War Information and then as director of Japanese Area and Language Studies at the University of Denver for the US Army. Due to the Yanaga couple's friendship with Charles Fahs, head of the Japan Desk, R&A, he became a part-time worker while serving as a visiting lecturer in foreign area studies at Yale University.[65]

As important as Hawai'i was, the continental United States proved equally fertile for the OSS recruitment. About three-quarters of the 127,000 Japanese on the mainland in 1940 resided in California, where the target language was widely used. In addition, the *kibei* population was equally large in 1935, with about a fifth of all American-born in the continental United States and Hawai'i. Half of them had spent eight years or more in Japan and had native facility in the Japanese language and together with those in Hawai'i, numbered an estimated 40,000 to 60,000 by 1935. Some had even accumulated sufficient social, cultural, and economic capital to dominate the Japanese community on the West Coast by virtue of their occupations as intellectuals, professionals, and businessmen with important commercial connections in Japan, which R&A could exploit. By 1909, they numbered some 2,000 but divided themselves along regional and occupational lines, if the Los Angeles Japanese Association is a guide. A handful of them were in occupational lines such as the export-import trade with Japan and had developed the personal connections the OSS was looking for. Some had the connections with politicians such as Takechiyo Matsuda, an Imperial Diet member, and Yōsuke Matsuoka, Japan's Foreign Minister in the years leading up the war, while others were connected by family to high-Imperial Japanese Navy officers.[66]

The main problem of recruiting Japanese Americans from the continental United States involved loyalty. Unlike their counterparts in Hawai'i, they did not enjoy the economic incentives that undergirded the loyalty of many Hawai'i Japanese toward the United States. Although those in San Francisco, San Diego, and to a lesser extent elsewhere witnessed an expanding military presence in their neighborhoods, they were not the beneficiaries since they were excluded by labor unions from construction jobs and other blue-collar and service sector jobs that an expanding American military presence stimulated. Japanese Americans also lacked the political influence their coethnics enjoyed in Hawai'i. Comprising only 1.4 percent of California's population and even less elsewhere, they attracted little attention from political parties normally wooing voters. With their immigrant parents' legal status as aliens ineligible for citizenship, they had no real political voice in local, state, or federal governments. Many of the working-class Japanese Americans therefore voted with their feet and moved out of the state, if not the country.[67]

Despite these disincentives, few Japanese Americans in the continental United States turned their backs on America and actively collaborated with Japanese intelligence operations. A few were journalists, such as Buddy Kazumaro Uno, who readily cooperated with Imperial Japanese authorities by propagating Japan's side of the conflict in China to the English-speaking world. But once propaganda was de-emphasized and tactical/operational intelligence collection was prioritized after 1939, Japanese Americans as a rule were not recruited to gather such information since high officials in Tokyo anticipated severe travel restrictions, if not outright mass internment, of all Japanese residents inside the United States after the outbreak of war. Thus, most of the Japanese on the mainland who collected tactical or operational intelligence were personnel working out of the established offices of the Imperial Japanese Navy and Army concentrated in New York and Washington. Numbering about fifty by 1936,these individuals confined themselves to collecting information from open sources to prevent possible arrest and deportation. Only a small handful of Imperial Japanese officers, posing as English-language students enrolled in American universities and their few trusted collaborators, engaged in the covert collection of tactical intelligence. They gathered information from various Japanese businesses, including fishermen, and paid a number of European Americans for information.[68]

Kazuo Thomas Tatsumi was one such trusted collaborator who served Imperial Japanese Navy interests. He immigrated in 1921 from Wakayama prefecture as a sixteen-year-old to join his father working in the fruit fields of California. His father returned to Japan in 1924 but Kazuo remained in Vacaville before taking up a position as a hotel clerk six years later in San Francisco. Working at the Yamato Hotel, he met Imperial Japanese Lieutenant Commander Inaho Ōtani and became the recipient and transmitter of intelligence gathered by the navy officer who was assigned as a "language student" to Southern California in 1936 to 1938. His association with Otani put Thomas in the counterintelligence crosshairs, since Ōtani was under constant FBI surveillance. In fact, his friend's claimed coverage was so complete that he played golf with those FBI officers. Tatsumi met several other navy officers who passed through the hotel. Given his close association with these officers, he was seen by the Office of Naval Intelligence as an important conduit of intelligence reports for the Imperial Japanese Navy: "He appears to have acted as a permanent espionage agent in San Francisco to whom each Japanese naval language officer reported while in that area. Subject is known to have supplied Lt. Comdr. Itaru TACHIBANA with information regarding movement of United States naval vessels." Before American officials could arrest him, Tatsumi and his wife

Daisy, a Denver-born Japanese American, left for Japan in early August 1941 whereupon—if one double agent's story is to be believed—he was reassigned to the lead attack submarine of the Imperial Japanese Navy at Pearl Harbor four months later.[69]

Unlike Tatsumi, most West Coast Japanese Americans were not collaborators. They did, however, become disaffected, especially after the mass removal and internment further narrowed their options for residing in the United States. By 1942, West Coast Japanese Americans had little reason to pledge loyalty to the United States. Three years earlier, Japanese merchants were vulnerable and virtually out of business after the Roosevelt Administration unilaterally abrogated the 1911 US-Japan Commercial Treaty. All Japanese Americans were subsequently affected by a series of punitive measures designed to slow the Imperial Japanese government's invasion of Southeast Asia, culminating in a freeze on economic assets of all Japanese nationals, including those of the immigrants. By fall 1942, Japanese Americans were removed from the West Coast and shunted into War Relocation Authority (WRA) camps for internment for the war's duration. During the first two years, most Japanese Americans in WRA camps likely interpreted their internment as the end of their lives in America and the beginning of new lives within the Japanese empire, given the apparent accuracy of the Imperial Japanese government's prewar warning that they would be mass interned. Hence, only a handful of individuals outwardly expressed loyalty toward the United States or the Allied war cause in the WRA camps, whether by volunteering for the army or by working in the camouflage net factories at much higher wages than what they earned as workers in the camps. The relatively small number of those who volunteered—less than 1,300, or about a sixth of what WRA officials anticipated—meant that the pool of potential recruits for the OSS would be small. Those who volunteered largely fell into two groups at the opposite ends of the WRA camp political spectrum. At one end were the leftists whose staunch adherence to the Allied war cause was unquestioned. At the other end were those with considerable stakes in the United States, with higher education and greater financial resources, whose political leanings were toward the Republican Party. Regardless, both groups had the higher education the OSS sought among its recruits.[70]

Fresh out of the WRA camps, Tokutarō Nishimura Slocum was a promising recruit for SI. In the first place, he was unquestionably loyal to the United States. Although he was born in Oyama, Shiga prefecture, he grew up in Minot, North Dakota, where his parents took up a homestead shortly after their arrival. Even though his family moved less than five years later to Antelope, Saskatchewan, and acquired Canadian citizenship, Nishimura stayed in North Dakota and was adopted by a local family named Slocum, who put him through a local high school. He attended the University of Minnesota for a year before enlisting in the army on February 18, 1918. His unit, the 328th Infantry under Colonel G. Edward Buxton, went with the American Expeditionary Force to France, where he took part in some of the heaviest fighting in the Meuse-Argonne and St. Mihiel campaign. Promoted to Sergeant Major after surviving trench warfare, Slocum suffered from bronchitis as a result of being wounded by poison gas.

Slocum's dogged pursuit of American citizenship following World War I provided further proof of his loyalty. He initially acquired his citizenship after he filed his request with the local court in Minot under the 1918 Act promising it to any alien who served in the US armed forces during World War I. He continued his education, going to Columbia University to earn a degree in history, with a minor in economics, in 1924. Slocum entered Columbia's law school, only to find a year later that the US Supreme Court invalidated his and other Asian American World War I veterans' citizenship papers in *Toyota v. the United States,* based on the law being applicable only to "white persons." Outraged, he lobbied for special congressional legislation granting American citizenship to him and other Asian immigrants who had served the US armed forces. He hoped to salvage his legal career, which required US citizenship prior to taking the bar exams. Slocum got his former infantry commander G. Edward Buxton and others to successfully press for passage of his bill through both houses of Congress in 1935, restoring American citizenship to the veterans.[71]

Slocum's experience with investigations provided an additional reason to recruit him. He worked as an interviewer for the California State Employment Service in Los Angeles from 1936 to 1938, and thereafter as a general clerk for the Department of Water and Power from 1938 to 1940 before transferring to the Department of Buildings and Safety. Once he was "evacuated" with other West Coast Japanese Americans to Manzanar, Slocum became a "special investigator" for the War Relocation Authority whose job was to "observe, analyze & report all subversive activities within the camp." He left this wartime job due to the riot at Manzanar on December 7, 1942, and joined the War Manpower Commission as a job analyst.[72]

By late summer 1943, Slocum was pulled into the MO division of the OSS. Herbert Little requested him, but it was Slocum's connection with Buxton, now assistant to OSS Director William Donovan, that sealed the deal. In August, Donovan officially requested Slocum's transfer from the War Manpower Commission to the OSS, stating that he had "particular qualifications both language and otherwise to assist us in some of our most confidential operations." He added that his assistant director G. Edward

Buxton's personal familiarity with Slocum in the same army regiment gave them "unusual confidence not only in his [Slocum's] abilities but in his fierce loyalty for our American institutions." Donovan's request was granted.[73]

George Kobayashi was another mainlander who volunteered for the OSS after leaving the WRA camps. Born in 1913 to a Japanese immigrant farmer in Fort Lupton, Colorado, Kobayashi grew up in El Centro, California after his father died and his mother Hideko remarried another farmer. After he graduating from the University of Southern California in 1935, he worked as a self-employed truck farmer in Niland until 1937, then moved to Oceanside where he was moderately successful, making about $200 a month until the Western Defense Command ordered the mass removal of West Coast Japanese Americans. Initially interned at Poston, Arizona along with other Japanese Americans in the Southern California region, Kobayashi left for Colorado and married Masaye Takemoto, a native of Colorado in October 1942, after being inducted into the army. Despite declaring his wife and parents-in-laws as his dependents, Kobayashi volunteered to join the all-Nisei combat team and was in training when he interviewed with Daniel Buchanan. His spoken Japanese proved sufficient, even though his reading and writing skills were not. Perhaps his strong identification with the United States, evident in his membership in the San Diego chapter of the Japanese American Citizens League (JACL), coupled with his resentment "against the unfair practices of white patriotic racketeers against the loyal Japanese Americans," motivated him to volunteer for a mission "more dangerous than combat."[74]

Chiyeko Nakamura was brought into the OSS for her linguistic skills. Recommended by Ryusaku Tsunoda, specialist on Japanese literature at Columbia University, Nakamura was rated as excellent in Japanese and fair in French. She hailed from Los Angeles, where she and her siblings were born and raised until their father passed away and her mother took the family back to Japan to live prior to the outbreak of war. Nakamura, however, stayed in the United States, along with her maternal uncle, who was interned with her at the Gila River WRA camp during the war. Prior to her incarceration, Nakamura had no other attributes of interest to the OSS. Although she had lived in Japan for four years in the late 1920s, she was trained in the world of haute couture. She attended Tokyo Women's Institute for Dressmaking from 1933 to 1935, finishing her education at the Los Angeles Fashion Academy in 1940. She worked for several different dressmakers, wholesalers, and retailers. She taught a sewing class at the Adult Education Department of the Gila River WRA camp before relocating to New York. She then started some part-time work for Columbia University as an instructor in Japanese before accepting a position with the OSS office in New York, doing research work for R&A beginning on September 11, 1944.[75]

George Tetsuya Ishimaru's route to the OSS was paved with a mixture of talent, unquestioned loyalty, good connections, and a desire to escape. In the first place, Ishimaru was in good physical shape despite being forty years old when he was interviewed by Daniel Buchanan for possible assignment to SO. He was an all-city basketball star, was active in *kendō* or the Japanese art of fencing, and remained an advisor to a YMCA club and the Boy Scouts. Ishimaru also had good Japanese language skills. Born and raised in California, Ishimaru acquired the language in part from his two trips to Ehime prefecture, where his parents were from. After graduating from the University of California, he kept up his language skills by servicing a Japanese-speaking clientele, opening an optometry office in the heart of Little Tokyo in Los Angeles. He was active in the Japanese community, serving on the Nisei board for the Southern California (Japanese) Orphanage. As part of his work with the national kendo association, he officially joined other Japanese-speaking community leaders in welcoming the Imperial Japanese Navy when it visited Los Angeles prior to 1941.[76]

Despite his public appearance with the Imperial Japanese Navy, Ishimaru was unquestionably loyalty to the United States. He joined the Anti-Axis Committee, a self-appointed watchdog group formed in December 1941 with leftists such as Shūji Fujii, editor of the Los Angeles *Dōhō*, and political conservatives like Tokutarō Slocum. Together they coordinated their search for individuals who "in words or by deeds connive with or defend the enemy." Even after Ishimaru lost his entire business practice and was interned at Poston in 1942, he remained loyal to the US government and willingly served as chairman of the Temporary Community Council. That November he attended the JACL's annual convention in Salt Lake City where, along with other delegates, he strongly supported a resolution calling for the reinstitution of selective service for Japanese Americans. When he returned to Poston, Ishimaru faced a hostile crowd of internees who forced him, Saburō Kido, and Sim Togasaki to retract the resolution under the threat of physical beating as an *inu* (spy). Ishimaru managed to avoid violence despite being an informant for the FBI. Probably the fear of eventual discovery of this fact led him to seek an early exit from Poston.[77]

High political connections allowed Ishimaru to join the OSS. Through his work on evacuating the Japanese orphans into the WRA camps, Ishimaru developed relationships with General John DeWitt, Colonel Karl Bendetsen, and John McCloy, Undersecretary of the War Department. He cultivated these relationships by sending copies of his correspondence, which he did so reliably that John Powell of Community Services in Poston observed that Ishimaru "would no more omit sending Washington copies of his correspondence than he would omit his trousers in dressing for dinner." Ishimaru wrote McCloy requesting a loyalty segregation program in December 1942, which the undersecretary turned into the Loyalty Registration Program of 1943. Under this program, Ishimaru was declared loyal and released from Poston in 1944.[78]

Thereafter, Ishimaru joined the OSS. Although on indefinite leave to the Eastern Command district, he was not fully trusted by the Japanese American Joint Board, which judged his participation in Japanese martial arts as potentially disloyal. Nevertheless, Ishimaru was able to reach Washington, DC, where he stayed with his friend Tokutarō Slocum, who probably introduced him to Daniel Buchanan. Although Buchanan found him "too demanding," Ishimaru became a replacement for a translator at the Eastern Research Institute, a cover for the OSS's large radio broadcast transmission monitoring station in Reseda, California, where Slocum served.[79]

Other individuals who left the WRA camps also joined the OSS. Among them were Hatsumi Yamada, recruited by R&A. Yoneo Bepp. Bepp was fingered by other Japanese Americans in the Manzanar WRA camp as an *inu* for the FBI and was eager to depart from the camp to escape bodily harm. He happily joined Fred Nitta, Tadami Tachino, Fred Kobayashi, Thomas Miyamoto, and Robert Takukawa at SI's Eastern Research Institute, where they monitored radio broadcasts originating from East Asia. Susumu Kazahaya and Takao Tanabe were among the handful of Los Angeles OSS members who joined Norwood Allman's Institute after Daniel Buchanan recruited them while in training for the 442nd Regimental Combat Team in 1944. They entered the OSS in 1944 believing, as had others recruited by Buchanan, that their chances of survival were low.[80]

Other Japanese American recruits came from New York, a safe haven for many Japanese American leftists before and during the war. The city had a small number of highly successful trading companies that pioneered American-Japanese trade beginning in 1876. Although fewer than a thousand before 1898, by 1920 they numbered nearly 5,000, with most Japanese engaged in business, professional service, or academic study, unlike the agricultural working class on the West Coast. During the Great Depression their numbers declined, and with the 1911 Commercial Treaty with Japan terminated in 1939, the Japanese export-import business collapsed. By 1940, the Japanese consulate found only 3,171 Japanese in the entire state of New York and their numbers in the city dropped to 2,000 by mid-1942, only to rise with the influx of a thousand new settlers in 1943–1944, most of them American-born Japanese leaving the WRA camps. Among the newcomers were intellectuals and artists who formed the Japanese American Committee for Democracy, an organization with close ties to the Communist Party USA (CPUSA). They attracted the interest of MO because their membership contained many with the required linguistic and educational qualifications. In addition, their firm commitment to a leftist ideology and experience in propaganda work made them reliable candidates; they were not likely to sell out to the Axis side.[81]

However, among these recruits were a few political conservatives. Of the fifty-five Japanese Americans in MO, a small number of them were passionately anti-communist, including Kay Keiichi Sugahara. Born in Seattle, he was the second child to Japanese immigrants from Sendai and of *samurai* lineage but was raised by the Hayakawa family, operators of a small fruit stand in Los Angeles, after being orphaned at the age of twelve. With his family broken apart he became independent early in life, sleeping in a local Methodist Church dormitory during his teen age years. At age eighteen he renounced his Japanese citizenship and matriculated at UCLA. Working to pay his way through college, he graduated with an undergraduate degree in business administration in 1932 and a year later he founded an export-import company called Universal Foreign Service. His business career was immensely successful until trade relations with Japan collapsed after the Commercial Treaty came to an end in 1939. Once the war started, Sugahara became unemployed and then was interned at Santa Anita WCCA camp in spring 1942. Clashing with Shūji Fujii over camp labor issues, he transferred to the Granada WRA Camp in Colorado, where he met Maxwell Kleiman, recruiter for MO. Sugahara then accepted Kleiman's offer to join, was inducted in the last week of March 1943, and left in care of his wife their children and substantial property holdings, including his 1942 Chrysler New Yorker sedan valued at $1,200.[82]

Most New York Japanese were not like Sugahara but further to the left of the political spectrum. Married couple Atsushi Jun and Tomoe Iwamatsu were among the early leftist recruits from the city. The former, an author of a pictorial novel, *The New Sun*, was a Japan Communist Party member connected with the leftist underground inside Japan. He took up the pen name Tarō Yashima, while Tomoe, also a committed Party member, became known as "Mrs. Y" to those in the Japanese-American Committee for Democracy and other New York City leftist circles. They arrived in 1939 and after the OSS established a New York office two years later, the couple volunteered to do research work at Columbia University for the

R&A branch, with the hope of expediting the formation of a "People's government" for postwar Japan. Mrs. Y also volunteered to spy on Japanese Americans:

> She feels that she could help . . . as an intelligence agent operating amongst her Japanese friends and acquaintances. . . . She proposes to work entirely under cover and apparently is quite cheerful at the thought of deceiving her friends in the obtaining of information which they might otherwise be reluctant to give. By the same token, she feels that she could be of use in indicating undesirable individuals.

With Bradford Smith of the OWI's recommendation, the Iwamatsu couple was able to join R&A on a full-time basis in early 1943.[83]

Karl Akiya's friendship with the Iwamatsus led to him joining the OSS. Born in San Francisco to Japanese immigrants from Chiba prefecture, Akiya spent only the first five years of life in the city before his father sent him to Japan to live with his maternal aunt and uncle in Kobe. He attended primary and secondary school there before matriculating in 1926 at Kansai Gakuin Academy in Osaka to study literature. Among other things, he studied Lenin and Marx and was arrested once for participating in a student demonstration against Japanese militaristic activities in Asia in 1928. He graduated in 1931 and two years later had renounced his Japanese citizenship. In 1935, he worked for Sumitomo Bank's San Francisco branch office and continued until the federal government closed it immediately after Pearl Harbor was bombed. Once San Francisco Japanese were interned at Tanforan WCCA camp in April 1942, Akiya worked for its finance department before moving with others to the WRA camp in Topaz, Utah in November 1942. There he worked in the adult education section teaching an Americanization course to Japanese immigrants and *kibei* like himself, since he was fluent in both Japanese and English. His other qualification—experience in intelligence-gathering—made him attractive to the OSS, and he admitted later that he had "helped many people in interpreting both into Japanese & English, especially assisted FBI, WRA, Naval Intelligence since the outbreak of war." After leaving Topaz, Akiya joined the faculty of the University of Michigan, where he became a Japanese language instructor for intelligence officers in training, and where he met and married a fellow instructor in June 1944. When his friend Atsushi Jun Iwamatsu approached him about joining the OSS in the spring of 1945, Akiya resigned from the University of Michigan and went to Washington, DC.[84]

Shūji Fujii was recruited in New York, after being born in Los Angeles and spending his early years in Tokyo, where he went to high school from 1925 to 1931. He left Japan in 1931, renouncing his Japanese citizenship, and attended Fairfax High School in Los Angeles from 1931 to 1933 without receiving a diploma. Lacking educational degrees, Fujii worked at various low-paying jobs from 1933 to 1939, in the nursery and produce business as a nursery can distributor and produce driver. He joined the produce drivers and workers' union, became a CIO organizer, and adopted various leftist causes as his own. His political activism led him to edit the leftist newspaper *Dōhō* [Comrade] from 1939 to 1942. Code-named "Jim Saito," Fujii received orders from his Communist International (COMINTERN) superiors in Moscow to move his newspaper to Colorado. But those orders were suddenly cancelled, and he was confined at the Santa Anita WCCA camp from May 1942 until he left that fall for New York. There he immediately joined the Japanese American Committee for Democracy. After months of unemployment, Fujii finally became a kitchen helper and a clerk in a book bindery before accepting a head position in the Japanese section of the Bureau of Overseas Publication for the Office of War Information. He was dropped from the OWI and, while waiting for his next job, was contacted by Herbert Little, who determined that Fujii was "a very valuable man." The recruiter was sent to his apartment doorstep with an offer to join the MO section. Fujii accepted.[85]

Another COMINTERN agent recruited by the OSS was Nobumichi Ukai, also known as Joe Teiji Koide. Unlike Fujii, Ukai was a Japanese citizen who entered the United States through Seattle in 1925 to attend college at the University of Denver. Upon graduation in 1929, however, he went to New York to join the Communist Party USA. He met Earl Browder, head of the Party, who sent him to Moscow for training at the Lenin International School in 1930. At this point Ukai switched identities to "Tanaka," a name he used with Party officials. After returning to New York, Koide was sent to Sam Darcy on the West Coast, who handed him over to Harrison George. He began translating articles into Japanese to incite average Japanese against their militarist leaders, rather than promote the interests of the Japan Communist Party. Harrison George left the work in Koide's hands but turned over operations to Rude Baker, a man with links to the Russian political intelligence agency NKVD. Koide chafed under Baker's authority and claimed to have quit the Party's activities, yet continued to take orders from COMINTERN in Moscow, as evidenced by his work on the printed Japanese editions of the history of the Communist Party. Once the West Coast Japanese were mass interned in spring 1942, Koide lost contact with his COMINTERN handlers and was confined in Heart Mountain WRA camp in Wyoming, where he participated in the largest draft resistance movement among interned Japanese Americans. As the spokesman for the Block Leaders' Council, he invited Spanish Consulate officials to report on the unfairness of drafting American-born Japanese males into the US armed forces while holding their parents and siblings hostage in WRA camps. With a bogus identity and his break with the COMINTERN less than transparent, Koide left himself vulnerable to postwar accusations that his loyalty to the United States was a sham.[86]

COMINTERN recruited other Asian Americans for intelligence work besides Joe Koide. At least two other individuals were known COMINTERN agents and thus served Russian, not American, governmental interests. Yotoku Miyagi assisted master spy Richard Sorge in his mission to determine Japan's capabilities and intentions in the Soviet Far East by acting as Sorge's "good left hand." Miyagi was born in Okinawa and emigrated to the United States in 1919 to join his father, but also to improve his health and study art. After a year in Imperial Valley, California, Miyagi moved to Los Angeles in 1926, where he became involved with other radical students from Okinawa, among them Paul Kōchi, who would join the OSS's MO section. In 1931, Miyagi joined the CPUSA, was given the name "Joe," and the following year was ordered to return to Japan for a three-month unspecified assignment. As an oil painter, he arrived in Yokohama in October 1932 and began surreptitiously gathering intelligence for Sorge, who in turn passed on the information to Moscow. Miyagi recruited others to spy on the Imperial Japanese Army, including the confidential secretary to General Kazushige Ugaki, former governor-general of Korea and vice-minister of the army. Miyagi and the Sorge spy ring gathered important intelligence, but would Stalin share such information on Japan with the American armed forces? Before that question could be answered, members of the Sorge spy ring, including Miyagi, were arrested by Japanese authorities less than two months before the Pearl Harbor attack.[87]

The other artist was Hideo Ben Noda. Born in 1908 to Japanese immigrant parents working in Santa Clara, California, Noda grew up in Kumamoto prefecture in Japan until 1926, when he returned to Oakland to attend high school. He proved so successful at oil painting that by 1930 the master muralist Diego Rivera of Mexico took him under his wing and nurtured his talent. Noda impressed Whittaker Chambers, who saw in Noda fulfilling the three requirements for John "Don" Sherman's spy ring—US citizenship, CPUSA membership, and high government connections. The artist gave Chambers the impression that he was "extremely intelligent, alert, personable and likeable" and had important family connections with Prince Fumimaro Konoye. "I introduced him to Don," Chambers recalled, "and, at a conversation in my presence, Noda readily agreed to go to Japan to work as a Soviet underground agent." Although all the principal components were set in Tokyo by the end of 1934, Sherman's spy ring was terminated by 1936 and Noda returned to New York thereafter. Their mission failed but Noda died in 1939 of natural causes; he was not executed by Soviet agents, as Chambers had predicted.[88]

Other Asian Americans served foreign entities other than COMINTERN, of whom Herbert Erasmus Moy was best known. Moy was in the employ of the German government and later the Imperial Japanese government as a radio broadcast propagandist in Shanghai during the war. He came from a prominent Chinese American family in New York, where he was born in 1911. His father had immigrated to Chicago around 1882 as a merchant and worked at various odd jobs in the New York area to provide for his family, pulling lottery numbers for the gambling houses during the weekdays and teaching the Chinese language to children on the weekends. His mother was a highly educated woman—allegedly the only Chinese woman of her generation in New York to be able to read and write Chinese—and her love of Chinese opera was passed on to her eldest children. Moy's older brother Ernest became famous in his own right as an important customs collector in Shanghai, a general for the Chinese Nationalist government forces during its war with Imperial Japanese forces after 1937, and an associate of Claire Chennault after the war. Herbert Moy, however, was less distinguished and became known within the family as its black sheep. He attended public school in Newark, New Jersey, before transferring to Mount Herman Preparatory School in Massachusetts, known for sending its graduates to Harvard University. He was allegedly married to a Ruth Taylor, who did not accompany him when he departed in fall 1932 for Shanghai to become a journalist with a Chinese publication. Claiming a Harvard pedigree, Moy landed a managerial post in the Overseas Broadcasting Company, owned by C. V. Starr's *Shanghai Evening Post and Mercury*, but quit to join the German radio propaganda team on XGRS in Shanghai in early 1940 because he was "completely sold on the German way of life." His "One Man's Comment for the Day" during the dinner hours in Shanghai were clearly pro-German, anti-American, and anti-British. Deemed a success by his German employers, he became their highest-paid employee at CN $14,000 a month or US $1,800—big money in Shanghai at the time—because his broadcasts reached a wide audience in China and because he lambasted the British "colonial policies and domineering ways." As Ulysses Harkness of the OSS testified, "As a newscaster over station XGRS[,] MOY took a pronounced pro-Axis viewpoint. He had a sarcastic manner of announcing and kept the Americans in Shanghai incensed at his broadcasting."[89]

Moy's collaboration with the Germans was instructive for the OSS in their recruitment of Asian Americans. Cognizant of divided loyalties among many Asian Americans, MO recruited Chinese American and Japanese American leftists to help boost the morale of the Chinese while at the same time undermining the Japanese. MO pulled in individuals like Joe Koide and Shūji Fujii, knowing that they strongly opposed the Axis powers. MO also took in others with politically conservative views such as Kay Sugahara and Tokutarō Slocum, creating in the process a group of workers united in their strong opposition to the Axis powers and thereby ensuring the unlikelihood of a Trojan Horse penetrating their ranks. SI and SO also sought out linguistically competent individuals, but required their recruits have the correct racial uniforms to slip behind enemy lines. Race therefore counted positively for these Asian Americans, but as SI recruiter Daniel Buchanan had determined, loyalty was a matter of the heart and the Asian Americans he selected had plenty of that quality. Buchanan pulled some Japanese Americans out of training for the 442nd Regimental Combat Team, while other SI recruiters tapped Chinese Americans in New York, such as Lincoln Kan, for their work. SO also required not only linguistically competent Asian Americans having the right racial uniforms to slip behind enemy lines and gather tactical intelligence, but also other technical skills to assist operations. Archie Chun-Ming was a medical doctor and Donald Eng a wireless communications expert, skills Eifler found crucial to his field unit's success in Burma.

But SO also recruited individuals with important social connections with the targeted region. Eifler got Ilhan New, whose pharmaceutical conglomerate's many offices were important contact points for operating in Japanese-occupied Korea and Manchuria. Eifler also pulled in Kunsung Rie despite doubts about his loyalty, since Rie's house in Korea was to provide a base of operations from which Detachment 101 would operate. For all sections of the OSS—MO, SI, and SO—the risk of inadvertently allowing into their ranks an enemy agent still existed, less so for MO and more so for SO. How each section dealt with these risks as they carried out operations is the subject of the following chapters.

CHAPTER 3

cVo

Morale Operations and Talking Their Way Into Japan

The Morale Operations section (MO), the group Joe Koide was assigned to, was responsible for handling propaganda. It was tasked exclusively by the Joint Chiefs of Staff to conduct psychological warfare with its primary aim to undermine Japanese morale and uplift the Chinese morale, according to JCS Directive 115 11/D. "OSS morale operations," Kay Halle, chief of the Section's Reports Office, wrote in spring of 1945, "were undertaken with two primary objectives: to overcome Japanese unwillingness to surrender and to strengthen Chinese opposition to the invaders." To accomplish these aims, the OSS quickly organized its own production and distribution systems with the assistance of about seventy Asian Americans like Joe Koide, who were fluent in the target languages. They required professionals to draft pictorial illustrations for literacy-challenged audience as well as others experienced in typesetting Chinese characters for the printed materials. Others with radio broadcast skills were recruited to help with the distribution.[1]

Uplifting Chinese morale proved no easy task. MO had to first counter Imperial Japanese propaganda claims that the conflict it was participating in was about racialism and colonialism. The OSS struggled with the Imperial Japanese officials' accusations that the Allies treated all Asians as racially inferior, requiring Allied colonial control over the region's population and resources. It was threatened by Japanese propaganda leaflets disseminated across China declaring that Japan's aim was "to liberate Asia from the white man's prison" and that it was the local populace's "natural duty"

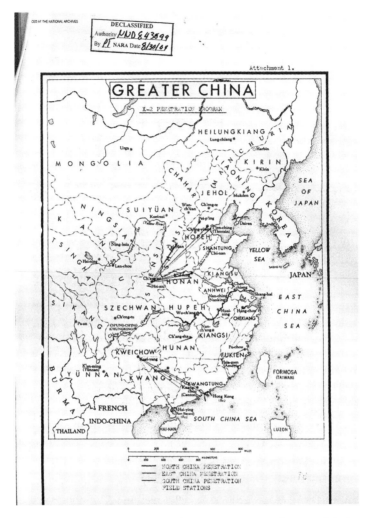

Figure 3.1 Map of China, X-2 ca. December 1944. Courtesy of National Archives and Records Administration II.

to join in the war against the Allied powers: "All of you Asiatics who have groaned under the yoke of the white man, unite!" The office was confronted with an equally effective enemy propaganda distribution system that spread Chinese-language magazines, colored posters, pictured leaflets, radio and letter campaigns, and rumors further portraying the Imperial Japanese troops as liberators and extolling their virtues of leadership of Asia against the West. MO could not truthfully deny that their British, French, and Dutch allies sought "imperial recovery," but they needed to act because Japanese propaganda was effective in keeping large portions of the

Chinese public away from supporting the Allied cause. If MO failed with Chinese morale, the US forces would pay a stiff price once they went on the offensive in China. Conversely, if it could elevate people's morale from indifference or collaboration with Imperial Japanese forces to cooperation with American forces and resistance against the Japanese, the OSS could then play a decisive role in forcing the Japanese to draw men and materiel away from the Pacific Ocean Theater to Asian continent.[2]

MO therefore assigned its Chinese and Chinese American personnel to develop propaganda materials. With a literacy rate of only 15 to 25 percent, it created materials to convey their message to a Chinese audience that primarily communicated by word of mouth or visual with limited writing. MO in China got Low Won Chan, Henry P. Wong, Albert Seely, Kwong Wai Lo, Wang Yun, Dekon (or Deacon) Tsai, and Tsung Wei, all of them fluent in Chinese, to gather and analyze Japanese propaganda targeting the Chinese populace before enacting its own countermeasures. In some instances where the Japanese appeared to be inciting panic among the local populace, MO countered with the truth, disseminated by word of mouth. In other instances, however, MO spread deliberate lies to advance its own ends, believing that rumors played an important role in the formation of popular opinion. It created fictitious oppositionist groups, ostensibly inside Japanese-controlled territory, to encourage Chinese resistance in those regions as well as to discourage collaborationists.[3]

Since the Japanese used colorful posters and leaflets to proclaim their message, MO had to produce equally effective visual materials, such as posters, leaflets, and cartoon strips. It portrayed the Imperial Japanese soldiers as stealing gold or silver fillings out of the mouths of local Chinese, exploiting the labor of hard-working Chinese males, and rapaciously kidnapping of Chinese females to serve in the brothels of the Imperial Japanese Army as sex slaves under the euphemistic label of "comfort women." Their aim in underscoring the ultimate victory of the American forces over the Japanese was also, as Kay Halle noted, to "persuade Chinese to desert bomb-target areas used by Japs."[4]

MO used various means to distribute their propaganda inside China. It used (to a limited extent) radio broadcasts to directly appeal to the Chinese populace under Imperial Japanese control. In Kunming, for example, the OSS had a group of fifteen Chinese supervised by two OSS officers and one enlisted man to distribute radio broadcasts in eleven dialects from a 500-watt transmitter beamed into the Canton area. In most cases, MO instead chose human agents to deliver their propaganda leaflets behind enemy lines. Having the right racial uniforms, Chinese Americans were entrusted

Figure 3.2 OSS Morale Operations' propaganda leaflet to Chinese, 1943. Courtesy of National Archives and Records Administration II.
Line 1:
If you smile (to the Japanese), they will pull out your gold tooth for sure, and you should have to shut your mouth and never smile again.
Line 2:
If you are hardworking, they will snatch you for heavy labor work, so you should do nothing and be free.
Line 3:
If you are seen (by the Japanese), they will take you away as a comfort woman even if you are ugly. So you should either hide or run away.

with the task of penetrating Occupied China and delivering the propaganda materials.

Mack Shin was one such Chinese American who infiltrated behind enemy lines in the Canton region. With Charles Fenn, Shin was assigned to counteract Japanese attempts to create a panic among the Chinese at the forward headquarters in Patpo, a city southwest of Kweilin. He and Fenn first established an underground headquarters in the area and equipped it with a small printing press. While one group was sent to Macao, Shin took his group, code-named "Mack," into many areas where the Chinese were downbeat after a recent successful Japanese military campaign in the region. Mack and a half-dozen students were trained, then sent to Canton with instructions "to pass certain rumors, gather strategic intelligence and report back on the completion of their assignment." In July 1944, Mack and the students worked with their own professor from Soochow University to plant fake intelligence documents, circulate leaflets exaggerating the Allied strength, and deliver poison-pen letters to sow dissension and confusion among the Japanese soldiers.[5]

Another Chinese American in MO was Dekon Tsai, who was sent in March 1945 to the forward headquarters in Hingning, in Canton Province. From there, Tsai and others infiltrated Japanese-controlled territory to spread their propaganda leaflets and rumors to a large Chinese audience in the Canton, Swatow, Waichow, Sheklung, Kitjang, Chao An, and Hoifung areas. Tsai's group created a nonexistent Chinese underground called the "Brotherhood of Patriots" or the "Great East Asia Youth Movement," with an organ called the *Canton Overseas Daily*. They encouraged Chinese workers, especially those in Swatow, to commit acts of sabotage to dishearten the 82,000 Imperial Japanese troops and an unspecified number of Chinese troops supporting them.[6]

When the correct racial uniform was insufficient, the OSS resorted to bribery to deliver their propaganda materials behind enemy lines. They initially hired a Chinese businessman as one of their agents, who used a company boat to make his regular "business trip" to Amoy (Xiamen). But when that boat was "marked" suspect by Imperial Japanese authorities, the OSS turned to smugglers sanctioned by the Japanese:

> After this it was necessary to enlist the cooperation of the smugglers for transportation over water. The Japs run their own smuggling boats so as to control smuggling. Thus it was necessary to bribe puppet officials. One man who was right hand man to Chief of Japanese Intelligence in this area was "bought" into our employ. This man then allowed our materials through the Japanese

controlled smuggling channels. For distribution in Amoy four additional sub-agents were employed who in turned [*sic*] hired others.[7]

Perhaps the most innovative approach MO used to deliver its propaganda leaflets involved setting adrift downstream brightly colored bamboo floats bearing its message. The idea originated from a similar tactic used by a commanding general who defeated his enemy in China some 500 years earlier. Under the banner "Sweep [away] the Enemy Society," the MO group of one civilian administrator, three Chinese artists, and an editor constructed tiny, brightly-colored bamboo floats loaded with a propaganda message and dropped into the Yangtze River every ten minutes, day and night, near Japanese lines.[8]

Despite the OSS restricting itself to black propaganda in China, Tai Li and Marion Miles deliberately undermined the OSS. The Chinese spymaster delivered outdated and at times false intelligence data to MO. When the OSS proposed establishing black radio stations farther north, Li selected sites directly in the path of advancing Imperial Japanese forces. After radio broadcasting equipment was brought into Chungking, Tai Li further disrupted MO's plans by denying entry permits for Low Won Chang, Henry P. Wong, Albert Seely, Kwong Wai Lo, Wang Yun, Dekon Tsai, and Tsung Wei, all Chinese Americans of the Collingwood group in Washington, DC assigned to work with Gordon Auchincloss on the black radio program in Chungking. In April 1945, Tai Li succeeded in having Auchincloss write Li's own scripts for the "Charlie" black radio propaganda program and have them all translated into Cantonese by Li Chi-wei, instead of the OSS Chinese Americans, to effectively terminate OSS Chinese American participation.[9]

Overcoming the Imperial Japanese soldiers' reluctance to surrender was the MO' other task. It agreed with top American military brass that an effective psychological warfare campaign might reduce Japanese resistance, resulting in saved American lives and shortening the war with Japan. But Imperial Japanese soldiers still would not surrender. They had explicit orders not to surrender when Premier Hideki Tōjō issued a *senjinkun,* or code of battlefield conduct, on January 8, 1941 requiring all soldiers to "not take on the embarrassment of being a living prisoner." They faced penalties even if they were involuntarily captured alive, such as falling into enemy hands after losing consciousness during combat. Their only hope was a reduced prison sentence of twenty-seven years if they brought back valuable intelligence on the enemy. The soldiers faced social pressures, both from their comrades-in-arms within their units as well as from society in general; their families back home would likely face persecution if it became known they were captured. They could not feign sickness, since those who became too ill to perform their duties were also viewed as disloyal. Worse, soldiers were aware that many Allied combat units at the battlefront refused to take as prisoners while others captured the Japanese only to torture them. Hence they had only victory or death as options, with the latter the likeliest outcome as the American forces advanced steadily toward Japan across the western Pacific.[10]

MO, however, believed Japanese soldiers could be induced to surrender. In late 1943 they viewed their opponents as rational, not insane, and reluctant to throw their lives away, the opposite of what some frontline American commanders and soldiers believed about the Japanese when faced with *banzai* charges. "These Nips Are Nuts," the *American Legion Magazine* titled one of its essays by an American Marine with stories from the warfront, a view rejected by MO. Instead, they asserted that the Japanese soldier chose death only under certain conditions and could be induced to surrender despite the penalties levied against him and his family:

> The Japanese soldier may be willing to die for the Emperor, but he is not anxious to do so. When circumstances have determined his fate, he is resigned to death, and once resigned, he would rather die as a hero, a credit to his family, than as a cripple on a hospital bed. Considerable effort has been expended to implant this resignation in the soldier. It has been most successful, but in practice acts of heroism are likely to be the product of a desperate situation, group morale, and the commands and threats of superior officers. When not under the eye of his superior or surrounded by the members of his group, the Japanese soldier's desire to live may assert itself like that of any other soldier, and may even overcome the fact that surrender will bring loss of citizenship and family status.[11]

Moderate success by a faction within the Japan Communist Party encouraged MO to adapt similar methods and principles for their own work. Some members of the Party gathered around their cofounder Sanzō Nosaka, who was assigned by COMINTERN to Yenan, in Shensi Province in China, to assist the Chinese Communist Party in 1940. As part of his duties with the Chinese communists' Eighth Route Army, Nosaka and his band of Japanese communists were tasked with conducting psychological warfare against the Imperial Japanese forces and management of Japanese prisoners. His group developed a strategy different from the American military—treat all Japanese prisoners with kindness and invite them to join his "Japanese People's Emancipation League," a group dedicated to overthrowing the wartime leadership of Japan. Nosaka treated the wounded Japanese prisoners, allowed them to freely move about Yenan, and even permitted them to return to their own units if they chose, all to demonstrate that the Eighth Route Army did not capture and kill all Japanese soldiers. He even sent some courageous volunteers like US Army Sergeant Kōji Ariyoshi of Hawai'i to the Japanese soldiers' encampment to shout invitations to defect by calling out those soldiers' personal names. Nosaka told the Japanese soldiers that it was their duty to live and to help usher in a new Japan, one based on justice and equality and the absence of militarists who were responsible for Japan's wartime loss. By blaming the "military clique" that ruled Japan, Nosaka exempted the emperor from responsibility for the war, a method that proved successful. While precise figures are not available, the OSS estimated in late July 1944 that Nosaka's deserting Japanese soldiers numbered no less 1,200, or from 2 to 4 percent of all Japanese prisoners of war taken by the Western Allies before the end of the conflict.[12]

Nosaka's other aim was much larger than getting Imperial Japanese soldiers in China to surrender. He planned to surround the entire island nation of Japan with his propaganda and infiltrate the country with his own agents posing as Korean laborers. His idea of "burrowing from within" was first developed when he worked with Joe Koide in California from 1934 to 1938, producing their own communist propaganda with their own typesetters and then smuggling their materials into Japan on merchant ships stowed away by communist sympathizers among the seamen. Nosaka was especially keen on working with the Japanese American Committee for Democracy (JACD) in New York City. His plan was presented to the American observers who visited Yenan in the summer of 1944 to consult with Mao Tse-tung and Chou Enlai. In it, Nosaka proposed to form a battle line encircling Japan from the east in Yenan, where his league was based; from the south in India, where a number of Japanese American leftists were working for the OSS developing propaganda materials; and from the west in New York, where the JACD was headquartered. "We are asking to connect up with the Japanese who are anti-fascist in America and India," Nosaka told American members of the Dixie Mission. He then sent a formal request of support for his plan to John Emmerson of the State Department.[13]

Sergeant Kōji Ariyoshi conveyed to the OSS the specific details of the Nosaka propaganda plan. The first step was to convene a Japanese soldiers' delegates conference with a core of "trusted" Japanese prisoners and American personnel. The aim was to re-educate these deserters:

> Our first task would be to give them hope in the future. We should convince them that they would be able to return to Japan with honor when the militarists

are overthrown. We should tell them that they (the Japanese) will have a people's government and they must take part in it. If we can make them think that they can act upon their world in such a government, we shall have gone a long way in our program.

The second step, Ariyoshi reported, was to inculcate within those former soldiers a sense of responsibility for postwar Japan: "Their dignity and faith in themselves must be restored and we should re-create their sense of responsibility." The way to do this, he believed, was to hold round-table discussions to allow these former soldiers to air their grievances to gain propaganda material:

> The discussion of the grievances would make the soldiers realize that they had suffered, had been used by the war leaders, and that Japan is not on the right track. All the grievances should be collected and the best ones chosen for propaganda use. They could be treated individually or collectively. Whenever the prisoners express grievances, specific examples and the reasons for the grievances should be obtained. These are very useful.

The third step was to expose them to photographic exhibits on the war, providing the kind of information denied to them by their own officers. In particular, they were shown photographs of Japanese American soldiers in American uniforms, fighting for the Allies, to underscore their message that the war was not about race. Having implanted these images in their minds, Ariyoshi moved to the final step—convincing the soldiers of the Allied war aims. He sought to accomplish this by getting the soldiers to discuss and criticize the OSS propaganda leaflets with the assistance of Japanese American translators: "The American personnel, particularly the *nisei* group, should explain our war aims to the prisoners."[14]

Ariyoshi's plan for the soldiers' conference, however, never materialized. State Department officials expressed enthusiastic support not for Nosaka but for the idea of using Japanese POWs for propaganda purposes. McCracken Fisher, who later became head of the China Division of the OWI, gushed: "It need not be more than a moderate secret that John Emmerson [State Department], John Davies [Political Attache to General Joseph Stilwell] and myself have been tremendously impressed with the possibilities of working among Japanese prisoners and are interested in seeing what high-level Allied support of the idea can be obtained." Others within the State Department, including Emmerson, thought Nosaka's dream of a communist Japan was unrealistic: "The United States could never support communism, and Mao and Nosaka were committed, respectively, to a Communist China and a Communist Japan."[15]

The State Department therefore turned to other alternatives. Emmerson pointed the OSS in the direction of two other Japanese nationals with potential for propaganda campaigns against Japan. One was Kazuo Aoyama, who worked with the Chinese Nationalist government, the British, and the Office of War Information (OWI). Although on the left and having membership in the Social Problems Research Club and the Atheists League, Aoyama had worked with Tai Li, the OSS nemesis inside China. The other was Wataru Kaji, who was linked to Chang Chen, the minister of war, and was the founder of the Anti-War League, which rallied Japanese residents in China to resist Imperial Japanese policy. Kaji had six Japanese prisoners of war working with him to produce radio broadcast propaganda and already had some assistance from Japanese Americans. Thus, the OSS chose Kaji as the main propaganda producer and believed his group could serve as the Provisional Government of Japan.[16]

Yet the Kaji project never became the Japanese Provisional Government envisioned by Emmerson. Although they were MO' noncommunist alternative to Nosaka's group, Kaji and his band of Japanese Americans ran afoul of the Chinese Nationalist government and Tai Li. Originally, Kaji called for utilizing five to ten Japanese POWs acquired from Tai Li. These POWs were to produce materials with the assistance of New York Japanese Americans sequestered in the OSS base in Washington, DC. Although Tai Li insisted on control of the production process, MO was able to retain its independence by remaining confined to Happy Valley near Chungking, where Tai Li and the Chinese Nationalist government were headquartered. Since the Sino-American Cooperative Organization (SACO) was housed in Chungking, Kaji was able to get Howard Furumoto, an enlisted man from Hawai'i, to handle the POWs received from Tai Li. He also was able to pull in funding from the Chinese Government's Political Training Bureau. Kaji's group started off with only four POWs. He insisted on the removal of two but then requested and received an additional ten POWs to assist in his propaganda work. He divided them into two groups, with Kaji directing the production of the "B" group in Kunming and his wife the "A" group in Happy Valley. Kaji then tasked Furumoto with being the liaison between both groups of POWs and the Chinese Nationalist government.[17]

Suspicions about the Kaji project brought about its demise. Furumoto seemingly did little liaison work, as measured by his lack of travel between Kunming and Chungking, a distance of about 400 miles. Instead, he and another Japanese American enlisted man, Calvin Kobata, spent half their time with the four POWs, ostensibly drafting materials to be used in leaflets, postcards, and letters. Furumoto characterized two of the POWs as "uncooperative" but the other two, Shinji Komada and Minoru Seiki, he deemed "extremely cooperative." He and Kobata worked closely with them, finding their background particularly useful for propaganda work. Komada was highly educated, a graduate of Tokyo Imperial University with a major in Chinese philosophy, who was alienated from the army because he had been drafted out of his well-paid high school teaching position and into the military. "A prisoner of the Army," Komada described himself in 1991. His alienation turned to hatred when he developed an amoeba infection and could not keep up with his own unit. They abandoned him in a wooden shack, leaving him with only a small packet of food and a bullet to commit suicide. "Those damn jerks," Komada bitterly recalled five decades later. He felt death was near until a Japanese American soldier, Calvin Kobata, got him reassigned to the Kaji project.

Seiki, on the other hand, displayed relief, not bitterness, over his re-assignment to the Kaji project. He was initially captured by the Chinese Nationalist forces when he was on a mission to procure food, something the Honolulu-born and bred Japanese American never imagined doing. Howard Furumoto explained that Seiki's linguistic and cultural knowledge made him "invaluable" to the Kaji Project, despite his Imperial Japanese Army uniform:

> At the outbreak of the war between Japan and the United States, SEIKI was studying in Japan after graduating from McKinley High School, Honolulu, Hawaii, and owing to his dual citizenship status he was promptly conscripted for service in the Japanese Army. . . . SEIKI has been most cooperative and en-thusiastic in his work. In spirit he is still a citizen of the United States. It is only through a very unfortunate circumstance that he was compelled to serve in the Japanese Army.[18]

Tai Li, however, was suspicious and pulled the plug on the Kaji Project. Although MO Director Herbert Little agreed to strictly adhere to the SACO Agreement, Li's observation of the behavior of the principals in the Kaji Project raised doubts. He knew the Kaji couple left the employ of the Chinese Nationalist government ostensibly because of insufficient funding for their propaganda operations. Li then may have guessed that Kaji had sold his services to the Americans, not knowing that Kaji in fact refused to sign OSS papers until it recognized his and the group's principled demands to be treated neither as POWs nor as an employees of the American gov-ernment but rather as independent "agitators of a democratic Japan." Moreover, Tai Li observed a curious lack of interest on the part of the MO in Chungking for printing presses, while being obsessed with acquiring more Japanese POWs. He was probably aware that John Emmerson recommended the formation of a Free Japan movement that would encourage cells inside Japan to spread defeatist propaganda, transmit radio propaganda broadcasts from a communist base area in Shantung to broadcast to Japan, Korea, and Manchuria, and to train units of Japanese for Occupation operations. Furumoto's and Kobata's seeming lack of interest in liaison work, coupled with a request for permission to bring in another Japanese American named Kenny Yasui, may have caused Tai Li to oppose the Kaji project. Tai Li knew Yasui had in the past received intelligence data on the design and specifications of a Japanese military aircraft from Kaji and surmised that Yasui's addition involved something more than propaganda work. Tai Li, therefore, concluded these Japanese Americans' ultimate aim was to train the Japanese deserters on Chinese territory to serve as part of the Allied Occupational forces, all without Chiang Kai-shek's knowledge or approval.[19]

Despite the loss of the Kaji project, MO refused to give up reaching Japan. If agents could not penetrate the home islands, MO officials reasoned, they could still send radio transmissions to a civilian population of an estimated five to six million with medium-wave radio sets. Those listeners, MO hoped, they would spread demoralizing rumors heard in the radio broadcasts to their neighbors. By giving voice to the anti-militarist Japanese living abroad and offering hope for a democratic Japan after the war, MO sought to embolden Japanese civilians and soldiers alike to resist their leaders' urging for greater sacrifice in the war. The section created fictitious organizations to air those views over the radio. At first, their plan called for transmitting black propaganda from fishing boats out of the Alaska region, but the ease with which Imperial Japanese forces could triangulate the broadcasts meant the approach was too vulnerable to attack. So MO opted for broadcasting from Saipan in the Marianas Islands, once American forces took the island in the summer of 1944. They targeted the early evening hours as the optimal time for Japanese listeners.[20]

The Collingwood group was established to create black propaganda for the radio broadcasts. This group of Japanese American propagandists, named after the country club turned camp outside of Washington, DC, had as its core members a group of leftist-leaning individuals recruited by Bruce Roger and supervised by Betty MacDonald. Among them were journalists Jin Konomi and Yoneo Sakai, picture book writers Atsushi and Tomoe Iwamatsu, labor union activist Seiji Takeda, and former CPUSA member Joe Koide. Around them were the recruits from Topaz, Gila River, Poston, and other concentration camps whose annual salary was $2,800, a figure more than ten times what they would make from employment inside those WRA camps.[21]

Collingwood Japanese Americans wrested control over the contents of their black propaganda away from their European American supervisors. Initially they refused to engage in black propaganda, since they—led by Joe Koide—opposed deception of the Japanese public when the ultimate defeat of the Imperial Japanese government and its forces seemed inevitable by July 1944. They also found European American plans for demoralizing the Japanese ineffective and juvenile at best. For example, they watched as European American planners came up with a plan to use foxes to scare the Japanese prior to the attack by the American forces, based on the assumption that the Japanese feared this animal. Their European American counterparts developed other variations of this fox plan, with one calling for launching a large fox-shaped balloon, another with six foxes from the New York zoo painted with radium and affixed on their skulls propaganda pamphlets, and still another dipping two foxes in phosphorus and releasing them near Japanese coastal positions. Japanese Americans saw these schemes fail when the two snarling foxes dropped into the water swam out to sea instead of the shore. Even their European American supervisors treated their fox plans with levity, stuffing a fox in a paper bag and presenting it to Tokutarō Slocum "to see if he had any 'throwback reactions.'"[22]

MO reached a compromise with the Collingwood Japanese Americans. They would not accede to the demands of Joe Koide and others to cease production of black propaganda, but conceded that the aims should be toward reducing the number of casualties through positive means of encouraging surrender rather than negative satirizing of the Japanese Emperor or attempting to instill fear in the public. Furthermore, they gave control of production to Japanese Americans who played upon the Japanese soldier's desire to return to his family. But MO won a concession—to have all materials translated and checked for final approval by a panel of specialists, all European Americans, with the right to revise the final product for dissemination in China and Burma, or via radio broadcasts from Saipan. Once OSS headquarters decided to close the Collingwood facilities, it temporarily merged Koide's group with another group of Japanese Americans brought in from New York, then moved them to San Francisco in December 1944, where they were joined by ten European Americans and three Imperial Japanese POWs.[23]

Renamed "Green," Joe Koide's new group developed radio broadcast programs to be disseminated from a black radio station in Saipan. Koide oversaw the entire Green project and laid out the main outlines of what the radio broadcasts should and should not cover. Henry Tsurutani directed the contents of each thirty-minute episode, which opened and closed with the song "The March of the Returning Soldiers." They portrayed themselves as a group of patriotic Japanese broadcasting from an undisclosed location, calling for the overthrow of the military clique in power. In its place, they sought the establishment of a constitutional monarchy for Japan, led by "the old liberal parties who are in favor of individualism of democracy as opposed to communism or military dictatorship." The group reported on the Allies' unconditional surrender clause in such a way as to encourage surrender and tweaked the Japanese military order prohibiting surrender to encourage Japanese soldiers not to fight. They often presented talk programs accompanied by music with prewar favorites. To appear authentic they created fictitious characters to discuss various news topics, but with the aim of conveying the idea of the inevitability of Japan's defeat. Dorothy Ogata anchored the episodes as the program announcer. Yoneo Sakai did the voice for a "Mr. Fujiwara," while Ujinobu "Jin" Konomi played the role of a "Dr. Matsumura," an elderly physician. Tomoe (Mitsu) Iwamatsu provided a matronly voice to appeal to the female audience. Francis Ōshita and Shigeo Yoshitsugu also added their voices to the program. To ensure that talks carried the latest information, the Green group tapped the OWI wire service information, daily press, periodicals, FCC monitoring reports, and captured soldiers' diaries, the latter of which often contained some of the best material for "dramatic and nostalgic features." Charles Mori and George Nishi handled much of the research, while Kiyoshi Saka, Toshimi Toda, and Takeshi Sayama, all Imperial Japanese Navy POWs, checked the contents to ensure usage of the most recent Japanese idiomatic expressions. Florence Farquar, head of Oriental Language Department at University of California, D. B. McKinnon, and S. O. Thorlaksson conducted the final review and approval, after which the materials were recorded on sixteen-inch records for air shipment to Saipan. From April to August 1945 they produced 124 episodes, of which at least 115 were broadcasted into Japan. However, they learned that the Imperial Japanese government immediately began radio jamming to prevent their broadcasts from reaching the Japanese public after the first one aired on April 23, 1945.[24]

Producing the radio broadcasts, however, was far from smooth. The Japanese American personnel encountered problems with their paychecks. Although their annual salaries were increased to $3,000, they saw too many errors in their paychecks, creating a "barrier of resistance" the ten European American personnel could not overcome. Their main complaint involved European American control over the final product. Joe Koide led the revolt, criticizing the discrepancies in their paychecks, the

European American editing of their work, the target of their propaganda (the Japanese militarists, not the Japanese soldier), and the message (the hope for a new, democratic Japan, not the coming destruction). Herbert Little agreed with Koide that the final review by Farquar and others sent the wrong message to Japanese American personnel that their episodes were checked for subversive messages to Japan. "In other words," Little explained, "it might have been better to have recognized at the start the fact that by virtue of their security clearance (which, God knows, is tough enough for a Japanese) they were completely trustworthy and accordingly, treated them as such." Japanese American personnel were indispensable for Green, as Little realized, because any propaganda idea made by a Caucasian and translated by a Japanese produced a "poor enough result" and should be avoided "like poison." Hence, Little and Project Chief Bogart Carlaw went with "rule by indirection" and worded their policy directives in the form of suggestions, not orders. Moreover, they had to accept Japanese American ideas and not impose their own, so that the entire program was "typically and completely Japanese." Little reported that this loss of control meant the end product that was "softer" than the line taken by Stanley Hornbeck and the State Department toward Japan:

> To get the Japanese personnel to cooperate, we had to bend to their ideas, not the other way around. The Japanese were NOT interested in an overwhelming victory over Japan, but in ending the war and building for a democratic future. They distinguished between the Japanese military clique and the Japanese people themselves and so our propaganda therefore emphasized the inevitability of defeat, the advantages of cessation of hostilities, and the hope for a democratic and peace-loving Japan in the future.[25]

Print was the other medium Japanese American propagandists used to demoralize Imperial Japanese soldiers. Code-named "Marigold," another group of Japanese propagandists took aim at the Japanese forces in China and Southeast Asia. This team began forming in February 1944, as they gathered in a secure building in New York. Takeshi Haga, former employee of the Yokohama Species Bank, Yoshitaka Takagi, and Shūji Fujii formed the core of the group. The latter pulled in two more of his Dōhō staff members, Shinsei Kōchi and Nobuyoshi Nakamura, while Haga and Takagi added typesetters Naotada Shimomura and Sumi Tanimoto and painter Chūzō Tamotsu to the group. The core members expanded the team to include their friends from the CPUSA, Go Kamikawa and Aisaku Kida, but also took in the political conservative export-importer Kay Sugahara and Christian minister Yoshinobu Kuroda. Given their close Communist

Party affiliation, Marigold members took a different approach to demoralizing Japanese soldiers than what MO initially conceived. As Takeshi Haga recalled, "As for us, of course we can say that we stand loyally with America (but) we don't hate Japan. For this (OSS) agency, (their aim) was the victory of the United States but for us the aim was to move the hand of the Japanese people to end the war and (to have) a situation where Japan is born again into a new democratic nation."[26]

Despite their loyalty, security over Marigold propaganda production was tight. Team members were not permitted to enter the building in groups larger than a pair and had to wait five to ten minutes while the security guard unlocked the chain on the door, checked their passes, and inspected their personal belongings. They were not permitted to tell family or friends the nature of their work, even though core members like Fujii and Haga earned an annual salary of over $3,000, or close to twenty times higher than the highest paid Japanese American worker in the WRA camps. Once they finished producing their counterfeit train tickets, doctored POW letters, and faked Japanese soldiers' manuals with "revised" surrender sections and bogus soldiers' magazines, their work was submitted to Harvard University's Serge Eliseef, Eugene Dooman of the State Department, Charles Nelson Spunks of ONI, John Maki of OWI, and others for final approval.[27]

The Marigold team created four basic black propaganda materials. It was moved out of New York in late 1944, renamed "Vicks," and before deployment overseas was temporarily housed at Georgetown University, where it worked on black propaganda in earnest. The first was known as the Princeton plan, a nonpolitical pocket library collection of poems; the second, the Dartmouth plan, a political monthly; the third, the Harvard plan, created a popular home monthly; and the fourth, the Yale plan, involved writing a magazine for the Japanese businessman that presented a cold, factual analysis of Japan's economy, markets, and production. The plans drew on analyses of Federal Communications Commission intercepts, reports, and policy guidance as well as Yaemichi Sugimachi's personal library of over 5,000 books. With all four plans, Marigold had two basic aims. One was to blame the *gunbu*, or the Japanese military, and fashion it and not the emperor as "the real enemy of the Japanese people" that because of their miscalculation, brought Japan an impending defeat. The other was to convince the average individual "not die for the *gunbu* but to live with the hope that the end of the war means the end of Japan's military, not the Japanese people." A new "peaceful, democratic Japan" would emerge, they declared, bringing "a new life based on peace, freedom, and progress."[28]

Atsushi Iwamatsu produced one of the drawings for Marigold to convey their message in pictorial form. Iwamatsu, who worked for Marigold while his wife worked for Green, depicted the wife of a soldier with a little child standing out in the field, looking depressed. The caption reads: "Mother, why do I not have a father. I want a father." Iwamatsu then conveyed to Japanese soldiers his message of not forfeiting their lives for a lost cause:

> Do not have these words come from your child on the day when the Japanese military is swept away and the bright day of a democratic Japan, an enjoyable day when the rebirth of the family [comes]. In the end, this is your responsibility to live, father, wife. Seize the opportunity! This chance will surely come.[29]

Marigold's hopeful outlook notwithstanding, working conditions were far from ideal. Like Collingwood, its members experienced pay slip problems. While waiting for their passport and visa clearance from the State Department, they heard that only twenty-seven of the forty-five members on the team were cleared. Furthermore, they learned that there were no guarantees of re-entry into the United States for the Japanese nationals, because the War Department had issued a directive against such individuals traveling to the China-Burma-India Theater. After months of bureaucratic delay the team finally departed for Calcutta on June 1, 1945, only to experience racial discrimination in the British Commonwealth they were partnered with. Upon arrival on July 9, they were immediately confined and kept under guard in their appointed camp compound, an arrangement that Kay Sugahara found reminiscent of his time spent at the Amache WRA camp. Others complained to their friends in Green that their restriction to the camp compound was reinforced by the electrified wire fence. Once clearance was received for the Marigold team to fly over the Himalayas (known as "the hump") to Kunming, only Shūji Fujii and four others were sent on August 1, while twenty-two Japanese Americans remained in Calcutta until August 20, awaiting orders to join the Kaji project, which never materialized. With budget cutbacks impending as the war was winding down, these Japanese Americans were shipped back to the United States without ever joining the Free Japan Movement. Fujii and his small team, however, were assigned to a heavily secured camp outside the city on a small island in a lake. But the war ended before Fujii's team was able to carry out its intended propaganda work.[30]

Although Marigold and Green made little impact in the field, they were not without influence in Washington. They pushed the War Department further down the path toward humanizing rather than demonizing the enemy. Japanese Americans provided their superiors with additional

Figure 3.3 OSS Morale Operations' propaganda leaflet to Imperial Japanese soldiers, urging them not to sacrifice their lives in battle, 1945, by Atsushi Iwamatsu (Tarō Yashima). Courtesy of National Archives and Records Administration II.

reasons why a humane approach to the Japanese was the best course of action. Their indispensability for producing propaganda materials for MO also forced that section of the OSS to counter the War Department's prohibition against OSS Japanese nationals traveling to the theater of operations in Asia. They accomplished this with a conceptual distinction between "Japanese" (the enemy) and "Japanese Americans," based on a loyalty that transcended nationality and race.

Yoneo Sakai's plan to end the war illustrates how far these Japanese Americans pushed the OSS toward a new understanding of Japanese and

Japanese Americans. Although a latecomer to the Collingwood group, Sakai established himself quickly as someone whose ideas must be heard. As a former journalist for *Asahi Shimbun* from 1931 until the outbreak of war, he was one of few Japanese to witness firsthand the Spanish Civil War, which he covered as a correspondent. Commanding the respect of his superiors in Collingwood, Sakai boldly proposed a plan to end the United States' war with Japan in three secret letters dated July 30, August 3, and August 6, 1945. He believed that some influential leaders inside Japan could be enlisted to persuade the emperor to negotiate for Japan's surrender. Among them were Shigeyoshi Kobatake, the foreign minister; Kichisaburō Nomura, former ambassador to the United States; Shigeji Kasai, Imperial Diet member; Toyotarō Yūki, finance minister; Aiichirō Fujiyama, president of Dai Nippon Sugar Manufacturing Company, who had helped topple Hideki Tōjō's from power in 1944; as well as a number of influential opinion-makers from the mass media, including Taketora Ogata, vice president of the *Asahi Shimbun* and a member of the Imperial Rule Assistance Association. He then proposed that three Japanese Americans, with these individuals' assistance, parachute into the Imperial Palace grounds in Tokyo to negotiate directly with the emperor for an acceptable surrender that would involve no loss of face for His Majesty. Upon hearing of it, Sakai's work colleague Jin Konomi stated: "Although I thought it was a dream-like fantasy, it had persuasive power."[31]

Persuasive or not, the OSS considered a variation on this plan. But it could not send MO folks like Yoneo Sakai, Jin Konomi, or Atsushi Iwamatsu, since many of them were already known inside Japan as spies, ensuring their untimely demise should they be captured. To carry out the penetration of Japan itself, the OSS had to develop other agents with the correct racial uniform, the right training in the tradecraft, and assurances that those being sent out were not double agents, since the stakes in the field for these agents were higher.

CHAPTER 4

✧

Fighting Like a Man, Special
Operations Style

Kunsung Rie was accorded greater trust by his Special Operations (SO) superiors than his civilian counterparts received from Morale Operations (MO). At first glance, however, one would expect opposite, since the consequences were greater for misinterpreting the loyalty of Asian American field operatives than for propaganda agents. The Marine Corps refused them, US Navy vessels had only Filipino galley stewards, and the army scattered Chinese and Koreans across various units while keeping Japanese Americans in segregated units overseen by European American officers. All services expressed the belief that Asian Americans in their ranks would hurt morale and increase the risk of placing a Trojan Horse in their midst. Yet the navy and the army accepted small numbers of Chinese Americans and Korean Americans and integrated them into their units without the stigma of segregation. With the rarest exceptions, however, they did not promote them to officers. The opposite was true for Asian Americans in SO, where as commissioned officers they were accorded respect not experienced in the wider society. European American enlisted men had to—at a bare minimum—salute them and obey their orders, or risk a court-martial.

Why this seeming aberration took place involves the nature of special operations. Normally sent behind enemy lines to destroy or capture certain objectives, they relied on team members' ethnic/cultural knowledge to assist them in their penetration behind enemy lines. Faced with an enemy's superior firepower, the unit members depend on each other to carry out their assigned roles in launching the surprise attack. During withdrawal, when the enemy may fire blindly at anyone, friend or foe, during the first few seconds of the attack, all shared the same risks of injury as they provided cover for each other. Regardless of racial uniform, any member with special linguistic skills enhances the group's combat effectiveness and ability to survive, strengthening unit cohesiveness. They are unlike those in the army or navy who serve on the front lines of combat, where dependence on their own superior numbers and firepower for success and survival affords them the luxury of disliking a fellow combatant based on race.

Another important factor was SO's success in achieving strong, measurable results in its early stages. Unlike MO, which could not point to any objectives attained, SO's effectiveness was easily seen in missions successfully executed and, more important, the number of casualties and deaths they inflicted upon enemy combatants. Credited with inflicting large losses on the enemy relative to their own losses, SO became William Donovan's favorite group as they validated to the Joint Chiefs of Staff his agency's importance to the war effort.

SO's initial experiment in Burma with Asian American agents proved a resounding success. Under Carl Eifler and Raymond Peers's leadership, the SO team originally known as Detachment 101 became a highly effective guerrilla unit behind enemy lines in northern Burma. At its peak of less than 900 Americans, of whom 22 were Asian Americans, this unit worked with some 11,000 locals, a force that comprised well under 2 percent of all Allied personnel committed to the fighting war in the region. Together, they killed 5,447 of the 316,700 Japanese soldiers counted in March 1944, wounded an estimated 10,000 more, and captured 64. They destroyed 51 bridges, 9 railroad trains, 277 military vehicles, and 2,000 tons of supplies. More important, they supplied 90 percent of the intelligence for General Joseph Stilwell's Northern Combat Area Command, which resulted in successful bombing runs that killed over 11,000 and wounded an additional 885 enemy combatants, while at the same rescuing close to 600 Allied combatants trapped behind enemy lines. Against this total, they lost 184 local agents and 22 Americans.[1]

Detachment 101's success was due to a number of factors. Although the unit's original area of responsibility covered China, Korea, Burma, the Malay States, Indo China, Hainan Island, and Japan proper, the team's initial operations were confined to Burma in early 1942. Various political factions seized the opportunity to grasp control over the country after the decisive defeat of British troops by the Imperial Japanese forces paved the way for independence from British ruling authority. Many of the ethnic Burmese, numbering some ten million of a total of seventeen million in the country, collaborated

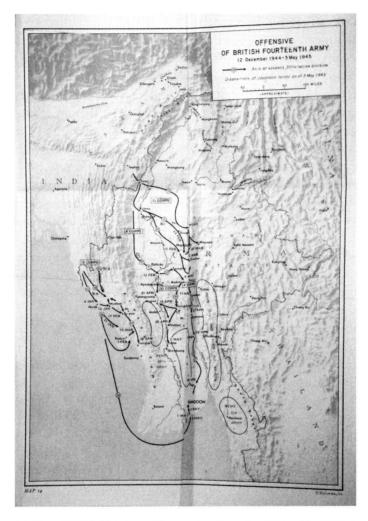

Figure 4.1 Map of British 14th Army Offensive, late December 1944 to May 1945. Courtesy of the National Archives and Records Administration II.

with the Japanese in driving out the British, Asian Indians, and the Chinese. With the Burma Independence Army, they launched a "race war" against the four million Karens and two million Shansi hill tribes in central and southern parts of the country. They expelled some 350,000 Asian Indian refugees who fled by land to India, passing through the Northwest Territory where Kachins, Nagas, Mons, and Chins resided. Since these ethnic minorities were the traditional enemies of the central and southern plains Burmese, they retaliated by assisting the refugees and nearly 11,000 of them enlisting as Kachin to join the Detachment's guerrilla force of 13,000.[2]

Detachment 101's success was also the result of Eifler blending guerrilla warfare tactics learned from a variety of sources. Although he trained in basic British commando tactics at Camp X, Eifler chose not to engage in pitched battles with Imperial Japanese forces once the element of surprise was lost. He instead favored immediate withdrawal of his forces to lure the pursuing enemy into his booby traps. His traps, often *punji* or sharpened bamboo spears, were tactics and weaponry learned from his Kachin personnel. Instead of using swift flying military aircraft for delivery of supplies and agents behind enemy lines, Eifler chose slower, smaller, lower-powered single-engine aircraft with skilled pilots trained in low-altitude, terrain-hugging flights as the means to avoid detection, a lesson he had learned from chasing smugglers as a customs service agent. Acquiring local labor to haul supplies and equipment behind enemy lines, Eifler used opium, gold, silver, cloth, knives, and salt as his currency, which locals favored over the Japanese military script the enemy used to pay for their services. "Payment is the best pull for native recruits," Eifler concluded, a principle he used to induce cooperation of the village headman in his areas of operation.[3]

Yet Eifler's approach toward dealing with the northern Burmese were probably not the reasons for Detachment 101's success. Eifler and his successor, Ray Peers, believed that the ends justified the means, even if they bordered on criminality. Peers stated, "Agents can recognize no rules in the kind of war we fight: cheating, lying, and 'unfair' means of striking the enemy are perfectly permissible." Deception, however, was reserved for the enemy, not for allies, only because Eifler believed his local recruits were like children:

> Should say that natives be recognized as human beings and treated as such. Will find that the average is like a child. Use same principles as father does with child. Do not lie to him and never let him lose confidence in you.

Eifler meted out stern discipline to "misbehaving children" who failed to collaborate with his team. He was utterly ruthless in such matters and called in air strikes against uncooperative villages, as he stated in a letter to one of his unit team members in 1943: "If there is any village that is giving trouble and you want it rubbed out, then say so in so many words and we will get it just as soon as the weather clears." The colonel's remorselessness spurred Orde Wingate to write him a stinging letter about his execution of Burmese collaborators:

> From the military point of view, it tends to create distrust in the minds of these very timid people, and they logically argue that the only safe thing is to have

nothing whatever to do with either side. I would rather risk loss of men through treachery, and enjoy co-operation, than isolate myself completely by action designed to frighten possible traitors.[4]

Kindness, rather than stern measures, was the most likely way to win Burmese cooperation, as Archie Chun-Ming discovered. His medicinal contributions were crucial to winning over northern Burmese to the American side and thus became a major reason for Detachment 101's success. Captain (later Major) Chun-Ming also had duties unrelated to medicine while serving in the Detachment. He had to secure communications by instructing all radio operators in the art of cryptography, in order to prevent the transmission from being compromised. Chun-Ming was in charge of morale and handled the postal censorship too. His regular medical-related duties for the unit involved providing the portable medical kits each team member and trainee carried on operations. He also inspected each camp, including those behind enemy lines, to ensure they met his health and sanitation standards. As the only medical officer servicing 89 officers, 227 enlisted men, and 4,000 local agents spread out over an area covering several thousands of miles, Chun-Ming's responsibilities were enormous and so was his success: the unit enjoyed the lowest percentage of illness of any organization in the entire region. Despite his busy schedule, Chun-Ming volunteered his medical services to help local villagers surrounding the Detachment's various bases. His superior in Washington, DC, General John Magruder, offered this praise: "Courageously and boldly he voluntarily participated in many errands of mercy into territory occupied by the enemy and natives of unknown affiliation." As for why he was nominated for the Legion of Merit medal, Magruder testified to the "great value" Chun-Ming gave to the Allied cause:

> Despite the hardship of enemy action, distance between camps, terrain and weather conditions, Major Chun-Ming not only rendered required medical service to the personnel and agents assigned to the detachment, but also unselfishly devoted himself to the native population in the surrounding areas. His splendid achievements developed friendliness and goodwill which richly rewarded the American Government by favorably influencing the natives toward Americans and enlisting their valuable aid to our cause.

Carl Eifler also recognized the initiative Chun-Ming took in rendering medical service: "It should be remembered that his primary duty was the health of the American contingent. His medical services to the natives were voluntary and beyond the call of duty."[5]

Other Asian Americans also had a hand in Detachment 101's success. Some played a supportive role in the unit's first mission, such as Sukyoon Chang, who was initially tasked to serve as the liaison officer between the team, the Korean Provisional Government, and the Korean underground. Fluent in Japanese and Chinese and native in Korean, Chang was a trained radio instructor and was immediately promoted to the rank of sergeant within days of his enlistment in May 1942. His important liaison assignment was soon switched to surveillance of Indira Gandhi and the independence movement: "For two months he did military intelligence work under the supervision of Colonel John Coughlin in New Delhi and Calcutta concerning the Mahatma Gandhi Movement in India and smuggling operations between Calcutta, India and China, by Chinese," Eifler reported to his superiors. Once Chang reached northern Burma, however, he was assigned the seemingly innocuous task of procuring food supplies for the detachment. In the process he learned Hindi and Burmese. When not on mess hall duty, he translated "secret papers written in Chinese and Japanese" brought in by agents and "some other sources of intelligence services." He also forged Japanese passes for OSS agents slipping into Japanese sections of Burma and interrogated the only captured Japanese fighter pilot in the Theater.[6]

Hong Richard Chan, another Asian American in the detachment, was the most likely source for some of the intelligence reports Sukyoon Chang received. Chan's role was also transformed by the unit's sudden deployment in Burma. Originally a worker in a New York City Chinatown restaurant, Chan was recruited to serve as the unit's only undercover agent operating inside India. After enlisting in the army and being immediately promoted to sergeant, Chan was sent by submarine to India ahead of detachment members to establish what was anticipated to be the unit's supply routes behind enemy lines. After arrival Chan extracted information from Chinese smugglers and Japanese spies, which he forwarded to Sukyoon Chang at the Indian detachment base in Nazira, Assam. The undercover agent was also tasked with establishing a smuggling operation in Rangoon to get rubber out while smuggling in supplies for their own covert operations in the region. As Carl Eifler reported: "I also have a man inside the smuggling activities out of Calcutta and I am attempting through him to open a second line into Burma, utilizing only the services of professional smugglers."[7]

Another indispensable Asian American was Don Eng, who was crucial to the team's communications system. Arriving in October 1942 at the team base in Nazira, he took charge of the unit's entire communication equipment. Eng realized that Eifler planned to send part of his team into the

Myitkyina area, where the Japanese maintained a fighter intercept group to attack American supply planes flying over the Hump. To relay their information by radio, however, the group needed a transmitter powerful enough to reach Nazira—a distance of 400 miles, when most radios had a range of only thirty to fifty miles. The master sergeant also understood that the radio and its generator had to be portable, preferably less than fifty pounds. Working under Captain Philip Huston, in two months Eng designed a new radio set with parts Allen Richter purchased in New York, and a generator that exceeded the ideal maximum weight by only three pounds. Eng, Richter, and Technical Sergeant Fima Haimson provided Detachment 101 with a radio that had an effective range of 1,200 miles, turning the group into an effective intelligence-dissemination unit. Frank Heck, however, credited only Eng with the invention:

> Don Eng was probably an outstanding radio man—he could make his radio sets reach much farther than any previous sets in China. Communication systems in 1942 were rudimentary with the best radio sets operating in China could only go no more than 30–50 miles. Eng exceeded this by quite a bit as I recall.

Eng's service to Detachment 101 also included flying into enemy territory on a single-engine aircraft to reach forward bases to repair radio sets. He often worked eighteen to twenty hours straight to maintain radio communications between seven forward units and three base stations in Ledo, Calcutta, and Chittagong. It was on one of those repair missions that he crash-landed, suffering severe nerve damage that earned him a medical discharge and a return trip to Seattle for convalescence.[8]

Given Detachment 101's success in its guerrilla warfare, Imperial Japanese forces were understandably concerned with locating and destroying Eifler's forces. But its radio directional finding equipment was inaccurate, so they were unable to locate his forces. Hence, they resorted to issuing threats. As Eifler reported, "They know who I am and who my men are. They just haven't got us. They threaten death to any native that plays [along] with us." Further, the Japanese forces placed a bounty of three bags of salt on the head of the colonel and sent word through the grapevine "to quit fighting like I am fighting and come out and fight like a man."[9]

"Fight like a man" is precisely what happened next under Peers's command. As Detachment 101 expanded its guerrilla operations and Eifler was assigned to another mission in Europe, Peers opened up his detachment to a dozen Japanese Americans. They were initially assigned to Secret Intelligence (SI) where, after receiving infantry training at Camp Shelby, they entered the army's Military Intelligence and Language School to take courses on translating Japanese military language documents and radio intercepts. Thereafter, the American-born Japanese recruits studied radio, cryptography, and other forms of the field craft at Camp McDowell near Napierville, Illinois. For in-country training, they went to Catalina Island off the coast of Los Angeles. They were then assigned to Detachment 101 in February 1945. The fourteen—ten from Hawai'i and four from the mainland—included four officers (Captain R. K. Betsui, First Lieutenant Chiyoki Ikeda, Lieutenant Junichi Butō, and First Lieutenant Ralph Yempuku), with eight enlisted men, all above the rank of private (Sergeant Dick Hamada, Sergeant Calvin Tottori, Sergeant Thomas Baba, Technical Four Shōichi Kurahashi, and Corporals Fumio Kido, William M. Kishinami, Calvin Tottori, and Takashi Nagaki). Three more, also at Camp Shelby, came from the WRA camps: Sergeant Susumu Kazahaya, Sergeant George Kobayashi, and Private Takeo Tanabe. Upon arrival in India, they were split into three groups, with Lieutenant Chiyoki Ikeda, Sergeants Susumu Kazahaya and George Kobayashi, Corporal Tadashi Nagaki, and Private Takeo Tanabe being sent to Detachment 202 in China. Captain Betsui and Corporal William Kishinami of the second group remained in New Delhi. Meanwhile, Lieutenants Junichi Butō and Ralph Yempuku, Sergeants Thomas Baba, Dick Hamada, and Fumio Kido, and Technical Four Shōichi Kurahashi and Corporal Calvin Tottori of the third group were assigned to Detachment 101 inside Burma. The latter group was split again, with Ikeda staying in the headquarters at Bhamo and the others assigned to the field.[10]

Some of these Japanese Americans avoided combat situations in central Burma. Thomas Baba snuck behind enemy lines in the central region with his commanding officer Oscar Milton, a radio operator, and two Burmese agents, but evaded the enemy while gathering intelligence. Shōichi Kurahashi spent his time near the front making propaganda leaflets for distribution over the Lashio area in central Burma. Others, like Chiyoki Ikeda, Susumu Kazahaya, George Kobayashi, and Takeo Tanabe, were all assigned to the rear area of New Delhi before being reassigned to Kunming in February 1945, rear areas away from combat. Fumio Kido stayed in a very safe location far from the fighting and spent some of his time translating documents and filing them away. Kido devoted the rest of his time to establishing a museum displaying captured Japanese equipment to orient people new to the Theater. Remembering only his quiet time spent in the rear area, Kido credited his ability to escape unscathed from a war that brought death to many of his Japanese American cohorts in the 442nd Regimental Combat Team to being in "the right place at the right time."[11]

Others, however, found themselves in places where they indeed had to fight like a man. To prevent them from being shot at, SO Japanese

Americans were defined as Americans and not Japanese, despite their physical features resembling the enemy. Lieutenant Ralph Yempuku, for example, joined the First Battalion of Kachin Rangers, led by Captain Joe Lazarsky. Their mission was to cut enemy communication and supply lines on the Burma Road, identify bombing targets, assist downed American aviators, and harass Japan's Thirty-Fourth Division in northern Burma, with close to 200 guerrillas armed with light weapons and mortars. Yempuku was assigned to lead Company C and to guard the flanks of Lazarsky and others. But Yempuku's Japanese physical features raised the possibility of mistaken identity on the battlefield, since he was five feet, three inches tall and weighed only 120 pounds. So Lazarsky undertook a special exercise for Company C to reinforce Yempuku's role as commanding officer. Yempuku recalled, "The Kachins were initially very wary about me because I was a Japanese-American. On the first day Capt. Lazarsky paraded me in front of the whole Battalion introducing me as 'American' and ordering them to study my face so that I would not be mistaken for and shot as an enemy Japanese." In fact, Yempuku was labeled a *duwa* or "white guy," as misinterpreted by Lazarsky, to ensure his safety. His racial reconstruction apparently was effective, since Yempuku was able to command his Kachin personnel to fight like men and hold their ground against Japanese mortar and tank fire, something these guerrillas were not trained to do. Despite this seeming liberal construction of his racial identity, Yempuku remained leery of his other commanding officers, since he felt they were too willing to risk his life. In one instance an officer sent him into a valley to persuade some 500 entrenched Japanese soldiers to surrender.[12]

Dick Hamada, however, required no such reconstruction, since his physical features were perceived as not Japanese. "Has Polynesian appearance, which is to our advantage," observed one anonymous trainer of the five-foot six-and-a-half-inch, 140-pound Hawai'i-born Japanese sergeant. Hamada, too, made little use of his Japanese language skills while in the field, as he explained: "I was never able to interrogate any enemy soldier for they were killed before I could get to them." Having joined a group of some 300 Kachin Rangers, Hamada was always accompanied by a European American soldier to protect him. He took the additional precaution of carrying a bullet to use on himself in the event of capture. He knew that the Imperial Japanese personnel would not treat him kindly, as reflected in the large bounty on the heads of all Japanese Americans in American uniforms. "If we were turned in and captured," Hamada recalled, "that individual would get rewarded $20,000. . . . Being in a jungle, being that we possess the face of an enemy, I was very much afraid of people that I didn't know. I was safe with my people, Americans." Like Yempuku, Hamada too was labeled *duwa* by the Kachins and accorded high respect. Hamada rewarded them with cigarettes and candies from his army allotment.[13]

Dick Hamada's amicable relations with the guerrilla soldiers saved his life in his next assignment to the Shan state in the central-eastern part of the country. Hamada and the 2,500-strong guerrilla force were assigned to secure the eastern flank of British General William Slim's Fourteenth Army drive toward Rangoon, but they were outnumbered by as many as 10,000 Imperial Japanese soldiers armed with artillery and tanks. In a small village between Lashio to the north and Loilem to the south in April 1945, the Japanese American sergeant found himself holding ground to protect his captain's flank, contrary to guerrilla warfare principles of surprise attack and rapid retreat. Their forces unexpectedly encountered Japanese soldiers encamped in a small village, and in the ensuing fire fight hundreds of the guerrillas deserted the battlefield. Outflanked and badly outnumbered, Hamada ignored the machine gun bullets flying about him and crawled his way to each of his twenty-five men's foxholes to encourage them to hold their ground:

> Our skirmish with the enemy forces never diminished and on the third night, I had to encourage and bolster my platoon's confidence. Crawling to them and assuring them with my presence and a pat on their back has indeed restored their faith to battle the enemy. Although communication was a major problem, knowing that I was there in the heat of the battle has certainly increased their faith and they battled with added confidence.

Hamada, however, faced communication problems with his men. So he used the Japanese language to communicate his desire that they hold their ground:

> Some of the soldiers understood Japanese and English which made communication great. For those who understood Japanese, "GANBATTE TATAKATTE KURE" [Hang in there! Fight!] was the most effective encouraging term for those that understood Japanese. Those who understood would convey the message to the others in their native language. For those that didn't understand, a pantomime action was the only means plus a pat on the back seem to work. Encouragement did the trick and they were able to hold their position.[14]

The OSS planned additional SO involving Korean Americans. Although their plans were delayed as much by interagency wrangling as by Korean political factionalism, the OSS had two insertion teams formed by early 1945 for intelligence and sabotage operations on the Korean peninsula, with Korean Americans playing a prominent role. OSS planning for both teams was fraught with complications beyond the question of loyalty of some of its members. Any planned operation inside Korea launched from China required the approval of the China Theater commander, who in 1945 was General Albert Wedemeyer. Wedemeyer's good working relationship with the Chinese Nationalist government was based on his willing consultation with Chiang Kai-shek before carrying out any operations inside the country. To consult with Chiang, however, meant the OSS ran the risk of compromising secrecy for its teams, since Chiang's government was known to be riddled with Japanese and Chinese Communist spies. In addition, the Imperial Japanese forces based in the Korean peninsula numbered over 86,000 and were well-positioned to counter sabotage committed by the teams. The OSS teams had doubts about the extent of cooperation they could secure in maintaining operations inside Korea, given that a large, unknown number of Korean collaborators existed. They had reason to pause, since 84 percent of the total population of Korea had Japanese surnames, in compliance with the Name Order law in late 1939. Even if they found sympathizers, those Koreans were under the scrutiny of the police force, which numbered 18,811 in 1930. Of that force, 40 percent (7,113) were Koreans whose role in the local station was to watch over an average of twenty small villages or 800 households. They even had to contend with some 350,000 Neighborhood Patriotic Associations, each local chapter responsible for ten households and assisted by village elders, tribal chieftains, and neighborhood heads.[15]

Operation Eagle was one of two OSS insertion teams headed for Korea. Eagle was defined as a SI mission that would become SO once the cooperation of the Korean underground was secured. The team's initial focus was on collecting tactical and strategic intelligence, with particular attention to "target data" to degrade Japan's war industry and military, and to have intelligence ready "in the event of an Allied landing on Korea." They targeted five areas—Suiho, Chinnanpo, Keijo, Genzan, and Seishin—and planned for twenty-two Americans to direct Eagle, of which fourteen of them were assigned to train forty-five Koreans to carry out the mission. At Hang-tu-ch'iao, China, the American trainers were to review 120 young Korean men, from which sixty were to be selected for training and forty-five chosen for the mission. Nine each were assigned to the five areas after three months of training under the direction of Colonel Willis Bird of the OSS office in Hsian. With the backing of both the Chinese Nationalist government and the Korean Provisional Government, Eagle appeared ready for its scheduled move from Hsian to Shandong on September 5, 1945.[16]

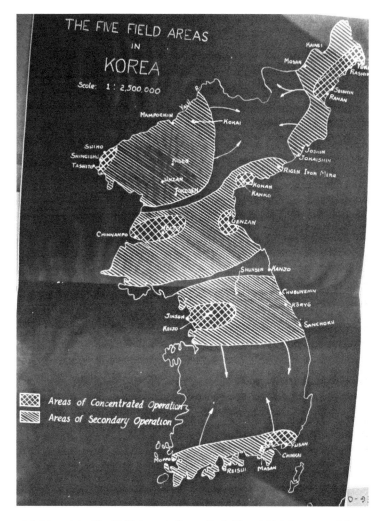

Figure 4.2 Map of the Five Field Areas in Korea, Eagle Plan, 1945. Courtesy of the National Archives and Records Administration II.

Asian Americans played a central role in Eagle. Aside from the handful of European American officers who staffed the headquarters, Asian Americans filled the most important positions on the team. In the rear, Susumu Kazahaya was tasked with drafting the maps Eagle members were to use after insertion, while Chiyoki Ikeda handled much of the counter-intelligence work in Hsian designed to keep the project a secret. Korean Americans, however, took center stage. They were tasked with training the forty-five team members, as well as leading the team into Korea. Their own training began in February 1945 in Washington, DC and Catalina

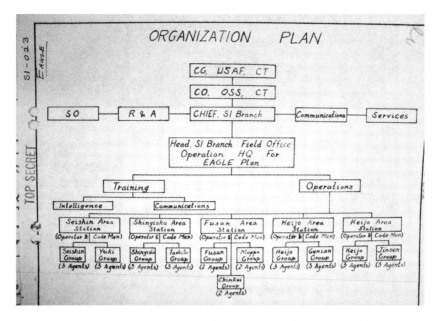

Figure 4.3 Organization Plan for Eagle, 1945. Courtesy of the National Archives and Records Administration II.

Island, before being shipped to Hsian in the China Theater in June 1945. The team was initially in high spirits, since it anticipated working with the Korean underground, using leader Captain Ryongi Hahm's high status and connections. In addition, nearly a dozen bilingual recruits from American colleges anticipated receiving favorable determinations on their US citizenship applications. Treated as special, they were excused from "kitchen police" duties to concentrate on teaching the art of intelligence-gathering and secret messaging to other team members. They were to instruct Korean deserters from the Imperial Japanese Army and extract information from recent émigrés from Korea to China. They sought knowledge of the courier routes to and from northern China and Korea that Eagle would use for its entry into Korea.[17]

Despite the preparations and William Donovan's backing, Eagle remained earthbound. British intelligence and Tai Li of Chinese intelligence opposed sending in the group, favoring other Korean groups instead. When he failed to insert his Koreans into Eagle, Tai Li sent Yang Yun-chu, director of the Department of Eastern Affairs, to ostensibly consult with Captain Clarence Weems on Eagle but in reality to spy on them: "[In] our talk with Mr. Yang," Weems reported, "he was trying to find out not only how much information we had relative to Korea, but what future plans we have in mind for the training and operating of Korean agents. We were

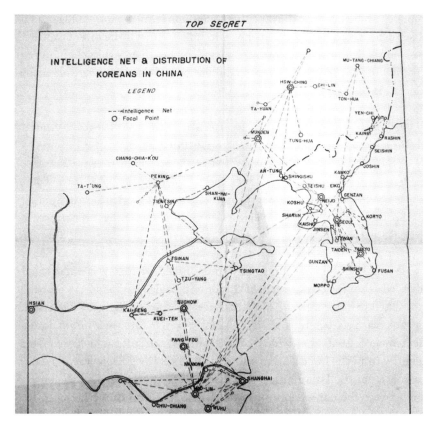

Figure 4.4 Intelligence Net & Distribution of Koreans in China, 1945. Courtesy of the National Archives and Records Administration II.

very careful not to make any commitments or promises, or to reveal to any extent any plans." Failing to secure the names of Eagle agents, Tai Li then spread rumors that the mission was funded through the OSS unvouchered funds to the tune of a half-million dollars a month and not the measly $8,000 a month it actually received —a relatively small sum compared with other operations funded by the OSS SI group.[18]

Eagle was also stymied by problems from within. The team suffered from low morale, although its sixty-one members had started off well in the eyes of their American trainers in early August 1945. They were, as one navy officer commented, not "real bloodthirsty" and shied away from dangers in field exercises that required, among other things, handling explosives and weapons. Instead of weeding out the "deadwood Koreans," Eagle team members were subjected to a battery of tests administered by expert psychologists, including two Chinese Americans, Robert Chin and Bingham Dai. The college-educated Eagle team members scored low in morale as field agents in part because their family members would stand to lose their privileges inside Japanese-occupied Korea if they were captured or identified. These same educated members, however, exhibited high motivation for Eagle when it came to discussions of their postwar role inside Korea. As the expert psychologists reported:

> Motivation in these men was high for work in the Korean postwar government. There was a general appreciation of the fact that they, as selected personnel of the Korean Independence Army and closely associated with the Korean Provisional Government, would have opportunities in that field at the end of the war. In a large percentage of the cases interest did not extend much beyond this; patriotism, defined as a willingness to sacrifice one's life for one's country, was all but absent.[19]

Eagle members' lukewarm response to their field training was understandable. Whether they were aware of this or not, Eagle members were probably not slated to enter into the fray until after most of the fighting had ceased or took place elsewhere. With less than a month before their target date of September 5, 1945, they had no counterintelligence unit to shield members' identity from the Imperial Japanese intelligence. Until Eagle was separated in July from the Hsian office, they had Chiyoki Ikeda keeping the enemy spies away. Their insertion route through China into Korea had also not yet been determined. They were plagued with infighting among the various political factions, including the Korean Provisional Government, all vying for control of the Korean insertion team to position themselves as heads of the postwar Korean government. "Their struggle was exactly like that of a roaring beast fighting for a piece of meat," one such trainee recalled. Another facetiously quipped he would volunteer for the Japanese Air Force so that he might bomb the Korean Provisional Government Building in Chungking. Moreover, these Korean trainees had little to fight for, given the possibility of another foreign occupation of Korea following the ouster of Japan. As Sygnman Rhee succinctly put it, "Why do you think the Koreans should revolt against the Japs and get killed, while the United Nations are [sic] plotting to force the Koreans to change from one master to another?"[20]

Unlike Eagle, however, Napko was the real OSS insertion team ready to risk their lives for operations deep behind enemy lines. Lacking assurances of a favorable postwar fate for Korea, these eight Korean Americans accepted the assignment of covertly landing via submarine near Seoul and Pyongyang on the west coast of Korea from their supply base in Okinawa to establish an intelligence network. After establishing temporary bases inside the country with the help of locals, they were then to recruit locals to assist with the rescue of downed American aviators, as well as to organize them into resistance groups that would engage in sabotage and guerrilla operations. Napko members were also to recruit, train, and dispatch other Koreans for espionage work inside the home islands of Japan. As Donovan reminded General Albert Wedemeyer, Commander of the American forces in the China Theater, "Ultimately, the goal is the projection of a secret intelligence network into Japan itself."[21]

Napko's officers were battle-hardened veterans who had proven their mettle. At the top was Carl Eifler, the former leader of Detachment 101. After being reassigned to another mission by Donovan in December 1943, Eifler spent 1944 recuperating and planning a daring raid to kidnap and smuggle out of Germany that country's top nuclear physicists working on the atomic bomb. Once that mission was scrubbed, Eifler returned to his original mission of initiating guerrilla warfare in northeast Asia. To assist in the development of these plans, he pulled in some of his former Detachment 101 team members, Robert Aitken, Floyd Frazee, Vincent Curl, and Sukyoon Chang. Eifler put Aitken in charge of his liaison work with headquarters in Washington, while Frazee handled all administrative matters in Los Angeles. The colonel then added Lois Poe to handle all the administrative paperwork as he began pulling the team together with the special assistance of Sukyoon Chang.[22]

Chang's role in the recruitment of Napko team members was crucial to the mission. After Eifler left the Burma Theater for the United States, Chang was assigned in May 1944 to Detachment 202 in Kunming, where he translated captured Japanese-language documents to determine bombing targets for the Fourteenth Air Force. In July, he was reassigned to Chungking to unspecified undercover work, which included planning with cabinet members of the Korean Provisional Government for future operations. Upon completion of this liaison work, Chang returned to Washington to join the Field Experimental Unit, a cover for Napko. Although Chang was tasked with handling mail and lecturing on conditions in Japan and its occupied territories, his most important work involved "recruiting Orientals for special missions." Chang appeared at Camp McCoy for about forty days, posing as a translator while checking on "conversations of prospective agents from recordings to judge their loyalty and security" among the confined Korean prisoners of war. Chang selected the Korean soldiers based on his perception of their level of patriotism toward Korea, intelligence, and hatred of the Japanese. He then signaled the camp commander to have those individuals surreptitiously smuggled out and taken to Catalina Island, where they joined "Einec" or "Charo," the first two teams to train for the mission.[23]

Leaders for Einec and Charo trained first, beginning in early March 1945. Under the supervision of Robert Carter, Vincent Curl, and Henry Keyes, they were divided into two groups of four and three each. For security purposes, they were trained out of sight from each other at Fourth of July Cove and Howland's Landing on the northwest end of Catalina Island, some twenty miles from Los Angeles. Over a three-month period, they practiced the collection and communication of intelligence. They learned aircraft identification, recruiting informants, photography, sketching, and observations of shipping vessels, as well as cryptography and radio transmission of their intelligence reports. They studied various covers, concealment, Imperial Japanese countermeasures, usage of secret ink, and propaganda, in addition to map reading, first aid, and landing by parachute, surface vessel, and undersea craft. To launch their guerrilla warfare campaign inside Korea, they mastered usage of various weapons—how to disassemble and reassemble them, how to engage in night firing and unarmed combat tactics, and how to set ambushes and explosives to maximize damage to the enemy.[24]

Napko team members demonstrated high morale during their early training period. Unlike Eagle, they were especially keen on action exercises involving explosives and weapons firing, as their trainer, Sergeant Vincent Curl, reported: "This group of students all seem to be in good spirits, and are quite interested in Demolition and Boat Work, as well as their Radio and Weapons. They pay good attention in their other classes, but don't seem quite as interested in them as they are in classes of action." "Einec," composed of Ilhan New, Jimmie Charr, Charles Lee (Charles Cho), and Earl S. Ben and scheduled to land near Seoul, threw themselves into the demolitions exercise with such alacrity that Vincent Curl had high praise for the Fourth of July Cove students' ability to slip past defenses and lay explosives: "The sentries were never aware that they were in the vicinity of the target, neither did they see them make their amphibious landing." "Charo," too, excelled in their training. Composed of Diamond Kimm, Kunsung Rie, and Jimmie Pyen, this three-man team was planning to land at Chinnampo Bay, not far from present-day Pyongyang, where Kimm's family resided. They performed well in both communications and demolition work. Kunsung Rie, for example, tested at a rapid twenty words a minute in his Morse Code radio transmitting exercises, while all three of them were graded "A" for their demolition work.[25]

Despite their enthusiasm, Napko had supervisory problems. Henry Keyes, chief instructor at the West Coast Training Center, believed he had the final say in training matters for Napko. He saw the entire team as nothing special and once told the other trainer, Robert Carter, that "he couldn't get overly excited about the Eifler unit, because they were all a bunch of flat-footed cops." Keyes in particular singled out Jimmy Pyen for his carelessness with camp fires, his "lack of guts" that almost caused him to lose his life during a boat landing exercise, and his unwillingness to keep up with the rest of the group on forced marches until the last twenty or thirty feet, at which he would sprint to catch up with the group. Keyes recommended to Curl that Pyen be dropped: "Keyes then went on to say that he thought Pyen was just impossible in everything he did, and that we had just as well get rid of him." But Vincent Curl thought otherwise, seeing Pyen's behavior as understandable in terms of cultural differences and Keyes as unduly harsh. In the end, Curl's opinion prevailed and Pyen was retained.[26]

A larger conflict over control, however, loomed between Vincent Curl and Einec team member Ilhan New. In New's eyes, his control over the Napko mission was normal, given his extensive experience in founding and directing scores of employees of his conglomerate, the YuHan Corporation, with pharmacies scattered throughout Korea and Manchuria. New was far more knowledgeable about Korea, with a book scheduled for publication that year. Since his business was the main conduit for getting intelligence out of Korea into Allied hands, New assumed the greatest risk of anyone on the team, which he felt earned him some control over Napko. New was also far more educated than the trainers, having an advanced graduate degree, and was more experienced in the ways of the world, being a decade older. His medical condition precluded him from keeping up with other Napko team members on long marches and runs, a physical conditioning that might prove necessary to flee pursuing Japanese. Thus, New quite "naturally" assumed he would be based in the rear headquarters, from which he could direct much of the Napko operations, and believed he should have all available information on "his" Napko mission to make informed decisions.[27]

Conflicts between New and the trainers surfaced over the former's attitude toward training. As head of Napko, New saw his training as a matter of formality, unlike his trainer, who faulted New for having "generally poor" physical conditioning and, worse, exhibiting "a habit of malingering." Curl found the special concessions his staff made to the businessman on one of their runs irritating: "On a compass run for the men at the 4th of July Cove, New was able to walk up one of the hills, but claimed he was giving out and could not go any further, so Lt. [Harry] Forbes let him walk around the road and meet them at the ravine." New became "a difficult person to handle at times," as Curl complained to Eifler, because of his preoccupation with private matters such as his income tax and his impending book manuscript deadline, for which he sought time off from training. Curl burned with resentment before the end of the second week of training:

> New has to be handled with kid gloves, but sometimes I think it would be better if he got the hell kicked out of him. . . . I know one thing, if he makes up his mind that he doesn't want to go through the training any longer, he can persuade or lead the other three men to follow. He mentions [this] quite often to me.[28]

A second clash occurred over security measures. Curl was insistent on strict adherence to Napko's established security measures. He threatened the OSS's own trainers with court-martials for security violations. As he reported to Eifler, "I went on to say that any individuals who may think this security unimportant had better change his mind now, because if any more remarks get back to me like I had previously been hearing, I would recommend they all be court-martialed for direct disobedience of orders." New, however, was inquisitive and violated the basic security principle of need-to-know. "Colonel Eifler has other groups on this Island training, doesn't he?" New asked. Furthermore, Curl learned through censoring Einec's outgoing mail that the group in general and New in particular violated his established security measures, warranting a reprimand:

> I warned the entire group of their breach of Security in continually mentioning their being or working with the Army and trying to pass it through in letters, and that all their letters would continue to be returned to them whenever any such break in Security was written. New, of course being the leader, concurred in this and stated that each of the men would have to restrict their letters to simple subjects, although he is one of the greatest offenders of all for breaking Security.

In fact, New admitted breaking the security rules but saw no harm in his actions since he was not being sent into Japanese-occupied Korea:

> New then stated that maybe he had talked a little too much, but he was a little perturbed when he read the letter from the censor, where the censor stated that he had mentioned travel to the Orient and being in the Army on numerous occasions. New said that he realized he had mentioned being in the Army after he had been told not to, but he had been careful not to since my third, repeat third warning. I informed New that he would have to get it through his head that Security was the most important factor in all their training, and that he definitely had to abide by the security rules laid down by Colonel Eifler. New then told me that [Harold] Cleveland had told the rest of the group that he was

not going overseas and he couldn't see where it mattered or where it hurt anything so much.

Curl then explained to New, code-named "Lan," that knowing too much
could endanger the lives of others:

> Lan, sometimes I think you have pipe dreams. You have been told not once but
> many times that there are plenty of people on this Island being trained, but who
> they belong to I don't know and don't care because it's none of my business. If
> everybody being trained would devote all their time trying to find out what the
> other fellow is doing, I am sure that it would be a waste of time trying to train
> them, and if every student would devote his time in trying to absorb all the
> instruction he received, he wouldn't have time to worry about other groups or
> what other students were doing. Being too inquisitive as everyone has been told
> many times, is one sure way of an agent being caught when he is inquisitive at
> the wrong time.[29]

An importance difference between New and Curl emerged over the former's
status within Napko. The Korean American businessman understood his
position within Napko as that of an advisor on par with Curl. He shared
the same understanding with Henry Keyes, the head of the West Coast
Training Center, who told Robert Carter that New was "merely out here
[at the Fourth of July Cove] to supervise," and was "just as responsible
for the training as Curl was" because he had originally recruited the Einec
members.[30]

The greatest difference between the two men, however, emerged over the
direction and depth of loyalty. For Curl, loyalty to the aim of the American
government was paramount, and fulfillment of the Napko mission required
exclusive quantities of it. Curl was, after all, a career officer in the army and
pledged, as had New, unqualified loyalty to defending the Constitution of
the United States against all enemies. He followed the American military's
chain-of-command concept and had learned from his combat experience
behind enemy lines in Burma that the Imperial Japanese forces were quite
adept at recruiting and using local collaborators, issuing them weapons for
guerrilla warfare against the Allied forces, and in some cases even having
some of their own officers marry into village headmen's families to cement
ties with locals. Curl knew that inside Korea there were many similar types
of collaborators and was well aware that the Imperial Japanese forces had
large numbers of Koreans within their ranks—over a quarter-million—
since he was scheduled to train a number of them who defected to the
Allies. The way to counteract these dangers, as Curl saw it, was to demand

unqualified allegiance and deal severely with collaborators by destroying their entire village by bombing, as they had done in Burma.[31]

The two men's differences surfaced over a discussion of the appropriate label OSS trainers should apply to Napko team members. New objected to Curl's characterization of Napko team members as "spies" in one of his lectures. "After the class was over," Curl wrote Eifler, "New said he wanted to talk to me a little, and asked me to please ask the instructor not to use the word, spies. He said that the Korean people had been spied upon for some forty years, and they even detested the thought of the word." Curl countered by claiming that he referred to Napko members as "agents," not spies, but New was not dissuaded and instead accused Curl of giving "the impression with the other students that they were spies" when, in fact, Einec members were "working only for a patriotic cause." While Curl allowed for Einec members serving a patriotic cause, which included the establishment of an independent Korea, he would not tolerate New or others having their own personal agendas, such as those he believed New held to interfere with achieving Napko's aims. "I told New," Curl informed Eifler, "that I realized that fact, but in my own mind I am fully convinced that New is not working for a patriotic cause but for his own selfish reasons." He then urged Eifler remove New from the team because of his poor attitude and its influence on others in Einec:

> The group would be a hundred percent better off, if he [New] were removed. By his actions and remarks, he feels far superior in everything to anyone in this organization. I have heard him make remarks about everyone but you, Colonel, and I am positive that he has gone as far as to make remarks about us. New definitely resents the fact when anyone asks him to do anything such as making his bunk, or any other minor thing. He will do them once when you kid him into it, but that is the last time it will be done until you set on them again. The rest of the students seem to follow him in his actions. When you ask them to do the same thing again, they will do it, but then they sulk for a few days.[32]

Resolution of the differences between Curl and New opened the door for more Korean Americans into Napko. Carl Eifler sent a message to New, the contents of which were unrecorded, but the immediate impact was evident—New backed off of his objections, and the Einec team members experienced an upward surge in morale before the end of March 1945. "They seem to be ready for anything," Curl confidently declared. Given that Einec and Charo's trainings were nearing completion, more Korean Americans were brought to Catalina in advance of the Korean POWs being recruited from Camp McCoy. They included six from Honolulu (Moo Pak Hyung, Hyen Il Kim, Pil Young Kim, Dong Pak Soong, Hong Rhee Chong, and Sil Rhee Chong), four from Los Angeles (Dr. Arthur Kim, Tai Mo Lee, Ki Buck Par, and Chin Ha Choy), and one each from Chicago and New York (Stanley Dunn Choy and Moon Duck Harr).[33]

Despite Napko surging forward with its training, the mission was delayed by opposition within the OSS itself. In late April 1945 the OSS's top secret intelligence officer in China, Paul Helliwell, labeled Napko as premature, its team members as woefully ignorant of current conditions inside Korea, and the plan defective because it "grossly underestimates the efficiency" of the Japanese security system in the country. Rather than Napko, Helliwell argued for sending in Eagle first:

> It is believed the Eagle Project can secure over a period of time sufficient current intelligence to permit successful implementation of the Eifler Plan; that through the Eagle Project, preliminary groundwork can be laid in Korea for the laying on of at least a reasonably adequate reception for the personnel involved in the Eifler Project; and that through the Eagle Project a general groundwork can be laid not only for intelligence activities but for the sabotage and guerrilla activities contemplated in the latter phases of the Eifler Plan.

In mid-July 1945 Richard Heppner, the top OSS officer in the China Theater, concurred with his secret intelligence chief, opposing Napko on grounds that the Theater lacked the gasoline supplies, personnel slots, and geographic proximity to insert Napko members by air. More important, Heppner believed Eagle should precede Napko: "If Napko is activated in this manner it could not achieve its objective before Eagle which is ready to take field in [a] few days." Only after William Donovan's strong insistence did Napko take precedence over Eagle and acquire approval to begin deployment in August 1945. Eifler was then sent to China, while the rest of the Napko team prepared for departure to Okinawa.[34]

Before Kunsung Rie could fulfill his destiny, however, Napko was terminated. Despite Rie and the Charo group's warning in early March to Curl that the war would end soon—"they had better go quickly, or it would be over," as Rie put it—Napko's deployment was delayed yet again until Imperial Japan's surrender on August 15. The Napko mission was officially terminated nine days later.

Rie's ulterior motive of fulfilling his destiny in Korea during Napko points to the complexity of Asian American loyalty. Like MO, SO needed Asian Americans whose loyalties and aims were wider than the Allied intent to establish a base from which to strike Japan. Unlike their propaganda counterparts, the guerrilla units trusted their Asian American members. Whether that faith in individuals like Rie was merited we may never know for sure, but the bond between SO members was cemented by their shared risks under fire. The same, however, was not true for those in SI.[35]

CHAPTER 5

✦

Knowing Your Enemies and Allies: Research & Analysis and Secret Intelligence

Lincoln Kan's radio messages in the spring of 1945 presented a problem for the OSS's Secret Intelligence (SI) section in the China Theater. Was he under control of the infamous Colonel Toyo Sawa and passing on disinformation to the Japanese? Or were there mundane reasons for Kan's odd answers to Captain Charles Ambelang's queries? Despite the possibility that Kan had fallen into enemy hands in the Macao region, his deployment and that of others behind and near enemy lines illustrates the OSS's willingness to trust Asian Americans with much-needed intelligence-gathering on Imperial Japanese forces, their leaders' intentions, the infrastructure and local terrain, and analysis of the residents. The agents had the requisite linguistic skills in addition to wearing the correct racial uniform.

Such Asian Americans were essential to the strategic intelligence business. Some were employed as secretaries by the Research and Analysis (R&A) division's field stations in Honolulu, San Francisco, Los Angeles, New York City, and Washington, DC. In addition to their linguistic skills, they were recruited for their familiarity with the geographic and personal names of East Asia, a necessity for accurately writing or typing up the reports for distribution. Not much is known about this small handful of administrators, except that they were female and carried out their duties competently. Mary Chan, for example, was a Chinese national recruited in June 1944 to initially serve temporarily as a clerk stenographer for the

SI office in Kunming. Her obvious skill in carrying out her duties earned her permanent employment and a promotion to senior clerk-stenographer. She was trusted because she was reliable and not in the service of Tai Li, who often placed his own spies inside American organizations disguised as lower-level administrators and service personnel. She faithfully served during the agency during its withdrawal of its personnel to Washington, DC and relocated there before resigning to joining her fiancé in Canada at the end of October 1945.[1]

Others worked as translators. With high levels of competence in the targeted languages, many were tasked with translating articles appearing in books, newspapers, magazines, and other open sources of information, including radio broadcasts for the R&A division for their strategic and tactical intelligence reports. These translators culled a large volume of materials on East Asia deposited at the Library of Congress and major universities such as Harvard, Yale, Columbia, the University of California, the University of Southern California, Occidental College, Claremont College, and the University of Hawai'i to extract information for strategic intelligence reports. They also used books and music records from private libraries, such as the office of the *Rafu Shimpō*, the bilingual Japanese—and English-language vernacular of Southern California, and Japanese-language publications from bookstores, since they lacked access to newspapers in Japan. With these materials, workers in the biographical records section of R&A, such as John Chung, were able to create profiles of leaders in Japan. "The discovery of the Rafu Shimpo newspaper reference library was perhaps the most important," an R&A supervisor explained, as it provided "a good many publications of interest to Biographical Records as well as several reference books later borrowed by the Far East Division."[2]

Some of the staff performed aural translations, working on radio communications in Japanese and Chinese. The employees of the Eastern Research Institute transcribed and translated commercial radio traffic from the western Pacific from which the SI/Far East section developed its strategic intelligence reports on political, economic, and social trends in East Asia. They also extracted from the radio traffic tactical intelligence, such as the movements of five Imperial Japanese Navy vessels in July 1945. Asian Americans assigned to the intercept unit were stationed in Reseda, California, where they monitored and transcribed a large volume of radio traffic each day. Charles Lee was the main translator who taught Zumruth Apcar and Adelia Larson the Japanese language, while Man Hee Fong handled the transcription of the Chinese-language radio transmissions. They started in September 1944, taking in about 150 messages a day, two-thirds of which were considered important. Their transcriptions were then passed on to Tokutarō Nishimura Slocum, head of security at the Eastern Research Institute. Six Japanese American translators—Tadami Tachino, Fred Nitta, Yoneo Bepp, Robert Takukawa, Thomas Miyamoto, and Fred Kobayashi—labored over the transcriptions under the supervision of Daniel Buchanan, who performed the final editing prior to transmission to SI's head in New York, Norwood Allman. Their work was initially heavy, beginning in September 1944 with a flow of transcript as high as 400 a day, reaching 800 a mere three months later. In that third month alone, the Institute's Japanese Americans produced sixty-seven translations of 7,500 radio intercepts from Japan's Dōmei news agency. In most instances the employees performed well, as was the case with Tadami Tachino. His work was deemed "accurate" and "painstaking" and his attitude "industrious, and willing," which Buchanan attributed to Tachino's "unquestioned loyalty to the United States."[3]

A few other Japanese Americans became informants for the OSS. For the most part, they shed light on farming conditions in places where they had traveled prior to the outbreak of war, such as Kumamoto or Gunma prefectures. Some submitted information to Edwin Sadler, special attorney for the Bureau of Economic Warfare, and John Eble, while still interned at the WRA camp in Heart Mountain, Wyoming. A few others provided tactical intelligence on military objectives that made its way to the army's Joint Chiefs of Staff as possible targets for bombing. For example, Robert Naka, who attended Meiji University from 1938 to 1940, volunteered his recollection of an ammunition dump in the Harajuku section of Tokyo. Rev. Yoshikazu Horikoshi provided Sadler with his recollections of military facilities in Korea he had discovered while serving as a missionary pastor in that country until 1942. Aware of the possible consequences of revealing such information to American authorities, Seattle-born Peggy Fujioka urged Sadler not to use the tactical information to bomb Japanese civilians indiscriminately: "The Allied Nations would never win the people over by mass bombings of cities and non-military objectives only." Given Japanese American concerns over how their information would be used, Ernest Price of SI urged the hiring of thirty-one Japanese Americans for postwar reconstruction of Japan in his report titled "Utilizing the Services of American Citizens and Friendly Aliens of Japanese Race for Post-War Planning."[4]

Okinawans in Hawai'i also offered their knowledge to the OSS. Rather than tactical intelligence, however, they provided R&A with essential background information on Okinawa and its resident population, including those who migrated to the Mandated Islands like Saipan and Tinian that the US Navy was planning to invade. An unspecified number of them volunteered facts and opinions to Honolulu R&A office director Alfred Tozzer, who in turn confirmed OSS speculation that Okinawans would not serve Imperial Japanese interests by supporting the Allied cause. "It is of increasing importance," Tozzer reported to R&A, "that the racial, linguistic, and cultural background of these people should be differentiated from corresponding features among the Naichijin or Japanese proper." To underscore this difference, his Honolulu office compiled a list of over 600 surnames that distinguished Okinawans from Japanese. "The ability to separate the two groups," Tozzer asserted, "together with a realization of the cleavage between them, is especially necessary in dealing with the Japanese after the war."[5]

Chinese Americans and Korean Americans also contributed to R&A's strategic intelligence collection. The San Francisco office of R&A used various means to elicit information from these two ethnic groups. In some cases it simply hired individuals graduate students, such as S. M. Yang of the University of California, to sift through and translate articles, editorials, and letters to the editors appearing in Chinese-language newspapers in San Francisco and Los Angeles. With Yang's translations, Dr. R. W. Scott's office was able to generate over 200 reports in December 1944 on the complex political landscape of war-torn China. These were assessed as having "a valuable contribution to our understanding of the political situation in China and the influence that will bear upon China," after the Political Subdivision of the Far East Division reviewed the first six reports. In other cases, the San Francisco office utilized materials on Korean Americans obtained through legally questionable means. To determine the relative political strength of various factions inside Japanese-occupied Korea, the Korean Unit of the Political section of R&A in Washington needed information on the underground movement, the collaborators, the Communist Party, and party affiliations of Korean Americans, especially of those planning to return to their homeland. The San Francisco office took copies of hundreds of overseas cable messages and international telephone conversations between Korean Americans, Chinese Americans in Hawai'i, and various individuals in East Asia. They were able to secure access with the help of the Office of Cable Censorship, since the US Attorney General had defined all cable traffic communication to and from Hawai'i as international and therefore subject to censorship until the policy changed on April 1, 1945. The San Francisco office staff then summarized their findings and sent them to Washington, DC, including two bundles of messages that were "carefully chosen collections of cables and international telephone conversations throwing light particularly on the policies of the Free Korean Government."[6]

SI targeted not only Korea but also the main islands of Japan for penetration. It particularly focused on two Japanese nationals, one of whom had spent most of his life in Illinois and the other part of the Japanese American community leadership in San Francisco and Seattle. Both were scheduled for repatriation to Japan along with diplomats, military attaches, and other important businessmen in 1942 and 1943, respectively. Katsuji Katō, who was headed to a position at a medical college in Tokyo, appeared a promising agent. He had spent most of his life in the United States after emigrating from Osaka in 1903. Katō received his undergraduate and graduate education in practical theology and medicine in the West, taught in the pediatrics department of Rush Medical College at the University of Chicago, and married and had a family with a local Japanese American named Dorothy. He had become an informant for the FBI when he slipped out reports on the conversations he overheard among Japanese diplomatic officials and Imperial Japanese Navy and Army attachés interned at the Greenbrier Hotel in West Virginia. J. Edgar Hoover assessed his reports as worthy of the OSS's attention and passed Katō's name on to Ernest Price, who recruited him secretly for the OSS just before Kato's departure to Japan aboard the first *Gripsholm* exchange in June 1942.[7]

Yahei Taoka, the other agent recruited for the OSS, was a branch manager of the shipbuilding company Nippon Yusen Kaisha. His normal responsibilities included travel outside of Japan, making him an ideal agent. Taoka's marriage to a British national named Kathleen Marguerite and his two Eurasian daughters suggested to OSS recruiters that he might sympathize with the Allied cause. As head of the Japanese Association of San Francisco, chairperson of the Japanese Association of America, and board member of the Japan Society, he had organizational ties that provided him with knowledge of and access to Japan's commercial world. As a close friend of the consul, he enjoyed personal connections with many important Japanese officials. His return aboard the *Gripsholm* with his family on September 2, 1943 seemed a unique opportunity to SI, even though he and Katō lacked SI training prior to departure.[8]

Yet the entire project failed before it began. Given the two potential agents' rapid departure, the OSS was unable to establish a secure communication link with them. Worse, Taoka's willingness to serve the Allied cause in some capacity was misinterpreted, as suggested by his name appearing on the Office of Naval Intelligence (ONI)'s list of "Suspected Japanese Formerly Active in the United States." As for Katō, SI tried to reconnect with him by reviving its spy network, known as Project X, with Egyptian-born Clement Hakim. But Hakim was not sent, despite having significant contacts in Japan after residing in Shizuoka for about eight years as a green tea merchant before moving to New York in 1940. Without specifying the reasons, Ernest Price agreed with Spencer Phenix's opinion that Clement Hakim "should be eliminated from consideration as prospective personnel to contact 'X' in Japan," turning instead to "certain American citizens of Japanese race." To keep Project X alive, Price pursued another unnamed American-born Japanese who sought "to be of service to the United States and who had expressed confidence that they could make their way into Japan itself." Despite these assurances, the whole project quietly died without producing a single intelligence report.[9]

Yet the dream of penetrating Japan with Japanese American agents did not fade. The OSS had another option to use Sanzō Nosaka and his group: to smuggle Nosaka's agents into Japan to revive the underground Communist Party prior to an Allied invasion. Nosaka had the credentials to lead Japanese leftists—he was a founding member of the Japan Communist Party in 1922, a COMINTERN agent in Moscow since 1931, and had helped draft the guiding document of the Party, known as the 1932 Thesis. He had consistently engaged in propaganda work against the Imperial Japanese Government from abroad, first on the West Coast of the United States, where he became good friends with Joe Koide. Moreover, from his forward area base in Yenan, Shaanxi Province, his Japanese People's Emancipation League succeeded in converting a relatively large number of Japanese POWs to the Allied cause. This caused no small excitement among American observers there: "Within the next week we will have interviewed 50 Japanese POWs, a number that is more than the whole Attu campaign and have on tap with permission to interview, several hundred. This is more than was available in the entire Pacific for the first 1.5 years of the war." Nosaka appeared amenable to the possible postwar policy of retaining the emperor rather than insist on his execution or abdication. However, he could not hide his close working relationship with the Chinese communists, so the OSS deemed him too risky to use.[10]

As a result, OSS Director William Donovan altered Nosaka's plan by proposing to insert Japanese Americans, instead of Nosaka's communist agents, inside Japan. In Spring 1945 he presented to the Joint Chiefs of Staff his own plan for placing a hundred Japanese nationals inside Japan, based on the assumption that the American bombing of Japan had wreaked havoc with local control to make the plan feasible. Donovan tasked those hundred Japanese volunteers with entering Japan covertly and gathering intelligence prior to the anticipated invasion of Japan. He called for an additional fifty Japanese Americans with "a knowledge of the Japanese language and people" to direct this spy network from inside Japan. While these supervisors were to come from army or navy ranks, the agents collecting the tactical intelligence were to be recruited from among the Japanese nationals living outside of the main islands, many of whom were associated with Sanzō Nosaka. Japan's sudden capitulation in mid-August 1945 occurred before the plan could go into effect.[11]

Joan Bondurant of the San Francisco R&A office proposed another plan for inserting additional Japanese American agents into Japan prior to Allied invasion. She thought that Japanese American women could undermine Japanese public's support for the war. Instead of continuing to write or broadcast appeals via radio, a small group of women could work on the ground in Japan. She noted that Japanese women were generally excluded from political decision-making in their country and thus formed "an untapped resource" for the OSS campaign to undermine Japanese morale. These women, Bondurant asserted, were never subjected to "rigorous propaganda training" and felt oppressed by the national polity. "I believe that the Japanese women," Bondurant told her superiors, "as a class, present just such a group which, if made the object of a specialized propaganda campaign would be highly useful in promoting a peace movement, providing a basis for certain post-war negotiations, and possibly even in speeding the final stages of the war with Japan." Why a woman would promote peace, the analyst claimed, was due to status: "Her own lot being of the lowest order a victory can mean but little to the Japanese woman; a peace, everything." Furthermore, Bondurant added, Japanese women had (as had women elsewhere in the world) understood that a fascist victory would not advance their interests as a group:

> Women wish for a just and righteous world where their children may grow to be useful and healthy members of society. They are little swayed by the vicissitudes of political conniving, they are less moved by the roll of drums than are their men, they are slower to choose arbitrary sides, quicker to lean towards sensitive judgment of what seems to them, individually, to be right. The intelligent Japanese who understand something of fascism (as some of them do—even today) are certainly not enthusiastic about victory itself, for they must realize as did Baroness Ishimoto that "Fascism with its strong militaristic flavor is no defender of feminism with its strong humanistic flavor."

Bondurant then proposed to initiate a whispering campaign to kick off the movement in a country tightly controlled by the police where women were disenfranchised:

> The best method, as I see it, would be the planning of a movement . . . in the form of a whispering-campaign, spreading through women's circles. Starting from

such women leaders as Miss Kawai and spreading through her friends, there should evolve some organization . . . which eventually would dare to speak out.

To reach key Japanese female leaders like Michi Kawai, a Bryn Mawr College graduate and YWCA Japan founder, the OSS needed an individual with strong prewar social and educational connections and a similar concern for the plight of Japanese women. Such an agent, Bondurant surmised, could only come from the ranks of Japanese American women:

> These women, above all others, must realize the sorry plight of their sisters in Japan. I know, personally, at least one young Japanese-American woman, educated partially in Japan, who thoroughly champions the rights of Japanese women and who is much distressed at the added burden they now are carrying. My suggested plan would involve careful selection of one or several of these young and loyal Japanese-American women until one be found willing to cooperate in the plan.

Infiltration of Japan would be accomplished by moving the designated agent to the front-line areas of the Pacific on the pretext that she was serving as a translator for Imperial Japanese prisoners of war. Once in contact with the POWs, she would feign being "intensely loyal" to Japan to learn from the soldiers how to contact Imperial Japanese forces, then "desert" the American forces to return to her family and relatives in Japan.[12]

Slipping agents into Japan proved too difficult for the OSS, so SI opted instead to gather intelligence in regions outside of Japan. In neutral countries such as Switzerland and Thailand, their Korean and Japanese American translators collected materials that would shed light on some operations undertaken by Imperial Japanese authorities. But prior to Eagle and Napko, they were prohibited by the Joint Chiefs of Staff from entering Korea and could not penetrate Manchuria or northern China without the assistance of the Chinese Communist forces, which would alienate them from the Chinese Nationalist government. Hence, SI's Far East section devoted most of their efforts toward gathering intelligence out of central and southern China, even though the State Department and General Albert Wedemeyer, Commander of the US Army in the China Theater, agreed to make the OSS, and not the army intelligence group, G-2, the lead in the region.[13]

To meet these increased expectations, the SI's Far East group became the central one within the OSS. It was reorganized in December 1944 and added new personnel to each of its five main sections: Japan-China, Southeast Asia, Order of Battle, Geographic Intelligence, and a temporarily organized Pacific. The China-Japan section under Duncan Lee anticipated a directive on Korea and raised its personnel requirements to 575, with forty-five individuals to be sent out into the field in May 1945. The entire SI Far East budget was increased to gear up for operations. It accounted for $4.6 million of SI's Theater total of $18.3 million, far greater than the $2.9 million devoted to the European Theater and only surpassed by the North Africa Theater's $5.5 million. Even at the Washington headquarters, the Far East section got the lion's share of the budget: $795,465 of a total $2.7 million, or more than six times the London section's. The section's field headquarters in Kunming was buzzing with activity, gathering intelligence in southern China and French Indochina in anticipation of an Allied invasion to open up a port in the Pearl River Delta region. J. B. deSibour observed of the China Theater headquarters in January 1945: "One feels the general atmosphere is good. They are all now looking forward to the future for everyone realizes that this Theater is 'THE' Theater for OSS activities."[14]

With the growth of the SI field headquarters in Kunming, Fumio Kido was among those sent to the office in anticipation of a deluge of Japanese-language documents during the summer of 1945. Leaving Burma, Kido and the other Japanese Americans were sent by truck convoy. During the ten-day journey, Kido and Dick Hamada were almost killed when their vehicle suddenly skidded over the edge of a mountain road. Hamada recalled: "Our

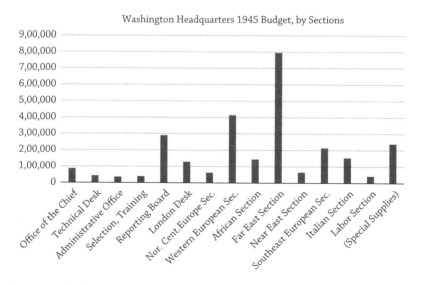

Figure 5.1 SI Budget Estimates, fiscal year 1945. *Source*: SI Budget, Folder 2, Box 42 Central Administration files, Entry 92, RG 226 Records of the OSS, NARA II.

convoy of trucks and jeeps proceeded routinely, until we were caught by a huge mudslide. The jeep Fumio and I were in was swept to the brink of the precipice. Had our jeep fallen over the cliff, we would have become a sad statistic." Despite the excitement, Kido, Hamada, Junichi Butō, and Ralph Yempuku all arrived safely in Kunming before being reassigned to different field stations inside China. Despite expectations, there turned out to be few captured Japanese-language documents to translate.[15]

Chinese Americans, however, had their hands full with covert intelligence work in southern China. Lincoln Kan and Pak Wong had dangerous encounters with the enemy while gathering intelligence for a mission code-named "Akron" in the Macao-Hong Kong area. Asian Americans joined the project to collect intelligence on the Pearl River Delta region in preparation for "Carbonado," a campaign in which thirty-nine Chinese Nationalist Army divisions aimed to seize control of Fort Bayard and an airfield at Tanchuk in order to open up a port for Allied supplies. After the initial twenty-day surveillance mission succeeded in netting maps, photos of the area between Hong Kong and Fort Bayard, and other information, Akron was extended to include coastal watching and establishing an intelligence net from Pakhoi to the border with Vietnam to keep tabs on Imperial Japanese Army troop movements. Charles Dewey and Charles Ambelang were brought in to do this work, as were Pak Hoy Wong and Lincoln Kan.[16]

Although on loan from the Fourteenth Air Force as a translator in early 1945, Pak Hoy Wong proved himself an invaluable asset. Previous attempts to penetrate the region had ended in the deaths of those agents at the hands of the Imperial Japanese Army's counterintelligence Colonel Toyo Sawa, who oversaw the area. Under Pak Wong's guidance, the first Akron team successfully spent about twenty days traveling behind enemy lines gathering intelligence, maps, and photos, including a hundred pounds' worth of Japanese-language books and periodicals, before returning to base. When Akron was extended in April, Wong joined the team permanently. He then guided another team into Japanese-held territory, but while passing through the area he was arrested by both the Chinese Communist and Chinese Nationalist troops before he reached enemy lines. He managed to escape, only to experience more hair-raising adventures after slipping behind enemy lines. "He has been close to death or capture a number of times" while collecting information, translating Chinese-language documents, and supervising field teams of local Chinese agents, his superior officer Major Robert Matthews testified. Matthews praised Wong "as near indispensable as any man I have seen in the army. No reward which seems likely, in the form of a decoration or promotion, could be too high, in my opinion." Wong's forays into enemy-held territory were well-known by locals, who considered him a hero, further compounding his dangers while in-country.[17]

Lincoln Kan, another veteran Asian American agent joining Akron, also raised expectations of success despite the dangers. Originally part of Air Ground Forces' Technical Staff, a joint intelligence-gathering venture of the Fourteenth Air Force and the OSS, Kan's group has a solid reputation as was "practically the whole [Allied intelligence] show in South China," according to Duncan Lee of the SI/Far East China-Japan section. Kan himself enjoyed personal success during his espionage foray into Shanghai, hiding in plain sight at his mother's home in June 1943 while he secretly gathered and relayed information on the deployment of enemy aircraft, shipping vessels, ammunition and food supply depots, troop staging areas, and other infra-structural details useful for planning aerial bombing by the Fourteenth Air Force. With important family connections on his father's side in the area, Kan was sent by the OSS with Wong and twenty other agents with the ex-pectation that his team would be able to gather vital intelligence needed for aerial targeting.[18]

Kan's early radio messages indicated success in intelligence-gathering in the Macao area. In April 1945, Kan was assigned to the region under the direction of Charles Dewey, a civilian, and Captain Charles Ambelang, once the Akron mission was extended. Initially, Kan was given orders be-fore departure to handle mundane matters, such as encouraging a Chinese Nationalist radio operator toward better performance in relaying radio messages. His boss, Charles Dewey, wanted Kan to push the man: "It is im-portant we make contact [with] his station before you leave. Between us, understand [the] radio man [is] very lazy. Try and get him on the beam." Kan was also asked to secure from the Chinese Nationalists additional in-telligence on Chinese officials collaborating with the Imperial Japanese and that military force's food production. All of this, after two months of traversing by foot to slip behind enemy lines, was in line with Kan's collec-tion of both operational intelligence and strategic intelligence "like polit-ical studits [sic], info[rmation] on economics condition, [and] documents." Once planted in the region southwest of Macao, the Chinese American spy reported the impending arrival of Imperial Japanese troops: "Am out now with team near Tongha as fifty thousand Nips reported on way thru this area. Have informed A[mbelang] of this move. Will keep you posted as to developments. Am keeping vigil at Kongmoon." He then was asked to pro-vide information to help the OSS prepare a "hot reception" (ambush) for Imperial Japanese troops believed to be headed for Kong Moon, Sun Wai, and Maoming: "Suggest you make every effort to identify troops, desti-nation and check number." Rather than send in additional information, however, Kan attempted to slow down the Imperial Japanese troops' arrival into the region by sending some disease-ridden prostitutes to delay their advance by an estimated two weeks. Such actions only earned him a reprimand from Ambelang: "It is hard for us to depend upon you, perhaps this is not your fault . . . due to many factors without your control. However, how are we to know[?]"[19]

Kan's superiors feared the worst when they lost contact with their Chinese American agent. Ambelang was dissatisfied with Kan's report on the so-called Chinese puppets, with his tardiness in relaying intelligence on available boats, and with his lack of details about the Japanese troops coming into his area. Dewey learned from radio messages allegedly originating from Kan that counterintelligence units of Colonel Toyo Sawa might be closing in on his group in Macao. On August 8, 1945, Dewey heard that the Kan spy ring in Macao was on the run and that Kan himself was already blacklisted by Imperial Japanese authorities. Although traveling incognito, Kan reported that he had been fired upon by Imperial Japanese troops when he traveled by boat to Siu Lam in the north: "NIPS in MAD Mood to suggest care when crossing river to Lucklow." Adding up these clues, Dewey, Ambelang, and Matthews considered the possibility that Kan had been captured by Sawa and that his incomplete, tardy messages were the products of an agent under duress, if not torture. Fearing the worst, Kan's superiors believed the intelligence was a deliberate deception planted by Sawa.[20]

Meanwhile, other Asian Americans were assigned to work in French Indochina, where the Japanese concentrated in order to repel Operation Carbonado. The Japanese had 44,000 troops deployed mostly in the southern portion of Southeast Asia but assigned enough of their troops to key checkpoints in the north such as Haiphong, Hà Giang, Lào Cai, Cao Bằng, Lạng Sơn, and Fort Bayard to wreak potential havoc with the operation. Their mission initially was to secure the rear of the Imperial Japanese Army forces invading Malaysia and Singapore in the early phase of the war and to defend the Imperial Japanese Navy base at Hainan Island, all of which ensured a steady flow of oil, tin, rubber, and other important materiel out of the Dutch East Indies for the Japanese war industry. But after catastrophic losses of their merchant marine, coupled with their retreat from Burma by winter 1944, the Imperial Japanese forces stationed in the region instead focused on regrouping their Southern Army's decimated ranks and preventing an Allied landing along the coast of southern China. Their opportunistic presence in French Indochina provided the Japanese war industry with locally grown oil seed, jute, peanuts, and cotton, which in turn made the northern section of the land dependent on the southern section for rice. This vulnerability became evident that winter when bad weather caused a famine that killed over a million locals. To maintain control over the region the Imperial Japanese forces left intact the French administration, which after June 1940 was staffed by the pro-Axis Vichy forces and included over 15,000 ill-equipped and badly demoralized French garrison troops. Imperial Japanese authorities solidified their grip on the region by recruiting spies among locals who were "ex-convicts and the lower elements." After the Allied invasion of North Africa in 1942, the Japanese took additional precautions against the French by backing some of the local groups pushing for independence. The head French intelligence director in Chungking reported that "the Japanese are using all means in their power to create among the 'Revolutionary Nationalists' in Cochin China an independence movement. Certain 'Revolutionaries' are enjoying the armed protection of the Japanese, and the situation thus engendered is becoming delicate."[21]

SI was caught in a complex situation in French Indochina. As in Burma and Korea, it was forced to grapple with the region's imperial forces. It knew that the future of French control over the region was not promising after the Imperial Japanese forces' takeover. Yet it watched the French levy high taxes, forcing farmers to devote 70 percent of their crops to paying, while those unable to pay became landless. SI was aware that the French planned to reassert their colonial authority over the land as soon as they became strong enough militarily to drive the Japanese out, something possible only with British and American assistance. SI knew that the British supported the French only to bolster claims for renewed imperial control over Hong Kong, Malaya, Singapore, and to a lesser extent, Burma. Moreover, it saw firsthand the Chinese Nationalist Government and the local Yunnan Provincial government's support for the French over indigenous groups struggling for independence. Yet SI was committed to President Franklin Roosevelt's anti-colonial policy, which contradicted other Allies' postwar imperial aims. Through an operational comity arrangement with the British, the OSS maintained a hands-off policy toward India and southern Burma, while the British promised to respect China and Korea as America's jurisdiction in military and intelligence matters. By mutual agreement, the OSS kept Southeast Asia a neutral zone, even though the region's Supreme Allied Commander, Lord Louis Mountbatten, was committed to reasserting British authority in Malaya, Hong Kong, and Singapore. Working against SI, the Chinese Nationalist Army's poor performance in late 1944 during "Ichigo," the Imperial Japanese offensive against southern China, combined with the improved British performance in Burma, emboldened hardliners within the Colonial Office to push

Mountbatten for imperial restoration of Hong Kong and support of the French in Southeast Asia.[22]

Yet working with the French brought additional problems. Numbering some 34,000 civilians and about 12,000 military personnel, by 1940 the French constituted a tiny minority within Indochina, at a ratio of only one to 544 Southeast Asians. Of these, only a small group remained loyal to the Vichy government, whose legitimacy ended in the eyes of many once the Allied invasion of Normandy succeeded in June 1944. The Vichy loyalists further promised to hand over downed Allied aviators to Japanese authorities and had, on occasion, turned over significant intelligence. But another faction, largely centering around General Zenovi Pechkoff and a lieutenant colonel in the French Military Mission in Chungking, followed the dictates of the Free French government under Charles de Gaulle. Yet General Henri Giraud, another French leader and a rival to de Gaulle, emerged after the successful American landing in North Africa in June 1942 against Vichy resistance, and retained the following of an estimated 80 percent the French troops in Indochina. Political factionalism notwithstanding, all French factions in East Asia were invested to some extent in the dream of reasserting colonialist rule over Indochina, which meant limiting American presence and influence. Experiencing difficulties slipping agents into the region and having no ethnic heritage speakers in the agency, SI director Norwood Allman had little choice but to depend on French intelligence. But in line with Donovan's wishes, he would not promise to keep OSS agents out of the region.[23]

Nevertheless, French connections in the region proved tempting for the OSS. One came in the form of a request by Milton Miles and Tai Li to arrange for the return of a local princess to the region as part of their intelligence-gathering network inside French Indochina. Thinh Katiou Do Huu, the wife of Robert Meynier, was spirited out of France through Spain and on to London, where she stayed at the Ritz Hotel under the pseudonym of Paula Martin, all arranged by the OSS London office. Thinh Katiou Do Huu was a princess from Annam married to the French submarine commander who refused to surrender after France fell in 1940. She rejoined her husband in North Africa, where he and a small number of Annamese soldiers gathered after they were liberated from the Germans. Meynier and the soldiers thought that Katiou might be able to exert influence in the region, since her wealthy father and uncle wielded considerable political influence. Thinh 's family name carried so much clout that Tai Li believed they could keep the factions focused on fighting the Japanese and not each other. With OSS funding and Mrs. Meynier's family wealth, the Meynier group was believed capable of gathering as many as 300,000 supporters.[24]

But the OSS plan for using the Meynier group was thwarted. The OSS funded Meynier and his wife for the first six months with about $15,000 and a promise of subsequent payments at the end of the war. SI received letters from both Charles de Gaulle and Henri Giraud to ensure cooperation from both factions. The French Military Mission accepted the first two (or $3,000 and the letters), but refused to cooperate. Without its support, Meynier's mission faced the difficult task of entering into the region from southern China where he, his wife, and troops were based. In addition, Meynier required time to recruit and prepare agents to gather intelligence when the OSS knew time was running short. The OSS cooled especially toward the Meynier group and sought an alternative that could provide good quality intelligence immediately, even if at a higher cost.[25]

The Gordon-Bernard-Tan (GBT) spy team of which Frank Tan was a key member offered the OSS a ready-made alternative to Meynier. Using the initials of the last name of each of their founders, the spy network of J. Laurence Gordon, Harry Bernard, and Frank Tan was established in 1942 and headquartered in Kunming. The three recruited agents from among the French expatriates residing in French Indochina, some of whom worked for British Tobacco Company, Shell Oil, and Charter Bank. By early 1945, the GBT had an estimated 2,000 agents and included a company of French troops at Seno. Moreover, the group willingly shared its intelligence data with other Allied intelligence agencies. Gordon passed on all information to the British Secret Intelligence Service that initially recruited, trained, and supplied him with the B-2 radios that agents used to relay their intelligence reports to the GBT headquarters. The GBT also enjoyed the full support of Tai Li, who received intelligence reports relayed to him by his own radio operator, Mac Shin. What the group lacked, the GBT thought, was sufficient funding and equipment, though SI thought it lacked sufficient training in intelligence-gathering techniques.[26]

SI funneled money into the GBT spy network and got Lieutenant Charles Fenn of Morale Operations to keep an eye on the group by serving as its liaison officer. The OSS provided a considerable amount of cash and supplies. In August 1944, Frank Tan acknowledged receipt of Chinese Nationalist dollars (CN) $450,000 (about US$1,660) and the following month, the group was given another CN$1,000,000 (about US$3,700). In addition, the OSS provisioned the group with luxury items such as cigarettes, boxes of candy, bottles of liquors, and pens, though GBT requested more—tubes of toothpaste, razor blades, soap, watches, cosmetics, and stockings. While their intelligence reports in the summer of 1944 were not considered to be of high quality, in the subsequent three-month period Frank Tan and the GBT agents earned high praise from the OSS for their upgrades in intelligence reports and preparations for sabotage operations. "The best intelligence agency now operating in the Far East," W. B. Kantack declared, as he recounted for his superiors how the group provided the Fourteenth Air Force with targeting information, while at the same time having trained at least a thousand agents for sabotage operations against bridges and other targets.[27]

Imperial Japanese authorities' takeover of administrative control of French Indochina on March 9, 1945 made Frank Tan's role in the GBT more prominent than those of his two European American colleagues. Anticipating a possible Allied invasion in conjunction with local French forces, Imperial Japanese authorities moved swiftly to round up all French troops and disarm and intern them, together with some French colonial administrators. Except for the handful who managed to escape with General Gabriel Sabattier to southern China, the Japanese also knocked out the GBT spy network with a single blow and deliberately created a vacuum in which local independence leaders would jockey for power, conditions not conducive for an Allied amphibious assault. Japanese authorities further encouraged King Norodom Sihanouk's declaration of Cambodian independence on March 13, followed by similar statements by King Sisavang Vong for Laos and Bảo Đại for the end of French rule in Indochina. Trần Trọng Kim took over the Japanese-founded Empire of Vietnam from March to August 1945, and under his government mass political participation was encouraged as a step toward national unity, which in turn opened up the government to an upward movement of local leaders and intelligentsia. The Indochinese Communist Party (ICP) led by Nguyễn Sing Cung, better known as Hồ Chí Minh, benefitted from the Japanese removal of the French forces in the north, demanded the end of Japanese fascism and French imperialism, and pressed for land reform.[28]

Frank Tan seized the opportunity to recenter the GBT spy network around Hồ Chí Minh. While Gordon attempted in vain to revive his independent, French–policy-friendly group, Tan and his OSS liaison officer Charles Fenn sought out pro-Allied, dependable, and promising indigenous leaders to work with. They developed a strong relationship with Hồ Chí Minh for a number of reasons. Tan's support for "Uncle Ho" was based on a mutually shared sense of discrimination. He had long resented the anti-Chinese discrimination he faced from European Americans while growing up in Boston, while Hồ experienced the same from the French while studying in Paris in the 1920s. In Fenn, Hồ Chí Minh saw an opportunity to secure arms, equipment, and training from the generous Americans, and Tan's wide network and knowledge of South Vietnam would prove useful in the coming struggle to oust the Japanese from the region. For Fenn, Hồ Chí Minh had some important qualities he was looking for in replacing the French: a strong following among the indigenous population, an agent inside the French Vichy military intelligence group, and the courage to risk his life and those of his group members to rescue downed American aviators without remuneration. Fenn also thought Hồ a genius whose usefulness to the Americans would outlast the immediate concern of preparing for Operation Carbonado:

> I was intrigued by this Indo-China "native," not only because he spoke excellent French and quite good English, but because of his impressive personality. Although of middle age (and indeed looking much worn), he had a remarkably vivacious personality, and the brightest eyes I'd ever come across; and I'd read that was a sure sign of genius![29]

With Gordon in Washington, DC, Tan and Fenn adopted the new Hồ Chí Minh spy network inside French Indochina. They met with the independence leader in Kunming that spring, whereupon they provided Hồ and his men with arms, equipment, and training, which upset Gordon. Fenn and Tan also began training Hồ and his men in the art of intelligence-gathering. Fenn taught the Vietnamese "the rudiments of military intelligence," and Tan offered to accompany Hồ on his return to French Indochina to help set up the network. When Hồ was ready to return home, Fenn had Claire Chennault's pilot fly him to the border, along with his thirty-two person entourage, their equipment, and two Chinese Americans, Frank Tan and Mac Shin. At night and under the cover of the jungle, Frank Tan began the long journey with Hồ, who arranged for horses for the two Chinese Americans to negotiate the muddy slopes. In April, Tan and Shin were in Pac Bo, sending reports to headquarters until Major Allison Thomas parachuted into the area with a supply of some of the latest rifles. The next month they went to Tan Trao with Hồ's group in a large party armed with Sten guns, Thompson machine guns, and communication gear. By then Gordon had lost control over the GBT while he was in Washington, DC, and the spy organization shifted its ties away from the British and the French and became closely linked with Hồ Chí Minh. When asked to return to headquarters, Tan and Shin refused, choosing instead to stay with the Viet Minh forces for the duration of the war. The pair of Chinese Americans camped at Ha Lua Hill and instructed Hồ's group in spy craft and radio operations. They radioed in their intelligence reports and assisted the Viet Minh forces in the rescue of downed American aviators. As a result of their work, other OSS agents were able to parachute into the region with the Viet Minh's prior approval, based in no small part to the life-long friendship Tan and Shin developed with Hô.[30]

Despite the pair's work inside French Indochina, the OSS dropped the GBT. The OSS realized that it no longer needed to secure French Indochina for Operation Carbonado, since the planned invasion of southern China became unnecessary after the successful American occupation of Leyte Island in the Philippines in late October 1944. With transoceanic shipping of Lend-lease supplies to Nationalist China now secure, the OSS focused its operations farther north in China and away from French Indochina. In addition, it was sensitive to the State Department's position, as US Consul William Langdon shared with others his low opinion of the future prospects for Hô Chi Minh and his Viet Minh movement.[31]

General Albert Wedemeyer was an important factor behind the OSS writing off the Gordon-Bernard portion of the GBT. Unlike his predecessor, Joseph Stilwell, Wedemeyer envisioned a large role for SI to play inside China. He placed all Allied operations, including the OSS, under his command. He then issued an ultimatum to Lieutenant Colonel Jacques deSibour, the OSS liaison officer, that independent spy organizations like the GBT would no longer be allowed to "play maverick." The colonel announced:

> The policy in the Theater seems to have changed. The Theater wants to know, quite rightly, who, where and how foreign agencies operate. GBT comes under this category and it is felt that they should be taken over completely by OSS. We don't know what reaction Gordon will have to this plan but if they don't acquiesce they are out completely.[32]

Wedemeyer further insisted that the OSS pressure the GBT to formally get on board with the China Theater by coming under the OSS, which J. Laurence Gordon had previously resisted. The general saw the GBT as essentially British, and preferred having far more experienced OSS officers conducting guerrilla warfare operations against Imperial Japanese forces in the region. Jacques de Sibour confided to his OSS colleagues:

> Gen. Wedemeyer also expressed his desire to make plans for extensive OSS operations in French Indo-China. He does not trust the GBT Group and on our explaining our relations with them, told us that we did not know the half of it and that he had it from sure sources that this Group was definitely forwarding British aims in Indo-China. We are therefore now beginning to hold back a bit on GBT and also thinking in terms of our own outfit in Indo-China.[33]

OSS termination of the GBT's service came abruptly. As early as late April 1945, when Frank Tan was in-country, Paul Helliwell, chief of SI/China Theater, wrote about GBT's tenuous future with the US military: "In the event that satisfactory arrangements can be worked out, a portion at least of the GBT Group will be used for FIC work." But Helliwell was also pre-pared to cut off all funding to the GBT and have OSS "proceed along dif-ferent lines." He felt strongly that the OSS was in a position to force the GBT to conform to OSS organizational and intelligence report distribution demands: "It is the opinion of this branch that the situation with relation to intelligence activities in Indo-China has now developed to the point where we can afford to take a much firmer position with GBT." Helliwell cut off supplies to the spy group on May 28:

> At the present time OSS is apparently supplying this group, and yet the group is devoting probably more time and energy to servicing AGAS than they are to servicing this organization. By the admission of Lt. Fenn they are still providing information to the Chinese. Lt. Fenn states that they are not providing infor-mation to the French and the British as they have in the past, although in my opinion this statement may be open to question.[34]

At that point Frank Tan became the only part of GBT to remain with the OSS. With "G" and "B" officially out as of June 1, 1945, the OSS proceeded to work freely with the Chinese American component of the organization. Richard Heppner, head of SI/China Theater, anticipated this development in late April and allowed Frank Tan and Mac Shin to be firmly embedded within the Indochinese Communist Party forces. The OSS then shifted its priority from solely intelligence-gathering to guerrilla warfare operations. To carry out these operations it used operational groups, small units of specially-trained combatants staffed with a translator, who maneuvered behind enemy lines to cut off or destroy communication and supply links. The OSS had taken this approach in the European Theater, and William Donovan was eager to apply the same method to the Imperial Japanese forces that had already proven effective in Burma. The OSS therefore armed, supplied, and trained some 5,000 Chinese commandos in parachuting, and they in turn inflicted more than 6,000 casualties on the Imperial Japanese forces, particularly in northern China. With the European Theater of Operation winding down, Donovan transferred operation groups to the China Theater, with a handful assigned to French Indochina.[35]

Dick Hamada was among the OSS personnel assigned to French Indochina. Initially detailed to Kunming, along with Fumio Kido, Tad Nagaki, Ralph Yempuku, Calvin Tottori, and Shōichi Kurahashi, Hamada trained at the parachute training school with other Chinese preparing for special operations. He was then assigned to a small group whose assignment was to parachute into French Indochina to demolish a bridge heavily used by the Japanese military. His mission was fraught with danger. He learned that the bridge was heavily guarded by troops encamped nearby; there were many rivers swollen from the monsoon rains; and local bandits with no affinity for Americans roamed the area. The day before departure, Hamada and the team captain surveyed the target area and determined, "This mission was certainly not to our liking." He recognized that the mission was suicidal, but his life was spared when the mission was scrubbed. Nevertheless, that realization prompted recurring nightmares for Hamada long after the war.[36]

Still other problems related to Asian Americans emerged. Uncertainty over Lincoln Kan's status was the only worry the intelligence collectors of SI and R&A faced. Kan may or may not have been under the control of Colonel Toyo Sawa and feeding SI false intelligence reports. But once the Allied planners decided to bypass the Macao region, Kan's reports decreased in value. When the war ended, questions of Kan's reliability vanished as OSS Asian Americans in SI, not R&A, confronted a new and more complicated problem related to loyalty. Sent on POW rescue missions, they were tasked with investigating war crimes committed by Imperial Japanese forces and local collaborators. In particular, they were to probe Asian Americans who shared the same racial and ethnic uniform but wore a different military uniform—that of the Imperial Japanese forces. In confronting their coethnics, the OSS Asian Americans could not avoid grappling with the meaning of loyalty.

CHAPTER 6

∽

Countering Enemy Spies, Rescuing POWs, and Dealing with Collaborators

Even if Lincoln Kan had not turned, or Kunsung Rie had not become a double agent, OSS operations involving Asian Americans were always at risk of discovery by the enemy. As with any operation behind enemy lines, these agents were aware that their presence and mission could become known to the enemy. Their enemy, after all, had its own means for gathering information and often did not have to cultivate double agents, since some of the information was readily obtainable from Americans or the Allies. Allied military personnel had a reputation for inadvertently blurting out valuable pieces of information after consumption of alcohol or during an intimate conversation with a member of the opposite sex. To prevent such leaks, X-2 or counterintelligence recruited Asian Americans to shore up security breaches, ferret out double agents, and search for potential sleeper agent cells deliberately left behind by the Imperial Japanese authorities immediately after the war ended.

Solving the problem of information leakage, however, proved difficult for the OSS in the China Theater. In places like Burma, the solution was simple but cruel. Officers like Carl Eifler swiftly executed collaborators and other locals who passed information to Imperial Japanese forces. But in China, X-2 was helpless in preventing the Japanese from intercepting and deciphering radio communications by the Chinese Nationalist Army, their leader Chiang Kai-shek, and the US military attaches' encrypted communications from Beijing to Washington, DC. X-2 monitored the movements of merchants, large and small, knowing that the Imperial Japanese Navy used commercial businesses to provision its forces and gather intelligence. It also kept watch over local entertainment establishments such as bars and brothels frequented by off-duty American personnel, since the Imperial Japanese Army was known to send in local entertainers, predominantly female, to gather intelligence from the unsuspecting. It could not, however, monitor all individuals, since the Japanese Army recruited many locals with exclusive privileges. As the OSS noted about local spying for Japan, "Agents in occupied areas had the right to control opium, gambling, prostitution and to smuggle within certain areas." In addition, counterintelligence officers faced the added complications of guarding against information brokers—individuals who collected information of military value, often by bribing or blackmailing local employees at American installations and selling the information to the highest bidder. They could not simply execute collaborators and spies, but were required to hand over such agents to the Chinese Nationalist government. Once the suspects were surrendered they knew that Chinese authorities treated alleged collaborators with leniency, viewing such behavior less a sign of political affinity and more of antipathy toward the Chinese Nationalist government.[1]

Chinese intelligence also presented challenges to X-2's guardianship of OSS secrets. Tai Li, head of the Bureau of Investigation and Statistics, operated a large spy agency with an estimated 325,000 employees, one of which was inside the OSS headquarters in Washington. His agents were known to be ruthless assassins who murdered American agents operating without tacit Nationalist government approval inside China. They also kept a close watch over the activities of the Japanese in occupied territories and moved quickly to reassert the Nationalist government's authority in places like Shanghai after the war. Bureau agents rounded up Japan's secret atomic energy researchers and offered them Chinese citizenship and privileges in exchange for developing the atomic bomb for Nationalist China. But the bureau was also infiltrated by moles, such as Yen Bao, who kept the Chinese Communists in Yenan informed. Li's agency may have been infiltrated by spies for Imperial Japanese authorities, since the highest circles of the Allied command in East Asia knew that information from the inner circles of the Chinese Nationalist government were leaked to the enemy. Lord Louis Mountbatten, writing to Albert Wedemeyer some three decades later, reminisced how information that was shared with Chiang Kai-shek would inevitably reach Imperial Japanese ears: "Indeed nobody knows better than you that anything sent to the Generalissimo was passed on to the Japanese within ten days!"[2]

The British presented problems for X-2 as well. Their Secret Intelligence Services (SIS) and Special Operations Executive (SOE) ignored the operational comity arrangement with the OSS and sent in espionage and sabotage agents into China. They hoped to position enough of their own personnel to recapture Hong Kong, actions not explicitly endorsed by their own Foreign Ministry. With much of their spy network destroyed by the Japanese at the beginning of the war, SIS took a back seat to the SOE in northeast Asia and concentrated on Southeast Asia, but retained forty-one agents inside China, half of whom were case officers supervising some 400 other spies throughout China. The SOE used Lindsay Ride's British Army Aid Group (BAAG), an organization committed to rendering aid to British and Canadian prisoners of war held by the Japanese in Hong Kong but in reality a front for slipping their agents in to prepare for an imperial recovery of Hong Kong. SOE's G. Findlay Andrew further established a toehold for their sabotage operations in China by supplying Ping-Sheng Wang, advisor to Chiang Kai-shek, and his Resources Investigation Institute with about £20,000 annually, or roughly a third of the institute's budget, with the stipulation that the institute would engage in subversive activities and economic sabotage. Hence, the SOE saw the institute as a beginning step for its own espionage and sabotage operations: "All the activities of R.I.I. are a direct charge on S.O.E. and heretofore have been run on lines approved by London and later also by the Commander of Force 136. With the expansion of Force 136 activity in China it is possible that special operations may be undertaken through R.I.I." Aware they were violating their agreement with the Americans, the SOE opted for silence: "Our policy is to retain quietly what we have and calmly deal with each hit and miss affair . . . as it arises."[3]

Without fanfare, the SOE prepared for a British takeover of Hong Kong in 1945. The SOE launched Walter Fletcher's Operation "Remorse," a trading company with large interests in essential goods such as quinine that reaped staggering profits—some £2 billion sterling—to finance BAAG operations. It also used the money to buy influence of local officials away from the Kwangsi (Guangxi) provincial government, an important obstacle to the recovery of Hong Kong. SOE officials also began Operation "Oblivion" in late 1944 to get around Chiang Kai-shek and Albert Wedemeyer's objections to the presence of armed British military personnel inside China. The SOE proposed bringing in enough captured German weapons from Europe to arm 30,000 Chinese guerrillas, all trained and led by sixty British officers in mid-December 1944. By early 1945, Oblivion had dozens of Cantonese or Hokkien-speaking Canadians waiting in Melbourne for aircraft to insert them into the Hong Kong area as radio operators, translators, and interpreters for the various guerrilla units. Until Oblivion was terminated on June 1, 1945, the SOE remained opposed to any American advance on Hong Kong.[4]

Relations between the OSS and the British deteriorated rapidly. As the tensions mounted between the summer of 1943 and 1944, the British expressed their reservations about their American allies. SOE's John Keswick wrote Donovan in London the year prior: "Hong Kong is being isolated from us in a very marked degree . . . [and] Americans are anything but co-operative and appear to seek elimination of British influence in China." The following summer, his OSS counterpart Richard Heppner likewise reported coolness: "Relations with the British are cordial on the surface, only." By February 1945, tensions reached a breaking point. Colin MacKenzie of SOE threatened to withdraw from the China Theater altogether, believing the Americans wanted to push the British out of the country. Heppner accused the British Military Mission in Chungking of trying to infiltrate the OSS, and three months later claimed to have proof of two or three such instances. He submitted a copy of a document to Washington proving SOE intent to infiltrate the OSS and the US Army Air Force. By late June 1945, Heppner concluded that BAAG was a mere front for SOE agents operating in the Hong Kong area "against American and Chinese personnel."[5]

Yet OSS counterintelligence relied on a working relationship with the British prior to 1945. X-2 was the last section of the OSS to organize, had the smallest budget, and employed the fewest personnel. It therefore required British assistance in tracking down enemy spies and plugging leaks within the organization, since they often faced the same opponents prior to 1945. As late as October 1944, X-2 worked with its British counterparts to compile a list of over 200 names of possible enemy agents and collaborators in the Kunming area.[6]

Despite the problems the British posed, X-2 concentrated its efforts on other threats to OSS security. First, it expanded its ranks to about 500 personnel to improve detection and neutralization of Japanese espionage networks at General Albert Wedemeyer's request in January 1945. It also established new offices so that within the next two months counterintelligence had seven offices inside China, located in Kunming, Chungking, Kweiyang, Chengtu, Yunnan, Chihchiang, and Hsian, with plans to open another in Yenan. Work production increased substantially as 500 new names were added to the master card (3-by-5-inch) file, while adding pertinent information was added to another hundred cards already in the system. X-2 was confident it was successfully combating Japanese spies without the assistance of the Chinese Nationalist government, with whom it maintained a policy of no contact. For example, X-2 was working against many Japanese spies in the old imperial city of Hsian where Yoshiko Kawashima, the Japanese Mata Hari, had allegedly positioned her "honey traps" (spies under the cover of prostitutes) in the Temple of Love, about a half-block west of the Bell Tower, to extract information from unsuspecting off-duty American servicemen.[7]

Asian Americans were among those hired in the expansion. Three unnamed Chinese Americans were brought into Kunming as plainclothes agents. Hong Richard Chan from Detachment 101, Special Operations in Burma, was assigned to infiltrate the Chinese Nationalist Army, ostensibly to identify its spies. Chan accomplished this by securing a colonel's commission in July 1944 and serving on the Military Staff Committee in Yunnan at Chiang Kai-shek's order. He trained officers and others until May 1945. His work for X-2 was dangerous. As his superior officer remarked, "The personal courage of this man is unquestionably high and when he was finally discharged, not in the field in China as other agents were, but at Fort Meade, Maryland, unobtrusively and away from China to reduce the risk of bodily harm to the fifty-three-year-old spy at the hands of the Chinese Nationalist government."[8]

Yet Asian Americans were not integral to OSS spy catching efforts as they would later become in the post-war period under the Strategic Services Unit and its successor, the CIA. In one case, an individual turned in a less than stellar performance. Lincoln Mei initially started off in the China Theater, where he received high praise. Sidney Rubinstein, under whom he served after being recruited from the Chinese Nationalist Army's Z Force in Burma, stated:

> You have performed your duty in an excellent and efficient manner. Your loyalty and high devotion to duty have been particularly outstanding. The important and special character of the assignments which have been performed by you have been a real contribution to the war effort of the United States.[9]

Mei was then assigned, along with James H. Chu, to counterintelligence's office at Kweiyang and Kunming, respectively, in November 1944 where they began work as investigators for X-2. A month later, his superior officer Jack Brown recommended Mei for promotion from second to first lieutenant "for the good of the Service," despite his reservations about the Chinese American officer. In writing to Arthur Thurston, head of X-2 in Washington, Brown stated:

> I am enclosing a recommendation for Lincoln's promotion which I am quite serious about. This does not mean we are sleeping together in that he has suddenly become an angel. In fact, some of his old traits, which you and I have found objectionable in the past are still evident in a lesser degree. I think he is slowly learning and has shown some real improvement. . . . His buddies who went

through OCS [Officer Candidate School] with him are now 1st Lts. or Captains, and he naturally feels that he has been left behind because of conditions and circumstances that he could not prevent.

Despite these objections, Mei's fluency in both Mandarin and Cantonese, and his native ability in the Shanghai dialect and his English-language skills, made him seemingly indispensable for conducting background security checks and searching for Imperial Japanese spies.[10]

But in early 1945, Mei fell from grace. He was assigned to Chengtu in south-central China as counterintelligence's field representative. Although he worked in a small office with only a civilian worker, an army corporal, and his superior officer, Mei had the command authority over his European American office workers while conducting investigations into the backgrounds of various applicants for employment at the Army Air Force bomber base nearby. In late January, Mei was hospitalized with a disease. Thereafter, his performance of duty was questioned and his character condemned:

> Lt. Mei was found to be indiscreet, immature, of poor judgment, and rather completely unsuited for investigation work. Individually it was possible to use him only as an administrative officer . . . He contracted a . . . disease due to misconduct.

When the war suddenly ended in mid-August 1945, Mei was declared surplus personnel and with his consent, was sent home to the San Francisco Bay area in late October 1945.[11]

In contrast, John Kwock's performance elicited high praise from his superiors. Although he had never been to China before, Kwock became a model officer in counterintelligence work even if he was unable to break up large Japanese spy rings, such as those belonging to the Japanese Mata Hari. Assigned to the Security Division, Kwock took up the task of protecting OSS property against fire hazards, petty thefts, and enemy spies. As Deputy Chief, Security Branch for the China Theater, he inspected all OSS offices and made security recommendations. Kwock's most pressing problem was not enemy spies but thieves. In Kunming, Kwock found that somebody had dug into the brick wall of the warehouse and stole a quantity of arms, forcing him to build a wooden framed inner wall and detailing an enlisted man to sleep there. He had to guard against theft of the transmitter wires, handguns, and ammunition deliveries by requiring truck drivers to be armed. In the absence of steel desks with locks, Kwock brought in padlocks. He also conducted background security checks on

American military personnel transferring into the OSS and potential Chinese employees for all branches of the OSS working inside China. Even when he and his staff had already decided to recommend against hiring a particular job applicant, he made use of the interview to extract greater information about the individual and then added the new information to the X-2 files. He surreptitiously took photographs of the interviewees with the help of OSS's Reproduction Board. Sensitive to the problem of theft and information leakage, the Chinese American urged others, such as Clyde Sargent of "Eagle," to limit the number of local hires.[12]

Although Kwock was successful in securing OSS property in the China Theater, guarding against enemy spies was another matter. In places like Kunming, Kwock was unable to seal off American bases from enemy spies due to geographic and human factors. He could not deny enemy agents' entry into the region because the land routes in from neighboring Southeast Asia were open to foot traffic, railroads, and buses running from Mengtze to the border. He was unable to get local Chinese customs officers to inspect individuals carefully, since the local police failed to check on suspicious characters and kept surveillance on none of the local hotels. Given the large volume of human traffic relative to X-2's few counterintelligence personnel, Kwock and his small office missed some Japanese spies who had slipped past them. He and his staff, for example, failed to follow up on Mimi Lau, a young secretary to a British businessman in Hong Kong who was arrested in Kweilin in 1944 for espionage. "The last report heard," an OSS agent reported in June 1945, "concerning SUBJECT, was to the effect that she had been executed because of evidence of her enemy activity." Kwock therefore resorted to designating areas like the Eagle training grounds as "highly restricted" to prevent espionage.[13]

Despite the limitations, Kwock was deemed a valuable contributor to the OSS in China. The army's Counter-Intelligence Corps (CIC) credited the OSS with "the best security of any US agency in China," based on their survey in early August 1945, which X-2 superiors chalked up to improvements made by Kwock. They recommended that he be promoted to captain and be given the Bronze Star, both of which he received with considerable praise:

> During this entire period, due to the extreme shortage of personnel Captain Kwock fulfilled this duty with the help of no other American personnel. Even though short-handed, by devotion to duty, resourcefulness and an untiring effort he succeeded in protecting the security of the Office of Strategic Services in the China Theater. . . . By his untiring devotion to duty, and thorough comprehension of security problems, and the inspiring nature of his leadership,

Captain Kwock markedly contributed to the safety and efficiency with which the Office of Strategic Services was able to operate in the China Theater.

At the end of August 1945, Kwock was placed at the head of the OSS group headed for Shanghai to establish an office from which they hoped to monitor events inside China while searching for Japanese agents left behind.[14]

Although unable to expose many enemy spy rings, Asian Americans nevertheless played an important role in the OSS's immediate postwar work. In general, their duties, as determined by Director William Donovan, were multifaceted. Their first priority was to provide aid and relief to more than 140,000 Australian, British, Canadian, Dutch, and American military prisoners and 130,000 civilians in hundreds of Japanese camps. They arranged for the immediate evacuation of the critically ill and provision of food and medicine for those healthy enough to wait for their transportation out of the camps. Their task was urgent, given that the POW death rate in Japanese camps was about one-third. Moreover, the rescue teams went in unarmed to assist the army's Air Ground Aid Service immediately after Japan surrendered, even though Imperial Japanese military forces still had weapons and their willingness to cooperate was unclear. They operated on the assumption that the local Japanese commanders would comply with surrender orders received from their own headquarters, even if the latter suspected that the OSS teams came to investigate them of war crimes. The teams also arrived without guarantees of local cooperation, since they were tracking down local collaborators and agents left behind to spy on the incoming regime.[15]

A publicity stunt conceived of by a superior officer compounded the dangers an Asian American officer faced on one rescue mission. Three days after Japan's surrender on August 15, 1945, Captain Ryongi Hahm boarded an unarmed and unescorted C-47 air transport bound from Hsian to Seoul with his commanding officer, Colonel Willis Bird, deputy director of the OSS in China. Partly concerned for the welfare of Allied POWs, after receiving reports of riots in Seoul, Hahm joined Bird and a dozen others as the group's interpreter. On this mission, however, he was joined by thirteen individuals rather than the recommended eight, the lower figure set to facilitate the parachute drop of large quantities of food and medicine to the prisoners. Hahm found himself surrounded by an Office of War Information writer, photographer, and others aboard to record the historic event. Under Bird's authority, Hahm and the group flew to Seoul without permission, escort, or sufficient fuel for a roundtrip flight. Furthermore, Hahm had to convince the Imperial Japanese commander to allow them to land. Successful, Hahm and Colonel Bird were escorted away at gunpoint to meet with the region's army commander. After convincing the Japanese officer the war had ended, they were provided with enough gasoline for their return flight, in addition to a beer and sake party during which each group sang its own national anthem. Having received assurances all prisoners and civilians were well, Hahm, Bird, and the rescue team flew to Weihsien, Shandong to connect with another rescue mission taking place at that location. Upon return, General Albert Wedemeyer court-martialed Bird for failing to deliver medical and food supplies to American POWs and for fraternizing with the enemy, in clear violation of his standing orders "to remain aloof, firm, and authoritative." Hahm escaped censure, however, since he was acting under Bird's orders.[16]

Fumio Kido became entangled in a dangerous espionage caper while carrying out a POW rescue mission. He was an SI agent in Kunming working with Detachment 202 when his assignment for a POW rescue mission came on August 16. Kido volunteered, as had Dick Hamada, Ralph Yempuku, and other Japanese American SI members in Kunming, and left the next day on a B-24 bomber for Mukden, Manchuria. He was the Japanese interpreter for the POW rescue team code-named "Cardinal" that was led by Major James Hennessy. Kido was aboard the aircraft with Major Robert Lamar, the medical doctor, Sergeant Edward Starz, the radio operator, Sergeant Howard Leith, the Russian interpreter, and Major Cheng-shi Wu, Chinese Nationalist Army officer interpreter. They parachuted into a field near the Hoten POW camp, only to be met by a Japanese platoon of soldiers. At Kido's suggestion, Cardinal members surrendered without a fight and allowed the Japanese to blindfold them during their detention. They were forced to face a wall and kneel, which Cardinal members took to be their final moments before execution. Despite Kido's explanation of Cardinal's peaceful intent, he was singled out for beatings with rifle butts and was intensely interrogated because he was perceived to be a Japanese in an American uniform. "Kido must have known," team member Roger Hilsman reminisced almost a half-century later, "when he volunteered for this mission that it was much more dangerous for him as a Japanese American than for others. It took extraordinary courage." Kido's torture ended, however, when the Imperial Japanese Army's commanding officer appeared on the scene, accepted them formally, and housed them at the Yamato Hotel, the best accommodations in Mukden. The Cardinal team then announced the end of the war to the POWs, brought in the airdropped food and medical supplies, and arranged for transportation for all POWs back to the United States. It also conducted its own investigation and determined that the Japanese commander and his troops committed no war crimes against the Allied POWs. They also learned that the American General Jonathan

Wainwright and British General Sir Percival were housed in another camp. Extracting those 1,500 prisoners would require considerable care, since Cardinal "encountered unceasing rifle and machine gun fire for four days" from August 20 to August 23 in the streets of Mukden to the Hoten POW Camp. Kido and the rest of the team, as well as the newly arrived Captain Roger Hilsman, remained to ensure the safe departure of all American POWs. But they faced greater danger with the arrival of Soviet troops on August 20. After ensuring that the last Allied POW had left Port Arthur safely, Kido and the team returned to their duty station in Kunming to begin their own demobilization and return to the United States. In his own recollection of events over a half-century later, Kido overlooked his beating and downplayed the dangers, claiming he was simply fortunate to be "in the right place at the right time."[17]

Kido's recollection did more than understate the dangers for Cardinal. He conveniently overlooked the fact that Cardinal's POW rescue provided a cover for other OSS agents, particularly those associated with Catholic Bishop Thomas Megan, to monitor the Soviet occupation of Manchuria, a land defined as part of China and whose physical assets were to remain intact by the terms of the Yalta Conference. Even though most of the 1,500 Allied POWs had already evacuated, Kido and Cardinal stayed well into September 1945, making sure the Allied POWs were transported by train to Port Arthur and loaded on ships bound for the United States, a process that took more than two weeks. His new commanding officer, Major Leo Brady, arrived with orders to stay in Mukden until expelled by force. Kido appropriately learned an important phrase in Russian for use when misidentified as an Imperial Japanese Army soldier: "Nyet Nipponaky soldat! [I'm no Japanese soldier]." Given their lingering inside Manchuria, Kido and Cardinal were harassed by angry Soviet troops who correctly surmised that the Americans were reporting on their (mis)appropriation of Japanese machinery and supplies. They were held at gunpoint numerous times and robbed of their pistols, watches, and other private possessions. They witnessed a three-day looting binge by the Russians, presaged by a Russian tank smashing through a building wall. They watched in horror as Russian soldiers looted, raped, and stole property, while local Chinese attacked residents in the Japanese section where they were housed. The team's rescue of the sickest prisoners was delayed when a Russian soldier bayoneted the tire of the American aircraft sent to airlift the former prisoners.[18]

Like Cardinal, Ralph Yempuku's team was assigned to do more than rescue POWs. Code-named "Pigeon," Yempuku and his team were sent in to rescue close to 600 Dutch and Australian military prisoners and two civilians, who were dying at a rate of two a day in a camp near Sanya at the southern end of Hainan Island in the South China Sea. Although John Singlaub was appointed the team's commanding officer and Leonard Woods its executive officer, Yempuku was their equal as captain and also served as the team's Japanese-language interpreter. Pigeon was also tasked with gathering Order of Battle intelligence data on the local Imperial Japanese Army forces in the event these soldiers continue fighting after Japan's surrender. Parachuting in on August 27, Pigeon started off badly with Woods and Yempuku both sustaining injuries during the jump, and the team's radio damaged beyond repair. Their situation deteriorated as they were approached on one side by local Chinese seeking to "liberate" the supplies dropped by the American bomber, and on the other by armed Imperial Japanese troops advancing toward them with fixed bayonets. Yempuku, only five feet three inches tall, took charge of the situation, translating Singlaub's orders to the Japanese in the same authoritative tone that Singlaub delivered them and demanding protection from the Chinese locals. To Yempuku's relief, the Japanese soldiers complied by chasing away the approaching locals and compelling others to assist with the move of the entire Allied POW population. Thus Yempuku and Pigeon successfully moved the group, half of them sick with beri-beri, malnutrition, malaria, or tuberculosis, from their inadequate housing in the POW camp to permanent, clean buildings in Sanya. Yempuku further aided in the organizing and administering of a 200-bed hospital to care for these sick prisoners. He then worked with other team members to gather evidence of war crimes by the local commander against the POWs under his control. The team found 356 emaciated Dutch and Australian POWs who had been tortured, beaten, and nearly starved to death, surviving only by trapping and eating rats and other rodents. They also searched for evidence that the local commander had ordered the execution of nine downed American aviators, five of whose demise was witnessed by local Chinese residents. As a result of his work with Pigeon, Yempuku was commended for volunteering for this dangerous mission; he was awarded a medal for demonstrating "tact and diplomatic handling of the Japanese," and credited "immeasurably" for Pigeon's success.[19]

As commendable as Yempuku and Pigeon team members' actions were in rescuing Allied POWs, they overlooked a greater atrocity committed by the Imperial Japanese forces. After the Japanese invaded Hainan in early February 1939 and took control, they built their own navy and air bases on the island from which to launch their attacks on the supply shipments to the Chinese Nationalist Government coming over the Burma Road. Chinese Nationalist forces and the Chinese Communist forces, each with about 4,000 men apiece, and a nonaligned group of over 3,000 armed men on the island, combined in 1944 to outnumber the Imperial Japanese forces and take control over substantial portions of the interior region. Instead of pitting the Nationalists against the Communists, as they had on the continent, the Japanese carried out the "three-all" campaign of killing all, looting all, and burning all. They did so in areas of the island where resistance was strong. With some 10,000 Japanese marines, Imperial Japanese authorities wiped out an estimated third of all resident males on the island, a war crime that made Pigeon's investigation look insignificant by comparison.[20]

On his mission Yempuku overlooked another important matter—his own brother, Donald. After his family returned to Hiroshima and the war broke out, Ralph assumed that his brothers would be conscripted for the Imperial Japanese forces and die while in service. His brothers assumed Ralph was probably dead, given the high casualty rates the Nisei soldiers experienced in Europe. When the last Allied POW was shipped out of the island, Ralph and the Pigeon team took a British warship to Hong Kong, where they arrived in time to witness the Royal Navy formally receive the Japanese surrender on September 16, 1945. Unbeknownst to Ralph, his brother Donald was a soldier and interpreter for the Imperial Japanese Army who attended the same ceremony at the Peninsula Hotel. He was spotted by Donald, who vividly recalled:

> I saw my oldest brother Ralph's back. He was in an American uniform. I knew it was Ralph right away. Immediately, I was happy he was alive. But almost in the same breath, I was embarrassed because he was on the side of the enemy. . . . For a brief second, I felt the urge to call out. But I couldn't let myself do that. I just couldn't do it. In my mind the war was still going on and we were still enemies. It was the most trying moment of my life as I marched past Ralph and past the crowd. I was so glad Ralph was distracted at that moment and didn't see me.[21]

Donald's perception of his brother Ralph belonging to "the other side" was not uncommon for many foreign expatriates in war-torn East Asia. Many chose to collaborate, some unwillingly, but others did so voluntarily, despite their home government's war against the Axis powers. Former Royal Navy gunner John Kenneth Gracie, for example, wrote his own anti-British radio broadcast scripts for XGRS, the German radio station in Shanghai. Australian national Gene Raymond, a former horse jockey racer, launched the "Free Australia" movement advocating an Australia free to ally itself with Imperial Japan rather than remain with Britain. Americans also collaborated, most notably freelance writer Don Chisholm, who was one of about fifty American citizens arrested after the war to stand trial as a war criminal. In Chisholm's case the evidence was quite damaging, as investigators had recordings of his radio broadcasts made on behalf of Japan and eyewitness reports on Chisholm's voluntary collaboration with the enemy. He became known as the "Lord Haw-Haw of the Orient" for anti-American and pro-Japanese broadcasts. Chisholm's actions were construed as giving aid and comfort to the enemy and were attested to by at least two witnesses. He was therefore deemed liable for prosecution under the treason statute. In his own defense, the son of a college dean from Baltimore, Maryland claimed he had to collaborate with Imperial Japanese authorities, lest he be interned and repatriated to the United States, leaving his wife, a White Russian, behind in Shanghai to fend for herself. When asked by one of his accusers why he made such blatantly anti-American radio broadcasts, Chisholm replied, "We all must eat."[22]

Among the many Chinese Americans residing abroad, a small handful of them also collaborated with Imperial Japanese authorities. Their existence is hardly surprising given the large numbers residing in China during the war. Bard College professor Gloria Chun estimated that a fifth of 30,868 American-born Chinese counted in the 1930 US Census lived in China. The majority of Chinese Americans probably resided in southern China, where their extended family connections were the strongest. A handful of them worked for the Chinese Nationalist Government in Chungking in an official capacity, such as Pearl Chen of Oakland, California, who became an English-language assistant to Mayling Soong, wife of the generalissimo. Others were gainfully employed by the US Army in Kweilin, where the Fourteenth Air Force under General Claire Chennault was based. Most in southern China worked locally, having arrived prior to the Pearl Harbor attack, and searched for employment since the cost of living, particularly food, was exorbitant. With American citizenship and command of the English language, Chinese Americans hoped to secure employment with the US Army, where monthly wages were three times higher than the average CN$2,000 (about US$72), barely enough to buy food. Lacking connections, some of them resorted to busing tables at the Four Musketeer's Café in Liuchow, hoping they might develop personal connections and eventual employment with the US Army through connections with off-duty American military personnel who frequented the place.[23]

Others, however, used their status and positions within China to collect information for the Imperial Japanese forces. Some, such as Peggy and Mabel Wong, exploited their friendships with other Chinese Americans in the Fourteenth Air Force to report to Imperial Japanese authorities on the movement and deployment of American military personnel moving from

India to southern China, according to their San Francisco-born sister, Mrs. T.H. Oh. In another instance, Henry Sing of New York reported that his own estranged wife, Shiao Shee, admitted to him that she was engaged in espionage for the Japanese in the Hong Kong area, behavior he saw as comparable to Ching Wei Wang, the leader of the so-called puppet government in Nanking who "endangered China and sold out the Chinese race."[24]

Other Chinese Americans found the Imperial Japanese government's pan-Asian stance appealing. Ling Kum of New York and Jimmy Chang of Boston were military police officers serving in India. They both were attracted to the Imperial Japanese government's call for unity among Asians to expel Westerners from East Asia, after seeing how badly the British treated local Asian Indians. Ling told an informant he was eager to go to China, where he hoped to see Asians rise up against "whites":

> If and when I survive after this war, I'm going to preach to the Chinese in China to rise up against the Whites. I hope the next war will be between the yellows and the whites. What a pity I cannot write Chinese!

Chang too believed that an alliance between China and Japan against whites was a desirable outcome of this war.[25]

Herbert Moy was among those Chinese Americans residing abroad who favored an Axis power victory. Moy's passionate stance against the Britain and the United States in their war against Germany help land him a well-paid radio broadcasting position with Station XGRS, operated by the German Embassy. His radio broadcasts attracted a wide audience and in 1940 and 1941, he became known in Shanghai as one of the most successful news commentators. On the radio, he defended the Axis powers' struggle to survive while criticizing the Allied powers' naked imperialist aims:

> The Axis nations, for instance, know precisely what they are fighting for. They are bound together by the same need of gaining a victory without which they must perish. They are the have-not nations fighting for their very existence. Their war aims and peace aims are simple: the right to live, to work and to share in the riches of the world hitherto denied them by the Allies. But on the Allied side, what do we find? England is at war allegedly to defend the territorial integrity of Poland, but in the course of time that has been so thoroughly forgotten that England has now consented to the incorporation of Poland into the Soviet Union after the war. Then, there is much ballyhoo about the Atlantic Charter and the Four Freedoms, but that has been scrapped in favor of outright imperialism. The Allies declared they are out to destroy totalitari[an]ism and they have allied themselves with the most terrible dictatorship in the world's history.

Out to defend Christianity they have allied themselves with a strong enemy of religion.[26]

In another, he lambasted President Franklin Roosevelt "as the best [of the] faker 'crumb' artists seen on the stage of world politics in modern times. . . . So you might keep an eye open for them [fakers], and know how much the world is being poisoned by his [Roosevelt's] dreams of world conquest and how far China is being diverted from her natural character by him."

The American Consulate in Shanghai revoked Moy's US citizenship in 1941, prior to the Pearl Harbor attack, though he still retained his Chinese nationality. Undeterred by the punishment, Moy continued his propaganda broadcasts until Germany surrendered, and thereafter he and the radio station were handed over to Imperial Japanese authorities. Moy stayed on the air until Japan surrendered in mid-August 1945.[27]

Why Herbert Moy chose to become an Axis propagandist was rooted in a complex set of motives. To be sure, ideology played an important role, as did his mistaken belief that the Axis powers would be victorious in the war. But Sergeant Gerald Finn of the US Marine Corps revealed Moy's personal reasons for willingly working for German propaganda. In prewar Shanghai, Moy told Finn that he'd started working for the Germans because the Imperial Japanese authorities placed his brother Ernest's name on their blacklist after 1937. His elder brother had taken files and receipts from the Chinese Customs office, which the Japanese interpreted as aiding the Chinese Nationalist government. That meant once Ernest stepped outside the bounds of the international settlement, he was marked for assassination. By working for the Germans, the New York native claimed that his new employers promise to remove Ernest's name from the blacklist and grant large German purchase contracts for his soybeans, and turn Moy into a well-paid radio broadcasting journalist. "I would be a fool," he told Finn, "to turn down such a good offer." The Chinese American may have then convinced himself that the propaganda was true after doing it for a few years. As Matthew Ford stated, "After MOY had gotten under way with his invective program against the British and the war-mongering United States he had no alternative but to continue it, and after a while had undoubtedly sold himself on what he was saying."[28]

Moy's motive for working with the Japanese was equally complicated. His German employers had turned over the entire radio station to Imperial Japanese authorities. Moy personally witnessed how bad German-Japanese relations were in Shanghai during the war, as his own superior, L. Ehrhardt, admitted: "It was very difficult to establish contacts with the Japanese, not to mention the difficulty to inspire confidence. . . . Relations between the Japanese and the Germans in Shanghai were tense, as the latter were considered friends of Chungking." Under the Japanese, Moy was denied a car, gasoline, and a curfew pass. After the Pearl Harbor attack, he told friends his choice was the lesser of two evils—continued employment with the Germans prevented the Japanese from arresting him. Herbert's fears turned to near panic when the Japanese invited him to work in Tokyo as a guest commentator. Moy excused himself by explaining that he needed to take care of his aging parents in Shanghai. "He was," as one observer noted, "deathly afraid that should he go to Tokyo that he would never be permitted to return." But Moy had ideological reasons too for not wanting to serve Imperial Japanese interests. As a matter of principle, he opposed working for them. When the Germans wanted him to do some work for Wang Ching Wei's collaborationist government, Moy refused, stating that such an act would be "traitorous to China." He therefore felt compelled to do propaganda work for the Japanese, but made sure the broadcasts contained a hint of incredulity. His broadcast content for the Japanese was at times overstated. Paul M. Anderson knew Moy and said that the Japanese even smirked at the mention of his name because he would say crazy things and make absurd claims, such as that the Japanese not only bombed Pearl Harbor but were bombing New York City and setting it ablaze, or that Imperial Japan would strike the United States multiple times, not just once at Pearl Harbor.[29]

Moy had committed suicide by the time Robert Chin was assigned to investigate the Chinese American radio broadcaster. After looking into Moy's background, inspecting the alleged suicide scene, interviewing the police investigators, and seeing the corpse, Chin concluded that Moy had slashed his own throat and jumped out of the third-story window of his radio station. Among those Chin interviewed were Marquita Kwong, Moy's common-law wife, who told the police that when Japan surrendered, Moy became despondent and talked of suicide, stating: "When a man has been playing the type of game I have, there is only one thing for him to do should he lose." Moy had been warned before by his friend Floyd Sylvester Jump, who repatriated to the United States during the war, that he would be "hanged or shot" if he returned to the United States to which Moy replied, "One must catch the rabbit first." Chin learned the police had found blood on the window from which he fell and on his chair, together with razor blades belonging to his father, on the floor. "There was no sign of disorder in the room," Chin reported, dismissing homicide as the cause of death. Despite the absence of a suicide note, Chin told the OSS that Moy had taken his own life. His report closed the case against Moy, since the Department of Justice's case against him, initiated as early as 1943, had already determined before the end of August 1945 that "prosecutive action [against Moy] would not be instituted at this time."[30]

The collaboration of Japanese Americans presented an even greater problem for OSS Asian American investigators than that of Chinese Americans. Their numbers residing abroad meant the potential number of collaborators was larger. In 1940, the Japanese government counted 2.5 million Japanese (citizens and their offspring) living overseas, with another 1.2 million in Korea, Formosa, and Karafuto, many of whom were dependents of Japanese nationals on the eve of the Pearl Harbor attack. In places like Manchukuo, where over 1.5 million Japanese resided, some 2,000 American-born Japanese were living and working there, because the opportunities for employment in white-collar and blue-collar positions were greater than in the American West. Many Japanese Americans who experienced racial discrimination in Depression-era America saw Manchukuo as a beacon of hope, especially given the absence of racial discrimination. Other regions in Asia also appealed to Japanese Americans, such as Kwantung or Shandong, where most of the 345,733 Japanese counted in 1940 China resided. Still other Japanese found the international city of Shanghai more appealing. As Imperial Japanese control extended further into the city's political life after the outbreak of war with China in 1937, the number of Japanese increased rapidly. Shortly after Pearl Harbor, they numbered close to 100,000 and many lived in a ghetto section of the city that fostered a strong sense of intraethnic solidarity and isolation from the local Chinese and foreign population. Here too an unknown number of Japanese Americans migrated to the city, hoping their common bond of being Japanese, together with their educational degrees and fluency in the English language, might land them meaningful employment. Some 40,000 Japanese Americans—about a fifth of the entire Japanese American population in 1940—had by 1935 already spent years living in Japan, bringing the total to thousands who moved to the western rim of the Pacific to carve out a future there.[31]

Conscription by the Imperial Japanese Army raised further the number of Japanese American collaborators. Many of them were subject to Japanese military conscription, which drafted all males from age twenty to forty, without regard to their American citizenship. Many were liable because they were still Japanese citizens—local governments continued to register their names in their respective family registries despite the central government's threat in 1924 to curtail dual citizenship. For those reasons, some 2,000 to 7,000 Japanese American men were conscripted into the armed forces of Imperial Japan, and an unknown number of Japanese American females served in military intelligence.[32]

Morihiko Takami was one such conscripted Japanese American. Born in Brooklyn in 1914, he grew up enjoying wealth and privilege, never experiencing the pain of racial discrimination or the intoxicating visions of utopia that attracted some of his coethnics to the Japanese empire. His father was a medical doctor, a community leader, and a founding member of the Japanese Association of New York. His mother also held high status as a Mount Holyoke College graduate. Takami himself was on an elite track, educated at Lawrenceville Preparatory School and Amherst College, before he dropped out to travel throughout Europe. His father disciplined him by sending him to Japan to attend Dōshisha University in March 1935 to study Japanese language and culture. In August 1937 he was drafted into the Imperial Japanese Army as a private and was promoted to the rank of corporal before being discharged in December 1940 and listed as a reserve. To avoid being redrafted, Takami moved to Shanghai and joined a friend's company before starting his own film company and dabbling in oil and merchandise trading. In 1943 Takami married socialite Rajkumari Sumair of Patiala, India, and became an advisor to the Imperial Japanese Expeditionary Forces in China, an action which many, including FBI Director J. Edgar Hoover, considered treasonous. Takami increased his likelihood of prosecution when he assisted his Amherst College friend Kichizō Ikushima, an officer in Japanese Naval Intelligence in Shanghai, with reading intelligence documents. At Ikushima's request, he joined an Imperial Japanese Navy mission to Manila to ferret out Filipino spies reporting to the Allies on Japanese ship movements. Takami, however, used the opportunity to sell medical merchandise in the city. Trapped in Manila when the American forces arrived, he was captured and imprisoned until the Department of Justice determined that he had already expatriated himself by serving in the Japanese Army, a generous application of the law that exempted him from prosecution under the treason statute.[33]

Hajimu Masuda was another Imperial Japanese Army soldier under OSS investigation. Although an American citizen, he was dragooned by authorities and sent to China as a private in the Imperial Japanese Army. Born in 1915 in Los Angeles, Masuda graduated from Venice High School before boarding the *Tatsuta Maru*. He arrived in Japan just after war broke out between Japan and China in July 1937 and proceeded to go on tour as a musician. The twenty-two-year-old performed at various locations throughout the main island of Japan and in Korea, Manchuria, and northern China, and despite the American consulate warnings, stayed in Japan to marry a fellow performing artist from Nagoya. In October 1942 his luck ran out when he was arrested for evading military conscription. During his month-long detention, the police beat him and accused him of being an American spy. He broke and applied for Japanese citizenship once they took away his US passport. Masuda was allowed to return to his wife's home in Nagoya for a year before being taken away for military training in January 1944. He then departed with the South China Expeditionary Force to Shanghai. But Masuda's refusal or inability to speak, read, and write Japanese well, along with a bad knee, got him reassigned to work with German government officials on the island of Shameen, near Canton, in August 1944. After reporting in the Twenty-Third Japanese Army Headquarters in Canton, Masuda worked with German intelligence in the Bureau Ehrhardt and began monitoring US Army Air Force and Chinese Nationalist Air Force radio communications, providing intelligence that would allow the Japanese fighter pilots to intercept and destroy American aircraft:

> I was assigned to monitor certain broadcast bands of the United States and Chinese Air Forces. My job was to take down every word that was spoken during these air-ground radio transmissions. I wrote down word for word the conversations concerning take-offs, plane number identifications, how many planes in flight, cargos they carried, and landing times and places. At first I didn't know what this was all about. I just did my job. . . . Mr. Heise had the American and Chinese codes with which to analyze the information I intercepted in these broadcasts, and so I came to know that we were plotting all the American and Chinese plane movements, cargo movements and troop traffic which was coming over the Hump from India into China. This was my most important job until May 1945.[34]

Even after Germany surrendered in May 1945, Masuda admitted in his sworn affidavit that he continued this work monitoring Allied ship movements, intelligence necessary for the suicide attack units to better target American naval vessels approaching the home islands of Japan:

> I took down all sorts of intercepted communications concerning "Boogies" and "Bandits" and "damaged ships" and "floating docks" and "repair work is going on here" or a certain ship is being towed from a certain place to a certain dock. I had to write out every word. . . . I remember listening in. It was all over the circuit that the Japs had quit. Nobody in the [Erich] Heise Office would believe me. Every day they used to bring these things to Mr. [Erich] Heise—right up until the day the Japanese formally announced the surrender.[35]

For Masuda, the war's end only added to his misery. When his German superiors finally accepted the fact that Japan had surrendered, he was released from the consulate office and worked as a chauffeur. The US Army arrived shortly thereafter and treated him as one among many Japanese soldiers waiting to be transported home to Japan. But when Marine Corps Captain Frank Farrell arrived in Shanghai to conduct war crimes investigations, he had all German Consulate employees including Masuda placed in temporary custody at the Ward Road Jail in Shanghai. All Germans, as Farrell saw it, had forfeited their diplomatic immunity by their continued surveillance of American air transports, fighters, and bombers after Germany had surrendered. Although his other three Japanese colleagues were released, Masuda was held while Farrell checked the Japanese American's claim to American citizenship, something that Masuda did not foresee would bring more trouble. Farrell revealed his intention:

> There were four Japanese working with [Erich] HEISE. MASUDA was one of them. I did not charge these Japanese with espionage because they were military personnel, in uniform and under orders from a Government with whom we were still at war. However, if Major Ware receives confirmation from the US that Masuda is an American citizen, as he claims, I am going to arrest him for treason and demand the death penalty.[36]

Fortunately for Masuda, Junichi Butō was also assigned by the OSS to investigate possible war crimes committed by Imperial Japanese military personnel at the Ward Road Jail. As part of his Secret Intelligence duties, Butō gathered documents left behind by Imperial Japanese forces to better understand how Japanese intelligence operated in the city. He collected information on economic conditions and its impact on Japanese civilians. When it came to war crimes investigations, Butō was not shy in laying responsibility for torturing Allied POWs on Japanese personnel, identifying seven Japanese personnel in the Ward Road Jail of torturing Allied POWs while exonerating only one. He also investigated and exonerated three Japanese Americans working as civilian employees of the Imperial Japanese governmental news agencies—Kay Miura and his wife, both of radio station XGOO in Shanghai, and David Hiroshi Inoshita of Dōmei News. Butō then recommended that the three be employed by the translation section, given their prior work experience in the Japanese embassy in Shanghai and the Japanese Consul office in Hangchow, respectively, and their knowledge of Japanese intelligence and consular activities. He advised against prosecution since the three had, in his view, no other alternative but to work for the Japanese. Butō, another SI agent reported, said that "his contacts believed these men are pro-American, and that there is no question regarding their security." Butō's recommendations for all four Japanese Americans prevailed, Farrell's investigation of Masuda notwithstanding.[37]

Masuda was not Captain Frank Farrell's only Japanese American target. He handled the OSS investigation into Ray Morio Uyeshima, another alleged Japanese American collaborator in Shanghai. He first heard of Uyeshima's allegedly treasonous behavior from a convicted criminal named Istvan Iritz, who told the Marine captain, "If you are looking for collaborators, this Uyeshima is one of the biggest." Farrell then investigated Uyeshima and secured sworn statements from twenty individuals, which prompted the Marine captain to emphatically declare Ray Morio Uyeshima as a true collaborator:

> Evidence contained in this report will show conclusively that Ray Uyeshima, a citizen of the United States prior to the Japanese attack on Pearl Harbor, who is now protesting vigorously his absolute loyalty to the United States during the period of his absence from the United States and his residence in an enemy Japanese-occupied zone and who is endeavoring frantically to regain his United States citizenship, was, in fact, an active and voluntary collaborator with the Japanese, both in plying war materials for the enemy and in furnishing intelligence to the enemy.

Farrell therefore recommended Uyeshima's arrest.[38]

But Farrell's case against Uyeshima was largely circumstantial. Some of the alleged eyewitnesses offered testimony that was only suggestive of his collaboration. Philip Kikuta, a former interpreter for the Imperial Japanese Naval Attaché in Shanghai, observed how Uyeshima had an abundance of food despite the severe rationing program imposed on Shanghai residents; how he personally observed the Japanese American broker drive a car around the city despite gas rationing and limitations on driving permits; and also noted his residence at the Pershing Apartments, where only the very wealthiest lived. Given these unusual privileges, Kikuta concluded that Uyeshima must have collaborated with Imperial Japanese authorities.[39]

Other eyewitnesses, however, produced testimony that was more than suggestive. Major Kenjirō Anami of the Japanese Gendarmerie headquarters, Western District, Shanghai, revealed his organization specifically targeted seventy to eighty American-born Japanese with offers of employment and privileges and threats of internment if they refused:

> It was the policy of the Japanese authorities to use the Nisei whenever in any way possible rather than intern such persons. Every effort was made to persuade the Nisei to work for the Japanese. Some Nisei were employed by the Japanese

authorities prior to the outbreak of war in the Pacific, and others offered their
services to Japan after the war began. Each Nisei was interviewed and when a
decision was finally made to intern nationals of countries at war with Japan
each Nisei was given the choice of working for the Japanese or being interned.

Major Anami's sworn statement further revealed that Uyeshima's wartime relationship with his organization followed the normal pattern
of incorporating American-born Japanese into collaborative work—
screening their loyalty to Japan, placing them on probation while the
collaborators gathered intelligence, and finally making lucrative offers of
Imperial Japanese Army or Navy supply contracts to those in businesses.
On top of Uyeshima's "normal" collaborative process, Anami recalled that
he was "one of the very first of the Nisei in Shanghai to go to work for the
Japanese authorities after the outbreak of war in the Pacific," and with his
experience in the brokerage business, had the knowledge of the location
of war materials and supplies the Imperial Japanese armed forces needed.
With an office inside the Gendarmerie headquarters, Anami too decided
that Uyeshima must have been a valued collaborator.[40]

Farrell had more evidence against Uyeshima beyond what Major Anami
supplied. Some of his witnesses pointed to the Japanese American broker's
usage of three offices, all within the jurisdiction of the Imperial Japanese
Navy, as proof of Uyeshima's guilt. Tatsuo Nakada, a former civilian broker
who worked directly under navy, told Farrell that operating any office in
Shanghai required a permit from the consulate office, or from the army
or navy. Seiichi Yamasaki, a former Japanese translator for the Italian
Embassy in Shanghai, was even more specific—Uyeshima must have had
strong connections to the Imperial Japanese Navy and convinced them of
his loyalty to Japan to get those offices. Yamasaki noted that Uyeshima had
three such offices in the naval zone of the city, one each in the Hamilton
House, the Chase Bank Building, and the Ezra Building. Getting permission from the Enemy Property Control Committee was difficult, prompting
Yamasaki to question how Uyeshima acquired them:

> It was difficult for a Japanese with a Japanese passport to obtain office space in
> any of these buildings or to obtain other favors from the Japanese authorities,
> and a Nisei without a Japanese passport must of necessity have had extremely
> close connections with the Japanese authorities, especially the Navy, in order
> to obtain the same things. The loyalty and activities of such a Nisei would be
> subjected to the closest scrutiny, and permits and special credentials would be
> issued only when the Japanese authorities were satisfied and then only with
> very powerful support from high Japanese authorities in the Army or Navy.[41]

Still others pointed to Uyeshima's provisioning of the Imperial Japanese Navy with much-needed materials. Heitarō Ogino, another former broker in Shanghai, swore that Uyeshima purchased a large quantity of welding rods from Raynold Boussuett for seven million dollars and then resold them to the Imperial Japanese Navy for ten million dollars. FBI investigators confirmed the claims of one detractor of Uyeshima—he had imported 30,000 tons of oil into Shanghai, only to have the Imperial Japanese Navy impound the entire supply and pay him compensation at a price considerably higher than the market value for the consignment. "Apparently he did buy materials and sell them to the Japanese Navy at huge profits for himself. He lavishly entertained Japanese naval officers who later gave him high prices for the materials that he sold to them."[42]

Finally, Farrell presented evidence that Uyeshima tried to change his nationality. One witness claimed that he applied for Japanese citizenship as early as spring 1943, only to be told by the Home Ministry in Tokyo that they couldn't grant his request but would still protect him during the war as a Japanese. Another quoted Uyeshima's own conversation with a Lieutenant Miwa of the navy in January 1943, when he was assured his application would meet approval: "Ray has applied for a Japanese passport which will be given to him very soon. He is a fine fellow who is willing to go to the front tomorrow as a Japanese soldier." Another testified he had heard directly from Uyeshima himself in the summer of 1944 that he had applied for Japanese citizenship.[43]

Why Farrell was quick to believe Uyeshima was guilty of treason requires an explanation. The Marine captain's willingness to accept at face value some of the hearsay testimony underscored his lack of legal knowledge, even though he had completed a year of law school prior to becoming a Marine. As a child, he had taken part in a few racialist incidents, such as shouting "Chinkee-chinkee-Chinaman" at a Chinese American laundryman and administering a beating with a baseball bat to some Italians from "Woptown" (his term) for stealing his bicycle. But as an adult he had an African American traveling companion named Charlie Porter, and displayed no racial antagonism toward the Japanese, distinguishing between the "Nisei," on the one hand, and "Japanese," on the other, during the war. Perhaps Farrell was jealous of Uyeshima, since the broker had succeeded in marrying a Japanese movie actress and lived a life of luxury during the war while Farrell himself, despite his movie-star looks, was never able to marry any of the Hollywood actresses he dated while covering them as a feature writer for the New York *World Telegram*.[44]

Farrell's views on citizenship was probably the determinative factor in his stance toward Uyeshima. He believed that American citizenship provided equality of opportunity for all, but mistook it for equality of condition. Born in 1912 in Brooklyn to a working-class Irish immigrant, Farrell saw Uyeshima as having the same opportunity to better himself that he had. At age six, Farrell and his siblings were expelled from the household after the father remarried. Farrell then worked many part-time jobs, paying his way through school and graduating from New York University before becoming an associate editor of the *World-Telegram*'s metropolitan magazine. Only by working hard—covering everything in downtown Manhattan twenty-four hours a day, seven days a week—did Farrell become the self-made success that he believed was possible in a country like the United States. For him, American citizenship was worth fighting for, and so Farrell volunteered for service right after hearing the news of the Pearl Harbor attack and gave up his high society lifestyle for what he hoped would be an adventurous, albeit dangerous, assignment on Patrol Torpedo boats. After receiving his training, however, Farrell was assigned to the Marine Corps and sent to Guadalcanal, where he experienced some of the bitterest fighting of the war. Farrell also fought at Peleliu, where he "voluntarily and with utter disregard for his own personal safety, led numerous small patrols into enemy territory to secure vital information of the enemy and to ascertain enemy activity." This Silver Star he received for this was only one of sixteen commendations he earned during the Pacific campaign. The sacrifices he made and the blood his fellow Marines shed made him intolerant of civilians hobnobbing with the Axis enemy. His anger boiled over when Farrell was in postwar China and learned of Kirsten Flagstad, the Norwegian performing artist who, with her husband, applied for American citizenship after being branded as "Quisling" for supporting Nazi Germany during the war. Farrell recalled giving her a tour of New York and listening to her spend "most of her time goddaming the not Barb-aryans at the Met." When Congress voted favorably on Flagstad's American citizenship, Farrell was livid:

> If Flagstad attains the status of American citizenship . . . I shall seriously consider giving up mine—because in the next war I should hate to contemplate that I was shedding blood for Flagstad. I speak not for just myself—but I dare to speak for all those Marines who served with me and died for their country in the Solomon Islands, in New Guinea, in New Britain, in the Palau Islands and China. We willingly paid whatever price the gods decreed for the honor and benefits of American citizenship—but we never imagined it could be regarded so cheaply that Flagstad would ever be considered for it.

With such an outlook, it is unsurprising that Farrell found Uyeshima guilty of betraying his American citizenship.[45]

Others, however, found Uyeshima innocent of the charges. American intelligence officer Albert H. Mackenzie, for example, made it clear to Farrell that when he heard rumors of Uyeshima's alleged complicity with the Japanese, he confronted the broker directly about the accusations:

> I asked him pointblank what he had to say to such an accusation, adding that if this were true I considered it very serious. His reply was an emphatic denial and with clenched fists he protested that he would like to meet the person face to face who made such a statement.

Mackenzie recommended Uyeshima conduct a hearing to clear his name but also checked further into the broker and found an absence of derogatory information against Uyeshima, which he deemed as significantly in favor of the accused:

> Considerable information has reached this Office concerning Niseis who found themselves in China at the outbreak of the Pacific War but in all of it, I have heard no word of condemnation against Mr. Uyeshima. I do not feel any hesitancy in suggesting that an absence of unfavorable reports is of some significance.

Mackenzie further assured Farrell of Uyeshima's loyalty to the United States by pointing out how cooperative and useful the broker has proven in his own investigation of Japanese assets in Shanghai: "Further, he has been most helpful in procuring 'subjects' for our interrogation, notably TAO and KITAHARA whose value, both to FEA and to G-2, cannot be overestimated. In other matters also, Mr. Uyeshima has gone out of his way to help us."[46]

Several eyewitnesses also added their sworn statements in favor of Uyeshima. Imperial Japanese Navy's purchasing section official Toshio Namba testified that during the war Namba worked in the navy's section overseeing all purchases of supplies and materials, and had met Uyeshima prior to the Pearl Harbor attack. He was in a position to know firsthand if the broker had sold provisions to the navy or entertained its officers after the Pearl Harbor attack. Namba denied knowledge of the former and scoffed at the latter, calling Farrell's claim "a little bit far-fetched."[47]

C. L. and Jean Huang, an elderly couple, also testified on Uyeshima's behalf. They had befriended Uyeshima and his wife and were so close to them that they viewed them as their own children. Uyeshima's regular visits to the couple several times a week positioned the Huang family as the best to judge his wartime behavior. Jean characterized Ray as a "true American" in the face of considerable Japanese pressure to serve their interests:

He always said that no matter what the consequences may be, he is an American, and will remain so, and I know for a fact, that Mr. Uyeshima was forever being pestered by the Japanese Gendarmeries and other Japanese authorities.

Jean recalled that the one time when Ray failed to show, she learned he had been taken into the infamous Bridge House, where he was subjected to physical and mental torture. When he never visited, she said "I could not restrain my tears when I saw his physical condition. He was a completely broken man both mentally and physically." Jean knew Uyeshima's unwavering belief that the United States would win the war undergirded his resistance toward Japanese authorities:

> I knew him even at the height of Japanese victories, and he always told in confidence, that even [if it] took ten years, the tide would turn against the Japanese, because he knew America too well to take it lying down.

Jean was certain Ray was innocent and his accusers simply malicious: "There positively must be some unjust character, who for some petty jealousy or other is accusing him of something which he has never committed."[48]

Army Captain Michael Shigeo Yasutake's belief in Ray Uyeshima's innocence was the deciding factor. Yasutake took a personal interest in the case after arriving in Shanghai as part of his counterintelligence work investigating Japanese wartime activities in Shanghai. As had MacKenzie, the army captain directly confronted Uyeshima regarding the case Farrell was preparing against the Japanese American broker and came away convinced of Ray's innocence. In his own report of December 12, 1945, Yasutake struck at the weakness in Farrell's case against Uyeshima— the issue of coercion. Yasutake knew, from his own intelligence work on Imperial Japanese military authorities' methods elsewhere, that Japanese Americans like Uyeshima were bullied into collaboration:

> From the time I met him on 14 September 1945 until the time he has related in detail exactly what he has been doing the past four years of [the] war in the Pacific. After hearing his story I am fully convinced that he has told me the truth and that he has in no way helped or collaborated with the Japanese voluntarily, and whatever he did for the Japanese during their occupation was forced upon him.

Furthermore, Yasutake credited Uyeshima with resisting Imperial Japanese authorities' pressure, a finding he came to after talking with many individuals in the course of his investigation:

All the people who know the American Japanese have only praise for Ray because of the fact that he did not help the Japanese materially and for flatly
refusing to take out formal Japanese papers. I admire him greatly for retaining
his American citizenship status even though he had to spend [a] great number
of miserable and trying days in the famous Bridge House undergoing torture by
the Japanese Gendarmerie.

The Japanese American captain then concluded that Uyeshima had committed no crime intentionally, was a man of good character, loyal to the
United States, and innocent of all charges, requesting that he "be given due
consideration and be cleared as soon as possible because I believe that he
is loyal as I am."[49]

The similarities in the two men's backgrounds undoubtedly help shape
Yasutake's belief in Uyeshima's innocence. Both hailed from large farming
families, and their respective parents followed the common immigration
pattern of males entering the continental United States from Kyūshū prior
to the gentlemen's agreement of 1906 and females thereafter. They were
born just a year apart and grew up working on their family farms. They
were educated in the same schools in Moneta, California, and were even
playmates. Their paths diverged when Ray left for Japan in 1932 to study
at Tenri University. Meanwhile, Yasutake gave up his dream of attending
the University of Southern California to continue supporting his parents
on the farm. He was drafted into the US Army in January 1941 and had to
remain in uniform after the Pearl Harbor attack. Even if their individual
paths diverged, both men faced the same challenge of loyalty to the United
States—the Uyeshima and Yasutake families lost their accumulated property at the hands of the federal government and were forcibly removed
and interned in WRA camps for the duration of the war.[50]

Wartime experiences were another factor that made Yasutake favorably inclined toward Uyeshima. Unlike the Japanese Americans in the
442nd Regimental Combat Battalion, Yasutake enjoyed comparatively
high status as a soldier. As an enlisted man, he dug his own foxhole every
night and shared the front-line dangers of shifting battle lines with other
American soldiers in one of the bloodiest campaigns in the Pacific. Yet he
was assigned a European American sergeant to serve as his bodyguard while
he volunteered to undertake dangerous missions, such as crawling into a
tunnel where Imperial Japanese soldiers were hidden to induce them into
surrendering, an act that earned him a medal. Reassigned to Fort Benning
in Georgia to teach jungle warfare, Yasutake was promoted to lieutenant.
Thereafter, he was assigned to Camp Savage as an instructor, whereupon he
served on the court-martial board dealing with a large number of delinquent

Japanese American soldiers. Yasutake found they did not share the Nisei culture that sociologist Tamotsu Shibutani observed in the 442nd—the desire to show themselves as better soldiers than others and success in becoming "an integral part of American life." Yasutake was sympathetic toward those who did not fully share that Nisei culture, and thus favored leniency for all Nisei brought up for court-martial, a stance that upset his superiors. Therefore, the Japanese American captain was already predisposed to treat Uyeshima in the best possible light when he was assigned to escort some Japanese officers to China and then on to Shanghai in September 1945 to collect intelligence-related documents and assist the OSS in war crimes investigations.[51]

Yet it was the FBI that closed the door on Ray Uyeshima's case. The Department of Justice's decision to not prosecute the Japanese American broker paved the way for his reacquisition of American citizenship. The department made its decision in part because the eyewitness accounts were contradictory:

> Some believed that he was an informer and collaborator openly and actively cooperating with the Japanese. Others stated that he remained loyal to the United States doing only what he had to do in order to stay alive during the Japanese occupation of Shanghai.

While admitting that Uyeshima purchased supplies for the Imperial Japanese Navy before and during the war, they found his actions prior to the war legal and his wartime activity of not much benefit to the enemy, since he charged much higher prices than the market value. Moreover, due to his actions, a couple of the Imperial Japanese Navy officers were forced to resign their commission once the scandal became known. Elwood Olsen, the department official, therefore concluded: "In the light of this uncertainty as to his citizenship I do not believe a treason case is presented here."[52]

For the OSS investigating officers, however, the case's closure brought mixed results. For Yasutake, the Department of Justice's admission that they had no case against Uyeshima reaffirmed the Japanese American captain's faith in his childhood friend and his conception of loyalty to America as broad enough to allow for cooperation with the enemy under duress. The case's closure also meant that Yasutake could forge ahead with his plans to marry Uyeshima's sister-in-law, with whom he had become acquainted in Shanghai while working for the OSS.

For Frank Farrell, however, the case's closure underscored his relative powerlessness in dealing with his own bosses in the OSS. After serving as an investigator and special prosecutor for the International Military Tribunal for the Far East in Shanghai, Farrell returned to the *New York World-Telegram* in 1947 an unhappy man. While still serving as special prosecutor, he penned an essay in mid-April 1945 titled "Seven Axis Agents Are Seized in Shanghai Coup," in which he claimed that seven Axis nationals gathered intelligence on Chinese and American troop, air, and fleet movements by "breaking, buying and stealing secret codes and transmitting information to Tokyo via clandestine radio stations." All of this resulted, Farrell claimed, in the loss of at least one American aircraft carrier, contributed substantially to the heavy casualty rates American forces experienced in Okinawa and elsewhere, and provided the Imperial Japanese forces with information on American planes flying the Himalayas Fleet. Once Farrell encountered difficulties prosecuting those he targeted as war criminals and collaborators, he turned to writing a novel, in which he placed the reader in the position of the fictional character Kenneth Steffens, an average American war veteran who reads up on what the protagonists "Mustang" (himself) and "Grendel" (Marvin Gray) did during their investigation and attempted prosecution of twenty-seven Nazi "werewolves" in China. Farrell was obviously criticizing the OSS for its failure to prosecute Ehrhardt, the German propaganda and intelligence organization for which Hajimu Masuda worked in Shanghai. "The verdicts of guilty against and the deportation of so few Nazis from China," Farrell wrote, "is a condemnation of the entire secret intelligence system of the United States." The Marine captain argued that

> OSS investigators whitewashed and closed the case against German Intelligence and Propaganda agencies. The OSS Counter-Intelligence Branch prohibits further investigations into their findings. The contradictory reports of Mustang and Grendel were never read. War Crimes Office does not want to consider a trial of Germans due to previous experiences with false arrests inspired by incompetent OSS men.

Farrell ended his story with an accusation of Michael Yasutake whitewashing Ray Uyeshima's alleged raitorous deeds: "A G-2 officer conceals the activities of his Nisei friend, an American traitor."[53]

Unlike Uyeshima in Farrell's fiction, Kazuo Thomas Tatsumi was a potential case for treason prosecution. In Farrell's book, Tatsumi is described as "a Japanese who was on the flag submarine in the attack on Pearl Harbor is uncovered as a former spy in the United States and is turned over to the FBI at Tokyo." Tatsumi in fact collected and transmitted strategic and tactical intelligence on the United States prior to December 7, 1941, for the Imperial Japanese Navy. While working as a clerk for the Yamato Hotel in downtown San Francisco, Tatsumi passed on numerous intelligence reports given him by Imperial Japanese Navy officers transiting between Tokyo and various points in the United States. He was close to Lieutenant Commander Inaho Ohtani, who probably got Tatsumi assigned as a naval attache to handle travel permits, passports, and German affairs in Shanghai, where Ohtani served as head of the Foreign Section, Liaison Office. There, Tatsumi met Eugen Hovans-Clige, a freelance agent who provided Farrell with details of the *yobiyose*'s alleged participation in the Pearl Harbor attack.[54]

Frank Farrell's allegations against Tatsumi's involvement at Pearl Harbor, however, are not proven. Farrell's only source was Eugen Pick Hovans, a White Russian intelligence broker in Shanghai who worked for both American and Japanese intelligence. Farrell learned from the Russian immigrant of a private conversation Hovans had with Tatsumi, in which the Japanese American revealed that he monitored American radio transmissions while aboard the lead submarine in the Pearl Harbor attack. While Pick Hovans's reliability is questionable, the details Hovan provided surrounding Tatsumi's alleged role were remarkably accurate even though he had no access to those details about the attack. With the absence of I-9 submarine records for that year, and a gap in similar records for the US Navy, it is difficult to verify the claim.[55]

Tatsumi's ability to escape investigation and prosecution points to how Asian Americans performed in spy-catching, POW rescue work, and war crimes investigations. On the one hand, trapping enemy agents proved nearly impossible even for talented agents like John Kwock. Even if they could not ferret out Yoshiko Kawashima, the Japanese Mata Hari, they were able to secure all the OSS stations in China against enemy agent infiltration. POW rescue work, however, was another matter.

Participating in at least five such operations, Asian Americans skillfully applied their knowledge of the language and culture to bring critically needed food, medicine, and exit transportation for Allied personnel confined in Japanese POW camps. By their actions, these Asian Americans saved hundreds of lives despite having, as Fumio Kido learned, the wrong racial uniform as far as the Japanese military personnel were concerned. Asian Americans handling the war crimes investigation were also beneficial to the OSS even if they missed some of the crimes, such as those committed by the Japanese forces on Hainan Island. Investigators like Junichi Butō and Michael Yasutake brought not only their language and investigative skills to bear on war criminals, but also salvaged some Japanese Americans who otherwise would have otherwise unfairly borne the brunt of other non-Asian American investigators bent on extracting vengeance on those whose understanding of loyalty differed from Frank Farrell's.

CHAPTER 7

༄

Race, Loyalty, and Asian Americans

The OSS rightfully dismissed Frank Farrell's case against alleged Asian American collaborators. The Marine captain ignored contrary evidence and law to justify his prosecution. He blindly accepted hearsay evidence against Uyeshima and forgot that the US government had expatriated all individuals who joined an army or had served in an official position governmental position of a foreign power since 1940. Farrell paid no attention to the OSS counterintelligence's operational definition of an "active collaborator" as "a person who aids the enemy only for his economic profit in regular business or who does so only under coercion is not considered a collaborator," a distinction that excluded Ray Uyeshima and other Japanese American civilians. In his blind fury against alleged war propaganda radio broadcasters, he disregarded the US government's definition of treason and made words equivalent to acts. In that regard Farrell resembled the Imperial Japanese government, which had lowered its own definition of treason to include mere words and, in the process, turned Japanese socialists such as those who joined Morale Operations (MO) into "non-nationals" or "traitors." Further, his rejection of "mixed" loyalty among those within the US Armed Forces contradicted his own commander-in-chief's acceptance of multiple loyalties and aims, such as African Americans who fought for a victory against the Axis powers abroad to achieve equality at home. The OSS he served was an organization that incorporated into its guerrilla operations individuals whose loyalty was not solely for the Allied cause. As pointed out by Dillon Ripley, chief of Secret Intelligence (SI) for Southeast Asia, locals joined the OSS not to defend abstract moral principles but out of personal loyalty to specific OSS officers. Finally, Farrell found treasonous only Japanese Americans while ignoring European American citizens like Don Chisholm, whose collaboration with the Germans and the Japanese was clearly voluntary and extensive. For the OSS, Farrell's singling out of Japanese Americans like Uyeshima appeared racially discriminatory.[1]

Admittedly, the OSS had its own problems with equating loyalty with race. Hatsumi Yamada of Research and Analysis (R&A) was denied access to secure areas of OSS buildings because of his race. In India, Japanese Americans in MO were confined under guard to the immediate compound where they worked, not unlike the WRA camps where some of their family members were still held. But it should be noted that their restrictions were imposed by British officials who governed the region, not the OSS. Many Asian Americans were unable to secure officers' commissions despite their outstanding field service, while lesser linguistically qualified European Americans had received such coveted ranks upon graduation from the Military Intelligence Language School.[2]

Yet for the most part, the OSS proved itself to be a racially liberal organization. William Donovan surrounded himself with minorities for his personal staff and racially liberal European American directors who hired Asian Americans for their professional staff. He refused to accept the Croix de Guerre medal from the French for rescuing his men under German heavy mortar fire during World War I until his Jewish sergeant at his side at the time also received the same award. His personal chauffeur was James Freeman, an African American whom he defended in at least one act of racial discrimination in wartime Washington, DC. He brought in Chinese American sergeants Yueh C. Tsai and H. Kuei Chang as his personal cooks. Donovan hired as his R&A China Director Joseph Spencer, who condemned as childish a lack of trust in Chinese Americans. MO employed many Asian Americans, including Joe Koide, and determined that their loyalty to the Allied cause was sufficient. SI/Far East signed up Asian Americans like Lincoln Kan, whose family connections to southern China proved invaluable. X-2 commended John Kwock for his language skills and ability to ferret out Chinese hired by the Japanese to penetrate the OSS. Special Operations (SO) defended Kunsung Rie and other Korean Americans as vital to their planned operations. Without these Asian Americans and their linguistic and cultural skills, their social and political connections to East Asia, and their correct racial uniforms, OSS officials knew that their operations in the region would have been severely hampered.[3]

In addition, the OSS had a gender problem overlapping their racial blemishes. Donovan's agency brought into their organization stellar European American females such as Cora DuBois, Jane Foster, Rosamund Frame, Joan Bondurant, and Betty MacDonald. But counterintelligence overlooked Mary Oyama, an experienced operative who worked for years prior to the war with Ralph van Deman, the so-called father of army intelligence. MO hired Japanese artists and writers from abroad, such as Tomoe Iwamatsu, but failed to bring in local residents like Louise Yim, Beulah Ong Kwoh, Mine Okubo, Loretta Chiye Mori, Chiura Obata, and Wakako Yamaguchi, all of them talented artists and writers. R&A found Los Angeles-born Chiyeko Nakamura, whose strong Japanese language skills impressed Professor Ryūsaku Tsunoda, the father of Japanese studies at Columbia University. They also brought in Korea-born Lois Woo-Ja Chung as another sharp research analyst. But they missed Tamie Tsuchiyama, a doctoral candidate in cultural anthropology at the University of California, Berkeley; Setsuko Matsunaga Nishi, a doctoral candidate in sociology and resident of New York City; and the upcoming University of Chicago doctoral student Rose Hum Lee. Yukiko Kimura, an established Japanese history specialist at the University of Hawai'i-Manoa, was another individual they missed, despite the fact that she was within a stone's throw of Alfred Tozzer's office in Honolulu. SI engaged five Asian American females, but only those who were already in military uniform. Corporal Anna Kim, of the Women's Auxiliary Army Corps and native of Oahu, was brought into SI for her fluency in Korean and Japanese and her work experience with photography. Kim joined the China Theater Headquarters with Hung Ngow Choy, Hisako Hirakawa, Chito Isonaga, and Fumiko Segawa, who combined had all the requisite skills. But SI missed some women not in uniform who could have proved invaluable. Miya Sannomiya, a journalist for the *Nichibei Shimbun*, was one such missed opportunity, as she had many important social and political connections within the Imperial Japanese government and lived just blocks away from their office in New York. Another was Flora Belle Jan, a Chinese American writer who greatly impressed University of Chicago sociologist Robert Park with her social observational skills and writing in the 1920s, and was already living in China. California-born Pearl Chen, the English-language secretary to Madame Chiang Kai-shek since the early 1930s, already had an established cover but went untapped.[4]

Why OSS recruiters missed so many Asian American females is a matter of speculation, but may involve a couple of factors. Race played a role in limiting the number of Asian Americans overall. Sexism was another factor, constructing Asian American females as linguistically capable of handling Asian language documents but little else. As with other OSS female employees, they were proscribed from combat assignments. But their understanding of loyalty was an equally important factor in limiting Asian American female recruitment. Joan Bondurant's construction of their loyalty as multiple rather than singular was a contributing factor, saying that like all women, Japanese American women have as their primary loyalty the "wish for a just and righteous world where their children may grow to be useful and healthy members of society." All else including political ideology, Bondurant claimed, were secondary considerations. With such priorities, Bondurant believed that Japanese American women had sufficient loyalty for admission into the OSS.[5]

But Bondurant's prioritized layers of loyalty were never acknowledged by OSS males such as Frank Farrell. The Marine captain believed that loyalty was singular, not multiple, and fixed rather than fluctuating according to conditions faced. Farrell's belief about loyalty became manifest with the Tokyo Rose case of 1948. Late that summer, Iva Toguri D'Aquino, an American-born Japanese, was imprisoned awaiting her treason trial, while others involved in the making propaganda radio broadcasts were not even charged. Farrell discussed "Rosie" with his radio audience and assured them that Attorney General Tom Clark didn't "play hunches" and had proof of her culpability. Farrell cited his own evidence of Rosie's treason in December 1943: she boldly predicted in her broadcast the coming defeat of his First Marine Division's impending attack on Cape Gloucester, New Britain after their victory at Guadalcanal:

> With your irritating tone of omniscience . . . you concluded smugly, "that our brave Japanese soldiers are fully prepared to repulse this insolent attempt. This time the jungles will run red with the blood of the Guadalcanal butchers." That gave us quite a jolt, Rosie. Nobody, least of all you, was supposed to know when or where we were to attack next. But you called the shots two weeks in advance and they were all bulls-eyes. . . . How did you know all these things, Rosie? The Japanese surely considered you one of their most valuable warriors.[6]

Farrell saw D'Aquino as a traitor in part because he believed American citizens owed loyalty in word and deed regardless of circumstances. His understanding was supported in 1949 by the Northern District of California's Federal District Court, which found Iva Toguri D'Aquino guilty of one "overt act" of treason in which she "gave aid and comfort to the enemy" in her radio broadcast about American war losses. After receiving a sentence of ten years' confinement and a $10,000 fine, her appeal reached the Supreme Court. Her conviction was upheld despite Justice William O. Douglas's doubts about the fairness of her trial. Farrell got his wish—D'Aquino was imprisoned in the federal penitentiary in Alderson, West Virginia until 1956.[7]

The Marine captain's stance on D'Aquino was based in part on his acceptance of the expanding power of the federal government in the first half of twentieth century. Prior to World War II, top federal government officials tolerated criticism of their actions during wars and opposed restrictions on individuals' rights to voice such opinions. They did so knowing that the Constitution guaranteed the right of free speech and that the bar was high for treason prosecution—as an overt act witnessed by two individuals. Top government officials could prosecute individuals for uttering words with potential damaging effects on their efforts to rally the public behind their war policies under the 1798 Alien and Sedition Act. But historically they did not, leaving the act dormant throughout the War of 1812, the War with Mexico, and even during the Civil War when no Confederate government official, including President Jefferson Davis, was tried for treason. But in the twentieth century federal government officials became increasingly intolerant of public criticism of their wartime policies and actions, as successful conduct of war depended on the public's willingness to support it. They turned to "constructive treason" as their means to suppress dissent and elevate war industries production. Federal legislators passed the Espionage Act of 1917 and its amendment, the Sedition Act of 1918, to criminalize utterance or publication of disloyal or abusive language concerning the US government or the Constitution. They received further support from the Smith Act of 1940, which forbade advocacy of armed revolution and violent overthrow of the federal government. Their stance was buttressed further by the Supreme Court, which allowed treason prosecution for words only. The Court moved past Oliver Wendell Holmes Jr.'s requirement in the 1919 case *Schenck v. the United States* for "clear and present danger" conditions to restrict usage of "constructive treason" in upholding statutory restrictions on freedom of speech and press. Hence, at the end of the Second World War, the Supreme Court justices were willing to uphold treason prosecution of any American citizen engaged in radio propaganda broadcasts for the Axis powers, including Herbert Moy and Iva D'Aquino.[8]

Frank Farrell also followed new rulings by the Supreme Court. Just months before he began investigating collaborators in Shanghai, the Court overruled the Court of Appeals' conviction in *Cramer v. United States*. In that case, the lower courts determined that Anthony Cramer, a German-born naturalized citizen, was guilty of treason. He was caught sharing a glass of beer with two German saboteurs planning to destroy munitions factories on American soil. The lower courts interpreted Cramer's actions as providing "aid and comfort to the enemy" in violation of the Treason Statute. On April 23, 1945, by a five-to-four decision, the US Supreme overturned the guilty verdict but upheld the Court of Appeals' emphasis upon intent as crucial for demonstration of an accused individual's actions as "adhering to the enemy." Accepting Court of Appeal Judge Learned Hand's premise that "aid and comfort to the enemy" required an overt act to reveal treasonous intent, the justices were left interpreting Cramer's acts as showing a similar destructive intent. Some judges concluded that Cramer's seemingly harmless behavior in sharing a conversation over a glass of beer revealed that the accused harbored similar hostile attitudes toward the United States as the German saboteurs he associated with. The justices further weakened the Constitution's two-witness requirement with their emphasis on intent, which demanded only one witness, to prove the prosecution's case. Fortunately for Cramer, the justices found the prosecution's case wanting. By relaxing the evidentiary requirements for treason prosecution, the Supreme Court opened the door for more treason cases going to trial which, since its founding in 1789, had totaled less than forty.[9]

Yet Farrell and the Court's reasoning on treason allegedly committed by D'Aquino and other Asian Americans was flawed. Farrell and the American judicial system, including the Supreme Court, broadened the understanding of overt acts to include words such as those used in propaganda radio broadcasts by D'Aquino and Herbert Moy, even though the Supreme Court had traditionally excluded planning and plotting from treason. If the intent of the writers of the American Constitution's Article III is to be upheld, then words expressed in a radio broadcast alone should not constitute treason. The US Constitution's Treason Clause was taken almost verbatim from an English statute of 25 Edward III, enacted in 1351. The phrases "levying war" and "adhering to their enemies, giving them aid and comfort" from this English statute defined treason as covering seven basic categories, of which thoughts or words could be construed as treasonous including "imagining the death of the king, queen, or their eldest son." The writers of the Constitution, however, deliberately restricted treason to "levying war" and "adhering to their enemies, giving them aid and comfort," preceded by the qualifying word "only." They also increased the burden of proof to two witnesses per treasonous act. Without a definition of levying war, American courts long before World War II insisted on demonstrable acts of war or rebellion, as attested to by Aaron Burr's acquittal in his 1807 treason trial. Written during the turbulent aftermath of the American Revolution, the Constitution's writers intended the law to prevent federal government officials from punishing dissenters whose treasonous activities consisted of words alone.[10]

Farrell and the courts were too quick to dismiss the duress Asian Americans faced within the Imperial Japanese empire. Michael Roche, the US District Court judge in D'Aquino's case, instructed the jurists to restrict duress to instances where an actual weapon was shown; verbal threats alone, he maintained, did not constitute duress. The jurists then determined that

D'Aquino was not under duress and had voluntarily made treasonous propaganda broadcasts. They ignored the fact that Asian Americans residing
within Japanese-controlled territory faced duress during the war—failure
to cooperate with Japanese officials meant family separation and confinement to an internment camp where physical beatings, torture, and death
were not uncommon, over and above police harassment of their relatives
in Japan. For D'Aquino, Ray Uyeshima, and other Asian Americans who
retained their American citizenship while residing in the Japanese empire,
duress was an ever-present reality.[11]

Moreover, Farrell ignored legal contingencies of residency and protection that came with allegiance. In *U.S. v. Hayward* (1815), the federal court
ruled that the American residents of Castine, Maine did not owe allegiance
to the United States while the British forces occupied the port during the
War of 1812. In fact, the court determined the American residents were
temporarily living in enemy territory where the United States' sovereignty
did not exist in terms of residence and protection, and thus loyalty was not
owed to the United States. Their interpretation was upheld as the courts
overturned the navy's successful prosecution of Samuel Shinohara, a
Japanese immigrant resident of Guam who serviced the Imperial Japanese
forces when they occupied the island during the war.[12]

At heart was the difference in view of loyalty and treason. Farrell's
thinking reflected many of the assumptions Columbia University law professor George Fletcher would later make. As had Farrell, Fletcher believed
D'Aquino was guilty because she owed allegiance to the United States by
virtue of her citizenship acquired at birth. Fletcher thought that she and
others had an understanding of self shaped over time through relationships
with other members of the same American society, resulting in partiality
toward and an identification with that society which is represented by its
government. Once this "historical self" is made, the citizen, as Fletcher saw
it, was required to reject "alternatives that undermine the principal bond."
Treason, therefore, was when a citizen or a permanent resident broke that
bond by going over to the enemy during a conflict, and thus was liable to
prosecution.[13]

Adopting the logic of the historical self, Farrell failed to see its in-
applicability to the Asian Americans he tried to prosecute for treason.
Admittedly, their "membership" in the United States was evident in
their American passports. But they and their respective families did not
share the historical self trajectory of Farrell's Irish American experience.
Farrell's parents became naturalized American citizens, while none of
these Asian Americans' immigrant parents could do so since they were
ruled aliens ineligible for citizenship by the Supreme Court, a position

that was not reversed until almost a decade after the war ended. If their parents were Japanese or Korean, they had faced tremendous economic and political insecurities since 1939, when the federal government unilaterally abrogated the US-Japan Commercial Treaty of 1911, stripping those immigrants of their last legal protection against expropriation and deportation, a fear that was realized in 1942 by the mass removal and internment of West Coast Japanese Americans. Uyeshima, Masuda, Yasutake, and other OSS Asian Americans were similarly affected by this federal government betrayal that did not extend to Farrell's parents or relatives. Farrell was able to parlay his college and graduate education into a comfortable white-collar position as a journalist during the Great Depression, whereas Asian Americans had few assurances that their American citizenship and college degrees would enable them to get positions beyond working at fruit and vegetable stands or the "kitchen police" of Chinese restaurants. Farrell could mix easily with America's social and cultural elites, whereas Asian Americans could not even swim in the same recreational pools as European Americans. It was racial discrimination in the same job market and the social outlets of Frank Farrell that led Herbert Moy, for example, to launch his own journalism career in Shanghai rather than New York prior to the war.[14]

Nor did Asian Americans share the experience of a "common culture" enjoyed by Farrell that led to an identification with and loyalty toward the American nation. Admittedly, Herbert Moy and others learned some of that common culture in their American public schooling. Yet their identification with the United States was less than complete. In Moy's case, as with so many Asian Americans living abroad when the war broke out, economic opportunism was the more important factor keeping them within the region where they encountered the political and social realities of the Imperial Japanese government control, working contrary to any ties they may have felt with the common culture of the land of their birth. If nationalism arises out of the growth of an "imagined community" wherein members of that group perceive themselves as moving through time and space together, then these alleged collaborators with the Japanese did not have loyalty to the United States in large part because they saw part of their lives as emerging in East Asia. For others, such as Hajimu Masuda and Ray Uyeshima, the common culture of Japan probably played little, if any, role in the appeal to Japanese Americans to collaborate because Japan had very little common culture in 1940, as reflected in strong regional identities and the absence of a standardized language. In short, loyalty is less about an essentialized culture than it is about the growth and nurturing of the perception of belonging to the same imagined community.[15]

Moreover, Farrell wrongly assumed that the historical self produces identification with and loyalty toward the United States. As philosopher Simon Keller shows, loyalty is unrelated to the historical self in his hypothetical example of an abused wife. The wife, as Keller asserts, is loyal to her ill-tempered husband but in the end she may leave him to discover her true self, illustrating how loyalty is unrelated to identity. In fact, loyalty expressed by the historical self appears in five different forms, according to Keller. The wife's loyalty is an expression of concern, while loyalty to a nation is a form of belief. The two expressions have different origins, since the latter is ostensibly supported by objective standards, whereas the former requires no such external validation beyond blood ties. Keller's understanding of loyalty makes greater sense of the evidence regarding Asian American collaborators such as Herbert Moy, who identified himself with the United States and socialized with others from the same country, suggesting that the historical self was in operation in his life but at the same time, he was loyal in belief to Nazi Germany. Moy's identification with Germany, therefore, probably sprang from a combination of economic opportunism and bitterness toward his own historical self that led him to employment with the German propaganda organization Kriegs. Finally, a loyalty of concern for his brother Ernest brought him to reluctantly collaborate with Imperial Japanese officials, whose country he despised and in no way identified with.[16]

Loyalty is not stable but fluctuates, especially during wars. It is also multilayered, with supra-national, national, and regional levels, with the former and latter often displaying competing claims. As sociologist James Connor points out, it is also an emotion, much like love or hatred, with either contractual or "natural" roots, the latter referring to kin, familial, or tribal connections. During World War II, national loyalty was viewed by most of the American public as primarily contractual and not natural, rendering it peculiarly thin in contrast to their Axis opponents, who believed themselves bonded together by the same blood lineage. Lacking such natural ties, national loyalty as viewed by the American public therefore involved reciprocity. For Asian Americans, that meant they needed a stronger sense of receiving benefits from American society, however imagined, to elevate a sense of reciprocity required to make personal sacrifices for the good of the nation on par with other Americans. That Herbert Moy and other alleged Asian American collaborators should be found lacking in the emotive and highly fluctuating sentiment called national loyalty is therefore no surprise.[17]

Farrell was not alone in misunderstanding loyalty. Later writers have also misunderstood the phenomenon as it applies to Asian Americans during World War II. Army historian James C. McNaughton and Asian American historian K. Scott Wong portray Asian American loyalty as singular and fixed, a result of cultural assimilation. Military historian Joseph D. Harrington understood Japanese American Army intelligence officers' devotion to duty as rooted in the opposite—their retention of a samurai heritage that made them fervent in their loyalty to the United States.[18]

Others have taken a different approach to Asian American loyalty. Japanese history specialist Howard Schonberger found that in MO the Japanese Americans' loyalty constant through the 1930s and 1940s, while the context changed. The MO leftists were defined by the US government as disloyal and their politically conservative opponents were understood as loyal in the 1930s, but this view was reversed in the 1940s. Japanese history specialist John J. Stephan and Asian American historian Yuji Ichioka have found that Japanese Americans in prewar and wartime China were loyal to Japan because they were attracted to a racial utopia under Imperial Japanese rule wherein they were privileged and not racially persecuted. Richard Kim finds Korean American loyalty initially dual, but it became increasingly singularly as the Korean independence movement leaders depended upon the American federal government to achieve Korean independence. Through their activities, they also sought recognition for themselves as an ethnic group and improve their status in America.[19]

As had Farrell, these writers also fall short in explaining Asian American loyalty. The cultural assimilation or ethnic heritage retention arguments by McNaughton, Wong, and Harrington do not explain why Hajimu Masuda faithfully carried out his translation duties as an Imperial Japanese soldier, nor Ray Uyeshima's resistance to collaborating with the Japanese Navy. Ichioka's and Stephan's "racial utopia" explanation fails to account for Morihiko Takami's behavior, as his prewar life was not scarred by racial discrimination. Kim's "quest for statehood" was limited to some Korean Americans in SO but inapplicable to other OSS Asian Americans, since China and Japan had established governments.

Where did Asian American loyalty originate? If we understand loyalty to a nation as a type of political belief undergirded by emotions and requiring an imagination of moving through time and space together with others, then Asian American loyalty was going to be divided and not be uniformly loyal to the United States, especially if they lived outside the US mainland. Understood in this way, Asian Americans who joined the Allied powers also had the genesis of their leftist political beliefs formed in Japan, where they were oppressed by the emerging militarist-like central government. The emotional motor to their loyalty was fueled by residing in and working among others of similar political belief in New York, Washington, and San Francisco. The Iwamatsu couple, Atsushi and Tomoe, is but one example of a number of Japanese leftists who fled Imperial Japan after their Japan Communist Party was defined as illegal and treasonous in 1925. In New York, and then in MO, they imagined themselves as moving through time and space together with others working to fight fascism. For other Asian Americans who were not politically left, their belief in the American democratic system was emotionally undergirded by the proof they saw around them—as the generation born in Hawai'i, they had American citizenship, could attain upward economic mobility into the blue-collar trades, and imagined themselves as part of a society that included many non-Asians. Or they could receive a college education and become an officer in the US Army, and compel European American enlisted men to obey their orders.

Asian Americans siding with the Axis powers had their loyalty formed in a similar manner. Herbert Moy's political beliefs began with his negative assessment of British imperialism and those who supported it, such as the American President Franklin Roosevelt. Germany, Britain's main enemy, became the object of Moy's loyalty and that inclination was further reinforced emotionally by the German propaganda office providing him with a well-paying job in journalism that he was unable to secure in New York. Once Germany surrendered, however, Moy transferred his employment over to the Japanese with the hope of protecting his older brother Ernest. For Hajimu Masuda, political beliefs played a lesser role in him joining the Imperial Japanese Army, since his original motive for going to Japan was to simply to give musical performances. That he continued residing in Japan and was married to a Japanese national helped him see that his life was linked with those on the western and not the eastern side of the Pacific Ocean. Serving as a conscript in the Imperial Japanese Army was therefore simply an unfortunate consequence of his residency, and thus military service was not entered into voluntarily.

Since loyalty was not fixed but changing, the OSS wisely sought ways to limit the entry of double agents into their ranks. The OSS as an organization followed the lead of its director William Donovan, who did not believe that race determined loyalty. Thus he went with the old boy network of hiring friends he was most familiar with and trusted for the top positions, and then gave them the latitude to determine the employment of those working under them. R&A followed Donovan's old boy network approach but also deliberately hired those on the political left, believing their loyalty was assured since these individuals had a proven track record of strongly opposing fascism. While Donovan's arrangement successfully kept Axis power agents out of his organization, it still left his group vulnerable to double agents of Allied and neutral nations, as the example of J. Arthur Duff illustrates.

The OSS should have exercised more caution, as the analysis of Asian American community shows. The Chinese Nationalist government had their agents among Chinese Americans, while Korean collaborators were a distinct possibility, as some were known to be paid informants of the Japanese consulate offices. Kunsung Rie was an informant out of convenience before the war, but once war broke out his loyalty to Korean independence was judged to supersede all else. Japanese Americans were the least likely to have foreign agents among them, as Joe Koide's example illustrates. Yet they still had the greatest number of individuals sympathetic to Imperial Japan's expansionist policy.

But not all sections within the OSS were equally susceptible to penetration by foreign agents feigning loyalty. Joe Koide's MO showed the greatest vulnerability since they recruited linguistically qualified individuals, many of them anti-fascist leftists committed more to the preservation of the Soviet Union than the Constitution of the United States. Kunsung Rie's SO too was uncomfortably exposed, since it had greater numbers of personnel involved in its operations with dual loyalties and whose commitment was less to the Allied cause and more to driving out foreign invaders from their homeland in northern Burma. The risk, however, was reduced in SO by virtue of the fact that the OSS was committed to an American foreign policy that matched the northern hill tribes' concerns for local autonomy. Lincoln Kan's SI was also susceptible to penetration by double agents. In places like China, spies, informants, and information brokers were not uncommon, with many of them engaged in espionage for reasons other than political beliefs. In a land plagued with inflation and other economic difficulties, SI simply applied the principle of redundancy or the hiring of more informants to draw upon multiple sources to corroborate information submitted by an agent in the field. With their rising budget and their enemies' declining economic fortunes, SI was therefore in a strong position to identify which of their own field agents were passing on disinformation planted by the enemy. Nevertheless, the possibility of Lincoln Kan and other OSS agents being hunted, captured, or even turned over to Japanese intelligence was a real possibility.

Despite loyalty providing clues to questionable individuals and information, at least one double agent was able to slip into the OSS operations in East Asia. The OSS failed to identify and apprehend this individual in part because they failed to understand that loyalty is contractual, multilayered, fluid, and not fixed. The OSS installed the wrong countermeasure of the old boy network and of trusting those with a longer and more accomplished family history in the United States than the immigrants and their America-born offspring. By adopting a narrow, essentialist definition of loyalty, the OSS and its war crimes investigator Frank Farrell misunderstood where Asian American loyalties lay, and thereby missed the double agent within their midst.

Epilogue

Unveiling the Trojan Horse

Who was the double agent inside the OSS? The OSS's recruitment of its top personnel was based on the principle of the old boy network, whereby Donovan picked his sections heads utilizing his personal connections and they in turn tapped their professional, social, and financial networks to find staff members. Donovan's approach not only infused the organization at the top with individuals he knew and trusted, but allowed the agency to fill its ranks with people of talent, having the requisite language, educational, and social skills necessary to carry out the task of centralizing strategic and tactical intelligence for the war against the Axis powers. While not foolproof, his methods prevented Axis agents from penetrating the OSS. The recruitment process of Asian Americans was driven largely by necessity, employing individuals with the right stuff: linguistic and cultural skills for the targeted areas and the requisite loyalty to ensure execution of their assigned tasks. This approach seemingly left the OSS vulnerable to double agents slipping in through the agency's back door. Among the various sections in which a double agent might have penetrated, Morale Operations was the most likely group, and Joe Koide was a prime suspect. Special Operations, where Kunsung Rie was assigned, appeared the least likely section for a double agent, given how their assignments were almost suicidal in nature. Research and Analysis (R&A) was another possible target for penetration by an agent of a foreign power, but its recruitment through the old boy network made Axis penetration difficult and their aim of strategic intelligence made the field less valuable to a foreign agent than Secret Intelligence, where the classified information was gathered. Except for Lincoln Kan's long period of radio silence, however, there were no indications of any Asian American agent being compromised or captured and turned. The X-2 or counteintelligence section was also not likely penetrated for the simple reason that its formation, also built upon old boy networks, made infiltration difficult. Additionally, given the section's relatively late formation, its lower prestige, and its involvement in the postwar search for war criminals and collaborators made it unlikely haven for Axis agents, Frank Farrell's accusations notwithstanding. Considering what treason and loyalty meant, the definitions the OSS used to determine which applicants would faithfully execute their duties shed little light on the identity of the double agent inside the OSS.

A SERIAL, NOT DOUBLE AGENT

On the surface, Joe Koide appears as the most likely suspect. Koide claimed to have quit COMINTERN prior to the Pearl Harbor attack and he may have done so, but his Party activities during the 1930s raised suspicions. He came under attack from James Oda, who accused Koide of deliberately obstructing distribution of Shūji Fujii's *Dōhō* newspaper by collecting subscriptions from Japanese readers but failing to turn in the collected money and of ordering George Hasegawa to compile a list of Party members' names, occupations, affiliations, cover or fictitious name, date of entry, and other information that later turned up as a blacklist of the Tokyo International Security Police without Joe Koide's name in 1938. When Koide's COMINTERN funding was cut off in the late 1930s, he and Nosaka turned to the crime syndicate Tokyo Club for funding, which Oda claimed was supported by Japanese intelligence. Once interned in Heart Mountain, Koide fomented draft resistance among US citizens, contrary to the Party's stance but in line with Imperial Japanese interests. After the war Koide became a federal government witness, fingering many of his former Party colleagues, resulting in their deportation. In short, Koide, as viewed by James Oda and other Party members, was a triple agent for the Soviet Union, Imperial Japan, and the United States.[1]

Yet the best available evidence indicates that Joe Koide was not a triple but a serial agent. It is true that he started off in 1930 as an agent of COMINTERN, but he quickly became disillusioned with it, first because of Stalin's Great Purge and then followed by the Party's support of mass removal and internment of Japanese Americans in 1942. With his original enthusiasm for worldwide revolution dissipating, Koide turned to the OSS and assisted the US government's persecution of alleged and real Communist Party members during the 1950s in exchange for his own immunity and permanent residency within the United States. Thus, in a limited sense, Koide could be considered an agent. But his service on behalf of the United States, beginning with the OSS in 1944 and possibly continuing on with the Strategic Services Unit and its successor, the CIA, took place only after he severed his ties with the Communist Party. As for his alleged associations with Imperial Japanese authorities, Japan Communist Party biographer Tomiya Watabe examined closely the 1938 Tokyo police list and found the name "H. Nishi" on it, the fictitious Party name Nobumichi Ukai used throughout the 1930s, after which he adopted the name "Joe Koide" to register safely under the Alien Registration Act of 1940. Watabe further discovered that the name "Joe Koide" was not the only significant Party member's name missing from the blacklist. Finally, the blacklist's misspellings of place names suggests that the author was unfamiliar with the city of Los Angeles, unlike "Joe Koide."[2]

AN AGENT FOR KOREA, NOT THE AXIS POWERS

Like Joe Koide, Kunsung Rie was not an agent for Imperial Japan. His service rendered to that government's authorities in the 1930s was understandable at the time. Rie feared possible arrest by Imperial Japanese authorities unless he cooperated with them. He had no hope for American naturalization, since Korean immigrants were defined as aliens ineligible for citizenship, making his visa status tenuous. He was at the mercy of the Japanese Consulate too, which could revoke his Japanese passport status. Once war broke out, Rie guessed correctly that the US forces would eventually defeat the Imperial Japanese forces, resulting in the liberation of his home country and even the possibility of acquiring US citizenship through service in the OSS. Rie then applied for citizenship after joining the OSS and spoke only of carrying out his "destiny" in life through Napko. He faced tremendous risks with Napko because many Koreans had collaborated with Imperial Japanese authorities, complicating determination of their loyalties. Over 80 percent of Koreans adopted Japanese family names, in contrast to 7 percent in Taiwan, and compliance with conscription notices reached about 85 percent, suggesting that the majority of Koreans were at least outwardly willing to comply with Imperial Japanese authorities. Over 360,000 served the Imperial Japanese forces from 1937 to 1945 including two princes, sons of the deceased King Kojong. Some even became war heroes, such as Major Sŏng-wŏn Kim, who was decorated by the emperor for bravery in leading troops into battle at the outbreak of war in China during the summer of 1937. Lieutenant Seiji Kawata, another Japanized Korean, made the ultimate sacrifice on behalf of Imperial Japan when he crashed his plane into a B-29 bomber over Mimaesaki, Shikoku Island, on May 29, 1945. Given the demonstrated loyalty of at least some Koreans, the Napko team members, including Kunsung Rie, were taking a risk entering the country. Moreover, he risked detection by the police, whose system within Korea was characterized as the "hands and feet" of the Japanese governor-general. With one police substation for every four *li* (about ten square miles) and an average of about three policemen for 800 households, Rie's odds of being discovered were uncomfortably high. As Paul Helliwell, chief of secret intelligence for the China Theater, saw it in spring 1945, the Napko plan "grossly underestimates the efficiency of Japanese police system and security checks which exist in Korea." Given his choice of re-maining or joining the mission, Rie's choice of the latter strongly suggests Eifler's confidence in Rie was sound.[3]

AN AGENT LOST, NOT COMPROMISED

More than Koide or Rie, Lincoln Kan deserved the benefit of doubt. Admittedly, Kan's chances of capture and torture were ever-present during his Akron mission. He played a cat-and-mouse game with the commander of Japanese intelligence, Colonel Toyo Sawa; slipped past the ruthless pi-rate Kung Kit Wong, who plied the local waterways he traversed; and skill-fully dodged Japanese radio detection units and local collaborators who regularly swept the area where he was stationed. Hence, Kan's temporary radio silence should not have been interpreted as capture, since other members of Akron got lost and wandered through the region for some time. He did not he deserve the negative assessments bandied about by some European Americans of Akron simply because he didn't maintain his regularly scheduled radio transmissions. For Kan, the Imperial Japanese authorities' tightening of security in the region in anticipation of a pos-sible Allied invasion, coupled with his cover being blown by a distant rela-tive, forced the Chinese American James Bond to improvise—he married the relative to "buy" her silence—and take longer to gather intelligence, especially after his key informant in Macao quit. Despite these problems, Kan carried out his mission, gathering information on Macao in prepa-ration for a possible Allied invasion code-named Carbonado. In addition, Lincoln followed Japanese troops, reporting their positions and sending them disease-ridden prostitutes, which he knew would slow down their advance by a couple of weeks. He further delayed their movements by floating downriver small, candle-lit wooden boats for the Japanese soldiers to shoot at night, thereby interrupting their sleep, which prompted some Imperial Japanese troops to fire on Kan when he was crossing the West River. After the war ended Kan remained in the Macao region, traveling incognito to avoid detection by enemies other than the Japanese, and continued to send reports to his OSS superiors.[4]

Lincoln Kan's postwar life offers proof his unwavering loyalty to the land of his birth. In the aftermath of the war, Kan faced many personal challenges but retained strong faith in the United States. His father's family property, as well as his mother's family wealth, was lost to the Chinese communists in 1949, leaving Kan to divide his mother's $100,000 estate with his stepfather. Kan finished his degree at the University of North Carolina before securing a job as a journalist reporting on agricultural news. His wife Maureen, a concert pianist from Texas, committed suicide, unable to adjust to the rural life in Georgia where they resided during the 1950s. Kan returned to school, earning his master's degree at Appalachian State University, and then remarried in 1960. Yet he could not secure a teaching job in the South, where it was illegal for a white woman to marry a Chinese. The couple then moved to upstate New York, where they both taught at the Rome Free Academy High School. While his wife taught English, Kan taught American history and political science. Ahead of his peers, Kan became a charter member of the city's NAACP chapter and pioneered the teaching of African American history to a high school student population that was overwhelming European American. In addition, Kan designed a program for African American studies that was used in the Rome Public School system. An early civil rights advocate, Kan proved by his postwar deeds not only that he was true hero, but a true patriot as well.[5]

A SOVIET AGENT

The foreign agents who penetrated the OSS were European Americans, not Asian Americans. They were not Axis power agents, but instead worked for another Allied country. Among them, Duncan S. Lee was an important informant for the Soviet Union. He was one of only a half-dozen such agents who reported to the Soviet Union from their positions inside the OSS. Lee was born in China to missionary parents whose ancestors included Confederate general Robert E. Lee and Richard Henry Lee, the American Revolutionary War leader. Duncan was educated at the University of

Virginia, Cambridge University, and Yale Law School before working
for Donovan at his New York law firm prior to the OSS. He became the
legal advisor to the OSS and then its chief of secret intelligence, Japan-
China Desk, by early 1945. As chief, he was privy to much of what Asian
Americans were doing for the OSS, from the R&A reports to the black radio
propaganda broadcasts produced by Joe Koide and the MO Green group in
San Francisco. He stayed abreast of the planning for Ryongi Hahm's Eagle
and Kunsung Rie's Napko insertion teams and was intimately involved in
Lincoln Kan's Akron mission. Prior to being unmasked, Lee's work earned
high praise from the director:

> You have put your brains, your imagination and your doggedness into every-
> thing you have done—even into devising ways of getting out of a jungle behind
> enemy lines after landing by parachute from a cracked up plane! From the early
> days when you added to the smooth functioning of the secretariat until these re-
> cent months when you were planning and staffing and implementing operations
> in China, your results have always been superior. You have reason to be proud of
> what you have done, and we are proud of you.

After the war, Lee was able to parlay his established wartime record of an
American patriot into a position within the C. V. Starr and Company, which
earned him millions of dollars and a life of comfort.[6]

Yet Lee betrayed the trust of Donovan and others. He submitted verbal
reports of top-secret documents he screened for Donovan to Soviet
couriers who visited his apartment in Washington, DC. His reports were
then communicated to the NKVD office in New York City, where they were
forwarded to Moscow in coded radio transmissions. Although some of
his OSS peers suspected him, Lee was never investigated during the war
and only after November 1945, when the Soviet's main courier Elizabeth
Bentley became an FBI informant, did he come under scrutiny from
Hoover's special agents. Yet he ably defended himself against espionage
charges before the House Committee on Un-American Activities in 1948,
portraying himself as a patriot and his accuser Bentley as a mentally un-
stable and vengeful acquaintance, a position he maintained until his death
in 1988. Lee died confident that his careful insistence about not leaving a
paper trail of his espionage activities and his self-termination of espionage
activities in late 1944 would protect his legacy, a belief shared by his own
children until 1995.[7]

However, evidence that Duncan Lee was a Soviet mole in the OSS
became apparent by the mid-1990s. The National Security Agency had
monitored the New York office radio transmission and determined

that a mole, code-named "Koch" or "Kokh," had passed on information from top-secret documents known only to the director and assistant directors of the OSS. However, the spy remained unidentified until Elizabeth Bentley reported to the New York office that "Koch" revealed to her an OSS plan to sneak Korean communists into Japan in 1945, information that carried a high probability of originating from Lee. Further evidence came from former KGB officer Alexander Vassiliev, who took notes of the Soviet intelligence agency NKVD records in which Koch took a trip to Chungking in late June 1943 and returned to the United States in October 1943. This spy's itinerary matched the exact location and time period registered on Duncan Lee's OSS personnel (duty station) card.[8]

Lee's life illustrates the important lessons American intelligence officers learned about loyalty. Lee, like Lauchlin Currie, Martha Dodd, Alger Hiss, Michael Straight, Donald Wheeler, and Harry White, had an elite education, was socially well-connected, and hailed from a family with long established roots in the United States. Yet Lee, as had others, embraced a supra-national loyalty to the cause of the working class, for which wartime survival of the Soviet Union became vital. As Captain Stanley Arnold of the Office of the Provost Marshal admitted after the war in his report on the mass removal and internment of Japanese Americans, loyalty was not determined by citizenship nor, one might add, by the historical self. Instead, individuals most likely to engage in espionage for a foreign power against the interests of the United States were those who hailed from well-established families. Applied to Duncan Lee, counterintelligence officials learned they should have examined high-level, elite European Americans before suspecting Asian Americans.[9]

An important lesson these officials failed to learn was the meaning of treason. In Duncan Lee's case, he was not a traitor even if the FBI sought to prosecute him as such, since some of the legal requirements were missing. True, he betrayed his oath of office by submitting top-secret information to Mary Price and Elizabeth Bentley, which was done knowing the information would reach Moscow. But the Constitution stipulates in Article III that an individual who owes allegiance to the United States must be engaged in "levying war" against the country. Even though he owed allegiance to the United States, Duncan Lee did not engage in levying war against it, and the requirement of two witnesses to his alleged treasonous act was never met. Admittedly, his actions knowingly provided "aid and comfort" to the Soviet Union, a country that was an ally, not an enemy. For Lee and for others who assisted Soviet intelligence during World War II, their motives were not at all treasonous, as Elizabeth Bentley revealed:

> They felt very strongly that we were allies with the Russians; that Russia was bearing the brunt of the war; that she must have every assistance because the people from within the Government, from what they had been able to dig up, were not giving her things that we should give her, things that we were giving to Britain and not to her. And they felt that it was their duty, actually, to get this stuff to Russia because she was hard-pressed and weakening, and someone must help her.

When one considers that Lee's passing of information to Moscow might have actually helped deter Stalin from making a separate peace treaty with Hitler, Lee may have actually saved the lives of countless American and British soldiers who would otherwise have had to bear the full brunt of the German forces had the Soviet Union withdrawn from the war.[10]

By focusing on Duncan Lee and other "underground" members of the CPUSA, attention is deflected from where blame—if any—should be placed. Although the FBI was successful in countering German espionage during World War II, it proved incompetent in dealing with other targets of its counterintelligence efforts. J. Edgar Hoover ignored the warning of an impending Imperial Japanese attack on Pearl Harbor by both British intelligence on August 14, 1941 and its British double agent Dusan Popov, code-named "Tricycle." Despite the bureau's multiplying its personnel devoted to counterintelligence sevenfold from 1936 to 1945, it failed miserably in detecting and maintaining surveillance over those Communist Party members who passed on classified information to Soviet intelligence. No doubt it was partly constrained by President Franklin Roosevelt, who did not want additional strains on the alliance, as fragile as it was, by exposing these foreign agents' activities. But Hoover's agents failed to keep track of them after the war ended, which attests to his poor skills in counterintelligence. As Mark Bradley, former CIA officer and Department of Justice attorney, points out, Hoover's persecution of the American Communists simply forced them to become adept at secrecy—techniques that would serve them and Soviet intelligence well when the latter turned desperately to them for assistance in the late 1930s, after Stalin executed many of their best intelligence officers. President Harry Truman should have fired J. Edgar Hoover for his incompetence, which might spared the nation the political convulsions and ruined careers with wrongful accusations that took place during the early years of the Cold War.[11]

A similar pattern of incompetence could be found in other federal government agencies as well. The State Department under Cordell Hull must share some of the blame. During the 1930s its security was dangerously lax, with sensitive diplomatic correspondence entrusted to regular foreign postal services carried on foreign-registered vessels sailing across the Atlantic, until 1935 when Congress passed appropriations for State to reinstitute its own courier service. Within the department's own offices security measures were equally lax, as Noel Field, Soviet mole inside the department where he worked since the 1920s, testified:

> The institution, and consequently, the mentality of the State Department, was rather provincial in my days. This was evident from the careless manner in which state secrets were managed. The most secret documents, sometimes in multiple copies, circulated from hand to hand. Thus, I saw not merely the telegraph messages, but almost everything concerning the department.

The OSS was not above reproach either. The OSS imposed strict security measures—secretaries typing research reports were assigned every third page to prevent them from seeing the entire document. Yet Donovan himself was careless at times, forgetting his briefcase full of classified documents in a cab once and leaving the door to his St. Regis suite open with secret papers spread over his bed. Worse, Donovan, along with many American leaders in high positions and those on the lower end of the OSS leadership, were seduced into thinking that a common elite background over many generations in the United States, buttressed by a similar physical or racial (i.e., white) appearance would be a sufficient guarantee of a loyalty. They failed to fully tap those with much shorter family histories and social connections to America, even as they discounted race in their recruitment of agents. After the OSS reconstituted itself into the CIA, they slowly but finally learned that loyalty does not require long historical roots and can flourish among the children of immigrant parents who came from the other side of the Pacific Ocean, in East Asia where that war, and later wars, would be waged.[12]

NOTES

PROLOGUE

1. Oath of Office, December 27, 1944, Folder Koide, Teiji, Box 415 Office of Strategic Services Personnel Files (hereafter OSSPF), Entry 224, Record Group 226 Records of the Office of Strategic Services, National Archives and Records Administration II, College Park, MD (hereafter RG 226 OSS/NARAII).

2. Jin Konomi, "Reminiscences of Joe Koide" (Part 1), *Pacific Citizen*, June 27, 1980, 8; Taketoshi Yamamoto, *Buraku Puropaganda: Bōryaku no Rajio* [Black Propaganda: Strategic Radio] (Tokyo: Iwanami Shoten, 2002), 140; Thomas J. McFadden to R. E. Simpson, October 14, 1944, Folder Koide, Teiji, Box 415 OSSPF, Entry 224, RG 226 OSS/NARA II.

3. James Oda, *Heroic Struggles of Japanese Americans: Partisan Fighters From America's Concentration Camps* (North Hollywood, CA: KNI Inc., 1981), 184 and his *Secret Embedded in Magic Cables: The Story of a 101 year old Japanese communist leader who served Japan, KGB and CIA* (Northridge, CA: KNI Inc., 1993), 43, 48–51.

4. Vincent Curl to Eifler, March 25, 1945 and C. W. Campbell and H. Kaplan to Paul McCallen, Student Progress Report Communications Training, March 31, 1945, Folder Curl's Rpts #1, Box 4, Carl Eifler Papers (hereafter CEP), the Hoover Institution, Stanford University, Stanford, CA (hereafter cited as HISU).

5. George Johnson, The NAPKO Project[:] Office of Strategic Services Field Experimental Unit March 30, 1945, Folder 29, Box 3 Honolulu OSS, Entry 139A, RG 226 OSS/NARA II.

6. Vincent Curl to Eifler, March 18, 1945, Folder Curl's Rpts #1, Box 4, CEP/HISU and Lt. (Robert) Carter, Evaluation, ca. March 1945, Folder Curl's Rpts #1, Box 4, CEP/HISU.

7. F(lorence) W[.] F(arquhar) to Files, January 23, 1945; C(arol) J[.] B(auman) to Files, January 13, 1945; and Security Officer (A. van Beuren) to Lt. Col. Donald Gregory, February 1, 1945, Folder 615 Security, Box 79, Entry 140, RG 226 OSS/NARA II.

8. Robert E. Clark, memo January 25, 1945, Folder 615, and Donald Gregory to O.C. Doering Jr., February 5, 1945 and Robert Clark to (blank), January 25, 1945, Folder 615, Entry 140 Box 79, RG 226 OSS/NARA II.

9. Wilfred Smith to Strategic Services Officer, China Theater [Richard Heppner], February 25, 1945, Box 84 OSS History Office, Entry 99, RG 226 OSS/NARA II; Lincoln Kan, Separation Process, March 19, 1946, Folders Kan, Lincoln, Box 389 OSSPF, Entry 224, RG 226 OSS/NARA II; John Whiteclay Chambers II, *OSS Training in the National Parks and Service Abroad in World War II* (Washington, DC: US National Park Service, 2008), 438–39; C. M. Parkin Jr. to Strategic Services Officer, CT (Richard Heppner), March 25, 1945, Folder 3172 Kunming-Akron

Mission, Box 185 Kunming, Entry 154, RG 226 OSS/NARA II; Paul Helliwell to Operations Officers, Communications Officer, Wilfred Smith, April 9, 1945, Folder 3172, Box 185 Kunming Office, Entry 154, RG 226 OSS/NARA II.

10. Ben Smith to Commanding Officer, Akron Mission, July 13, 1945, Folder 3172 Kunming-Akron Mission, Entry 154, Box 185 Kunming, RG 226 OSS/NARA II; Form of Chinese Certificate, December 27, 1924, File 23962/14–1 KAN Sat Hing, Immigration Arrival Investigation Case Files, 1884–1944, Archival Research Catalog (ARC) ID #296445, San Francisco District Office, RG 85 Immigration and Naturalization Service (hereafter INS), National Archives and Records Administration (hereafter NARA)/San Bruno, CA.; Lewis Reynolds, Statement by Lydia Kan, alleged mother, August 26, 1925 and John Zurbrick to the Chinese Inspector in Charge, August 1, 1925, Lincoln Kan, Case 25,282, Box 174 RG 85 Chinese Exclusion Index, NARA/New York; *The Columbian* (Shanghai American School, 1936), 114, Angie Mills Papers, Chicago; "China to Wilmington Is a Long Way, But They Have Mutual Friends" ca. June 2, 1942, Betty F. Kan Papers, Chapel Hill, NC; Charles Fenn, *At the Dragon's Gate: With the OSS in the Far East* (Annapolis, MD: Naval Institute Press, 2004), 81–82.

11. "Kentucky," Report YH/CK 142/45, June 11, 1945, Folder 283, Entry 140, Box 37; Indochina Intelligence Report G.B.T. Group, May 22, 1945, Folder 314, Entry 140, Box 40, RG 226 OSS/NARA II; "Kentucky," Report YH/CK 142/45, June 11, 1945, Folder 283, Entry 140, Box 37, RG 226 OSS/NARA II; Robert J. Antony, "We are Not Pirates," *Journal of World* History 28, no. 2 (June 2017), 258-60; Nom Wong, General View of the Military Espionage Organization of the Japanese General Staff with Notes on the More Important Branches, ca. November 7, 1945, Folder 410 Raw Intelligence–Disseminated "Tampa, Fla.," Box 51 Kunming-SI, Entry 140, RG 226 OSS/NARA II.

12. Wilfred Smith to Strategic Services Officer, China Theater [Richard Heppner], February 25, 1945, Box 84 OSS History Office, Entry 99, RG 226 OSS/NARA II.

13. Herbert Little to MO Reports Office, Asiatic War Diary, Washington/Far East 1945, 22–24, 27 and OSS MO Branch, History of "Blossom" Radio (Green's Project), n.d., 33–37, Folder 2500, Box 188 Wash-MO, Entry 139, RG 226 OSS/NARA II; Henson Robinson to Philip Allen, February 20, 1945, Robert Carter Jr. Papers, Catalina Island Museum, Records Center, Avalon, CA.; Vincent Curl to Eifler, March 4, 1945, Folder Curl's Rpts #1, Box 4, CEP/HISU; Eifler to Donovan, March 7, 1945, Folder 1, Box 521, Entry 92, RG 226 OSS/NARA II.

14. Wilfred Smith to Strategic Services Officer (Richard Heppner), March 25, 1945, Box 84 OSS History Office, Entry 99, RG 226 OSS/NARA II.

15. Duncan Lee to General Donovan, May 4, 1945, Subfolder WN 13222, Folder 7 WN 13320-13325, Box 340 OSS Washington Director's Office, Entry 210, RG 226 OSS/NARA II; Paul Helliwell to Turner McBaine, August 23, 1945, Subfolder WN 13323, Folder 7 WN 13320-13325, Box 340 OSS Washington Director's Office, Entry 210, RG 226 OSS/NARA II.

INTRODUCTION

1. Lon Kurashige, *Two Faces of Exclusion: The Untold History of Anti-Asian Racism in the United States* (Chapel Hill: University of North Carolina Press, 2016), 140–69; (William J. Donovan), "Remarks of Major General William J. Donovan, USA, Director of Strategic Services, at Final Gathering of OSS Employees," September 28, 1945, Folder YAMADA, HATSUMI, Box 856 OSSPF, Entry 224, RG 226 OSS/NARA II.

2. There are 414 Asian Americans among the 23,798 names listed in the OSS Personnel Index. Estimates of the actual number of OSS employees, however, vary considerably. Archivist Larry McDonald believes the total number is closer to 13,000, since this list includes many names of individuals not formally employed in the OSS. Yale historian Robin Winks thought the opposite, estimating they numbered about 26,000. The CIA's two-volume set titled "OSS Personnel List A-K and L-Z" contains 21,087. See Lawrence H. McDonald, "The OSS and Its Records," in *The Secrets War: The Office of Strategic Services in World War II*, ed. George C. Chalou (Washington, DC: National Archives and Records Administration, 1992), 85 and Robin W. Winks, "Getting the Right Stuff: FDR, Donovan, and the Quest for Professional Intelligence," in *The Secrets War*, ed. Chalou, 24.

3. Bradley F. Smith, *The Shadow Warriors: O.S.S. and the Origins of the C.I.A.* (New York: Basic Books, Inc., 1983), 130, 312, 379–80; Douglas Waller, *Wild Bill Donovan: The Spymaster Who Created The OSS and Modern American Espionage* (New York: Free Press, 2011), 5, 92, 364, 21, 80, 89.

4. J. R. Hayden to General [William] Donovan, April 15, 1943, Folder 0048, Box 001, CREST (CIA Records Search Tool), NARA II; Waller, Wild Bill Donovan (2015), 232–34. Joseph Hayden was the OSS's only agent on the Philippines. Sterling Seagrave and Peggy Seagrave, *Gold Warriors: America's Secret Recovery of Yamashita's Gold* (New York: Verso, 2005) claim Edward Lansdale was another OSS agent in the Philippines, and Max Boot's oral interviews with Lansdale family members assert the same, as presented in *The Road Not Taken: Edward Lansdale and the American Tragedy in Vietnam* (New York: Liveright Publishing Co., 2018). However, there is no documentary evidence to substantiate this claim. Both the OSS Personnel Database and the CIA Index of OSS personnel do not list him as part of the OSS. Furthermore, the claim that the OSS was involved in the secret confiscation of General Tomoyuki Yamashita's gold treasure allegedly buried in the Philippines is a myth. See Jose Eleazar R. Bersales, "Looking for Yamashita's Gold," *Philippines Quarterly of Culture and Society* 44, no. 3 (2016): 183–210. As for Thai Americans, they too are not covered in this study, as these students did not settle in the United States but joined the OSS only to establish themselves as part of ruling elite of Thailand. They are covered in E. Bruce Reynolds, *Thailand's Secret War: OSS, SOE, and the Free Thai Underground During World War II* (Cambridge: Cambridge University Press, 2005).

5. Yossi Shain and Aharon Barth, "Diasporas and International Relations Theory," *International Organization* 57, no. 3 (Summer 2003): 449; George P. Fletcher, *Loyalty: An Essay on the Morality of Relationships* (New York: Oxford University Press, 1993), 3–8, 24, 33–36, 57; Simon Keller, *The Limits of Loyalty* (Cambridge: Cambridge University Press, 2007), 21, 56–60; J. H. Leek, "Treason and the Constitution," *Journal of Politics* 13, no. 4 (November 1951): 608; Timothy Brook, *Collaboration: Japanese Agents and Local Elites in Wartime China* (Cambridge, MA: Harvard University Press, 2005), 1–2.

6. John Ferris, "Intelligence," in *The Origins of World War Two: The Debate Continues*, ed. Robert Boyce and Joseph A. Maiolo (New York: Palgrave Macmillan, 2003), 308; Jon Robb-Webb, "Anglo-American Naval Intelligence Cooperation in the Pacific, 1944–45," *Intelligence and National Security* 22, no. 5 (2007): 769; David Kahn, *The Codebreakers: The Story of Secret Writing* (New York: Scribner, 1996), xvi–xvii; Miles Copeland, *The Real Spy World* (London: Sphere Books, Ltd., 1978), 107, 109;

Nigel West, *Historical Dictionary of International Intelligence* (Lanham, MD: The Scarecrow Press, Inc., 2006), 89, 170; Lawrence C. Soley, *Radio Warfare: OSS and CIA Subversive Propaganda* (New York: Praeger, 1989), 25.

7. Brian Masaru Hayashi, *Democratizing the Enemy: The Japanse American Internment* (Princeton, NJ: Princeton University Press, 2004), 43-52.

8. Lawrence H. McDonald, "The OSS and Its Records," in *The Secrets War*, ed. Chalou, 78–79, 88.

9. Pierre Nora, "Between Memory and History: Les Lieux de Mémoire," *Representations* 26 (Spring 1989): 7–24; Kathryn L. Nasstrom, "Between Memory and History: Autobiographies of the Civil Rights Movement and the Writings of Civil Rights History," *Journal of Southern History* 74, no. 2 (May 2008): 334–35; Robert E. McGlone, "Deciphering Memory: John Adams and the Authorship of the Declaration of Independence," *Journal of American History* 85, no. 2 (September, 1998): 416–24.

10. Elizabeth P. McIntosh, *Sisterhood of Spies: The Women of the OSS* (Annapolis, MD: Naval Institute Press, 1998) and *Undercover Girl* (New York: Macmillan, 1947); Thomas N. Moon and Carl F. Eifler, *The Deadliest Colonel* (Springfield, MA: Vantage Press, 1975); Joe Koide, *Aru Zaibei Nihonjin no Kiroku: Renin Gakko kara Nichibei Kaisen made Jō* [Recollections of a Japanese in America, Volume 1: From the Lenin School to the Beginnings of the US-Japan War] and *Aru Zaibei Nihonjin no Kiroku Ge: Nichibei Kaisen kara Shusen made* [Recollections of a Japanese in American, volume 2: From the Beginnings of the US-Japan War until Its End] (Tokyo: Yushindo, 1970).). Section 523, Public Law 104–106, passed in 1996, released military intelligence personnel from their legal obligations to maintain secrecy. See James C. McNaughton, Kristen E. Edwards, and Jay M. Price, "'Incontestable Proof Will Be Exacted': Historians, Asian Americans, and the Medal of Honor," *The Public Historian* 24, no. 4 (Fall 2002): 16.

11. Asian American historian Yuji Ichioka urges historians to examine Japanese Americans who were loyal to Japan to under "the Nisei generation is all its complexities." See his "The Meaning of Loyalty: The Case of Kazumaro Buddy Uno," *Amerasia Journal* 23, no. 3 (Winter 1997–1998): 63.

12. John Dower, *War without Mercy: Race and Power in the Pacific War* (New York: Pantheon, 1986); Peter Schrijvers, *The GI War against Japan: Americans Soldiers in Asia and the Pacific during World War II* (New York: New York University Press, 2005); Michael Omi and Howard Winant, *Racial Formation in the United States: From the 1960s to the 1990s* (New York: Routledge, 1994); Lon Kurashige, *Two Faces of Exclusion: The Untold History of Anti-Asian Racism in the United States* (Chapel Hill: University of North Carolina Press, 2016).

CHAPTER 1

1. Wendell E. Pritchett, "A National Issue: Segregation in the District of Columbia and the Civil Rights Movement at Mid-Century," *Georgetown Law Journal* 93 (2005): 1328–330; David A. Nichols, "'The Showpiece of Our Nation': Dwight D. Eisenhower and the Desegregation of the District of Columbia," *Washington History* 16, no. 2 (Fall/Winter 2004/2005): 46.

2. Thomas F. Troy, *Donovan and the CIA: A History of the Establishment of the Central Intelligence Agency* (Frederick, MD: University Publications of America, 1981), 90; Anthony Cave Brown, *The Last Hero: Wild Bill Donovan* (New York: Times Books, 1982), 164–65.

3. Memorandum on the Functions of the Secret Intelligence Service of the Office of Strategic Services, October 24, 1942, Folder 2, Box 173 COI/OSS Central Files, Entry 92, RG 226 OSS/NARA II.

4. Robin W. Winks, "Getting the Right Stuff: FDR, Donovan, and the Quest for Professional Intelligence," in *The Secrets War: The Office of Strategic Services in World War II*, ed. George C. Chalou (Washington, DC: National Archives and Records Administration, 1992), 24–25 and John Whiteclay Chambers II, *OSS Training in the National Parks and Service Abroad in World War II* (Washington, DC: US National Park Service, 2008), 34, 465.

5. Shen Yu, "SACO: An Ambivalent Experience of Sino-American Cooperation during World War II" (PhD diss., University of Illinois-Urbana Champaign, 1996), 79; Maochun Yu, *OSS in China: Prelude to Cold War* (New Haven, CT: Yale University Press, 1996), 50–55, 73–75, 95, 97–98; Donovan Webster, *The Burma Road: The Epic Story of the Chinese-Burma-India Theater in World War II* (Waterville, ME: Thorndike Press, 2003), 24–25, 88–89.

6. Richard J. Aldrich, *Intelligence and the War against Japan: Britain, America and the Politics of Secret Service* (Cambridge: Cambridge University Press, 2000), 20, 215–16, 283; Keith Jeffery, *MI6: The History of the Secret Intelligence Service, 1909–1949* (London: Bloomsbury, 2010), 573; Tommy Drew-Brook to Herbert Sichel, July 27, 1944 and August 8, 1944, Folder HS 8/93; Herbert Sichel to B.P.B. Washington, July 31, 1944, Folder HS 8/98, Records of the Special Operations Executive, The National Archives, Kew, London (hereafter cited as SOE/NAKL); Brief History of OSS/CBI to 26 October, 1944, 1, Folder 1, Box 72, Entry 99, RG 226 OSS/NARA II; Turner McBaine to W.J. Donovan, August 3, 1944, 8–9, 5–6, Folder #1, Box 393 Declassified, Entry 210, RG 226 OSS/NARA II.

7. David Stafford, *Camp X* (New York: Dodd, Mead & Co. 1987), xiv–xvi; Chambers II, *OSS Training in the National Parks*, 417.

8. Troy, *Donovan and the CIA*, 84–85, 165–66, 222, 253; Barry M. Katz, *Foreign Intelligence: Research and Analysis in the Office of Strategic Services, 1942–1945* (Cambridge, MA: Harvard University Press, 1989), 5, 6, 9, 13, 21–22; Office of the Coordinator of Information, n.d., Folder 2:8,743 1942, Box 73 COI/OSS Central Files, RG 226 OSS/NARA II.

9. Alan M. Winkler, *The Politics of Propaganda: The Office of War Information, 1942–1945* (New Haven, CT: Yale University Press, 1978), 8–19; Brown, *The Last Hero*, 237; John Coughlin to Tom [Moon], December 5, 1971, Folder The Deadliest Colonel, Box 3 CEP/HISU.

10. Philip Phillips, "Alfred Marsten Tozzer, 1877–1954," *American Antiquity* 21, no. 1 (July 1955): 72–80; Alfred M. Tozzer, "History of Honolulu Outpost," ca. 1945, 2–4, 10–13, 5, Folder 790, Box 78, Entry 139, RG 226 OSS/NARA II.

11. J. R. Hayden to W. W. Haggard, June 26, 1941, Folder Correspondence-June 1941 and University of Michigan College of Literature, Science, and the Arts Faculty Record, ca. 1943, Folder Correspondence, 1943 Box 8, Joseph Ralston Hayden Papers, Bentley Historical Library, University of Michigan, Ann Arbor, MI (hereafter JRHP/UM); Joseph Ralston Hayden, *The Philippines: A Study in National Development* (New York: Macmillan, 1941) and *Pacific Affairs* (Minneapolis: University of Minnesota Press, 1937); Joseph Hayden, Application for Employment, Coordinator of Information, September 6, 1941 and COI to Joseph Hayden, September 2, 1941, Folder Joseph R. Hayden, Box 320 OSSPF, Entry 224, RG 226 OSS/NARA II; J.R. Hayden to William Donovan, October 9, 1943, Folder Correspondence, 1943, Box 8, JRHP/UM.

12. Personal Data Sheet; L. A. Peter Gosling and George Kish, "Professor Emeritus Robert B. Hall," ca. April 4, 1975; and Samuel Dana and Clark Hopkins, "In Memoriam Robert Burnett Hall 1896–1975," ca. April 4, 1975, Folder Faculty Material Robert Hall Obituaries 1975, Box 5 University of Michigan, Center for Japanese Studies, Bentley Historical Library, University of Michigan, Ann Arbor, MI; S.P. Poole to Commanding General, Officer Procurement Service, January 6, 1943, Box 14, RG 263 CIA Personnel Records, NARA II; Application and Personal History Statement, November 1, 1942 and Personal History Statement, November 1, 1942 and Personnel Action Request Form, OSS, October 8, 1942; William Donovan to Robert Hall, January 14, 1943, Box 306 OSSPF, Entry 224, RG 226 OSS/NARA II.

13. Captain Wyman H. Packard, *A Century of U.S. Naval Intelligence* (Washington, DC: Department of the Navy, 1996), 21, 43–44; Troy, *Donovan and the CIA*, 87, 90; Mark Fritz, "The Secret (Insurance) Agent Men," *Los Angeles Times*, September 22, 2000; Ron Shelp and Al Ehrbar, *Fallen Giant: The Amazing Story of Hank Greenberg and the History of AIG* (Hoboken, NJ: John Wiley & Sons, 2006), 49–50.

14. Writing Services Company, *Cornelius Vander Starr, 1892–1968* (New York: Starr Foundation, 1970), 6–9, 4–5, 8–9, 41; Shelp and Ehrbar, *Fallen Giant*, 28, 39, 49–50; "Men of Shanghai," *Fortune* XI, no. 1 (January 1935): 115.

15. Esson McDowell Gale, *Basics of the Chinese Civilization: A Topical Survey, with Reading* (Shanghai: Kelly and Walsh, 1934) and "Public Administration of Salt in China: A Historical Survey," *The Annals of the American Academy of Political and Social Science* 152, 1 (November 1, 1930): 241–51.

16. Application and Personal History, September 26, 1941; Application for Employment, ca. September 26, 1941. He terminated his OSS services as of September 30, 1942. See G. Howland Shaw to Donovan, n.d., Folder Gale, Esson, Box 258 OSSPF, Entry 224, RG 226 OSS/NARA II; William Donovan to Esson Gale, February 5, 1942, Folder China in World War II 1941–1942, Box 2, Esson Gale Papers, Bentley Historical Library, University of Michigan, Ann Arbor, MI (hereafter cited as EMGP/UM); John Simon Guggenheim Memorial Foundation, Fellowship Application Form, October 14, 1955, Anon., "Esson M. Gale Personal Data," n.d., and Anon., "Esson M. Gale, "Advanced Studies & Research Accomplished" n.d., Folder Gale Biographical and bibliographical information, Box 1, EMGP/UM; D. P. S. Roberts, Shanghai Municipal Police Report, September 26, 1939, RG 263 Shanghai Municipal Police Records, Microfilm M1750, Reel 58, File 9451, NARA II; Esson Gale to Daniel Poling, December 4, 1961, Folder Correspondence, 1961–65, Box 1 EMGP/UM; Esson Gale to Dorothy May Bell, August 15, 1955, Folder Correspondence, 1955; Esson Gale, "First Interim Report," February 26, 1958, Folder Correspondence, 1957, Box 1; (Esson Gale) to Mortimer Graves, February 15, 1935, Folder Correspondence, 1935; C.W. Nimitz to Doctor Gale, January 10, 1939, Folder Correspondence 1939; C.W. Nimitz to (Essen) Gale, October 25, 1941, Folder Correspondence 1941–45, Box 1, EMGP/UM. See also Esson M. Gale, *Salt for the Dragon: A Personal History of China 1908-1945* (East Lansing: Michigan State College Press, 1953). 5-6, 9, 13, 54-58, 73-77, 100-06, 146-50, 166-68, 180-90, 200-15.

17. Joseph Hayden to William Donovan, June 10, 1942, Folder 38, Box 2, Entry 92, RG 226 OSS/NARA II; G. Holland Shaw to Esson Gale, December 2, 1941, Folder Correspondence, 1941–45, Box 1 EMGP/UM.

18. Esson Gale to Joseph Hayden, February 7, 1942, Folder 38, Box 2, Entry 92, RG 226 OSS/NARA II.

19. Esson Gale to Joseph Hayden, October 23, 1941, Folder Gale Biographical and bibliographical information, Box 1, EMGP/UM; David Williamson to G. Howland Shaw, May 13, 1942; COI to (Esson) Gale, May 13, 1942; (Esson) Gale to (Joseph) Hayden, May 6, 1942, Folder 38, Box 2, Entry 92, RG 226 OSS/NARA II.

20. Esson Gale to Franklin Roosevelt, December 20, 1945, Folder Correspondence, 1941–1945, Box 1, EMGP/UM.

21. (Joseph) Hayden to (Esson) Gale, June 5, 1942, Folder 38, Box 2, Entry 92, RG 226 OSS/NARA II; Ernest Price to Hugh Wilson, September 12, 1942 and (Esson) Gale to J. McCracken Fisher, August 10, 1942, Folder 38, Box 2, Entry 92, RG 226 OSS/NARA II.

22. Shen, "SACO"; Michael Schaller, "SACO! The United States Navy's Secret War in China," *Pacific Historical Review* 44, no. 4 (1975): 527–53.

23. Charles Frederick Remer, *Foreign Trade of China* (Shanghai: Commercial Press, 1926), *A Study of Chinese Boycotts with Special Reference to Their Economic Effectiveness* (Baltimore: Baltimore, The Johns Hopkins Press, 1933), and *Foreign Investments in China* (NewYork: Macmillan, 1933).

24. Katz, *Foreign Intelligence*, 23; Charles Remer, Personnel Action Request, May 18, 1943, Folder Remer, Charles, Box 639 OSSPF, Entry 224, RG 226 OSS/NARA II; C.F. Remer, Supplementary Statement on International Investment in the Far East, Institute Secretariat Institute of Pacific Relations New York, November 1939, 1, Folder "International Investment in the Far East and Suggestions for Research" 1939, Box 3 and "The War in the Far East," ca. 1940, 3, Folder War in the Far East, Box 31, C. F. Remer Papers, HISU.

25. Charles Stelle, "Americans and the China Opium Trade in the Nineteenth Century." Ph.D. diss., University of Chicago (1938).

26. Howard Nelson, "In Memoriam," *Annals of the Association of American Geographers* 75, no. 4 (1985): 595–603 and *The Polar Front Blast: Official Journal of the U.C.L.A. Geographic Society* V, no. 2 (1 August 1944), 1–2, Folder 17, Box 1, Joseph Spencer Papers, Collection 1543, Special Collections, University of California, Los Angeles (hereafter UCLA).

27. Statement—J. K. Fairbank, October 31, 1951, Folder Military Review Board—October 31, 1951 Statement (Draft), Box 4 John King Fairbank Papers, Harvard University; John King Fairbank, *Chinabound: a fifty-year memoir* (New York: Harper & Row, 1982); Paul A. Cohen and Merle Goldman, eds., *Fairbank Remembered* (Cambridge, MA: John K. Fairbank Center for East Asian Research and Harvard University Press, 1992).

28. Passport United States of America, No. 16595, Folder Personal Material Passports, I.D. Cards 1929–1978, Box 2, IV 2B 44; Caroline Bailey, A Conversation with Charles Burton Fahs (August 1979) in Mrs. Charles Burton Fahs, "Charles Burton Fahs, Scholar, Diplomat, Humanist: Notes on the Life of an International Man," n.d., manuscript, 6; Jamie Ross Fahs, "A Short Personal Biography of Charles Burton Fahs," 67–68, Folder Draft of Biog of CB Fahs by Mrs. (Jamie) Fahs, IV 2B 44; Charles Fahs, Political Diary, January 29, 1932, Folder Personal Materials Political Diary 1932, Box 2 IV 2B 44; Charles B. Fahs, *Government in Japan: Recent Trends in its Scope and Operation* (New York: International Secretariat, Institute of Pacific Relations, 1940), I.P.R. Inquiry Series, Box 2 IV 2B 44, Charles B. Fahs Papers, Rockefeller Archives Center, Sleepy Hallow, NY.

29. Randall Gould, *Chungking Today* (Shanghai: The Mercury Press, 1941), 24–25, 29–30, Writing Services Company, *Cornelius Vander Starr, 1892–1968*, 12, 41, 44–45; Shelp with Al Ehrbar, *Fallen Giant*, 37, 47–48; "Men of Shanghai," *Fortune* Vol. XI,

No. 1 (January 1935), 115; Anon, New York, November 16, 1942, HS 1/165, SOE/ NAKL; N. F. Allman, History-Far East SI, ca. 1945, 23, Folder 6–17: "History—Far East, SI," Box 6, Norwood F. Allman Papers (hereafter cited as NFAP/HISU).

30. Duff family, James Arthur Duff (1996), 1–3, Folder 1–1; Certified Copy of an Entry of Birth within the District of the British Consulate at Kiukiang-China, Application Number 6528H, May 22, 1981, Folder 1–14; Passport Canada Number 3-14981, March 22, 1947, Folder 1–15, Box 1; Duff family, James Arthur Duff (1996), 3, Folder 1–1, Box 1; J. Arthur Duff, no title, ca1978, Folder 1–2, Box 1; Major S.V.C., To Whom It May Concern, March 31, 1938, Folder 2–4, Box 2, J. Arthur Duff Papers (hereafter cited as JADP/HISU); [JAD], Office of Strategic Services—JAD 1942–1943, July 1984, 1–4, Folder 2–4, Box 2; Randall Gould, News Letter No. 40 (February 14, 1942) to the Executives of the Starr Group and Other Friends, Folder 4–3, Box 4 JADP/HISU.

31. J. Arthur Duff, Notes on "Child of Empire," 1984, Folder 2–7, Box 2; J. Arthur Duff, Confidential—For General Wedemeyer Compliments of JAD, 6–7, August 17, 1943, Folder 2–6, Box 2, JADP/HISU.

32. (J. Arthur Duff), Office of Strategic Services 1942–1943, Folder 2–4, Box 2, JADP/HISU; David Bruce to Carolyn Copeland, October 10, 1942, Ernest Price to Kenneth Baker, September 30, 1942, and Kenneth H. Baker to N. F. Allman, October 26, 1942, Folder 11, Box 3, Entry 211, RG 226 OSS/NARA II; BB 232 (Major A. H. Samson) to O/X (London) and BB 100 (Meerut), July 5, 1943, HS 1/ 165; J. Arthur Duff to F.S. Crawford, June 12, 1943, Folder HS 1/165 OSS/SOE cooperation, 1942–44, HS 1/165 (Far East—China, OSS/SOE Co-operation, 1942 to 1944); O.111 (Crawford) to London, February 23, 1943, HS 1/165, SOE/NAKL; Certificate of Identification, No. 261, June 19, 1943, Folder 2–5, Box 2 JADP/ HISU.

33. (J. Arthur Duff), Office of Strategic Services—JAD 1942–1943, July 1984, 11–13, Folder 2–4, Box 2; Itinerary No. II, n.d., Wartime No. 2 Notes, 22–23, Folder 5–1: Memoirs Topics Wartime notes, Box 5; J. A(rthur) D(uff), The Morale of the Kwantung People, September 30, 1943, Folder 5–1 Memoirs Topics Wartime notes, Box 5, JADP/HISU; Agent BH-001 in Calcutta, India, report (secret) on Tai Li Operations in China, June 26, 1944, Folder 1, Box 72, Entry 210, RG 226 OSS/NARA II; J. Arthur Duff, Addendum to Starr/Donovan Relations, as per "Shadow Warriors" (Bradley F. Smith) 1984, Folder 2–7, Box 2, JADP/HISU.

34. New York Times March 2, 1987, D11; Bernard Wasserstein, Secret War in Shanghai: An Untold Story of Espionage, Intrigue, and Treason in World War II (Boston: Houghton Mifflin, 1999), 64; OSS Form 1193, Norwood Allman, Folder Allman, Norwood, Box 11 OSSPF, Entry 224, RG 226 OSS/NARA II.

35. N. F. Allman, History-Far East SI, ca. 1945, 1–14, Folder 6–17: "History—Far East, SI," n.d., Box 6, NFAP/HISU; Yu, OSS in China, 87.

36. Clare D. Kinsman, ed., Contemporary Authors Revised (Detroit, MI: Gale Research Co, 1967–68), Vol. 17–20, 108; Rev. D. C. Buchanan, "Inari: Its Origin, Development and Nature," Transaction of the Asiatic Society of Japan Second Series XII (1935); Daniel Crump Buchanan, Japanese Proverbs and Sayings (Norman: University of Oklahoma Press, 1965).

37. Ernest Price, "A Plan to Give Further Aid to China and Russia and to Establish Air Bases Behind the Japanese Lines," n.d., 4, 11, Folder 4–1, Box 4 Millard Preston Goodfellow Papers (hereafter cited as MPGP/HISU); Ernest Batson Price, The Russo-Japanese Treaties of 1907–1916 Concerning Manchuria and Mongolia

(Baltimore: Johns Hopkins University Press, 1933), 159; Director of the Consular Service to Ernest Price, May 5, 1914, Folder Biographical file, entry into the Foreign Service, Box 4; Price to William Calder, February 22, 1921, Folder Foreign Service Office Files Canton, China, American Consulate, 1920–1921, Box 9; Ernest Price to Hallett Abend, April 25, 1929, Folder Foreign Service Office Files Nanking, China, American Consulate, 1928–1929, Box 10, Ernest B. Price Papers (hereafter cited as EBPP/HISU); Ernest Price, A Plan to Give Further Aid to China and Russia and to Establish Air Bases Behind the Japanese Lines, n.d., 1,2, Folder 4–1, Box 4 MPGP/HISU; Ernest B. Price, "The Manchurians and Their New Deal," *Pacific Affairs* 8, no. 2 (June 1935): 165–67.

38. William Langer to William Donovan, March 3, 1942, Folder 4–1, Box 4 MPGP/HISU; Ernest Price to Allan Dulles, October 7, 1942, Folder 682, Box 49, Entry 168, RG 226 OSS/NARA II. See also Maochun Yu, *OSS in China: Prelude to Civil War* (New Haven, CT: Yale University Press, 1996), 80–81.

39. Yasutarō Soga, *Life Behind the Barbed Wire: The World War II Internment Memoirs of a Hawai'i Issei* (Honolulu: University of Hawai'i Press, 2008), 30–31; J. W. Stilwell to (Carl) Eifler, February 26, 1940, Folder The Deadliest Colonel, Box 3 CEP/HISU; Troy J. Sacquety, *The OSS in Burma: Jungle War against the Japanese* (Lawrence: University Press of Kansas, 2013), 18.

40. Personal History Statement, ca. 1943 and Acting Chief, MO Branch to Chairman, OSS Officers Board, December 8, 1943, Folder Kleiman, Max, Box 457 OSSPF, Entry 224, RG 226 OSS/NARA II.

41. Theater Service Record, August 20, [1945]; Emergency Addressee and Personal Property Card, August 30, 1943, Folder Kleiman, Max, Box 410 OSSPF, Entry 224, RG 226 OSS/NARA II; H.S. Prescott to D.C. Buchanan, Security Office Investigation Report, October 28, 1943, Box 19 RG 263 CIA Personnel Records, NARA II; H.S. Prescott to D.C. Buchanan, Security Office Investigation Report No. AA 8020-W, October 28, 1943, Folder Kleiman, Max, Box 410, Entry 224, RG 226 OSS/NARA II.

42. Elizabeth P. McIntosh, *Sisterhood of Spies: The Women of the OSS* (Annapolis, MD: Naval Institute Press, 1998), 52–53, 54–55, 197–98; Elizabeth P. MacDonald, *Undercover Girl* (New York: Macmillan, 1947), 5; Patrick Dolan to Morton Bodfish, January 20, 1944; Morton Bodfish to the Director, March 4, 1944, Folder 1 and Kenneth Mann to the Director OSS, February 1, 1945, Folder 2, Box 151 COI/OSS Central Files, Entry 92, RG 226 OSS/NARA II.

43. Morton Bodfish to the Director (Donovan), March 4, 1944, Folder 2 MO Allotments, Box 151, Entry 092, RG 226 OSS/NARA II.

44. Douglas Waller, *Wild Bill Donovan: The Spymaster Who Created The OSS and Modern American Espionage* (New York: Free Press, 2011), 21, 364, 5, 92, 89; William Donovan, Memorandum to the President, December 29, 1941, December 21, 1941, and Summary of Intelligence on South America, December 13, 1941, Folder Office of Strategic Services Reports: 12/ 18-27/41 #2, Box 147 Office of Strategic Services, Personal Secretary File, Franklin Delano Roosevelt Library, Hyde Park, NY (hereafter cited as PSF/FDRL).

45. (Donovan) Memorandum for the President, No. 258, February 17, 1942, Folder Reports: 2/12-20/42 #244-273, Box 148; Coordinator of Information, Memorandum for the President, December 15, 1941, Folder Reports: 12/12-17/ 41 #1, Box 147, Office of Strategic Services, PSF/FDRL.

46. Herbert Little, Personal History Statement, ca. 1943, Folders Little, Herbert, Box 457 OSSPF, Entry 224, RG 226 OSS/NARA II.

47. Daniel Buchanan, Application for Employment and Personal History Statement, June 19, 1943 and Daniel Buchanan, Personal Record, September 13, 1942, Folder 863, Box 50, Entry 92, RG 226 OSS/NARA II.

48. Brandon Palmer, "Images and Crimes of Koreans in Hawai'i: Media Portrayals, 1903–1925," in *From the Land of Hibiscus: Koreans in Hawaii, 1903–1950*, ed. Yŏng-ho Ch'oe (Honolulu: University of Hawai'i Press, 2007), 89–122; Craig S. Coleman, *American Images of Korea: Korea and Koreans as Portrayed in Books, Magazines, Television, News Media, and Film* (Elizabeth, NJ: Hollym, 1990), 65–76.

49. F.I.S. Directive—Far East—No. V—March 31–April 6, 1942, No. 24, frame 617, Roll 49; Ellery Huntington Jr., Memorandum to Mr. (no first name) Murphy, November 10, 1942, frames 216–17, Roll 66, M1642 Washington Director's Office Administrative Files, RG 226 OSS/NARA II.

50. Edwin Martin to William Langer, January 22, 1945, Folder 7, Box 4, Entry 1, RG 226 OSS/NARA II.

51. Norwood F. Allman, "China: Eyewitness 1916–1950," *Collier's 1953 Year Book*, 145, in Folder 6–4 "China: Eyewitness 1916–1950," 1953 Box 6, NFAP/HISU.

52. William Maddox to Charles Cheston, August 9, 1945, Folder 3, Box 275 Declassified, RG 226 OSS/NARA II; William Donovan to Secretary of War (Henry Stimson), February 17, 1942, Folder Office of Strategic Services Correspondence Jan. 1942–May 1942, Box 3, MPGP/HISU.

53. Aldrich, *Intelligence and the War against Japan*, 7; Ellery Huntington to Colonel Buxton, August 30, 1942, Folder WN 13658-13662, Box 344 OSS Washington Director's Office, Entry 210, RG 226 OSS/NARA II.

54. Ellery Huntington to Colonel Buxton, August 30, 1942, Folder WN 13658-13662, Box 344 Washington Director's Office, Entry 210, RG 226 OSS/NARA II.

CHAPTER 2

1. US Census Bureau, Reports on Population, Sixteenth Census of the United States: 1940, for Alaska, Hawai'i, Guam, and Samoa; and the Statistical Abstracts of the United States for the Philippines at http://1940census.archives.gov (accessed February 17, 2016).

2. Douglas Waller, *Wild Bill Donovan: The Spymaster Who Created The OSS and Modern American Espionage* (New York: Free Press, 2011), 79, 73; Robin Winks, "Getting the Right Stuff: FDR, Donovan, and the Quest for Professional Intelligence," in *The Secrets War: The Office of Strategic Services in World War II*, ed. George C. Chalou (Washington, DC: National Archives and Records Administration, 1992), 24.

3. Douglas W. Lee, "The Overseas Chinese Affairs Commission and the Politics of Patriotism in Chinese America in the Nanking Era, 1928–1945," *Annals of the Chinese Historical Society of the Pacific Northwest* (1984): 203–204, 208, 211, 216–20; Sherman Cochran, *Big Business in China: Sino-Foreign Rivalry in the Cigarette Industry, 1890-1930* (Cambridge, MA: Harvard University Press, 1980), 118–19, 270.

4. *The Chinese in Hawaii* Vol. 2 (September 1936), 58–59; I. H. Mayfield, "An Analysis of the Japanese Espionage Problem in the Hawaiian Islands," April 20, 1943, Appendix, A7, Folder Japanese Intelligence Activities—U.S. (Gen.), Box 1 Japanese Organization & Intelligence in US, Office of Naval Intelligence, Sabotage, Espionage, Counterespionage (SAC) Section, Oriental Desk, 1936-1946, Entry UD 29, RG 38 Office of the Chief of Naval Operations (hereafter cited as CNO)/NARA II; Brett de Bary and Victor Nee, "The Kuomintang in Chinatown," in *Counterpoint: Perspectives on Asian America*, ed. Emma Gee (Los Angeles: Regents

of the University of California and the Asian American Studies Center, 1976), 149–50.

5. K. Scott Wong, *Americans First: Chinese Americans and the Second World War* (Cambridge, MA: Harvard University Press, 2005), 188–89; Roger Daniels, *Asian America: Chinese and Japanese in the United States since 1850* (Seattle: University of Washington Press, 1988), 69, Table 3.1; Clarence E. Glick, *Sojourners and Settlers: Chinese Migrants in Hawaii* (Honolulu: University of Hawai'i Press, 1980), Table 10, 128.

6. "Table 2: Age, Race, and Sex for the Territory and for Honolulu City:1940 and 1930," 6, in US Census Bureau, *Reports on Population, Sixteenth Census of the United States: 1940, for Alaska, Hawaii, and Samoa* (Washingto, DC: US Government Printing Office, 1943) at http://1940census.archives.gov; Robert H. K. Chang, "The Military Record," in *The Chinese in Hawaii: Who's Who 1956–1957*, Vol. 3 (Honolulu: United Chinese Penman Club, 1957), 37; Romanzo Adams, *The Peoples of Hawaii* (New York: American Council, Institute of Pacific Relations, 1933), 33; Adam McKeown, *Chinese Migrant Networks and Cultural Change: Peru, Chicago, and Hawaii, 1900-1936* (Chicago: University of Chicago Press, 2001), 266–67; and Kum Pui Lai, "Occupational and Educational Adjustments of the Chinese in Hawaii," in *The Chinese of Hawaii*, Vol. II (Honolulu: Overseas Penman Club, 1936), 1–2.

7. Ernest S. Ing, "The Legal Status of the Chinese in Hawaii," in *The Chinese of Hawaii*, Vol. I (Honolulu: Overseas Penman Club, 1929), 26; F. Everett Robison, "Participation of Citizens of Chinese and Japanese Ancestry in the Political Life in Hawaii," *Social Process in Hawaii* IV (May 1938): 58; Glick, *Sojourners and Settlers*, 328–29; Francis Kang, "China's Plight Increases: Map and Comments," *The New Pacific*, October 1944, 17, 18.

8. *The Chinese in Hawaii*, Vol. 2 (September 1936), 37. The percentages were calculated based on the number of Chinese students enrolled in public and private schools with the numbers enrolled in Chinese language schools. See also Him Mark Lai, "Retention of the Chinese Heritage: Chinese Schools in America before World War II," *Chinese America: History and Perspectives* (2000): 10–31; Glick, *Sojourners and Settlers*, 23, 99–100 and Noriko Asato, *Teaching Mikadoism: The Attack on Japanese Language Schools in Hawaii, California, and Washington, 1919–1927* (Honolulu: University of Hawai'i Press, 2006), 114.

9. *Star Bulletin*, December 28, 1940; George F. M. Nellist, ed., *Pan-Pacific WHO'S WHO* (Honolulu: Honolulu Star-Bulletin, 1941), 1940–1941 edition; *Advertiser*, March 4, 1941; *Star Bulletin*, January 5, 1945; US Department of Labor, INS, Honolulu, File no. 4391/53 for CHUN MING, Archie, Applicant for a Certificate of Citizenship—Hawaiian Islands, April 15, 1937 and F. Arnold, Inspector, [Interview], April 15, 1937, National Archives and Records Administration, San Bruno, CA (hereafter cited as NARA/San Bruno); *The Chinese of Hawaii*, Vol. 2, 32; Franklin Odo, *No Sword to Bury: Japanese Americans in Hawaii during World War II* (Philadelphia: Temple University Press, 2004), 40; Thomas N. Moon and Carl F. Eifler, *The Deadliest Colonel* (Springfield, MA: Vantage Press, 1975), 36, 50, 112.

10. Kwock Lum Shee, "Family History," January 6, 1932 US Immigration Service, Honolulu, File 4380/3855 KWOCK, Lum Shee and Inspector C.B. Borella, Applicant for Form 432, August 15, 1931, File 4380/3855 KWOCK, Lum Shee, Case Files for Return Certificates—Lawfully Domiciled Chinese Laborers (4380), 1916-1938, Archival Research Catalog ID# 628298, Honolulu District Office, RG 85 INS, NARA/San Bruno; US Department of Labor, Immigration and

Naturalization Service, Receipt, July 10, 1939 and F. Arnold, Review and Findings, File 4500/3799, KWOCK, Yok San (John KWOCK), Case Files of US Citizens of Chinese Race Applying for Certificates of Citizenship—Hawaii Islands, Departing to the Continental US or Foreign Destinations (4500), 1924–42, Archival Research Catalog ID# 628463, Honolulu District Office, RG 85 INS, NARA/San Bruno; F. Arnold, Review and Findings, File 4500/3799, KWOCK, Yok San (John KWOCK), Case Files of US Citizens of Chinese Race Applying for Certificates of Citizenship—Hawaii Islands, Departing to the Continental US or Foreign Destinations (4500), 1924-42, Archival Research Catalog ID# 628463, Honolulu District Office, RG 85 INS, NARA/SB; Weston Howland, OSS Requisition by Name, November 16, 1943, to Chief, Personnel Procurement Branch/OSS; E. F. Connely to the Adjutant General, November 30, 1943; Lester Baylis, Security Office Investigation Report to C. J. Brown, February 14, 1944, Folder Kwock, John, Box 425 OSSPF, Entry 224, RG 226 OSS/NARA II.

11. L. Eve Armentrout Ma, *Revolutionaries, Monarchists, and Chinatowns: Chinese Politics in the Americas and the 1911 Revolution* (Honolulu: University of Hawai'i Press, 1990), 5–6, 10–11; Him Mark Lai, *Chinese American Transnational Politics* (Urbana: University of Illinois Press, 2010), 11–12, 14, 16–17.

12. The Nationalist Government followed the late Qing Dynasty practice of *jus sanguinis* or conferring citizenship upon Chinese regardless of residence and thereby defining Chinese Americans as Chinese citizens. For the late Qing era nationality law, see Tsai Chutung, "The Chinese Nationality Law, 1909," *American Journal of International Law* 4, no. 2 (April 1910): 407 and American Society of International Law, "Law on the Acquisition and Loss of Chinese Nationality," *American Society of International Law* 4, no. 2 (April 1910): 160. For the Nationalist Government making Chinese Americans into dual citizens through its nationality law passed on February 5, 1929, see Chiun Hungdah, "Nationality and International Law in Chinese Perspective with Special Reference to the Period Before 1950 and the Practice of the Administration at Taipei," in *Nationality and Internationality Law in Asian Perspective*, ed. Swan Sik Ko (Dordrecht, Neth.: Martinus Nijhoff Publishers, 1990), 36–37.

13. Renqiu Yu, *To Save China, To Save Ourselves: The Chinese Hand Laundry Alliance of New York* (Philadelphia: Temple University Press, 1992), 98, 79–80, 96–97; Madeline Y. Hsu, *Dreaming of Gold, Dreaming of Home* (Stanford, CA: Stanford University Press, 2000), 40; Mei Zheng, "Chinese Americans in San Francisco And New York City During the Anti-Japanese War: 1937–1945" (MA thesis, University of California Los Angeles, 1990), 59–60, 38–41; Yong Chen, *Chinese San Francisco, 1850-1943: A Trans-Pacific Community* (Stanford, CA: Stanford University Press, 2000), 236–37.

14. Hsu, *Dreaming of Gold, Dreaming of Home*, 177–78; Gloria H. Chun, "Go West . . . to China: Chinese American Identity in the 1930s," in *Claiming America: Constructing Chinese American Identities during the Exclusion Era*, ed. K. Scott Wong and Sucheng Chan (Philadelphia: Temple University Press, 1998), 173–75; Him Mark Lai, *Chinese American Transnational Politics*, 19–22.

15. Ernest K. Moy, "Sun Yat-Sen To Me: An Address by Ernest K. Moy," delivered at the Memorial Meeting to Observe the 30th Anniversary of the death of Sun Yat-sen, Sino-American Amity, Inc., March 12, 1955, 2–3, 5–7, Folder Ernest K. Moy, Box 128, Alfred Kohlberg Papers, HISU.

16. Charles Cheney Hyde, "The Nationality Act of 1940," *American Society of International Law* 35, no. 2 (April 1941): 318; Zheng, "Chinese Americans in San

Francisco and New York City During the Anti-Japanese War," 58–59, 47–48; G. B. Chin, "China's Leader and Her Military Situation in Pre-war Days," *U.S. Naval Institute Proceedings* (October 1944): 1263; Lai, *Chinese American Transnational Politics*, 26.

17. Personnel Attached to CBI, November 25,1944, signed by Lincoln Mei; Lincoln Mei to Edward Harding, August 28, 1945; Anon., 1st Lt. Lincoln Mei, n.d., Folder Mei, Lincoln, Box 515 OSSPF, Entry 224, RG 226 OSS/NARA II.

18. Harry Gordon Jung, Application for Employment and Personal History, November, 4, 1943; Charles Fisher to Naval Command/OSS, January 24, 1944; Security Office Investigation Report #10492, to L. W. Johnson, December 3, 1943, Folder Jung, Harry, Box 385 OSSPF, Entry 224, RG 226 OSS/NARA II; US Immigration Service Form 2505, December 12, 1932, File 35236/11-8, re: Chung Kay Quong, Immigration and Arrival Investigation Case Files, 1884-1944, RG 85 INS, San Francisco District, NARA/SB; Chung Kay Quong to Commissioner of Immigration/San Francisco, January 23, 1933.

19. D. M. Dimond to the Board of Review, November 7, 1944, Folder Eng, Don, Box 220 OSSPF, Entry 224, RG 226 OSS/NARA II; Richard Dunlop, *Behind Japanese Lines With the OSS in Burma* (Chicago: Rand McNally & Co., 1979), 77, 122–23, 151, 154.

20. David Kai-Foo Loa to Edgar Salinger, May 21, 1944, Folder 13, Box 3, Entry 168A, RG 226 OSS/NARA II; Fenn, *At the Dragon's Gate*, 148–51; John McAuliff, "Transcript of the OSS-Viet Minh 1995 Meeting" (Southampton, NY: The Fund for Reconciliation, 1997): 4, 7–11; DIO-3ND Section 16-B-5 of NYC, Intelligence Report, September 22, 1943, Report # 45,596, Box 512 R&A Intelligence Reports, Entry 16, RG 226 OSS/NARA II; Dixee Bartholomew-Feis, *The OSS And Ho Chi Minh: Unexpected Allies in the War Against Japan* (Lawrence: University Press of Kansas, 2006), 63–69, 155–56.

21. Abbreviated Service Record, n.d.; Theater Service Record, April 1945; Graham Campbell, Interviewer's Report, July 23, 1945, Folder Chan, Richard Hong, Box 345 OSSPF, Entry 1568, RG 226 OSS/NARA II; Chan Hong to C.R. Corcoran, July 24, 1945, Folder 57, Box173 OSS History Office, Entry 92, RG 226 OSS/NARA II.

22. Peter Pugliese to (Charles) Cheston, June 8, 1945; Emergency Addressee and Personal Property Card, June 28, 1945; Application Form for Commissions in Army, Navy, or Marine Corps (OSS Form), n.d.; Robert Handy, Joseph Spencer, S. W. Lintt to Adjutant, August 15, 1945; C. Martin Wilbur to Whom It May Concern, April 18, 1945, Folder Chin, Robert, Box 345 OSSPF, Entry 224, RG 226 OSS/NARA II.

23. (Charles Boynton), S.A.S. Students, 1912-1941, Folder SAS Newspaper (S.A.S. Nooze), Box 9, Charles L. Boynton Papers/HISU; (Charles Boynton), "The Growth of an Idea," n.d., Folder Shanghai Am. School The Growth of an idea, Box 3, Charles L. Boynton Papers, HISU; *The Columbian* (Shanghai American School, 1936), 66, 114, Angie Mills Papers (private), Chicago; Betty Kan, "Reliving His Glory Days," *Chapel Hill Magazine* 2, no. 6 (November/December 2007): 121, Betty F. Kan Papers, Chapel Hill, NC.; author, telephone interview with Betty Kan, at her home in Chapel Hill, North Carolina, February 21, 2011.

24. Zhong guo Kexue yuan Shanghai Jing ji Yan jiu suo [Chinese Academy of Sciences, Shanghai Institute of Economics], ed., *Nan Yang Xiong Di Gong Si Shi Liao* [Nanyang Brothers Tobacco Company Historical materials] (Shanghai: Shanghai Ren Min Chu Ban She, 1958), 2, 81–87, 100–102, 509; Chan Yuen Zang, "Mr. Kan Chiu-nam," *The Fuh-Tan Banner* VI (July 1924): 18; Cochran, *Big Business in*

China, 60–61, 63–64, 107, 115, 117, 195–96, 185–87, 197–98; Carol Benedict, *Golden-Silk Smoke: A History of Tobacco in China, 1550-2010* (Berkeley: University of California Press, 2011), 140, 146, 154; Statistical Record, ca. 1936 and Libel for Divorce, Floyd Superior Court, No. 1560, July 8, 1946, by C. H. Porter, Betty F. Kan Papers, Chapel Hill, NC.

25. Wayne Patterson, *The Ilse: First-Generation Korean Immigrants in Hawaii, 1903-1973* (Honolulu: University of Hawai'i Press, 2000), 5, 25, 29–30, 33, 72–73; Bernice B. H. Kim, "The Koreans in Hawaii" (Master's thesis, University of Hawai'i, 1937), 171, 177; Yŏng-ho Ch'oe, "The Early Korean Immigration: An Overview," in *From the Land of Hibiscus: Koreans in Hawaii, 1903–1950* (Honolulu: University of Hawai'i Press, 2007), 13, 19, 23, 25.

26. Jacob Kyung Dunn, "Cairo and Korean Independence," *The New Pacific,* February1944, 4–5, 32.

27. Patterson, *The Ilse,* 193; Legislative Committee of the Korean Civic Association, *We Who Fight the Common Enemy* (Honolulu: Korean Civic Association, 1945), 7, 8.

28. Edward Taehan Chang, "Korean Kaleidoscope: An Overview of Korean Immigration to the U.S.," *Korean and Korean American Bulletin* 11, no. 2 (2000): U12; Kim, "The Koreans in Hawaii," 205; Patterson, *The Ilse,* 118–19.

29. Donald Kang, "The Koreans in Hawaii," in *The New Pacific* (November 1944), 5 and Lili M. Kim, "The Pursuit of Imperfect Justice: The Predicament of Koreans and Korean Americans" (PhD diss., University of Rochester, 2001), 225, 220.

30. Carter J. Eckert, *Offspring of Empire: The Koch'ang Kims and the Colonial Origins of Korean Capitalism, 1876-1945* (Seattle: University of Washington Press, 1991), 77; Takashi Fujitani, "Right to Kill, Right to Make Live: Koreans as Japanese and Japanese as Americans During WWII," *Representations* 99 (Summer 2007): 17; Geoffrey Pharaoh Adams with Hugh Popham, *No Time For Geishas* (London: Corgi Books, 1974), 63.

31. (ONI), "Topic Study Analysis of the Korean Situation," ca. August 13,1943, 3–4, Folder Analysis of the Korean Situation, Box 15 CI on PI, Bonins, Korea, Okinawa, Formosa, RG 38 Office of Naval Intelligence, (SAC) Oriental Desk, 1936-1946, Entry UD 29, CNO/NARA II; John Sterling Adams, "Kilsoo K. Haan, with aliases," October 20, 1942, File No. 100-1718, Folder 1 of 3: Sino Korean Peoples League, Box 35 Security Classified Intelligence and Investigative Dossiers, 1939-1976, Entry 143A, RG 319: Records of the Office of Assistant Chief of Staff, G-2, Intelligence, NARA II; (H.C. Train), "Topic Study Analysis of the Korean Situation," Report #42,468, ca. August 13, 1943, Folder 42462-42469, Box 489 R&A Intelligence Reports, Entry 16, RG 226 OSS/NARA II; David K. Yoo, *Contentious Spirits: Religion in Korean American History, 1903-1945* (Stanford, CA: Stanford University Press, 2010), 42; Patterson, *The Ilse,* 192; The Korean Open Letter, Vol. 2 Number 28, March 5, 1945, Folder 120,425, Box 1374 R&A Intelligence Reports, Entry 16, RG 226 OSS/NARA II; (ONI), "Topic Study Analysis of the Korean Situation," 17–18, Folder Analysis of the Korean Situation, Box 15, Entry UD 29, RG 38 ONI, (SAC) Oriental Desk, NARA II.

32. Syngman Rhee to Leo Crowley, September 29, 1943; Carl Hoffman to William Donovan, June 15, 1943, frames 272–73, roll 066, Microfilm 1642, Washington Director's Office Administrative Files, RG 226 OSS/NARA II.

33. Sun Bin Yim, "The Social Structure of Korean Communities in California, 1903-1920," in *Labor Immigration under Capitalism: Asian Workers in the United States Before World War II,* ed. Lucie Cheng and Edna Bonacich (Berkeley: University of California Press, 1984), 519, 524, 542; Chang, "Korean Kaleidoscope"; Anne Soon

Choi, "Border Crossings: The Politics of Korean Nationalism in the United States, 1919–1945" (PhD diss., University of Southern California, 2004), 59, 73, 96.

34. J. Edgar Hoover to William Donovan, n.d., M1642 Microfilm reel 54, frame 492–93, RG 226 OSS/NARA II; *Chicago Daily News* 9 December 1941; Eugene (Oregon) *Register Guard*, February 23, 1944; *The Milwaukee Journal*, October 3, 1945; *The Sunday Morning Star* (Wilmington, Delaware), February 17, 1946; Syngman Rhee to Soon Kyo Hahn, April 6, 1942, Folder Hahn, Soon Kyo 1942, Box 1, MPGP/HISU; Stanley Hornbeck, Adviser on Political Relations to Mr. Soon K. Hahn, May 11, 1942, Folder Haan, Soon K., Box 197, Stanley K. Hornbeck Papers, HISU.

35. Security Office to Lt. Col. H. P. Goodfellow, Security Office Investigation Report, April 11, 1942, Folder 201 Chang, Sukyoon, Box 117 OSSPF, Entry 224, RG 226 OSS/NARA II; Chihō Kankokujin Chōsa [Regional Korean Survey], 1942, Korean Commission (Washington, DC), Koreans in Montana: 1942 census, Korean American Digital Archives, USC Digital Library (hereafter cited as KADA/USC) at http://www.trails.com/tcatalog_trail.aspx?trailid=HGR211-019, accessed September 1, 1913; (Sukyoon Chang), no title, n.d., Folder Chang, Sukyoon, and Card, Sukyoon Chang, n.d., Folder Chang, Sukyoon, Box 117 OSSPF, Entry 224, RG 226 OSS/NARA II; Moon and Eifler, *The Deadliest Colonel*, 48.

36. Ilhan New, *When I Was a Boy in Korea* (Boston: Lothrop, Lee & Shepard, 1928), 171–74, 5–11; Neil R. Grazel, *Beatrice: From Buildup through Breakup* (Urbana: University of Illinois Press, 1990), 46; (Clarence Weems), "A Report on the Progress of the Free Korean Movement (Part I)," March 24, 1943, 11, Folder 571, Box 72 Pacific Coast/Field Stations Files, Entry 140, RG 226 OSS/NARA II.

37. Dong-on Kim and Johngseok Bae, *Employment Relations and HRM in South Korea* (Hampshire, UK: Ashgate Publishing, 2004), 128; Eckert, *Offspring of Empire*, 254, 116–17, 177; Peter Conn, *Pearl S. Buck: A Cultural Biography* (New York: Cambridge University Press, 1998), 298.

38. Ilhan New to Members of the Korean Economic Society, December 1944, KADA/USC; (Clarence Weems), "A Report on the Progress of the Free Korean Movement Part I," March 24, 1943, 11, 16, Appendix II; Part II, June 18, 1943, 6, 15, 29–30, Folder 572, Box 72, Entry 140, RG 226 OSS/NARA II.

39. (Clarence Weems), "A Report on the Progress of the Free Korean Movement Part II," June 18, 1943, 22, 24, 26, 29, Folder 572, Box 72, Entry 140, RG 226 OSS/NARA II; *Daily Worker* September 9, 1955 and Diamond Kimm vs. Richard C. Hoy, No. 15,763 United States Court of Appeals for the Ninth Circuit, February 19, 1953, reprinted in reprinted in KADA/USC.

40. F(rederick) W(.) F(isher) to Files, January 23, 1945 and C(harles) J(.) B(rown) to Files, January 13, 1945, Folder 615, Box 79, Entry 140, RG 226 OSS/NARA II.

41. Alien Personal History and Statement, November 17, 1944; Daniel Buchanan to Chief, Personnel Procurement Branch OSS, November 16, 1944, Folder Hahm, Ryongi C., Box 304; Edgar Salinger to James McHugh, February 24, 1944, Folder 8, Box 3 Field Station Files, Entry 224, RG 226 OSS/NARA II.

42. Separation Process, December 17, 1945; Peter Namkoong to Robert Alcera, April 15, 1946; Engagement Sheet, n.d.; Daniel Buchanan, Request for Procurement of Personnel, January 30, 1945; Extract from Service Record, Folder Namkoong, Peter, Box 550 OSSPF, Entry 224, RG 226 OSS/NARA II.

43. W.E.W(alker), Personnel Officer, SI to Chief Personnel Procurement Branch, December 16, 1944; D.C. Buchanan to Chief Personnel Procurement Branch, Request for Procurement of Military Personnel, January 31, 1945, Folder Kim, David Chu-Hang, Box 404 OSSPF, Entry 224, RG 226 OSS/NARA II.

44. Lawrence Fuch, *Hawaii Pono: An Ethnic and Political History* (Honolulu: The Bess Press, 1961), 122–25; Yukiko Kimura, *Issei: Japanese Immigrants in Hawaii* (Honolulu: University of Hawai'i Press, 1988), 177, 112; Eileen Tamura, *Americanization, Acculturation, and Ethnic Identity: The Nisei Generation in Hawaii* (Urbana: University of Illinois Press, 1994), 231, 223–27.

45. Sixteenth Census of the United States: 1940, Population Second Series Characteristics of the Population Hawaii, "Table 1: Race, By Nativity and Sex for the Territory and for Honolulu City: 1910–1940," 5 in US Census Bureau, Sixteenth Census of the United States: 1940 Population Second Series Characteristics of the Population of Hawaii (Washington, DC: US Government Printing Office, 1943) at http://1940census.archives.gov; Tamura, *Americanization, Acculturation, and Ethnic Identity*, 227–28.

46. Fuchs, *Hawaii Pono*, 22, 247–49; Gary Y. Okihiro, *Cane Fires: The Anti-Japanese Movement in Hawaii, 1865-1945* (Philadelphia: Temple University Press, 1991), 184, 203; Tom Coffman, *The Island Edge of America: A Political History of Hawai'i* (Honolulu: University of Hawai'i Press, 2003), 50–51; Charles Hemenway to Ralph (Yempuku), May 23, 1942, Folder VVV Personnel: Personal Accounts, Box 37, AJA 002: Ted Tsukiyama Papers, Archives & Manuscripts Department, University of Hawai'i, Manoa, Honolulu (hereafter cited as TTP/UHM).

47. Kimura, *Issei*, 196–97; Odo, *No Sword to Bury*, 14, 20–21, 24, 36; Kyōhei Sasaki, "Military Expenditures and the Employment Multiplier in Hawaii," *Review of Economics and Statistics* 45, no. 3 (August 1963): 298.

48. Tomonori Ishikawa, "Okinawaken ni okeru Shutsu Imin no Rekishi oyobi Shutsu Imin Yōinron," [History of Emigration from Okinawa Prefecture and Theorizing the Reasons for Emigration] *Imin Kenkyū* 1 (March 2005): 11; Kimura, *Issei*, 22–23, 79; United Okinawan Association of Hawaii, *Uchinanchu: A History of Okinawans in Hawaii* (Honolulu: Ethnic Studies Program, University of Hawai'i, 1981), 42, 102, 128–31, 218.

49. Okihiro, *Cane Fires*, 106, 114–18; Kimura, *Issei*, 213.

50. Eric Robertson, *The Japanese File: Pre-war Japanese Penetration in Southeast Asia* (Singapore: Heinemann Asia, 1979), 90–91; Lt. General Fujiwara Iwaichi, tr. by Yōji Akashi, *F. Kikan: Japanese Army Intelligence Operations in Southeast Asia during World War II* (Hong Kong: Heinemann Asia, 1983), 9, 118–19 and Louis Morton, *The United States Army in World War II: The War in the Pacific: The Fall of the Philippines* (Washington, DC: Office of the Chief of Military History United States Army, 1953), Vol. 2, part 2, 118–19; H. N. Street, Memorandum for The Island Commander, 20 June 1945 and Enclosure (A) to A C of S G-2 Conf. Memo Serial 0203 to Is(land) Com(mander), Folder A17-15 (4) Guam "Confidential" May-Aug 1945, Box 1 Records of the Office of the Judge Advocate General (Navy), War Crimes Branch, Confidential Correspondence, 1945-1948, Entry 17 A1, RG 125 War Crimes Branch, NARA II.

51. Kimura, *Issei*, 206–207; John J. Stephan, *Hawaii under the Rising Sun: Japan's Plans for Conquest after Pearl Harbor* (Honolulu: University of Hawai'i Press, 1984), 30, 33, 37; Kenneth J. Ruoff, *Imperial Japan at its Zenith: The Wartime Celebration of the Empire's 2,600th Anniversary* (Ithaca, NY: Cornell University Press, 2010), 148, 156, 161; Stephan, *Hawaii under the Rising Sun*, 28–33, 49, 152–54, 164.

52. Stephan, *Hawaii under the Rising Sun*, 23–26; Teruko Kumei, "Senkyūhyaku sanjūnendai no Kibei Undō: Amerika Kokusekihō tono Kankei ni Oite," [The 1930s Kibei Movement: Its Relationship to the American Nationality Law] *Ijū Kenkyū*

[Migration Studies] 30 (March 1993), 152–53; and Tamura, *Americanization, Acculturation, and Ethnic Identity*, 86.

53. Ken Kotani, *Japanese Intelligence in World War II*, tr. Chiharu Kotani (Oxford: Osprey Publishing, 2009), 136–37; Gordon W. Prange, *At Dawn We Slept: The Untold Story of Pearl Harbor* (New York: Penguin Books, 1981), 72, 75–77, 148, 156, 254, 419–20; Special Agent 31987, Memorandum for the Officer in Charge, July 9, 1947, 3, Folder Pre-Pearl Harbor Espionage, Box 114 Entry 134, RG 319 G-2 Records of the Investigative Records Repository: Intelligence and Investigative Dossiers, NARA II.

54. Kimura, *Issei*, 219; Dennis M. Ogawa and Evarts C. Fox Jr., "Japanese Internment and Relocation: The Hawaii Experience," in *Japanese Americans: From Relocation to Redress*, ed. Roger Daniels, Sandra C. Taylor, and Harry H. L. Kitano (Salt Lake City: University of Utah, 1986), 135–41; Tetsuden Kashima, *Judgment without Trial: Japanese American Imprisonment during World War II* (Seattle: University of Washington Press, 2003), 78, 74–75.

55. Odo, *No Sword to Bury*, 2, 162–64, 182, 223, 228; Lyn Crost, *Honor by Fire: Japanese Americans at War in Europe and the Pacific* (Novato, CA: Presidio Press, 1994), 62–63.

56. Calvin Tottori, *The OSS Niseis in the China-Burma-India Theater* (Honolulu: privately printed, ca. 1997), 5; (Howard Furumoto), Recommendation (For Ralph Yempuku), DA Form 638, February 8, 1997, Folder Recommendation for Distinguished Service Medal; Ted Tsukiyama, "Ralph Yempuku: Remembrances," July 18, 2002, Folder Ralph Yempuku Memorial, 2002; "Ralph Tsuneto Yempuku: Varsity Victory Volunteer, MIS Veteran, Promoter," *Hawaii Herald*, August 2, 2002, Folder Ralph Yempuku Memorial, 2002, Box 40, Varsity Victory Volunteers (hereafter VVV), TTP/UHM.

57. Montague Mead to D.C. Buchanan, September 13, 1944, Folder "40," Box 54 OSSPF, Entry 224; Richard Betsui to Chief SI/CT, May 31, 1945, Folder 3435, Box 205, Entry154; War Department Pay and Allowance Account, April 30, 1944, Folder "40," Box 54 OSSPF, Entry 224; Charles Cheston to The Adjutant General, October 3, 1944, Folder "40," Box 54 OSSPF, Entry 224, RG 226 OSS/ NARA II; Military Intelligence Roster—Burma & India, n.d., Folder MIS Field Assignments: China-Burma-India Theaters, 1945-2001, Box 22, VVV, TTP/UHM.

58. Larry Y. Mizuno, ed., *Ka Palapala: University of Hawaii—1940* Vol. XXV (Honolulu: Associated Students of the University of Hawai'i), 210, 107; Bert Noboru Nishimura and Shonosuke Koizumi, eds., *Ka Palapala 1939* (Honolulu: Associated Students of the University of Hawai'i, 1939), 89, 87, 86, 85.

59. Personal History Statement, December 1, 1943, and Addendum, Folder Ikeda, Box 362 OSSPF, Entry 224, RG 226 OSS/NARA II; Gordon Kadowaki, ed., *Ka Palapala 1941* Vol. XXVI (Honolulu: Associated Students of the University of Hawai'i, 1941), "Track Section"; Eddie N. Chong and Sam N. Mukaida, eds., *Ka Palapala 1942* Vol. XXVII (Honolulu: Associated Students of the University of Hawai'i, 1942), 86, 87.

60. Separation Process, December 7, 1945, Box 28 OSSPF, Entry 224, RG 226 OSS/ NARA II; Odo, *No Sword to Bury*, 188.

61. Personal History Statement, December 6, 1943, Folder Yempuku, Ralph, Box 852 OSSPF, Entry 224, RG 226 OSS/NARA II; Honpa Honganji Hawaii Mission, Honolulu, funeral program for July 18, 2002, for Ralph Tsuneto Yempuku, Folder Ralph Yempuku Memorial, 2002; Ted Tsukiyama, "Ralph Yempuku: Remembrances," July18, 2002, Folder Ralph Yempuku Memorial, 2002; Curtis Lum, "Ralph Yempuku: Promoter and War Hero," *Honolulu Advertiser*, ca.

July 14, 2002, Folder Ralph Yempuku Memorial, 2002, Box 40, VVV, TTP/UHM; "Estimate of "Bey" on special personnel, n.d., Folder Yempuku, Ralph, Box 852 OSSPF, Entry 224, RG 226 OSS/NARA II; Ralph Yempuku Interview with Franklin Odo, March 28, 1985 at the Ethnic Studies Program, in Honolulu, Hamilton Library, UHM; Eddie N. Chong and Sam N. Mukaida, eds., *Ka Palapala 1942* Vol. XXVII (Honolulu: Associated Students of the University of Hawai'i, 1942), 102, 105, Special Collections, Hamilton Library, UHM.

62. Ted Tsukiyama and James Tanabe, Interview with Fumio Kido, September 18, 2002, Military Intelligence Service Veterans Club of Hawaii, Oral History Project, UHM.

63. Application for Employment and Personal History Statement, October 29, 1943, Folder Hamada, Dick, Box 308 OSSPF, Entry 224, RG 226 OSS/NARA II; Dick Hamada, "The Hawai'i Nisei Story: Americans of Japanese Ancestry During World War II," University of Hawaii, The Hawaii Nisei Project, 2006-07, UHM; Dick S. Hamada, January 16, 1944, Folder Hamada, Dick, Box 308 OSSPF, Entry 224, RG 226 OSS/NARA II.

64. Personal History Statement, October 30, 1943; Memorandum to Files, Estimate of "Bey" on special personnel, April 3, 1944, Folder Tottori, Calvin, Box 782 OSSPF, Entry 224, RG 226 OSS/NARA II.

65. Tottori, *The OSS Niseis in the China-Burma-India Theater*, 6; Author interview with Howard Furumoto, Honolulu, May 9, 2008; Chitoshi Yanaga to August Vollmer, January 1, 1944, Folder 699, Entry 140, Box 84 Pacific Coast/Field Station Files, RG 226 OSS/NARA II; Jamie Ross Fahs, "A Short Personal Biography of Charles Burton Fahs" (unpub., 1984), 50, Folder Draft of Biog of CB Fahs by Mrs. Fahs, IV 2B 44 Charles B. Fahs Papers, Rockefeller Archives Center, Sleepy Hallow, NY; Warren Tsuneishi, "Obituary," *Journal of Asian Studies* 45, no. 3 (May 1986): 669.

66. Brian Masaru Hayashi, *Democratizing the Enemy: The Japanese American Internment* (Princeton, NJ: Princeton University Press, 2004), 45–47; Eichirō Azuma, *Between Two Empires: Race, History, and Transnationalism in Japanese America* (New York: Oxford University Press, 2005), 119; Alexander Yoshikazu Yamato, "Socioeconomic Change among Japanese Americans in the San Francisco Bay Area" (PhD diss., University of California, Berkeley, 1986), 256–59; Hiroshi Yoneyama, "Rafu Nihonjinkai Yakuin Senkyō to Zairosuanzerusu Nihonjin Shakai no Henyō: Senkyūhyakujūgonen kara Senkyūhyakunijūichi [Los Angeles Japanese Association Board Members Election and the Change in Japanese Society in Los Angeles: From 1915 to 1921]" (unpub. manuscript, Ritsumeikan University, 2000), 6–9, 14–15.

67. Paul R. Spickard, *Japanese Americans: The Formation and Transformations of an Ethnic Group* (New York: Twayne Publishers, 1996), 46–47; Yuji Ichioka, *The Issei: The World of the First Generation Japanese Immigrants, 1885–1924* (New York: The Free Press, 1988), 253, 145; Daniels, *Asian America*, 115; Masao Suzuki, "Occupational Mobility of Japanese Immigrants to the U.S.: Evidence from War Relocation Authority Records (1942) and the Immigration and Naturalization Service" (report, Stanford University, Dept. of Economics, May 1992), 24–25.

68. Yuji Ichioka, "The Meaning of Loyalty: The Case of Kazumaro Buddy Uno," *Amerasia Journal* 23, no. 3 (Winter 1997–1998): 44–71; Anon. Office of Naval Intelligence [to] Office of the Chief of Naval Operations, June 11, 1941, Folder Japanese Intelligence Activities—U.S. (Gen.); (Anon.), Memo for Comdr. (Ellis) Zacharias, February 4, 1936, Folder 13th ND-Japanese Activities; I. H. Mayfield,

"An Analysis of the Japanese Espionage Problem in the Hawaiian Islands," April 20, 1943, 25–26, Folder Japanese Intelligence Activities—U.S. (Gen.), Box 1 Japanese Organization & Intelligence in US, ONI, (SAC) Section, Oriental Desk, Entry UD 29, RG 38 CNO/NARA II. See also Richard J. Samuels, *Special Duty: A History of the Japanese Intelligence Community* (Ithaca, NY: Cornell University Press, 2019), 54–55; Pedro A. Loureiro, "The Imperial Japanese Navy and Espionage: The Itaru Tachibana Case," *International Journal of Intelligence and Counterintelligence* 3, no. 1 (Spring 1989), 105–21 and Loureiro, "Japanese Espionage and American Counter-measures in Pre-Pearl Harbor California," *Journal of American-East Asian Relations* 3, no. 3 (Fall 1994), 197–210.

69. *Shin Sekai Asahi Nenkan* [The New World Sun Yearbook] (San Francisco: Shin Sekai Shimbunsha, 1941), 81, 29; (Frank) Farrell and (Marvin) Gray, Memo to Lt. Waldorf for FBI, July 3, 1946, Box 29, Frank Farrell Papers, Special Collections, The Library of Congress, Washington, DC (hereafter cited as FFP/LOC); Special Agents 4560 and 4604, Memorandum for the Officer in Charge, April 9, 1946, Research and Analysis, General Headquarters, United States Army Forces, Pacific, Office of the Chief of Counter Intelligence, Folder Inaho OTANI, Box 589 Investigative Records Repository, RG 319 Office of the Assistant Chief of Staff for Intelligence, Entry 134B, NARA II; ONI, Tatsumi, Kazuo Thomas, September 20, 1945, Counter-Intelligence Data on Japan Section VII: Suspect Japanese Formerly Active in the United States October 3, 1945, Folder no title, Box 20, CI Reports on Japanese organization and individuals, 1945, Entry UD 29, RG 38 CNO/NARA II; Captain Farrell and Mr. Gray, Memo to Lt. Waldorf for FBI, July 3, 1946, Folder 10, Box 29, FFP/LOC.

70. Hayashi, *Democratizing the Enemy*, 157–59.

71. Tokutarō Nishimura Slocum, Application for Federal Employment, August 21, 1943, Folder Slocum Nishimura Tokutaro, Box 718 OSSPF, Entry 224, RG 226 OSS/NARA II; Harry Maxwell Naka, "The Naturalization of the Japanese Veterans of the American World War Forces" (MA thesis, University of California, Berkeley, 1935), 73, 45–47.

72. Slocum, Application for Federal Employment, RG 226 OSS/NARA II.

73. William Donovan to Carroll Shartle, August 24, 1943, Folder Slocum Nishimura Tokutaro, Box 718 OSSPF, Entry 224, RG 226 OSS/NARA II.

74. Personal History Statement, for "George," October 29, 1943; MISLS Evaluation Sheet, May 6, 1944; Special Academic Report Sheet, July 12, 1944; Memorandum to Files, Estimate of "Bey" on special personnel, April 3, 1944, Folder Kobayashi, George, Box 414 OSSPF, Entry 224, RG 226 OSS/NARA II.

75. IRIS State Department, October 22, 1945; Oath and Declaration of Appointee, September 11, 1944; and Application for Federal Employment, April 5, 1944 and August 7, 1945, Report of Efficiency Rating, July 31, 1945, Folder Nakamura Chiyeko, Box 550 OSSPF, Entry 224, RG 226 OSS/NARA II.

76. The Rafu Shimpō, *Rafu Nenkan* [Los Angeles Yearbook] (Los Angeles: Rafu Shimpō, 1939), 36; Shirō Fujioka, *Ayumi no Ato: Hokubei Tairiku Nihonjin Kaitaku Monogatari* [Traces of Footsteps] (Los Angeles: Rafu Shimpō, 1957), 536; John Walker Powell, "Community Government in Poston—an informal discussion—," June 1, 1946, Folder J 3.16, Japanese American Evacuation and Resettlement Studies 67/14C, Bancroft Library, University of California, Berkeley; *Rafu Shimpō*, October 5, 1931, reel 70, JARP/UCLA; (Alexander Leighton), Interview with Head, Gelvin, and Henrietta Johnson, June 30, 1943, 12, Folder 11–62, Box 30, Restricted Access Materials, Japanese American Relocation Centers Records

#3830, Rare & Manuscripts Collection, Kroch Library, Cornell University, Ithaca, NY.

77. Bill Hosokawa, *JACL in Quest of Justice: History of the Japanese American Citizens League* (New York: William Morrow, 1982), 140; Hayashi, *Democratizing the Enemy*, 74–75; Edward Kirby, "Subversive Activities at War Relocation Centers," January 9, 1943, 21–22, Folder Section 3 Serials 30X3-55, Box 81, RG 65 Records of the Federal Bureau of Investigation, NARA II.

78. Richard Nishimoto, "Personalities," Folder **J 6.15G, JERS/UCB; (Karl) Bendetsen and (John) Weckerling, December 7, 1942, Record #26, 27, 28, by K. Russell, Folder Various Telephone Conversations on the Manzanar Riot, Box 56, RG 338 Western Defense Command (hereafter cited as WDC/NARA II); John Powell to John Provinse, July 18, 1945, Folder 66.010#4: March 1944, Box 401, Central Files WRA HDQS, Community Government(General), RG 210 Records of the War Relocation Authority Headquarters Subject-Classified General Files, NARA I; (Karl) Bendetsen to (John) Weckerling, December 7, 1942, Folder 323.3/ 32 Manzanar Riot, Box 56, RG 338 Records of the Western Defense Command, NARA II.

79. Adrian S. Fisher, Minutes, May 12, 1944, Folder Minutes of the Japanese American Joint Board from February 26, 1943 to May 12, 1944, Box 1759, Personnel Security Division Japanese-American Branch General File 1942-46, RG 389 Records of the Office of the Provost Marshal General, NARA II; DCB (Daniel Buchanan), [interview notes], n.d., Folder 10, Box 309 COI/OSS Central Files, Entry 92, RG 226 OSS/NARA II; Engagement Sheet, June 13, 1944, Employee Withholding Exemption Certificate, June 20, 1944, and Daniel C. Buchanan to Mrs. Casswell, October 26, 1944, Folder Ishimaru, Tetsuya, Box 365 OSSPF, Entry 224, RG 226 OSS/NARA II. The Board's negative evaluation likely stemmed from Ishimaru's kendo activities, see Eric L. Muller, *American Inquisition: The Hunt for Japanese American Disloyalty in World War II* (Chapel Hill: University of North Carolina Press, 2007), 47.

80. W. L. Langer, to Chief, Personnel Procurement Branch, January 6, 1944, Folder Yamada, Hatsumi, Box 856 OSSPF; Charles Ford to Eva Caswell Jones, September 27, 1945, Folder Nitta, Fred Hidetoshi, Box 561 OSSPF; Abbreviated Service Record/Card, Folder Kazahaya, Susumu, Box 304 OSSPF, Entry 224; (Takeo) Tanabe to (Daniel) Buchanan, June 7, 1945, Folder 2383, Box 112, Entry 92A, RG 226 OSS/NARA II.

81. T. Scott Miyakawa, "Early New York Issei Founders of Japanese American Trade," in *East Across the Pacific: Historical and Sociological Studies of Japanese Immigration and Assimilation*, ed. Hilary T. Conroy and T. Scott Miyakawa (Santa Barbara, CA: ABC Clio, 1972), 163; Mitziko Sawada, *Tokyo Life, New York Dreams: Urban Japanese Visions of America, 1890–1924* (Berkeley: University of California Press, 1996), 13–14, 16; Zaibei Nihonjinkai, *Zaibei Nihonjinshi* [History of the Japanese in America] (San Francisco, CA: Zaibei Nihonjinkai, 1940), 163; Greg Robinson, "Nisei in Gotham: The JACD and Japanese Americans in 1940s New York," *Prospects: An Annual Journal of American Cultural Studies* 30 (2005): 581, 584, 586; Daniel H. Inouye, *Distant Islands: The Japanese American Community in New York City, 1876–1930s* (Boulder: University Press of Colorado, 2018), 33–35, 82–84, 85–86, 138–53; Margaret Feldman to Colonel Kenneth Mann, May 4, 1945, Folder 6, Box 165, Entry 92, RG 226 OSS/NARA II.

82. Howard Schonberger, "Dilemmas of Loyalty: Japanese Americans and the Psychological Warfare Campaigns of the Office of Strategic Services, 1943–45,"

Amerasia Journal 16, no. 1 (1990): 25 and his *Japanizu Konekushon: Kainunō K. Sugahara Gaiden* [Japanese Connection: A Biography of the Shipping Magnate Kay Sugahara] (Tokyo: Bungei Shunjū, 1995), 74, 78, 16–17, 25–26, 36–37, 41, 48, 87, 117, 123, 126; L. F. Sloan to O. A. Blalock, March12, 1943 and L.F. Sloan to James Terry, March 25, 1943, Folder Sugahara, Kay, Box 5454 Evacuee Case Files, RG 210, War Relocation Authority Washington Office Records, NARA I, Washington, DC.

83. Document 24284: Eric Straight to Frederic Dolbeare, March 29, 1944, Folder 2, Box 22 OSS Classified Sources and Method File; Herbert Little to W. A. Kimball, August 22, 1944, Folder 6, Box 165 COI/OSS Central Files, Entry 92; John Roller to the Director, August 3, 1944, Folder 33, Box 460 COI/OSS Central Files, Entry 92; Eric Staight to Frederic Dolbeare, March 29 1944, Folder 5, Box 21 OSS History Office, Entry 211; Bradford Smith to [Alfred] Tozzer, October 14, 1944, Folder 776 Japan, Box 77, Entry 139, RG 226 OSS/NARA II.

84. Statement of United States Citizen of Japanese Ancestry, Folder 22, Box 5, Karl Akiya Papers, Tamiment Library, New York University, New York City; Karl Akiya, *Jiyūhe no Michi Taiheiyō wo Koete: Aru Kibei Nisei no Jiden* [The Road to Freedom (by) Crossing the Pacific: A Kibei Nisei's Autobiography] (Kyōto: Gyōjisha, 1996), 136, 222.

85. Shūji and Kikue Fujii, Personal History Statement, October 6, 1943, Folder Fujii, Shuji, Box 255 OSSPF, Entry 224; William Magistretti to William Langer, November 13, 1944, Folder Fujii, Shuji, Box 255 OSSPF, Entry 224, and Little to Van Halsey, September 22, 143, Folder 2173, Box 103 COI/OSS Central Files, Entry 168A, RG 226 OSS/NARA II.

86. Minoru Ōmori, *Sokoku Kakumei Kōsaku* [Revolutionary Maneuverings of the Ancestral Homeland] (Tokyo: Kōdansha, 1975), *Sengo Hisshi* Vol. 3 [Postwar Secret History], 26; Joe Koide, *Aru Zaibei Nihonjin no Kiroku: Renin Gakkō kara Nichibei Kaisen made Jō* [Recollections of a Japanese in America, Volume 1: From the Lenin School to the Beginnings of the US-Japan War], 18, 27–28, 161–64, 174, 184–88 and *Aru Zaibei Nihonjin no Kiroku Ge: Nichibei Kaisen kara Shusen made* [Recollections of a Japanese in American, Volume 2: From the Beginnings of the US-Japan War until Its End] (Tokyo: Yushindo, 1970), 66, 73, 141; S(pecial) A(gent in) C(harge), Los Angeles [FBI], "Teiji (Joe) Koide," July 13, 1951; FBI Report, File No. 100-30303, September 13, 1951; and SAC Report to the Director, January 2, 1952, Folder 8, Box 46, Josephine Fowler Papers, Charles E. Young Research Library, University of California, Los Angeles; US Congress, House of Representatives, Committee on Un-American Activities Investigation of Communist activities in the San Francisco area, "Hearing Investigation of Communist Activities in the San Francisco Area" (1954), Part 5; James Oda, *Heroic Struggles of Japanese Americans: Partisan Fighters from America's Concentration Camps* (North Hollywood, CA: KNI, 1981), 184, 159–60; Harvey Klehr and John Haynes, "Comintern's Open Secrets," in *The Cold War Vol. 4: Cold War Espionage and Spying*, ed. Lori Lyn Bogle (New York: Routledge, 2001), 301.

87. Gordon W. Prange, with Donald M. Goldstein and Katherine V. Dillon, *Target Tokyo: The Story of the Sorge Spy Ring* (New York: McGraw-Hill, 1984), 345, 126–28, 130, 418, 421–25; The Okinawa Club of America, tr. by Ben Kobashigawa, *History of the Okinawans in North America* (Los Angeles: Resource Development and Publications, Asian American Studies Center, University of California, Los Angeles, and The Okinawa Club of America, 1988), 28; Toshihito Obi, *Gendaishi*

Shiryō: Soruge Jiken [Modern History Sources: The Sorge Incident] (Tokyo: Misuzu Shobō, 1962), Vol. 3, 307, 311–12, 315.

88. Kunio Motoe, "Hideo Noda or the Unfinished 'Bridge'" in, *Amerika ni Mananda Nihon no Gakatachi: Kuniyoshi, Shimizu, Ishigaki, Noda to Amerikan Shin Kaiga* [Japanese Artists Who Studied in America: Kuniyoshi, Shimizu, Ishigaki, and Noda and the American Scene Painting], ed. Kenji Adachi Kenji and Michiaki Kawakita (Tokyo: Tokyo Kokuritsu Kindai Bijutsukan, 1982), 187–89; Helen A. Harrison, "John Reed Club Artists and the New Deal: Radical Responses to Roosevelt's 'Peaceful Revolution'," *Prospects* 5 (1980): 261; Seiichirō Kuboshima, *Hyōhaku: Nikkei Gaka Noda Hideo no Shōgai* [Bleaching: The Life of Japanese American Artist Hideo Noda] (Tokyo: Shinchōsha, 1990), 16–33, 42–44, 84, 177–84; Whittaker Chambers, *Witness* (New York: Random House, 1952), 291, 364, 366–67, 388.

89. Guy Iman, August 28, 1945, [Federal] Bureau [of Investigation] File #100-155291, Folder 146-28-648, Box 94, RG 60 General Records of the Department of Justice, Classified Subject Files, NARA II (hereafter cited as CSF-DOJ/NARA II); Eugenia "Beah" Chen Wing, "MY FAMILY HISTORY RECORD: A Genealogical Record compiled by Eugenia 'Beah' Chen Wing" (February 1981), 19–20, Jack Young Papers at Jolly Young King, Honolulu; (Herbert Moy), Passport Application, 560842, October 19, 1932; William Jones, FBI File No. 61-184, May 7, 1943; William James Burke, FBI report on Herbert Erasmus Moy File No. 61-267, March 5, 1943; George Atcheson Jr. to Secretary of State, August 7, 1943; T. Carter Gleysteen, FBI report on Herbert Erasmus Moy, File No. 100-16945, March 26, 1943; S. Herman Horton, FBI report on Herbert Erasmus Moy, File No. 61-165, April 29, 1943; T. Carter Gleysteen, FBI report on Herbert Erasmus Moy, File No. 100-16945, March 26, 1943; Benedict Cruise, FBI report on Herbert Erasmus Moy, File No. 61-184, May 27, 1943 Folder 146-28-648, Box 94, RG 60 CSF-DOJ/NARA II.

CHAPTER 3

1. Kay Halle, Memorandum of Information for the Joint U.S. Chiefs of Staff, April 23, 1945, Folder 5 General MO Fld. Ops., Box 60, Entry 99, RG 226 OSS/NARA II.

2. John W. Dower, *War without Mercy: Race and Power in the Pacific War* (New York: Pantheon Books, 1986), 207–11; Gerald Horne, *Race War!: White Supremacy and the Japanese Attack on the British Empire* (New York: New York University Press, 2004), 68-69, 77, 263..

3. John Roller to Charles Cheston, August 25, 1944, Folder 2 MO Allotments, Box 151, COI/OSS Central Files, Entry 92; Harold Faxon to Jacques de Sibour, January 25, 1945, Folder 2, Box 84 OSS History Office, Entry 99; W.B. Kantack, Report on OSS Activities for the Month of July 1944, Folder 2, Box 123, Entry 99; John Cavanaugh to Strategic Services Officer, March 25, 1945, Folder 4, Box 84 OSS History Office, Entry 99, RG 226 OSS/NARA II.

4. Barak Kushner, *The Thought War: Japanese Imperial Propaganda* (Honolulu: University of Hawai'i Press, 2006), 122–33; Implementation Study for the Over-all and Special Programs for Strategic Services Based in China, South China, April 5, 1945, Folder 1707 OSS Planning Group Implementation Studies, Box 127 Washington and Field Station Files, Entry 139, RG 226 OSS/NARA II; Kay Halle, Memorandum, op. cit.

5. W. B. Kantack, Report on OSS Activities for the Month of July 1944, Folder 2, Box 123, Entry 99, RG 226 OSS/NARA II; Anon., Addendum, Far East Theater Office

Report June 1944, Folder 1 OSS Activities June 1944, Box 123 History Office, Entry 99, RG 226 OSS/NARA II; Taketoshi Yamamoto, *Buraku Puropaganda: Bōraku no Rajio* [Black Propaganda: Strategic Radio] (Tokyo: Iwanami Shoten, 2002), 202–205.

6. Halle, Memorandum of Information for the Joint U.S. Chiefs of Staff; Major MO Achievements in FE—IBTO—CTO and U.S., ca. April 1945, Folder 304 General—MO, Box 60 OSS History Office, Entry 99, RG 226 OSS/NARA II.

7. MO Monthly Report—July 1945, Folder 3, Box 85, Entry 99, RG 226 OSS/NARA II.

8. Halle, Memorandum of Information for the Joint U.S. Chiefs of Staff, RG 226 OSS/NARA II.

9. Lawrene C. Soley, *Radio Warfare: OSS and CIA Subversive Propaganda* (New York: Praeger, 1989), 163, 172–82.

10. ATIS, SWPA, "Defects Arising from the Doctrine of 'Spiritual Superiority' as Factors in Japanese Military Psychology," Research Report No. 76, Part VI, October 10, 1945, 27, 19, Folder 1–2, Box 1 Charles Andrew Willoughby Papers, HISU; Dower, *War without Mercy*, 68–69.

11. Dower, *War without Mercy*, 45, 52–53, 144; Peter Schrijvers, *The GI War against Japan: American Soldiers in Asia and the Pacific During World War II* (New York: New York University Press, 2002), 165, 177; Special Military Plan for Strategic Services Activities against Japan, December 31,1943, Folder 1707 OSS Planning Group Implementation Studies and Over-all and Special Programs for Strategic Services Activities, Box 127, Entry 139, RG 226 OSS/NARA II; and Ann Todd, *OSS Operation Blackmail: One Woman's Covert War against the Imperial Japanese Army* (Annapolis, MD: Naval Institute Press, 2017), 97–99.

12. R&A Report #91224, July 30, 1944, Box 297 Research and Analysis Branch Central Information Division, Name and Subject Card Indexes to Series 16, Entry 1; J.S. Collins to Colonel (David) Barrett, July 29, 1941 [*sic*:1944/45], Folder 435 China, Box 583, RG 226 OSS/NARA II. For estimates of how many Japanese were taken prisoners, the lowest figure of 35,000 is by Ulrich Strauss, *The Anguish of Surrender: Japanese POWs of World War II* (Seattle: University of Washington Press, 2003), xiii, 24 and the highest figure of 50,000 Ikuhiko Hata, "From Consideration to Contempt: The Changing Nature of Japanese Military and Popular Perceptions of Prisoners of War Through the Ages," in *Prisoners of War and Their Captors in World War II*, ed. Bob Moore and Kent Fedorowich (Oxford: Berg, 1996), 263.

13. Mikio Haruna, *Himitsu no Fairu: CIA no Tainichi Kōsaku* [Secret Files: CIA Operations against Japan] (Tokyo: Shinchō Bunko, 2004), 210–12.

14. Koji Ariyoshi, "Japanese Soldiers' Delegates Conference[:] A Step Toward Effective Propaganda," Yenan Report #34, December 28, 1944, Folder 117, 111–17, 114, Box 1335 R&A Intelligence Reports, Reg. Series, Entry 16, RG 226 OSS/NARA II and Joe Koide, *Aru Zaibei Nihonjin no Kiroku Ge* [Recollections of a Japanese in American, Vol. 2], 262–70.

15. McCracken Fisher to George Taylor, James Stewart, Ralph Block, Porter McKeever, Bradford Smith, F.S. Marquardt, Army, Philippines, John Emmerson, n.d., Folder 117, 111–17, 114, Box 1335 R&A Intelligence Reports, Reg. Series, Entry 16, RG 226 OSS/NARA II.

16. John K. Emmerson, *The Japanese Thread: A Life in the U.S. Foreign Service* (New York: Holt, Rinehart and Winston, 1978), 193–203; John K. Emmerson, "Kazuo Aoyama (Kuroda): Japanese 'Revolutionary'," January 1, 1945, Folder 104 Dixie, Box 7, Entry 148; MO Reports Office to Director, Secretariat, April

23, 1945, Folder 5, Box 60 OSS History Office, Entry 99; Richard Heppner to Commanding General, United States Forces, China Theater, February 22, 1945, Fol. 5, Box 275 Declassified, Entry 210; Roland Dulin to Richard Heppner, March 25, 1945; R.E. Dulin to Richard Heppner, April 26, 1945, and SACO/MO Report for Period 26 February 1945 to 25 March 1945, Folder 4, Box 84 OSS History Office, Entry 99; SACO/MO Report for Period 26 April 1945 to 20 May 1945, Folder 1, Box 85, Entry 99, RG 226 OSS/NARA II.

17. Roland Dulin to Richard Heppner, March 25, 1945; R.E. Dulin to Richard Heppner, April 26, 1945, and SACO/MO Report for period 26 February 1945 to 25 March 1945, Folder 4, Box 84; Anon., Overall (SACO) Report for period 26 April 1945 to 20 May 1945, Folder 1; SACO/MO Report for period 21 May 1945 to 30 June 1945, Folder 2, Box 85 OSS History Office, Entry 99, RG 226 OSS/NARA II.

18. SACO/MO Report for Period 26 February 1945 to 25 March 1945, Folder 4, Box 84, Entry 99, RG 226 OSS/NARA II; Shinji Komada, *Watakushi no Chūgoku Horyo Taiken* [My Experience as a Prisoner in China] (Tokyo: Iwanami Bukkuretto No. 214, 1991), 8–9, 16–17, 25–27; Howard Furumoto to Major Donald Monroe, May 29, 1945, Folder 2 Japanese POW Matters, Box 1 Chungking-MO, Entry 148, RG 226 OSS/NARA II; *Hawai Nihonjin Jinmei Jūshoroku* [Hawaii Japanese Directory] (1937–38), 178; Nippu Jiji, *Hawai Nenkan Shōwa Shichi-Hachinen Tsuki Nihonjin Jūshoroku* [Hawaii Directory 1932–1933 with Japanese Directory] (Honolulu: Nippu Jiji, 1938), City of Honolulu section, 160, Box 359, Japanese American Research Project 2010 Special Collections, Charles E. Young Research Library, UCLA (hereafter cited as JARP/UCLA).

19. General Tai Li to Major (Herbert) Little, April 23, 1944, Folder 1; Howard Furumoto to Major Donald Monroe, May 29, 1945, Folder 2 Japanese POW Matters; Kaji Wataru to Col. (Harley) Stevens/OSS, July 31, 1945, Folder 2 Japanese POW Matters, Box 1 Chungking-MO, Entry 148; Overall Report for Period 21 May 1945 to 30 June 1945, Folder 2, Box 85 OSS History Office, Entry 99; John Emmerson, "Japanese Fear of Allied Psychological Warfare," November 7, 1944, Folder 104 Dixie, Box 7, Entry 148; Don Monroe to Strategic Services Officer, China Theater, August 8, 1945, Folder 2 Japanese POW Matters, Box 1 Chungking-MO, Entry 148, RG 226 OSS/NARA II.

20. Halle, Memorandum of Information for the Joint U.S. Chiefs of Staff, RG 226 OSS/NARA I; Soley, *Radio Warfare*, 163; Yamamoto, *Buraku Puropaganda*, 68.

21. Takeshi Haga, "Nyū Iku Rapusode: Aru Nihonjin Bei Kyōsantoin no Kaisō," in *Nihon Heiwaron Daikei*, ed. Saburō Ienaga (Tokyo: Nihon Tosho Senta, 1994), Vol. 20, 263; Herbert Little to MO Reports Office, Asiatic War Diary, Washington/Far East 1945, 1, Folder 2500, Box 188 Washington and Field Station Files, Entry 139; (Herbert Little), "Biography on "Marigold," 5–6, Folder 2500, Box 188, Entry 139; Anon., Notes on Telephone Conversation between Bruce Rogers and Major Herbert Little, June 23, 1944, Folder 1632 Collingwood Jap Personnel, Box 120, Entry 139; Thos. McFadden to the Board of Review, October 17, 1944, Folder 1632 Collingwood Jap Personnel, Box 120, Entry 139, RG 266 OSS/NARA II.

22. Jin Konomi, "Reminiscences of Joe Koide" (Part 1), *Pacific Citizen*, June 27, 1980, 8; Haruna, *Himitsu no Fairu*, 199–200; Elizabeth P. MacDonald, *Undercover Girl* (New York: Macmillan, 1947), 10–11; and Joe Koide, *Aru Zaibei Nihonjin no Kiroku Ge* [Recollections of a Japanese in American], Vol. 2 (Tokyo: Yūshindō, 1970), 289–90, 295.

23. Yamamoto, *Buraku Puropaganda*, 97–98, 102; Haruna, *Himitsu no Fairu*, 206–207; Herbert Little to MO Reports Office, Asiatic War Diary, Washington/Far East

1945, 22–24, 27, Folder 2500, Box 188 Washington and Field Station Files, Entry 139 and A.D. Mittendorf to MO Reports Office, May 29, 1945, 1,2, Folder 7, Box 149 Declassified, Entry 210, RG 226 OSS/NARA II.

24. Herbert Little to MO Reports Office, Asiatic War Diary, Washington/Far East 1945, 13–14, 17, 22–25, 27–30, Folder 2500, Box 188 Washington and Field Station Files, Entry 139; Richard Pratt to Lt. Col. H.S. Little, July 31, 1945 and (Richard Pratt), Green's Project, n.d., Folder 9, Box 573 COI/OSS Central files, Entry 92; MO Reports Office to Director, Secretariat, April 23, 1945, Folder 5, Box 60 OSS History Office, Entry 99, RG 226 OSS/NARA II; Yamamoto, *Buraku Puropaganda*, 175, 138–39; Howard Schonberger, "Dilemmas of Loyalty: Japanese Americans and the Psychological Warfare Campaigns of the Office of Strategic Services, 1943–45," *Amerasia Journal* 16, no. 1 (1990): 30.

25. Schonberger, "Dilemmas of Loyalty," 28; Little to MO Reports Office, 11–12, 20, 30–34, RG 226 OSS/NARA II.

26. (Herbert Little), "Biography on "Marigold," 3–4, Folder 2500, Box 188, Entry 139, RG 226, OSS, NARA II; Haga, "Nyuiku Rapusode," Vol. 20, 257–58, 262; Haruna *Himitsu no Fairu*, 196–97; Yamamoto, *Buraku Puropaganda*, 84–86.

27. Yamamoto, *Buraku Puropaganda*, 88–90; Schonberger, "Dilemmas of Loyalty," 28–29.

28. Soley, *Radio Warfare*, 161; "VICKS," "Analysis and Comments upon the Japanese Situation," August 24, 1945, Folder 1709, Box 127; Michael Choukas, "Summary Report—MO Plans and Production for Operations in the Far East," September 25, 1945, to Herbert Little, 2–6, 8, 19, 31, Folder 2500, Box 188; and Yaemitsu Sugimachi to Michael Choukas, April 3, 1945, Folder 1713, Box 127; Free Japan League, "Postwar Prospects for Japan," n.d., 1–4, Folder 1718, Box 126 Washington and Field Station Files, Entry 139, RG 226 OSS/NARA II.

29. Yamamoto, *Buraku Puropaganda*, 127; Shō Usami, *Sayonara Nihon: Ehon Sakka, Yashima Tarō to Mitsuko no Bōmei* [Farewell, Japan: The Political Exile of Picture Book Artist Tarō and Mitsuko Yashima] (Tokyo: Nihon Tosho Senta, 1994), Vol. 20, 466.

30. Captain Randall Clark to Roger Simpson, June 14, 1945, Folder 1713, Box 127 Washington and Field Station Files, Entry 139; Herbert Little to Roland (Dulin), April 17, 1945, Folder 6 SSO 31921, Box 550, Entry 92; Carleton Schofield, MO/SEAC Monthly Report, September 30, 1944, Folder 7 SEAC-Sept. 1944, Box 60 OSS History Office, Entry 99, RG 226 OSS/NARA II; Schonberger, "Dilemmas of Loyalty," 31–32; Howard Schonberger, *Japanizu Konekushon: Kaiunō Kei Sugahara Gaiden* [Japanese Connection: Kay Sugahara the Shipping Magnate], translated by Rinjirō Sodei (Tokyo: Bungei Shunjun, 1995), 146; Herbert Little to MO Reports Office, Asiatic War Diary, Washington/Far East 1945, 30–34, Folder 2500, Box 188 Washington and Field Station Files, Entry 139; Robert Ellis to Strategic Services Officer, July 26, 1945 and John Archbold to Strategic Services Officer, HQ, Det 404, July 27, 1945, Folder 2, Box 83 OSS History Office, Entry 99; Herbert Little to Roland (Dulin), April 17, 1945, Folder 6 SSO 31921, Box 550, Entry 92, RG 226 OSS/NARA II.

31. Folder 8, Box 8, Yoneo Sakai Papers 1426, JARP/UCLA; Haruna, *Himitsu no Fairu*, 189–92, 203–204.

CHAPTER 4

1. William Peers and Dean Brelis, *Behind the Burma Road: The Story of America's Most Successful Guerrilla Force* (Boston: Little, Brown, and Co., 1963), 223–28;

Louis Allen, *Burma: The Longest War, 1941–45* (London: J. M. Dent & Sons, 1986), 662; Troy J. Sacquety, *The OSS in Burma: Jungle War against the Japanese* (Lawrence: University Press of Kansas, 2013), 222; John Nunnely and Kazuo Tamayama, *Tales by Japanese Soldiers of the Burma Campaign, 1942–1945* (London: Cassell and Co., 2000), 10; Frank McLynn, *The Burma Campaign: Disaster into Triumph, 1942–45* (London: Vintage Books, 2011), 1; "Military Intelligence Corps Hall of Fame," *Military Intelligence* (April–June 1993): 47, Folder The Deadliest Colonel, Box 3 CEP/HISU.

2. Frank McLynn, *The Burma Campaign: Disaster into Triumph, 1942–45* (London: Vintage Books, 2011), 7, 8, 31–32; Mandy Sadan, *Being and Becoming Kachin: Histories Beyond the State in the Borderworlds of Burma* (New York: Oxford University Press, 2013), 262–63; Mary P. Callahan, *Making Enemies: War and State Building in Burma* (Ithaca, NY: Cornell University Press, 2003), 47, 75.

3. Peers and Brelis, *Behind the Burma Road*, 144–47; Carl Eifler to Colonel William Donovan, November 24, 1942, 25–26, Folder 3; (Carl Eifler) to William Donovan, Report covering period June 1 to June 30, 1943, July 1, 1943, 32, Folder 1, Box 65, Entry 99; "Interviews with Colonel Eifler, Some of Colonel Eifler's View on Training; Based on Talks en route to and at Areas A-4, E, and F, July 1944," Folder 28, Box 2, Entry 161; Carl Eifler to Carl (Hoffman), November 4, 1943, Folder 2, Box 65, Entry 99, RG 226 OSS/NARA II.

4. "Interviews with Colonel Eifler, Some of Colonel Eifler's View on Training; Based on Talks en route to and at Areas A-4, E, and F, July 1944," and Remarks of Colonel Carl Eifler (A-3)—January 31, 1944, Folder 28, Box 2, Entry 161; R. Davis Halliwell to General William J. Donovan, June 18, 1943, cover letter plus Colonel Eifler's report for April 30th to May 15th, p.6, Folder 2, Box 65, Entry 99, RG 226 OSS/NARA II; Wingate to Eifler, October 7, 1943, Folder The Deadliest Colonel, Box 3 CEP/HISU.

5. Thomas N. Moon and Carl F. Eifler, *The Deadliest Colonel* (Springfield, MA: Vantage Press, 1975), 112; (Carl Eifler) to General William Donovan, Report covering period May 16 to May 31, 1943, inclusive, June 1, 1943, 22, Folder 2, Box 65, Entry 99, RG 226 OSS NARA II; Carl Eifler to Citations Officer, September 25, 1945; John Magruder to The Adjutant General, War Department, October 30, 1945; (John) Magruder, Proposed Citation, Folder Chun Ming, Dr. Archie M., and Carl Eifler to The Adjutant General, October 3, 1945, Folder Chun Ming, Archie 0308700, Box 124 OSSPF, Entry 224; Remarks of Colonel Eifler in Mr. (James) Murdock's office, February 2, 1944, Folder 28, Box 2, Entry 161 RG 226 OSS/NARA II.

6. Card, Sukyoon Chang, n.d.; Extract from Service Record, October 3, 1945; Sukyoon Chang to Floyd Frazee, September 7, 1945; Carl Eifler to the Adjutant General, September 18, 1945; Outline of Duties which Justifies Promotion for Sgt. Sukyoon Chang, Folder 201 Chang, Sukyoon, Box 117 OSSPF, Entry 224, RG 226 OSS/NARA II.

7. Chan Hong to Capt. C. R. Corcoran, July 24, 1942, Folder 57, Box 173, Entry 92, RG 226 OSS/NARAII; Extract From Service Record, n.d. and Theater Service Record, April 1945, Folder Chan, Hong, Box 345 OSSPF; Carl Eifler to Colonel William Donovan, November 24, 1942, 20, Folder 3, Box 65, Entry 99, RG 226 OSS/NARA II. For smuggling activities in general, see Philip Thai, "Law, Society, and the War on Smuggling in Coastal China, 1928-1937," *Law and History Review* 34, no. 1 (February 2016): 75-114.

8. Peers and Brelis, *Behind the Burma Road*, 62–63; Moon and Eifler, *The Deadliest Colonel*, 79–81; Frank Heck, "Airline to China," in *The Army Air Forces in World War II*, ed. Wesley Craven and James Cate (Chicago: University of Chicago Press, 58), Vol. 7, 119; Captain [Jack] Neller to Colonel [Lawrence] Lowman, November 6, 1944; D. M. Dimond to the Board of Review, November 7, 1944; W. R. Peers to Commanding General, CBI, August 7, 1944, Folder Eng, Don, Box 220 OSSPF, Entry 224; (Carl Eifler) to William Donovan, Report covering period July 1 to July 31, 1943, inclusive, August 1, 1943, 4, Folder 1, Box 65, Entry 99, RG 226 OSS/ NARA II.

9. Remarks of Colonel Carl Eifler (A-3)—January 31, 1944, Folder 28, Box 2, Entry 161 RG 226 OSS/NARA II.

10. Jeffrey T. Richelson, *Spying on the Bomb: American Nuclear Intelligence from Nazi Germany to Iran and North Korea* (New York: Norton, 2009), 51; John Whiteclay Chambers II, *OSS Training in the National Parks and Service Abroad in World War II* (Washington, DC: US National Park Service, 2008), 173–74; F. M. Small to SSO, HQ, China Theater, February 25, 1945, Folder 3439, Box 203, Entry154, RG 226 OSS/NARA II; Calvin Tottori, *The OSS Niseis in the China-Burma-India Theater* (Honolulu: privately printed, ca. 1997), 6, 10–12.

11. Tottori, *The OSS Niseis in the China-Burma-India Theater*, 11, 14, 30; Ted Tsukiyama and Jim Tanabe, Interview with Fumio Kido, September 18, 2002, Military Intelligence Service Veterans Club of Hawai'i, Oral History Project, University of Hawai'i-Manoa, Honolulu.

12. Ralph Yempuku Interview with Franklin Odo, March 28, 1985 at the Ethnic Studies Program, in Honolulu, Hamilton Library, University of Hawai'i-Manoa, Honolulu; Tottori, *The OSS Niseis in the China-Burma-India Theater*, 21, 23–24; (Howard Furumoto), Recommendation (For Ralph Yempuku), DA Form 638, February 8, 1997, Addendum by Ralph Yempuku written on February 6, 1997, Folder Recommendation for Distinguished Service Medal, Box 40, Varsity Victory Volunteers, TTP/UHM; Tottori, *The OSS Niseis in the China-Burma-India Theater*, 25. The term "duwa" refers not to white persons but to officers or someone in authority. See Sadan, *Being and Becoming Kachin*, 239–40 and Hugh Tinker, "Burma's Northeast Borderland Problems," *Pacific Affairs* 29, no. 4 (December 1956), 328.

13. Memorandum for Files, Estimate of "Bey" on special personnel, April 3, 1944, Folder Hamada, Dick, Box 308 OSSPF, Entry 224 RG 226 OSS/NARA II; Tottori, *The OSS Niseis in the China-Burma-India Theater*, 12; University of Hawai'i, The Hawai'i Nisei Project, "The Hawai'i Nisei Story: Americans of Japanese Ancestry During World War II," The Dick Hamada Story, 2006–07, Honolulu.

14. Sacquety, *The OSS in Burma*, 207–208; Louis Allen, *Burma: The Longest War 1941–45* (New York: St. Martin's Press, 1984), 455; Field Marshal The Viscount (Sir William J.) Slim, *Defeat Into Victory* (New York: David McKay Co., 1961), 384; Captain Daniel Barneswell, Certificate, February 20, 1945, Folder Hamada, Dick, Box 308 OSSPF, Entry 224, RG 226 OSS/NARA II; Draft of Citation Bronze Star Medal; Dick Hamada to Author, August 3, 4, 2009.

15. Maochun Yu, *OSS in China: Prelude to Cold War* (New Haven, CT: Yale University Press, 1996), 274–76; OSS, Implementation Study for the Over-all and Special Programs for Strategic Service Activities Based in China, Korea, P.G. 108–1 15 May 1945, Folder 170, Box 29 Washington Planning Group, Entry 144, RG 226 OSS/NARA II; Ching-chih Chen, "Police and Community Control Systems in the Empire," in *The Japanese Colonial Empire, 1895–1945*, ed. Ramon H. Myers and Mark R. Peattie (Princeton, NJ: Princeton University Press, 1984), 223–26;

Carter J. Eckert, Ki-baik Yi, Yŏng-ik Yu, Michael Robinson, and Wolfgang Eric Wagner, *Korea, Old and New: A History* (Cambridge, MA: Korea Institute, Harvard University, 1990), 318, 321.

16. OSS/SI China Theater, The Eagle Project for SI Penetration of Korea, February 24, 1945, 1, 2, and Appendices, 7–8, 20–23, and (Clyde) Sargent to (Robert) Bowdler, NR 136, August 10, 1945 and NR 117, August 5, 1945, Folder 2887, Box 167, Entry 154, RG 226 OSS/NARA II.

17. OSS SI-FE, "Progress Report SI Branch Far East Division Japan-China Section," April 5, 1945, Folder 10, Box 78, Entry 99; (Clyde) Sargent to (Robert) Bowdler, NR 114, August 3, 1945, Folder 2887 Eagle, Box 167 Kunming, Entry 154; (Clyde Sargent) to Paul Helliwell, June 29, 1945, Folder 2, Box 85, Entry 99; Paul Helliwell to Richard Heppner, July 5, 1945, Folder 2, Box 85, Entry 99; Duncan Lee to Paul Helliwell, March 1, 13, 1945, Folder 6 YK-009/11 Eagle, Box 223, Entry 210, RG 226 OSS/NARA II.

18. Clyde Sargent to Deputy SSO, OSS Chief SI China Theater, and Chief SI, May 2, 1945, Folder 6, Box 223, Entry 210; SACO Report for Period November 26 to December 25, 1944, Folder 1, Box 84, Entry 99; Heppner to (John) Whitaker, June 8, 1945, Folder 3414, Box 201 Kunming Office, Entry 154; (Quentin) Roosevelt for Lee, Krause for Sargent, July 28, 1945, and (Clyde) Sargent (and) Helliwell to (Quentin) Roosevelt, August 2, 1945 and Quentin Roosevelt to Strategic Services Officer, China Theater, June 3, 1945, Folder 6, Box 223, Entry 210; Kim Yak-san and Lee Chung-chan to Willis Bird, May 30, 1945, and Quentin Roosevelt to Strategic Services Officer, China Theater, June 3, 1945, Folder 6, Box 223, Entry 210; (Clyde Sargent), Outline of the Plan for the Eagle Project, Folder 6, Box 223, Entry 210, RG 226 OSS/NARA II.

19. John Whittaker to The Intelligence Officer, OSS, Washington, DC, May 25, 1945, Folder 1, Box 85 OSS History Office, Entry 99; Bradford Hudson to Major [John] Handy and Major [Robert] Murray, August 10, 1945 and R. G. Bowdler, Hsian Trip Report, July 26, 1945 and August 10, 1945, YK-009/11 Eagle, Box 223 OSS Classified Sources and Methods File, Entry 210, RG 226 OSS/NARA II; The OSS Assessment Staff, *Assessment of Men: Selection of Personnel for the Office of Strategic Services* (New York: Rinehart & Co. Inc., 1948), v, vii, 386–89.

20. (Willis) Bird to (Richard) Heppner, NR 147, August 12, 1945, Folder 2887 Eagle, Box 167 Kunming, Entry 154, RG 226 OSS/NARA II; Chong-Sik Lee, *The Politics of Korean Nationalism* (Berkeley: University of California Press, 1965), 226–27; Robert T. Oliver, *Syngman Rhee and American Involvement in Korea, 1942–1960: A Personal Narrative* (Seoul: Panmun Book Co., 1978), 13. See also Richard S. Kim, *The Quest for Statehood: Korean Immigrant Nationalism and U.S. Sovereignty, 1905–1945* (New York: Oxford University Press, 2011), 68–73, 81–86, 159–61 and Chong-sik Lee, *The Politics of Korean Nationalism* (Berkeley: University of California Press, 1965), 226–28.

21. Paul Caraway to War (Department), May 23, 1945, Folder 237, Box 16 Field Station Files, Chungking, Entry 148; William Donovan to Albert Wedemeyer, March 12, 1945, Folder 3416, Box 201 Kunming Office, Entry 154, RG 226 OSS/NARA II.

22. Moon and Eifler, *The Deadliest Colonel*,173, 181–84, 214, 218; Edward Koch, Military Record and Report of Separation Certificate of Service, September 23, 1947, no folder; Anon., Medical Abstract ca. 1946, Folder Retirement Orders, Box 4; Carl Eifler to Lois Poe, November 9, 1945, Folder The Deadliest Colonel, Box 3 CEP/HISU.

23. Carl Eifler to the Adjutant General, September 18, 1945, Folder Chang, Sukyoon, Box 117, Entry 224; OSS, Field Experimental Unit, The NAPKO Project, March 30, 1945, Appendix "B ": Summary of Prisoners of War Interrogation, 15, Folder 29, Box 3 Washington and Field Station Files Honolulu, Entry 139A, RG 226 OSS/ NARA II; Moon and Eifler, *The Deadliest Colonel*, 217; Chambers, *OSS Training in the National Parks and Service Abroad in World War II*, 462.
24. E. G. Wilson to Planning Group, May 28, 1945, Folder 173: NAPKO Project-No. 269, Box 29, Entry 144, RG 226 OSS/NARA II; Vincent L. Curl to (Carl) Eifler, March 4, 1945, Folder Curl's Rpts #1, Box 4, CEP/HISU.
25. Vincent Curl to Eifler, March 25, 1945 and April 1, 1945; C. W. Campbell and H. Kaplan to Paul McCallen, Student progress Report Communications Training, March 31, 1945; Sergeant (George) Ghecas, Demolitions Evaluation, March 26– 31 [1945]; First Lieutenant Robert Carter to Major (Vincent) Curl, ca. March 1945, Folder Curl's Rpts #1, Box 4, CEP/HISU.
26. Vincent Curl, report to Carl Eifler, March 4, 1945 and March 11, 1945, Folder Curl's Rpts #1, Box 4, CEP/HISU.
27. Vincent Curl to Colonel Carl Eifler, March 11, 1945 and April 1, 1945, Folder Curl's Rpts #1, Box 4, CEP/HISU.
28. (Theodore) Russell, evaluation, n.d.; Vincent Curl, report to Carl Eifler, March 4, 1945 and March 11, 1945; Folder Curl's Rpts #1, Box 4, CEP/HISU.
29. Vincent Curl, report to Carl Eifler, March 4, March 11, and March 25, 1945, Folder Curl's Rpts #1, Box 4, CEP/HISU.
30. Vincent Curl to Eifler, March 11, 1945; Robert Carter to (Vincent) Curl, n.d. ca. March 1945, Folder Curl's Rpts #1, Box 4, CEP/HISU.
31. (Carl Eifler) to William Donovan, Report covering period June 1 to June 30, 1943, July 1, 1943, 32–33, Folder 1, Box 65, Entry 99, RG 226 OSS NARA II; Brandon Palmer, *Fighting for the Enemy: Koreans in Japan's War, 1937–1945* (Seattle: University of Washington Press, 2013), 123; Colonel Eifler's report for April 30th to May 15th, ca. June 18, 1943, 17, 6, Folder 2, Box 65, Entry 99, RG 226 OSS NARA II.
32. Vincent Curl to Eifler, March 25, 1945, Folder Curl's Rpts #1, Box 4, CEP/HISU.
33. Vincent Curl to Eifler, March 18, 1945, Folder Curl's Rpts #1, Box 4, CEP/HISU.
34. Paul Helliwell to Strategic Services Officer/China Theater, April 26, 1945, Folder 3416, Box 201 Kunming Office, Entry 154; (Richard) Heppner to 109 (William Donovan), May 8, 1945, Folder 237, Entry 148, Box 16 Field Station Files Chungking; and 109 (William Donovan) to (Richard) Heppner and (Otto) Doering, May 6, 1945, Folder 3416, Box 201 Kunming Office, Entry 154, RG 226 OSS/NARA II.
35. Indiv and Fiser from Stevens, NR 766, August 24, 1945, Folder 237, Box 16 Field Station Files, Chungking, Entry 148, RG 226, NARA II; Vincent Curl, report to Carl Eifler, March 4, 1945, Folder Curl's Rpts #1, Box 4, CEP/HISU.

CHAPTER 5

1. James Opsata, CSC Field Report, December 3, 1945; EAS, Office memorandum, November 30, [1945], Folder 39, Box 116, Entry 224, RG 226 OSS/NARA II.
2. Anon., Summary of Monthly Report, R&A, for October 1944, 10, Folder 99, 1 of 3 and Martin Easton to Donald Gregory, November 1, 1944, Folder 99–3 of 3; Anon., Central Information Division—November 1944, Folder 100–1 of 3, Box 115 OSS History Office, Entry 99; John Hughes to The Director, December 6, 1944, Folder 100–3 of 3, Box 115 OSS History Office, Entry 99; Janet McHendrie to (Martin)

Easton, January 9, 1945, Folder 618 General, Box 79 Pacific Coast Office, Entry 140; Alfred Tozzer, "History of Honolulu Outpost," ca. 1945, 27–39, Folder 790, Box 78, Entry 139; Martin Easton to Donald Gregory, November 1, 1944, Folder 99–3 of 3, Box 115 OSS History Office, Entry 99; (Janet McHendrie), History of R&A, Los Angeles Branch, ca. January 9, 1945, Folder 618 General, Box 79 Pacific Coast Office, Entry 140; E. P. Connely, Monthly Report-Pacific Coast Area-Month of March, 1945, April 9, 1945; (Edward Allen), Report of Seattle Regional Activities, Pacific Coast Area, 1st to 31st March, 1945; and Martin Easton by A. D. McHendrie to E. F. Connely, April 2, 1945, Folder 5, Box 573, Entry 92, RG 226 OSS/NARA II.

3. Intercept Translation Unit, Los Angeles- Personnel, caOctober 24, 1944, Folder 188, Box 14, Entry 146B; A. R. Lusey to H.S. Morgan, October 24, 1944, Folder 188, Box 14, Entry 146B; (A. R. Lusey) to (N. F. Allman), September 20, 1944, Folder 188, Box 14, Entry 146B; A. R. Lusey to S. J. Nicholson, October 21, 1944, Folder 188 Correspondence- Mr. A. Lusey, June 1944–Dec1944, Box 14, Entry 146 OSS History Office, RG 226 OSS/NARA II; N. F. Allman, History-Far East SI, ca. 1945, 16–18, Folder 6–17: "History—Far East, SI," n.d., 8, Box 6, NFAP/HISU; N. F. Allman, to C. R. Bohannon, August 1, 1945, Folder 4, Box 14, Entry 146 OSS History Office; Charles Ford to Eve Jones, September 27, 1945; Daniel Buchanan to B. Knollenberg, January 12, 1945; John Stacy to Winthrop Mayo, September 25, 1944, Folder Bepp, Yoneo, Box 50 OSSPF, Entry 224; Progress Report, FESI, December, 1944, 19, Folder 1, Box 79, Entry 140; Daniel Buchanan to Whom It May Concern, August 25, 1945, Folder Tachino, Tadami, Box 763 OSSPF, Entry 224, RG 226 OSS/NARA II.

4. Report #54,890; A. Cornell, Survey of Foreign Experts, Report #54,888, January 6, 1944, Box 660 R&A Intelligence Reports; Ewing Sadler, "Japanese Mind and War Effort," confidential report, February 20, 1943, to Fowler Hamilton, Report #29,893; Edwin Sadler, Memorandum for the files, February 20, 1943, Report #29,894; Edwin Sadler, Memorandum for the files, February 20, 1943, Report #29,895, Box 300 R&A Intelligence Reports; Ernest Price to Economic Warfare Unit, May 18, 1943, Report #37332, Box 415 R&A Intelligence Reports, Entry 16, RG 226 OSS/NARA II.

5. Alfred Tozzer, "History of Honolulu Outpost," ca. 1945, 7, 18, 25–27, Folder 790, Box 78, Entry 139, RG 226, OSS/NARA II.

6. Donald Gregory to William Cary, December 13, 194, Folder 100 3 of 3 Monthly Report November 1944 and R.W. Scott to D.M. Gregory, November 3, 1944, Folder 99–3 of 3, Box 115 History Office, Entry 99; R. W. Scott to W. L. Langer, April 26, 1945; Janet McHendrie to (Martin) Easton, (Edward) Stanton, November 23, 1944, Folder 619 R&A General, Box 79 Pacific Coast Office, Entry 140; R. W. Scott, "Report of R & A Activities in the Pacific Coast Area for March 1945," April 2, 1945, Folder 5, Box 573, Entry 92, RG 226 OSS/NARA II; Chas. Sullivan Jr. to District Cable Censor, San Francisco, June 30, 1943, Folder San Francisco-Cable June 1943, Entry 1A, Box 671; A History of the Office of Censorship, Volume VI: Office of the Chief Cable Censor, 16, Box 6, Entry 4, RG 216 Record of the Office of Cable Censorship, NARA II.

7. Katsuji Katō, *The Psychology of Oriental Religious Experience: A Study of Some Typical Experiences of Japanese Converts to Christianity* (Menasha, WI: George Banta Publishing Company, 1915), 102; Katsuhiro Fukutake, "In Memory of Prof. Dr. Katsuji Kato," *Blood: News and Views* 19 (1962): 123; US Census, 1940, roll T627_931, 2B, enumeration District 103–331; R&A Report #15388

C, as indicated in card index in Box 297 Research and Analysis Branch Central Information Division, Name and Subject Card Indexes to Series 16, Entry 1; J.R. Hayden to Robert Cresswell, June 20, 1942, Far Eastern Progress Report— Summary through June 13, 1942, Folder 7, Box 80 COI/OSS Central Files; J.R. Hayden to Robert Cresswell, Far Eastern Progress Report, July 6, 1942, Folder 24, Box 78, Entry 92, RG 226 OSS/NARA II.

8. ONI, "Taoka, Yahei," September 20, 1945, Counter-Intelligence Data on Japan Section VII: Suspect Japanese Formerly Active in the United States October 3, 1945, Folder no title, Box 20, CI Reports on Japanese organization and individuals, 1945, Entry UD 29, RG 38 CNO/NARA II; Spencer Phenix to Ernest Price, June 25, 1942, Folder 39, Box 82, Entry 92, RG 226 OSS/NARA II; *Shin Sekai Asahi Nenkan* [The New World Sun Year Book 1941] (San Francisco: Shin Sekai Shimbunsha, 1941), 81.

9. Ernest Price to Project Officer, September 5, 1942; Progress Report for Week Ending September 5, 1942, Far East Desk; Ernest Price to Project Officer, September 21, 1942, Ernest Price to Project Officer, August 31, 1942, J. R. Hayden to Robert Cresswell, Far Eastern Progress Report, July 6, 1942 and June 22, 1942, Folder 24, Box 78; Progress Report for Week Ending August 22, 1942, Far East Desk, Folder 24, Box 78, Entry 92, RG 226 OSS/NARA II; www.nytimes. com/1996/06/24/nyregion/clement-m-hakim-a-tea-importer84.html (accessed November 10, 2013); Ernest Price to Project Officer, August 3, 1942, Far Eastern Progress Report—Week Ending August 1, 1942, Folder 7, Box 80 COI/OSS Central Files, Entry 92, RG 266 OSS/NARA II.

10. Carolle J. Carter, *Mission to Yenan: American Liaison with the Chinese Communists, 1944–1947* (Lexington: University Press of Kentucky, 1997), 64, 67–69; Haga, "Nyu Iku Rapusode," Vol. 20, 96–98; Ray Cromley, Personnel Needed for China Order of Battle Work, July 31, 1944, no folder title, Box 564 Kunming Field Station Files, Entry 154, RG 226 OSS/NARA II; Douglas Waller, *Wild Bill Donovan: The Spymaster Who Created The OSS and Modern American Espionage* (New York: Free Press, 2011), 283–88, 278–80.

11. Director of Strategic Services, Memorandum for the Joint Chiefs of Staff, July 18, 1945, Folder 11, Box 81, Entry 92; Roger Sanford, S. B. Mitsunaga, Michael Murphy, Memorandum for the G-2 Appendix A, April 26, 1945, Folder 11, Box 81, Entry 92, RG 226 OSS/NARA II.

12. Joan Bondurant to Merrill Spaulding, June 17, 1943, Folder 638, Box 80, Entry 140; C.J. Francis to Joan Bondurant, September 28, 1945, Folder Bondurant, Joan V., Box 67, Entry A1 224; OSS Pacific Coast Area, Reports Prepared by the Research and Analysis Branch, ca. June 12, 1945, Folder 704, Box 85, Entry 140; Joan Bondurant to Robert Hall, July 9, 1943, Folder 638, Box 80, Entry 140, RG 226, OSS/NARA II; Rumi Yasutake, *Transnational Women's Activism: The United States, Japan, and Japanese Immigrant Communities in California, 1859–1920* (New York: New York University Press, 2004), 43–44.

13. Duncan Lee to Chief SI/CT, May 14, 1945, Progress Report for April 1945 and Progress Report for May 1945, June 11, 1945; Progress Report SI Branch Far East Division Japan-China Section, Progress Report for March 1945, April 5, 1945, Folder 3, Box 81, Entry 92; Progress Report, FESI December 1944, p.1, Folder 1, Box 79, Entry 92; OSS SI-FE, "Progress Report SI Branch Far East Division Japan-China Section," April 5,1945, Folder 10, Box 78, Entry 92, RG 226 OSS/NARA II.

14. Progress Report, FESI December, 1944, 1, Folder 1, Box 79; Duncan Lee to Chief SI/CT, May 14, 1945; Progress Report for April 1945, Folder 3, Box 81; Progress

Report SI Branch Far East Division Japan-China Section, June 6, 1945 Progress Report for May 1945, Folder 10, Box 78; Summary of Budget Requirements SI Branch Fiscal Year 1945, Folder 2, Box 42; Duncan Lee to Chief SI/CT, June 11, 1945, Progress Report for May 1945, Folder 3, Box 81, Entry 92; J.B. de Sibour to Strategic Services Officer, HQ, OSS/China Theater, January 29, 1945, Folder 2, Box 84, Entry 99, RG 226 OSS/NARA II.

15. Calvin Tottori, *The OSS Niseis in the China-Burma-India Theater* (Privately printed, Honolulu, ca. 1997), 28; Ted Tsukiyama and Jim Tanabe, Interview with Fumio Kido, September 18, 2002, Military Intelligence Service Veterans Club of Hawai'i, Oral History Project, University of Hawai'i-Manoa, Honolulu.

16. Charles F. Romanus and Riley Sunderland, *Time Runs Out in CBI* (Washington, DC: Office of the Chief of Military History, Department of the Army, 1959), Vol. 9, pt.3, 361–62, 366; Paul Helliwell, to Wilfred Smith, April 9, 1945, Folder 3172 Kunming-Akron Mission, Box 185, Entry 154, RG 226 OSS/NARA II.

17. Texas to (Paul) Helliwell, NR 656, June 16, 1945, Folder 3172 Kunming-Akron Mission, Box 185, Entry 154; John Whiteclay Chambers II, *OSS Training in the National Parks and Service Abroad in World War II* (Washington, DC: US National Park Service, 2008), 438–39; C. M. Parkin Jr. to Strategic Services Officer, CT, March 25, 1945 and William Davis to Chief OSS/CT, March 8, 1945, Folder 3172, Box 185 Kunming Office, Entry 154; Akron to Repo & Texas, June 15, 1945, Folder 2935, Box 170 Field Station Files Kunming, Entry 154; Robert Matthews Jr., Report on Field Duty, October 3, 1945, Folder 3172 Kunming-Akron Mission, Box 185, Entry 154, RG 226 OSS/NARA II.

18. Maochun Yu, *OSS in China: Prelude to Cold War* (New Haven, CT: Yale University Press, 1996), 155–56; Lincoln Kan to Jesse Williams, June 22, 1943, Folder Naval Group China Chapter 7, Box 10, Entry 332, RG 38 CNO/NARA II; Author, telephone interview with Betty Kan, February 21, 2011.

19. Paul Helliwell to Wilfred Smith, April 9, 1945, Folder 3172, Box 185 Kunming Office, Entry 154; YKB-2672, (handbook #2, Dewey to Kan), n.d., 2; YKB-2672, (handbook #2, Dewey to Kan), n.d., 3, Folder 445, Box 55, Entry 140; YKB-2672, (handbook #2, Kan to Dewey), August 8, 1945, 17; Mat(thews) to Kan, n.d., YKB-2672, (handbook #2, Dewey to Kan), n.d., 1, Folder 445, Box 55, Entry 140, RG 226 OSS/NARA II; Author, telephone interview with Betty Kan, February 21, 2011; YKE-2672 Exercise Book From Ambelang, n.d., 1–3, Folder 445, Box 55, Entry 140, RG 226 OSS/NARA II.

20. YKB-2672, (handbook #2, Kan to Dewey), August 8, 1945, 17 and YKB-2672, (handbook #2, Dewey to Kan), n.d., 11, Folder 445, Box 55, Entry 140, RG 226 OSS/NARA II.

21. Dixee Bartholomew-Feis, *The OSS And Ho Chi Minh: Unexpected Allies in the War Against Japan* (Lawrence: University Press of Kansas, 2006), 26–27, 30, 33; Martin Thomas, 955–56; Robert Larson, Memorandum for Commander (David) Wight, March 7, 1944, Folder 3, Box 35; Lt. Col. [first name] Emblanc, Information Bulletin Number 16, 2nd week of September 1943, Folder 5, Box 36, Entry 332, Record Group 38 Office of the Chief of Naval Operations, Naval Group China and Milton E. Miles, National Archives and Records Administration II, College Park, MD (hereafter CNO/NGC/NARA II).

22. Bartholomew-Feis, *The OSS And Ho Chi Minh*, 11; Martin Thomas, "Silent Partners: SOE's French Indo-China Section, 1943–1945," *Modern Asian Studies* 34, no. 4 (2000), 947–49; James T. H. Tang, "From Empire Defence to Imperial Retreat: Britain's Postwar China Policy and the Decolonization of Hong Kong,"

Modern Asian Studies 28, no. 2 (1994), 318–22; Steve Tsang, *A Modern History of Hong Kong* (London: I. B. Tauris & Co., 2004), 130–31.

23. Douglas Porch, *The French Secret Services: A History of French Intelligence from the Dreyfus Affair to the Gulf War* (New York: Farrar, Straus and Giroux, 1995), 202–202, 295–97; Julia Alayne Grenier Burlette, "French Influence Overseas: Rise and Fall of Colonial Indochina" (MA thesis, Louisiana State University, 2007), 62; Bartholomew-Feis, *The OSS and Ho Chi Minh*, 126; R&A Report #91838, July 31, 1944, Box 304, Entry 14, RG 226 OSS/NARA II; D.D. Wight, Memorandum for (Joseph) Dickey, May 11, 1944, Folder 2, Box 35; (Milton Miles), Summary of Meynier Group, August 31, 1943, Folder 4 French Indo-China Group, Box 36, Entry 332, RG 38 CNO/NGC/NARA II; Thomas, "Silent Partners," 952–53; N. F. Allman to Ward Delaney, April 9, 1943; WJD (William J. Donovan) to DKEB (David K. E. Bruce), December 3, 1942; and DKEB to WJD, November 20, 1942, Folder 6, Box 173, Entry 92, RG 226 OSS/NARA II.

24. Thomas, "Silent Partners," 960–61; Yu, *OSS in China*, 117; (Milton Miles), Report on the Activities of "SACO" Directed Towa6t5rd Indo China, n.d., Folder 4 French Indo-China Group, Box 36, Entry 332, RG 38 CNO/NGC/NARA II.

25. Milton Miles to Colonel William Donovan, May 7, 1943; Milton Miles to William Donovan, September 21, 1943; (Marion Miles), Summary of Meynier Group, August 31, 1943; Robert Larson to (Marion) Miles, September 21, 1944; and R. Davis Halliwell to J.C. Metzel, July 19, 1943, Folder 4 French Indo-China Group, Box 36, Entry 332, RG 38 CNO/NGC/NARA II.

26. Charles Fenn to Jacques de Sibour, November 25, 1944, Box 72, Entry 99, RG 226 OSS/NARA II; John McAuliff, "Full Transcripts of the OSS-Viet Minh Meeting organized by the Fund for Reconciliation in Southampton, New York, 1997," 9, 19–20, 66; Commander, US Naval Unit, 14th Air Force to Chief of Naval Operations, December 6, 1944, Folder 3 French Indo-China Group, Box 36, Entry 332, RG 38 CNO/NGC/NARA II; Archimedes L. Patti, *Why Vietnam?: Prelude to America's Albatross* (Berkeley: University of California Press, 1980), 44–45; John Coughlin, "Comments on Gordon Plan," n.d.; John Coughlin, "The Gordon Plan," September 20, 1944 and T. G. Hearn to Commanding General, USAAF, India-Burma Theater, November 4, 1944, Folder 669 TS 29, Box 44, Entry 148, RG 226 OSS/NARA II.

27. Frank Tan to Gunnar Mykland, August 11, 1944, Folder 151 Advances; Gunnar Mykland to Colonel Robert Hall, August 28, 1944 and September 7, 1944, Folder 154, Box 007 Kumning Special Funds Financial Records, Entry 197; Charles Fenn to Paul Helliwell, May 11, 1945, Folder 3453 Projects YK-009/2 GBT, Box 203, Entry154; W.B. Kantack, Report on OSS Activities for the Month of July 1944, Folder 2, Box 123 History Office, Entry 99; Summary by W. B. Kantack, Folder 5, Box 123, Entry 99, RG 226 OSS/NARA II. The US dollar to Chinese Nationalist dollar exchange rate was about 1 to 277 in 1944.

28. Vu Ngu Chieu, "The Other Side of the 1945 Vietnamese Revolution: The Empire of Viet-Nam, March-August 1945," *Journal of Asian Studies* XLV, no. 2 (February 1986): 294–98, 304, 312–16; Kiyoko Kurusu Nitz, "Independence without Nationalists? The Japanese and Vietnamese Nationalism during the Japanese Period, 1940–1945," *Journal of Southeast Asian Studies* 15 (March 1984): 120–22, 132–33; Patti, *Why Vietnam?*, 57.

29. John McAuliff, "Full Transcripts of the OSS-Viet Minh Meeting organized by the Fund for Reconciliation in Southampton, New York, 1997," 20–22, 50; William J. Druicker, *Ho Chi Minh: A Life* (New York: Thenia, 2000), 288, 294; Charles Fenn to Richard Heppner, April 24, 1945, Folder 5, Box 84, Entry 99, RG 226 OSS/

NARA II; Charles Fenn, "Remembering Frank Tan," Indochina News Summer 2002, http://www.ffrd.org/indochina/summer02news.html (accessed June 14, 2008).

30. Charles Fenn, "Remembering Frank Tan," Indochina News Summer 2002, http://www.ffrd.org/indochina/summer02news.html (accessed June 14, 2008); John McAuliff, "Full Transcripts of the OSS-Viet Minh Meeting organized by the Fund for Reconciliation in Southampton, New York, 1997," 32, 33, 10–11; Vu Ngu Chieu, "The Other Side of the 1945 Vietnamese Revolution," 306; David G. Marr, *Vietnam 1945: The Quest for Power* (Berkeley: University of California Press, 1997), 284: Patti, *Why Vietnam?*, 126.

31. Thomas, "Silent Partners," 962–64; Maochun Yu, *OSS in China*, 207; OSS SI-FE, "Progress Report SI Branch Far East Division Japan-China Section," April 5, 1945, Folder 10, Box 78, Entry 92, RG 225 OSS/NARA II. See also Susan C. Seymour, *Cora Du Bois: Anthropologist, Diplomat, Agent* (Lincoln: University of Nebraska Press, 2015), 199–201.

32. Chin-tung Liang, *General Stilwell in China, 1942–1944: The Full Story* (Shanghai: St. John's University Press, 1972), ix, xii–xiii; J.B. de Sibour to Strategic Services Officer, HQ, OSS/China Theater, January 29, 1945, Folder 2, Box 84, Entry 99, RG 226 OSS/NARA II.

33. J. B. de Sibour to Strategic Services Officer, Headquarters China & India-Burma Theaters, December 26, 1944 and SACO Report for Period November 26 to December 25, 1944, Folder 1, Box 84, Entry 99; J. B. de Sibour to Strategic Services Officer, Headquarters China & India-Burma Theaters, December 26, 1944, Folder 1 China-Dec. 1944, Box 84, Entry 99, RG 226 OSS/NARA II.

34. Paul Helliwell to Colonel Richard Heppner, April 28, 1945, Folder 5, Entry 99 Box 84; Paul Helliwell to Strategic Services Officer, May 22, 1945 and Paul Helliwell to GBT Group, May 28, 1945, Folder 3453 Projects YK-009/2 GBT, Box 203, Entry154, RG 226 OSS/NARA II.

35. Waller, *Wild Bill Donovan*, 330; Francis B. Mills, Robert Mills, and John W. Brunner, *OSS Special Operations in China* (Williamstown, NJ: Phillips Publications, 2003), 365–88; Patti, *Why Vietnam?*, 126–29.

36. Jonna Doolittle Hoppes, *Just Doing My Job: Stories of Service from World War II* (Santa Monica, CA: Santa Monica Press, 2009), 308–27; Dick Hamada to author, August 29, 2009; http://nisei.hawaii.edu/object/io_1193532373937.html (accessed February 26, 2016).

CHAPTER 6

1. Ken Kotani, *Japanese Intelligence in World War II* (Oxford: Osprey Publishing, 2009), tr. by Chiharu Kotani, 12–19, 125, 72, 6–7, 48–50; Strategic Services Unit, "Japanese Intelligence Organizations in China," June 4, 1946, Section I: 87–88, 179–80; Section II, 1–2, 48–50, 174–75, 184, at CIA's website http://www.foia.cia.gov/document/519cd81a993294098d515f19 (accessed August 15, 2015).

2. C. Lester Walker, "China's Master Spy," *Harper's* (August 1946), 1–2, in Folder China, Box 2, Richard Harris Smith Papers, HISU; Frederic Wakeman Jr., *Spymaster: Tai Li and the Chinese Secret Service* (Berkeley: University of California Press, 2003), 5; Agent BH-001 in Calcutta, India, report on Tai Li Operations in China, June 26, 1944, File No. 5, Box 72, Entry 210; BH/215, Local file no. YEX-1187, January 28, 1946, Folder 140, Box 26, Entry 182, RG 226 OSS/NARA II; Dickie (Mountbatten) to Al (Wedemeyer), November 21, 1974, Folder 52.21 Mountbatten, Louis, Box 52, Albert Coady Wedemeyer Papers, HISU.

3. Keith Jeffery, *MI6: The History of the Secret Intelligence Service, 1909–1949* (London: Bloomsbury, 2010), 573–95; O.125 (G. Findlay Andrew), R.I.I. Origin— Scope—Objectives, September 30, 1942; O.125 [G. Findlay Andrew] to O/X, April 12, 1944; BB.100 (Colin Mackenzie) to O.125 (G. Findlay Andrew), March 4, 1944; O.125 to F. A. (New Delhi), January 17, 1945, HS 1/140; O/X (George S. Moss) to AD/O (John Keswick), May 6, 1943; D/U to BB 100 (Colin Mackenzie), October 21, 1942; HS 1/165, SOE/NAKL.

4. Robert Bickers, "The Business of Secret War: Operation 'Remorse' and SOE Salesmanship in Wartime China," *Intelligence and National Security* 16, no. 4 (Winter 2001): 11–12, 17, 27, 29; B /B100 and A. D. to C. D., November 1, 1945, Folder HS 1/180; G. Findlay Andrew to Admin. HQ Force 136, February 20, 1945, Folder HS 1/180; B /B100 and A. D. to C. D., November 1, 1944, Folder HS 1/ 180; JH to KANDY, January 10, 1945 and KANDY to London A.D.4, January 15, 1945, Folder HS 1/180; Minutes of Meeting Held at Meerut 8th November '44 to Discuss Requirements for the Formation of a Resistance Movement in China, November 30, 1944, Folder HS 1/180; H.M. Sichel to Hugh (Legg), December 1, 1944, HS 8/80; Mike (Kendall) to Herbert (Sichel), January 23, 1945 and JRL to TGDB, October 9, 1944, HS 8/86 (Chinese recruits for India training, Part 4, January 1, 1944 to December 31, 1844); JRL to TGDB, June 20, 1945 and Mike (Kendall) to Herbert (Sichel), May 29, 1945 and HMS to TGDB, May 19, 1945, HS 8/86 (Chinese recruits for India training, Part 4, January 1, 1944 to December 31, 1944); London "O" telegram no. 253, May 27, 1945, HS 8/86 (Chinese recruits for India training, Part 4, January 1, 1944 to December 31, 1944), SOE/NAKL.

5. A. D. O. (John Keswick) to CD., May 31, 1943, HS 1/165, SOE/NAKL; W. B. Kantack, Report on OSS Activities for the Month of July 1944, Folder 2, Box 123, Entry 99, RG 226 OSS/NARA II; Richard Heppner, Report of the Strategic Services Officer, China Theater, for 26 February 1945 to 25 March 1945, 5, Folder 4, Box 84, Entry 99; Richard Heppner, Report of the Strategic Services Officer, China Theater, for 26 February 1945 to 25 March 1945, Folder 4; Richard Heppner, Report of Strategic Services Officer, 25 March to 25 April 1945, Folder 5, Box 84, Entry 99; W.B. Kantack to Director, May 14, 1945, Folder 5, Box 84 OSS History Office, Entry 99, RG 226 OSS/NARA II.

6. James R. Murphy, Monthly Report of Activities for October 1944, n.d., Folder 99, 1 of 3, Box 115, Entry 99, RG 226 OSS/NARA II.

7. X-2 Branch to Jacques de Sibour, January 24, 1945, Folder 2; Monthly Report of Activities, X-2 Branch, China for February, 1945, February 22, 1945, Box 84, Entry 99; Anon., Monthly Report of Activities X-2 Branch, China for March, 1945, March 24, 1945, Folder 4, Box 84, Entry 99; Amos W. Melton to Commanding Officer Hsian Field Unit Command, May 30, 1945, Folder 1, Box 85, Entry 99; BH/044, BH/030, Report No. YKX-2623, June 14, 1945, Folder 3; BH/030 Report YKX-1650, March 14, 1945, Folder 5, Box 1, Entry 182, RG 226 OSS/ NARA II. This spy network was not likely set up by Kawashima despite her use-fulness in intelligence gathering for the Japanese in the early 1930s but more likely a product of another individual. For English-language accounts of Yoshiko Kawashima, see Louise Edwards, *Women Warriors and Wartime Spies of China* (Cambridge: Cambridge University Press, 2016), 91–116 and Phyllis Birnbaum, *Manchu Princess, Japanese Spy: The Story of Kawashima Yoshiko, the Cross-Dressing Spy Who Commanded Her Own Army* (New York: Columbia University Press, 2015), 116–25, 158, 179-80, 218-9..

8. Edward Harding to Richard P. Heppner, July 31, 1945, Folder 3, Box 85 OSS History Office, Entry 99; Anon., Monthly Report of Activities X-2 Branch, China for March, 1945, March 24, 1945, Folder 4, Box 84, Entry 99; Chan Hong to C.R. Corcoran, July 24, 1942, Folder 57, Box 173, Entry 92; Theater Service Record, April 1945 and R.R. Oliver to The Adjutant General, July 30, 1945, Folder 57, Box 173, Entry 92, RG 226 OSS/NARA II.

9. Sidney S. Rubenstein, Personal Report to William Donovan, September 1, 1944, Folder 3, Box 73, Entry 210; Sidney Rubenstein to Lincoln Mei, September 5, 1944 and Personnel Attached to CBI, November 25, 1944, Folder Mei, Lincoln, Box 515 OSSPF, Entry 224, RG 226 OSS/NARA II.

10. X-2 Branch to Jacques de Sibour, November 24, 1944 and OSS SU Det. 202, CBI, (List), November 29, 1944, Folder 1, Box 72, Entry 99; Jack Brown to Arthur Thurston, December 13, 1944 and Jack (Brown) to Art (Thurston), December 13, 1944, Folder Mei, Lincoln, Box 515 OSSPF, Entry 224, RG 226 OSS/NARA II.

11. Edward Harding to Personnel Committee, August 18, 1945, Folder Mei, Lincoln, Box 515 OSSPF, Entry 224; Lincoln Mei to Louis Kubler, July 11, 1945, Folder 100, Box 13, Entry 182A; William Weiss Jr. to Commanding Officer, Det. 202, January 25, 1945; and W.B. Kantack to Secretariat, February 12, 1945, 40, 83, Folder 2, Box 84 OSS History Office, Entry 99; Anon., 1st Lt. Lincoln Mei, ca. October 1945 and Separation Process Sheet, ca. November 1, 1945, Folder Mei, Lincoln, Box 515 OSSPF, Entry 224, RG 226 OSS/NARA II.

12. John Kwock to Commanding Officer, Detachment 202, January 24, 1945, Folder 2; John Kwock, Monthly Report, Security branch for Period 26 January–25 February 1945, Folder 3; John Kwock, Monthly Report, Security branch for Period 26 January–25 February 1945, Folder 3; John Kwock, Security Report Special Programs and Other Authorized Activities, ca. May 1945, Folder 5, Box 84 OSS History Office, Entry 99; John Kwock, to Captain Clyde Sergent thru (Gustav) Krause, June 14, 1945, Folder 3542, Box 203, Entry 154, RG 226 OSS/NARA II.

13. George White, X-2 Branch Report, January 28, 1945, Folder 5, Box 1 Shanghai Intelligence Files, Entry 182, RG 226, OSS/NARA II; BH/011, Report No. YKX-2680, June 25, 1945, Folder 31-00-101 to 1-00-237 Sect. II, and BH/011, Report untitled, March 18, 1945, Folder 5, Box 1 Shanghai Intelligence Files, Entry 182, RG 226, OSS/NARA II; John Kwock, to Clyde Sargent, June 14, 1945, Folder 3542, Box 203 Entry 154, RG 226 OSS/NARA II.

14. Department of State Interim Research and Intelligence Service, Research and Analysis Branch, Monthly Reports to the Outposts, August 4, 1945, Folder 9, Box 21, Entry 1; NA, Citation (for John Kwock), n.d., Folder Kwock, John, Box 425 OSSPF, Entry 224; Robert Delaney, Circular No. 14 HQ, OSS, China Theater, August 30, 1945, 3, 5, 7, 11, Folder 2838 Circulars, Box 164 Kunming, Entry 154, RG 226 OSS/NARA II.

15. Gavan Daws, *Prisoners of the Japanese: POWs of World War II in the Pacific* (New York: Quill William Morrow, 1994), 17–18, 360–61; Bernice Archer, *The Internment of Western Civilians under the Japanese, 1941–1945: A Patchwork of Internment* (London: Routledge Curzon, 2004), 5.

16. Maochun Yu, *OSS in China: Prelude to Cold War* (New Haven, CT: Yale University Press, 1996), 233–35; (Robert) Helm to (Ray) Peers, August 17, 1945, NR 369, Folder 3188, Folder 3185, Box 186 Field Station Files, Kunming, Entry 154, RG 226 OSS/NARA II; COM(manding) GEN(eral) China to COMGEN SOS for Heppner OSS and AGAS Cipion, August 24, 1945, Folder 3185, Box 186 Field Station Files, Kunming, Entry 154, RG 226 OSS/NARA II.

17. Ted Tsukiyama and Jim Tanabe, Interview with Fumio Kido, September 18, 2002, Military Intelligence Service Veterans Club of Hawai'i, Oral History Project, University of Hawai'i-Manoa, Honolulu; Yu, *OSS in China*, 242–45; Douglas J. King to Deputy SSO, OSS/CT, September 3, 1945, Folder 3185, Box 186 Field Station Files, Kunming, Entry 154, RG 226 OSS/NARA II; Hal Leith, *POWs of Japanese Rescued!: General J.M. Wainwright* (Trafford Publishing, 2004), 11–25; Roger Hilsman, *American Guerrilla: My War Behind Japanese Lines* (London: Brassey's, 1990), 232–35, 237–40; Ted Tsukiyama, "OSS-Detachment 101: Nisei Guerrilla Fighters of World War II," manuscript, November 1, 2006, TTP/UHM; Yu, *OSS in China*, 242–44. See also James C. McNaughton, *Nisei Linguists: Japanese Americans in the Military Intelligence Service during World War II* (Washington, DC: US Department of Army, 2006), 399–400 and Ann Todd, *OSS Operation Black Mail: One Woman's Covert War against the Imperial Japanese Army* (Annapolis, MD: Naval Institute Press, 2017), 168–69.

18. Hilsman, *American Guerrilla*, 245–50; Yu, *OSS in China*, 242–47; McNaughton, *Nisei Linguists*, 400; Daws, *Prisoners of the Japanese*, 342.

19. John K. Singlaub with Malcolm McConnell, *Hazardous Duty: An American Soldier in the Twentieth Century* (New York: Summit Books, 1991), 82–101; Report Mission: POW Mission to Hainan Island, September 15, 1945, Folder 456, Entry140, Box 56, RG 226 OSS/NARA II; Captain Leonard Wood to OSS Commander, China Theater, September 12, 1945, Folder Ralph Yempuku Recommendation for Distinguished Service Medal, Box 40, Varsity Victory Volunteers; Ted Tsukiyama, "OSS-Detachment 101," manuscript, TTP/UHM; Personal History Statement, December 6, 1943; Thomas Smart to Director of Strategic Services Unit/Washington, DC, December 17, 1945, Folder Yempuku, Ralph, Box 852 OSSPF, Entry 224, RG 226 OSS/NARA II.

20. R. T. Phillips, "The Japanese Occupation of Hainan," *Modern Asian Studies* 14, no. 1 (1980): 95, 97–98.

21. Ted Tsukiyama, "Ralph Yempuku: Remembrances," July 18, 2002, Folder Ralph Yempuku Memorial, 2002, Box 40, Varsity Victory Volunteers, TTP/UHM; Steve Tsang, *A Modern History of Hong Kong* (London: I. B. Tauris & Co. Ltd., 2004), 135–38. See also Tomi Kaizawa Knaefler, *Our House Divided: Seven Japanese American Families in World War II* (Honolulu: University of Hawai'i, 1991), 92–93.

22. "Yanks in Shanghai for War Trial," *The Milwaukee Journal*, November 28, 1945, 29; "US Haw-Haw Suspect Held," *Stars And Stripes*, November 1, 1945, Folder 6, Box 22; Donald Chisholm, Statement to the Swiss Consulate General, January 15,1943, Folder 6, Box 22; Ernest Leroy Healey, (sworn statement), September 13, 1945, Folder 6, Box 22, Frank Farrell Papers, Library of Congress (hereafter FFP/LoC); Greg Leck, *Captives of Empire: The Japanese Internment of Allied Civilians in China, 1941–1945* (Bangor, PA: Shandy Press, 2007), 360–66; Bernard Wasserstein, *Secret War in Shanghai: An Untold Story of Espionage, Intrigue, and Treason in World War II* (Boston: Houghton Mifflin, 1999), 171–72; Timothy Brook, *Collaboration: Japanese Agents and Local Elites in Wartime China* (Cambridge, MA: Harvard University Press, 2005), 7–8, 10–13, 162, 172.

23. Gloria H. Chun, "'Go West . . . to China': Chinese American Identity in the 1930s," 174, in *Claiming America: Constructing Chinese American Identities During the Exclusion Era*, ed. K. Scott Wong and Sucheng Chan (Philadelphia: Temple University Press, 1998); Hannah Pakula, *The Last Empress: Madame Chiang Kai-Shek and the Birth of Modern China* (New York: Simon & Schuster, 2009), 462; Roger Daniels, *Asian America: Chinese and Japanese in the United States since 1850*

(Seattle: University of Washington Press, 1988), 69, Table 3.1; Link, Harry & BH-012, Report, untitled, October 1, 1944, Folder 2, Box 1 Shanghai Intelligence Files, Entry 182, RG 226 OSS/NARA II.

24. George White, X-2 Branch Report, Calcutta, January 22, 1945, Folder 4, Entry 182, Box 1 Shanghai Intelligence Files, RG 226 OSS/NARA II; Counter Intelligence Corps, Branch Office #4, India-China Wing Air Transport Command, February 1, 1945, Folder 5,, Box 1 Shanghai Intelligence Files, Entry 182, RG 226 OSS/NARA II.

25. George White, Report, June 31, 1944, Folder 4 and George White, X-2 Report, Calcutta, January 31, 1945, Folder 5, Box 1 Shanghai Intelligence Files, Entry 182, RG 226 OSS/NARA II.

26. Guy Iman, August 28, 1945, 28,29, 32, Bureau File #100-155291, Folder 146-28-648, Box 94; Henry Franklin, FBI report on Herbert Erasmus Moy, File 61–139, April 1, 1943, Folder 146-28-648, Box 94; William Jones, FBI File No. 61-184, May 7, 1943, Folder 146-28-648, Box 94; T. Carter Gleysteen, FBI report on Herbert Erasmus Moy, File No. 100-16945, March 26, 1943, Folder 146-28-648, Box 94; S. Herman Horton, FBI report on Herbert Erasmus Moy, File No. 61-165, April 29, 1943, Folder 146-28-648, Box 94; John Adams, FBI report on Herbert Erasmus Moy, File 61–213, March 4, 1943, Folder 146-28-648, Box 94; Transcript of Shortwave Broadcasts, May 22, 1943 but transcribed on August 24, 1943, by Herbert Moy, Folder 146-28-648, Box 94, RG 60 General Records of the Department of Justice, Classified Subject Files, NARA II (hereafter CSF-DOJ/NARAII).

27. John Hoover to Tom Clark, August 7, 1944, and Transcript of April 24, 1944 broadcast recorded by the FBI; KR/IS (X-2/China Theater), Report No. YKX-466, November 5, 1945, Folder 146-28-648, Box 94, Folder 146-28-648, Box 94, RG 60 CSF-DOJ/NARA II.

28. KR/IS (X-2/China Theater), Report No. YKX-466, November 5, 1945, Folder 146-28-648, Box 94; John Ansley, FBI Report File No. 61-150, November 22, 1943, on Herbert Erasmus Moy, Folder 146-28-648, Box 94; T. Carter Gleysteen, FBI report on Herbert Erasmus Moy, File No. 100-16945, March 26, 1943, Folder 146-28-648, Box 94, RG 60 CSF-DOJ/NARA II.

29. L. Ehrhardt, Translation of Report on "K.O." (Kriegs Organization), October 7, 1945 and Walter Richter, Report Nr. 2, October 4, 1945, Folder 67, Entry 182, Box 10 Shanghai Intelligence Files, RG 226 OSS/NARA II; BH/023, File No: YKX-902, January 12, 1945, Folder 4, Entry 182A, Box 1 Shanghai Office, RG 226 OSS/NARA II; T. Carter Gleysteen, FBI report on Herbert Erasmus Moy, File No. 100-16945, March 26, 1943 and Sidney Thwing, FBI report, June 15, 1943, Folder 146-28-648, Box 94, No Entry #, RG 60 CSF-DOJ/NARA II.

30. Robert Chin to Mr. (Arthur) Horton, September 26, 1945 and Inspecting officers of 3rd sub-department, Hwa Shan Road Police Station, Suicide Case of Herbert Moy, August 16, 1945, Folder 454, Entry 140, Box 56, RG 226 OSS/NARA II; KR/IS, Report No. YKX-466, November 5, 1945; Guy Iman, August 28, 1945, Bureau File #100-155291; Guy Iman, August 28, 1945, 32, Bureau File #100-155291, Folder 146-28-648, Box 94, RG 60 CSF-DOJ/NARA II.

31. Ken J. Ruoff, *Imperial Japan at its Zenith: The Wartime Celebration of the Empire's 2,600th Anniversary* (Ithaca, NY: Cornell University Press, 2010), 148; John J. Stephan, "Hijacked by Utopia," in Ichioka, Yuji, ed., "Beyond National Boundaries: The Complexity of Japanese-American History," *Amerasia Journal* 23, no. 3 (Winter 1997–1998): 3; Joshua A. Fogel, "'Shanghai-Japan': The Japanese

Residents' Association of Shanghai," *Journal of Asian Studies* 59, no. 4 (November 2000): 940–42; Brian Masaru Hayashi, *Democratizing the Enemy: The Japanese American Internment* (Princeton, NJ: Princeton University Press, 2004), 45.

32. Edward J. Drea, *Japan's Imperial Army: Its Rise and Fall, 1853–1945* (Lawrence: University Press of Kansas, 2009), 232; Stephan, "Hijacked by Utopia," 23, 40.

33. Mitzi Sawada, *Tokyo Life, New York Dreams: Urban Japanese Visions of America, 1890–1924* (Berkeley: University of California Press, 1996), 19–21, 37; T. Scott Miyakawa, "Early New York Issei: Founders of Japanese-American Trade," in *East Across the Pacific: Historical and Sociological Studies of Japanese Immigration and Assimilation*, ed. Hilary T. Conroy and T. Scott Miyakawa (Santa Barbara, CA: American Bibliographic Center Clio Press, 1972), 156–86; *Nyūiku Nihonjinkai Jiseki Yōran* [Summary of New York Japanese Association's Achievements] (New York: Nyūiku Nihonjinkai Henshū (Iinkai), 1934), 14, Folder New York, Box 37 and T. Scott Miyakawa, "Earlier East Coast Issei (Experiences of Pre-World War II Issei" (unpub. mss., ca. 1971), 2, Box 15, T. Scott Miyakawa Papers (1296), Special Collections, Young Research Library, UCLA; First Counter Intelligence Corps/Manila, Memo, November 20, 1946, Folder 146-28-2057, Box 13, Department of Justice, Division of Communications and Records, RG 60 DOJ/NARA II; John Edgar Hoover to T.L. Caudle, February 5, 1946; Memorandum for Files, September 6, 1945; Theron Caudle to the Director, FBI, June 19, 1946; Tom Clark to the Director, FBI, November 27, 1943; J. Edgar Hoover to Tom Clark, November 8, 1943, Folder 230-B-13-1, Box 94, General Records of the Department of Justice, Class 146–28 Litigation Files, RG 60 DOJ/NARA II; Shanghai Municipal Police Crime Branch report, October 9, 1941 and D.S.I. McKeown, Shanghai Municipal Police Report, November 29, 1940, File H 1656c Princess Sumaire, 190-24-44-1, Box 119, Entry A12, RG 263 CIA Shanghai Municipal Police Records, NARA II. See also Wasserstein, *Secret War in Shanghai*, 250–55 and Daniel H. Inouye, *Distant Islands: The Japanese American Community in New York City, 1876– 1930s* (Boulder: University Press of Colorado, 2018), 75–76, 79, 118.

34. Hajimu Masuda to Ivan Ware, October 8, 1945, Folder 12, Box 25; Attachment #27: Hajimu Masuda, A Certified True Copy (*sworn affidavit), March 13, 1946, Folder 14, Box 29, FFP/LoC.

35. Attachment #27: Hajimu Masuda, A Certified True Copy, March 13,1946, Folder 14, Box 29, FFP/LoC.

36. Hajimu Masuda to Ivan Ware, October 8, 1945, Folder 12, Box 25; Attachment #27: Hajimu Masuda, A Certified True Copy, March 13, 1946, Folder 14, Box 29, emphasis retained; F.T. Farrell to Capt. Miller for (Ivan) Ware, November 5, 1945, Folder 12, Box 25 FFP/LoC.

37. J. Buto to Capt. (Robert) Buckley, October 3, 1945, Folder 458, Box 56, Entry 140, RG 226 OSS/NARA II; J. Buto to Capt. (Robert) Buckley, October 6, 1945 and J. Buto to Capt. (Robert) Buckley, October 2, 1945, Folder 458, Box 56, Entry 140, RG OSS, NARA II; J. Buto to R. E. Buckley, October 11, 1945, Folder 458, Box 56, Entry 140, RG 226 OSS/NARA II; BH/204 and BH-027 to BH-068, Memorandum, undated, Folder 7, Box 1 Shanghai Intelligence Files, Entry 182, RG 226 OSS/NARA II.

38. (Frank Farrell), (Notes), on (Tajiri), ca. December 24, 1945, Folder 10 and (Frank Farrell), (Report on Ray Uyeshima), ca. December 25, 1945, Folder 14, Box 29 FFP/LoC.

39. Attachment #11: Philip Y. Kikuta, (Statement), February 18, 1946, Folder 14, Box 29, FFP/LoC.
40. Attachment #15: Major Kenjirō Anami, (Statement), March 9, 1946, Folder 14, Box 29, FFP/LoC.
41. Attachment #12: Tatsuo Nakada, (Statement), January 18, 1946; Attachment #13: Seiichi Yamasaki, (Statement), February 19, 1946, Folder 14, Box 29, FFP/LoC.
42. Attachment #7: H. Ogino, (statement), February 22, 1946, Folder 14, Box 29, FFP/LoC; Elwood Olsen to Nathan Elliff, October 2, 1946, Folder 146-28-2057, Box 13, Department of Justice, Division of Communications and Records, RG 60 DOJ/NARA II; Memo, March 20, 1947, Folder 36, Box 8, OSS History Office, Entry 216, RG 226 OSS/NARA II.
43. Attachment 2: Major Kenjirō Anami, (Statement), March 9, 1946; Attachment 8: Kazumi Shinohara, (Statement), February 23, 1946, (Frank Farrell), (Report on Ray Morio Uyeshima), ca. December 25, 1945, Folder 14, Box 29, FFP/LoC.
44. (Frank Farrell) to Guy, April 23, 1942, Folder 12; Lee Mortimer, "Star Guiders: Escorting the Visiting Filmites Is Nice Work If You Can Get It," *Sunday Mirror* magazine Section, April 27, 1941, Folder 11; and Dorothy Kilgallen, "The Voice of Broadway," November 14, 1940, Folder 11, Box 43, FFP/LoC.
45. (Frank Farrell) to Guy, April 23, 1942; "Silver Star for Frank Farrell," *New York World-Telegram*, ca. November 1944, Folder 12; WABC RADIO American Broadcasting Company, Biography, Frank Farrell, May 1954, Folder 15; Walter Winchell, "In New York," March 26, 1947, Folder 12, Box 43, FFP/LoC.
46. Attachment #29: Albert H. MacKenzie to Briggs Howard, December 8, 1945, Folder 14, Box 29, FFP/LoC.
47. (Frank) Farrell, interview with Toshio Namba, February 14, 1946, Folder 14, Box 29, FFP/LoC.
48. Attachment #30: Jean Huang, To Whom It May Concern, (Statement), December 14, 1945, Folder 14, Box 29, FFP/LoC.
49. Attachment #31: Shigeo Yasutake, To Whom It May Concern, December 12, 1945, Folder 14, Box 29, FFP/LoC.
50. Rafu Nihonjin Ryojikan Kiroku, cards # 2301-2305, ca1920, Box 214; cards #236-245, Box 209, JARP/UCLA; Shig Yasutake, Tape 1, Interview, The Hanashi Oral History Video Archive, Go For Broke Museum, Torrance, CA., accessed 2010; Michael Shigeo Yasutake, Interview by Ron Ikejiri, May 13, 2004, Asian American History: South Bay/Los Angeles Nisei, The Virtual Oral/Aural History Archive, California State University, Long Beach, Interview Disc1 Track1 Segment 111 and Segment 113, December 28, 2011, http://www.csulb.edu/voaha (accessed 2010).
51. Shig Yasutake, Tapes 2 to 5, Oral Histories, Go For Broke Museum, Torrance, CA.; Michael Shigeru Yasutake, Interview with Ron Ikejiri, May 13, 2004, Asian American History: South Bay/Los Angeles Nisei, The Virtual Oral/Aural History Archive, California State University, Long Beach. Interview Disc1 Track1 Segments 115, 116, 118, and Segment 211, http://www.csulb.edu/voaha (accessed December 28, 2011); Tamotsu Shibutani, *The Derelicts of Company K: A Sociological Study of Demoralization* (Berkeley: University of California Press, 1978), 80–82.
52. Elwood Olsen to Nathan Elliff, October 2, 1946, Folder 146-28-2057, Box 13, Division of Communications and Records, RG 60 DOJ/NARA II.
53. Shig Yasutake, Tape 5, Oral Histories, Go For Broke Museum, Torrance, CA.; "Seven Axis Agents Are Seized in Shanghai Coup," April 16, 1945, (World-Telegram),

Folder 12, Box 43; (Frank Farrell), untitled manuscript, summaries for Chapter One, Eleven, and Twelve, Folder 3, Box 78 FFP/LoC.

54. (Frank Farrell), untitled manuscript, summary for Chapter Twenty-three, Folder 3, Box 78; Captain (Frank) Farrell and (Marvin) Gray, Memo to Lt. Waldorf for FBI, July 3, 1946, Box 29, FFP/LoC; (Frank) Farrell, interview with Toshio Namba, February 14, 1946, Folder 14, Box 29, FFP/LoC; General Headquarters United States Army Forces Pacific, Office of the Chief of Counter Intelligence, February 14, 1945, Folder Inaho Otani, Box 589 Investigative Records Repository, Entry 134B, RG 319 Office of the Assistant Chief of Staff for Intelligence; Special Agents 4560 and 4604, Memorandum for the Officer in Charge, April 9, 1946, Research and Analysis, NARA II.

55. (Frank) Farrell and (Marvin) Gray, Memo to Lt. Waldorf for FBI, July 3, 1946, Folder 10, Box 29, FFP/LoC; Kaigun Bunkan Meibō [Roster of Naval Annex], Vol. 1 (1943), 38; General Headquarters United States Army Forces Pacific, Office of the Chief of Counter Intelligence, February 14, 1945, Folder Inaho OTANI, Box 589 Investigative Records Repository, RG 319 Office of the Assistant Chief of Staff for Intelligence, Entry 134B, NARA II; *Nihon Kaigun Sensuikanshi* [History of Submarines of the Japanese Navy] (Tokyo: Nihon Kaigun Sensuikanshi Kankōkai, 1979), 391–92, lists those aboard the I-9 for 1942 and 1943, but has no data for 1941, the year Tatsumi would have been listed.

CHAPTER 7

1. DH/001, X-2 FETO Operational Manual, 3–4, Folder 89, Box 8 Schools & Training, Entry 211, RG 226 OSS/NARA II; Naoyuki Umemori, "The Historical Contexts of the High Treason Incident: Governmentality and Colonialism," in *Japan and the High Treason Incident*, ed. Masako Gavin and Ben Middleton (New York: Routledge, 2013), 54–55; Lawrence R. Samuel, "Dreaming in Black and White: African-American Patriotism and World War II Bonds," in John Bodnar, *Bonds of Affection: Americans Define Their Patriotism* (Princeton, NJ: Princeton University Press), 1996, 192, 209; Dillon Ripley, Monthly Report of SI Branch SEAC, July 31, 1944, Folder 1 SEAC-July 1944, Box 60 OSS History Office, Entry 99, RG 226 OSS/NARA II.

2. Bradley F. Smith, *The Shadow Warriors: O.S.S. and the Origins of the C.I.A.* (New York: Basic Books, 1983), 380; Charles McGehee to Strategic Officer, January 27, 1945, Folder 5, Box 78 OSS History Office; Robert Ellis to Strategic Services Officer, July 26, 1945, Folder 2 IBT-July 1945, Box 83; Oliver J. Caldwell to Herman Harjes, January 22, 1944, Folder 1, Box 71, Entry 99, RG 226 OSS/NARA II.

3. Douglas Waller, *Wild Bill Donovan: The Spymaster Who Created The OSS and Modern American Espionage* (New York: Free Press, 2011), 21, 5, 92; William Donovan, Memorandum to The President, December 29, 1941, December 21, 1941, and Summary of Intelligence on South America, December 13, 1941, Folder Office of Strategic Services Reports: 12/18-27/41 #2, Box 147 Office of Strategic Services, Personal Secretary File, Franklin Delano Roosevelt Library, Hyde Park, NY (hereafter cited as PSF/FDRL).

4. Ann Todd, *OSS Operation Black Mail: One Woman's Covert War against the Imperial Japanese Army* (Annapolis, MD: Naval Institute Press, 2017), 39, 43, 48, 70–71; Alfred W. Coy, *Policing America's Empire: The United States, the Philippines, and the Rise of the Surveillance State* (Madison: University of Wisconsin Press, 2009), 330–32; Henry Yu, *Thinking Orientals: Migration, Contact, and Exoticism in*

Modern America (New York: Oxford University Press, 2001), 125–33, 155, 17–71, 205, 208–11; Valerie J. Matsumoto, *City Girls: The Nisei Social World in Los Angeles, 1920–1950* (New York: Oxford University Press, 2014), 87–91; Lane Ryo Hirabayashi, *The Politics of Fieldwork: Research in an American Concentration Camp* (Tucson: University of Arizona Press, 1999), 13–21, 159–60; Eriko Yamamoto, "Miya Sannomiya Kikuchi: A Pioneer Nisei Woman's Life and Identity," *Amerasia Journal* 23, no. 3 (winter 1997): 72–101; Capt. W. R. Moore, Attached Interviewer Report, February 5, 1945; William Beale, Request for Procurement of Military Personnel, OSS Form 802, to Chief, Personnel Procurement Branch/OSS, February 17, 1945; Maj. S. H. Parkins to Major Ulmer, February 23, 1945, Folder KIM, Anna, Box 404 OSSPF, Entry 224, RG 226 OSS/NARA II; George Why Chen, "Biography of George W. and Pearl L. Chen in War Time China," https://masterchensays.wordpress.com/biography-of-george-w-and-pearl-l-chen-in-war-time-china/ (accessed August 9, 2020).

5. D'Ann Campbell, "Women in Combat: The World War II Experience in the United States, Great Britain, Germany, and the Soviet Union," *Journal of Military History* 57, no. 2 (April 1993): 302, 306; Todd, *OSS Operation Black Mail*, 38, 59–60; Joan Bondurant to Merrill Spaulding, June 17, 1943, Folder 638, Box 80, Entry 140; C. J. Francis to Joan Bondurant, September 28, 1945, Folder Bondurant, Joan, Box 67, Entry A1 224, RG 226, OSS/NARA II.

6. Frank Farrell to Mrs. Iva Toguri d'Aquino, radio script, ca. August 1948, Folder 6, Box 37, FFP/LoC.

7. Masayo Duus, *Tokyo Rose: Orphan of the Pacific* (New York: Kodansha International/USA, 1979), 134–35 and Frederick P. Close, *Tokyo Rose/An American Patriot: A Dual Biography* (Lanham, MD: Scarecrow Press, 2010), 438–39, 443, 455, 469.

8. J. H. Leek, "Treason and the Constitution," *Journal of Politics* 13, no. 4 (November 1951): 613–19.

9. J. Woodford Howard Jr., "Advocacy in Constitutional Choice: The Cramer Treason Case, 1942–1945," *American Bar Foundation Research Journal* 11, no. 3 (Summer 1986): 391, 402–406; Leek, "Treason and the Constitution," 617; William Hurst, "Treason in the United States: III. Under the Constitution," *Harvard Law Review* 58, no. 6 (July 1945): 806, 822.

10. Carlton F. W. Larson, "The Forgotten Constitutional Law of Treason and the Enemy Combatant Problem," *University of Pennsylvania Law Review* 154, no. 4 (April 2006): 869–73, 902–904, 908–909, 912, 925.

11. Greg Leck, *Captives of Empire: The Japanese Internment of Allied Civilians in China, 1941–1945* (Bangor, PA: Shandy Press, 2006), 419–20. Leck notes that violence and torture was not uncommon for Allied civilians captured by the Imperial Japanese forces, especially at the Bridge House in Shanghai where Ray Uyeshima was taken.

12. Jeremy Duda, *If This Be Treason: The American Rogues and Rebels Who Walked the Line Between Dissent and Betrayal* (Guilford, CT: Lyons Press, 2016), 45; Tim Maga, *Judgment at Tokyo: The Japanese War Crimes Trials* (Lexington: University Press of Kentucky, 2001), 108–109; Keith L. Camacho, *Sacred Men: Law, Torture, and Retribution in Guam* (Durham, NC: Duke University Press, 2019), 153–79.

13. George P. Fletcher, *Loyalty: An Essay on the Morality of Relationships* (New York: Oxford University Press, 1993), 3–7, 24, 33–36, 42, 46, 57, 101.

14. Paul R. Spickard, *Japanese Americans: The Formation and Transformations of an Ethnic Group* (New York: Twayne Publishers, 1996), 80–82, 85–88.

15. Benedict Anderson, *Imagined Communities: Reflections on the Origin and Spread of Nationalism* (London: Verso, 1983, rev. ed.,1991), 6–7, 24–26.
16. Simon Keller, *The Limits of Loyalty* (Cambridge: Cambridge University Press, 2007), 11–14.
17. James Connor, *The Sociology of Loyalty* (Canberra: Springer, 2010), 8, 134–42, 90 47–48; John Bodnar, *Bonds of Affection: Americans Define Their Patriotism* (Princeton, NJ: Princeton University Press, 1996), 14; Keller, *The Limits of Loyalty*, x. Judith Shklar argues that political obligation is less fluctuating than loyalty because it is based on law whereas the loyalty is an emotion that rapidly changes over time. See Judith N. Shklar, "Obligation, Loyalty, Exile," *Political Theory* 21, no. 2 (May 1993), 183–84, 187.
18. James C. McNaughton, *Nisei Linguists: Japanese Americans in the Military Intelligence Service during World War II* (Washington, DC: US Department of Army, 2006); K. Scott Wong, *Americans First: Chinese Americans and the Second World War* (Cambridge, MA: Harvard University Press, 2005); Joseph D. Harrington, *Yankee Samurai: The Secret Role of Nisei in America's Pacific Victory* (Detroit: Pettigrew Enterprises, Inc., 1979), 242–43;
19. Howard Schonberger, "Dilemmas of Loyalty: Japanese Americans and the Psychological Warfare Campaigns of the Office of Strategic Services, 1943–45," *Amerasia Journal* 16, no. 1 (1990): 35. See also Howard Schonberger, *Japanizu Konekushon: Kaiunō Kei Sugahara Gaiden* [Japanese Connection: Kay Sugahara the Shipping Magnate] (Tokyo: Bungei Shunjun, 1995), translated by Rinjirō Sodei; Yuji Ichioka, "The Meaning of Loyalty: The Case of Kazumaro Buddy Uno," *Amerasia Journal* 23, no. 3 (Winter 1997–1998): 53–60; Richard S. Kim, *The Quest for Statehood: Korean Immigrant Nationalism and U.S. Sovereignty, 1905–1945* (New York: Oxford University Press, 2011).

EPILOGUE

1. James Oda, *Secret Embedded in Magic Cables: The Story of a 101-Year-Old Japanese Communist Leader Who Served Japan, KGB and CIA* (Anaheim, CA: KNI Inc., 1993), 43, 48–51, 58–59, 62–63, 97–98.
2. Tomiya Watabe, *"Roy" Nosaka Sanzō Setsu ni Ketsugi wo Tsuketa gojūnenme no Jijitsu: Soruge Jiken de Gokushita Gaka Miyagi Yotoku wo Nihon ni Hakkenshita Roi to Yobareru Otoko wa Nikkei Kyōsantoin Kimoto Denichi da!* [The "Roy" Sanzō Nosaka Explanation Resolved in the Fiftieth Year of the Truth: The One Who Sent the Artist Yotoku Miyagi to Prison for the Sorge Affair was the Japanese American Communist Party Member Denichi Kimoto!] (Tokyo: Shakai Undō Shiryō Senta, 2001), 8–12.
3. Brandon Palmer, *Fighting for the Enemy: Koreans in Japan's War, 1937–1945* (Seattle: University of Washington Press, 2013), 41, 131, 64, 83; Ching-chih Chen, "Police and Community Control Systems in the Empire," in *The Japanese Colonial Empire, 1895–1945*, ed. Ramon H. Myers and Mark R. Peattie (Princeton, NJ: Princeton University Press, 1984), 222–25, 236–39; Paul Helliwell to Strategic Services Officer/China Theater, April 26, 1945, Folder 3416, Box 201 Kunming Office, Entry 154, RG 226 OSS/NARA II.
4. (Paul) Helliwell to Texas, May 3, 1945, Folder 3172 Kunming-AKRON Mission, Box 185, Entry 154, RG 226 OSS/NARA II; (Richard) Moore to (Paul) Helliwell, August 3, 1945, NR 141, Folder 3436, Box 203, Entry154, RG 226 OSS/NARA II; Author, telephone interview with Betty Kan, February 21,2011; YKB-2672,

(second handbook, Dewey to Kan), ca.August 18, 1945, Folder 445, Box 55, Entry 140, RG 226 OSS/NARA II.

5. "Former Reporter Heir To Estate," *Goldsboro News-Argus*, August 12, 1954; Henry Balk to Linc(oln Kan), ca.January 28,1949; Jennifer Musgrove to Betty Kan, April 21,1998 cover letter and copy of articles from *The Asheville Citizen* June 25, 1956; June 26, 1956; and January11, 1953; Certified Certificate of Marriage, Helen Underdown, Register of Deeds and custodian of marriage records for the County of Watauga, North Carolina, May 2, 1976; Mohawk Valley Community College (Rome, NY), "The Black Experience," n.d., Betty F. Kan Papers, Chapel Hill, NC.

6. Douglass Waller, *Wild Bill Donovan: The Spymaster Who Created The OSS and Modern American Espionage* (New York: Free Press, 2011), 355; Allen Weinstein and Alexander Vassiliev, *The Haunted Wood: Soviet Espionage in America—the Stalin Era* (New York: Random House, 1999), 257–59; Duncan Lee to Paul Helliwell, March 1, 1945, Folder 3452, Box 203, Entry 154, RG 226 OSS/NARA II; William Donovan to Duncan Lee, September 28, 1945, Folder Lee, Duncan Lt. Col. Army, Box 441 OSSPF, Entry 224, RG 226 OSS/NARA II; Mark A. Bradley, *A Very Principled Boy: The Life of Duncan Lee, Red Spy and Cold Warrior* (New York: Basic Books, 2014), 2, 251–52, 260–61..

7. Bradley, *A Very Principled Boy*, 113–15, 172–73; Yu, *OSS in China*, endnote 40, 301–302.

8. Bradley, *A Very Principled Boy*, 203–204; MAKSIM [xv] to VIKTOR, New York to Moscow, No. 880, June 8, 1943 and Maksim to Viktor, New York to Moscow, May 26, 1943, Folder 7: Addition Hayne File New York KGT—1943 p.1–180, Box 7, Alexander Vassiliev Papers, Library of Congress, Washington, DC; Personnel Card, ca. 1945, Folder Lee, Duncan C. 0912627, Box 441 OSSPF, Entry 224, RG 226 OSS/NARA II.

9. Joseph E. Persico, *Roosevelt's Secret War: FDR and World War II Espionage* (New York: Random House Trade Paperbacks, 2002), 293–300; John Earl Haynes and Harvey Klehr, *In Denial: Historians, Communism & Espionage* (San Francisco: Encounter Books, 2003), 141–92; Brian Masaru Hayashi, *Democratizing the Enemy: The Japanese American Internment* (Princeton, NJ: Princeton University Press, 2004), 212.

10. J. H. Leek, "Treason and the Constitution," *Journal of Politics* 13, no. 4 (November 1951): 608, 610–11; Larson, "The Forgotten Constitutional Law of Treason and the Enemy Combatant Problem," *University of Pennsylvania Law Review* 154, no. 4 (April 2006): 874–878, 865, 902–904, 921–22; Bradley, *A Very Principled Boy*, 156, 267–68.

11. Rhodri Jeffrey-Jones, *The FBI: A History* (New Haven, CT: Yale University Press, 2007), 110–11; Athan Theoharris, *Chasing Spies: How the FBI Failed in Counterintelligence But Promoted the Politics of McCarthyism in the Cold War Years* (Chicago: Ivan R. Dee, 2002), 11–12, 34, 42–46; Bradley, *A Very Principled Boy*, 248–49.

12. State Department Historian's Office, *History of the Bureau of Diplomatic Security of the United States Department of State* (Washington, DC: Global Publishing Solutions, 2011), 36; Haynes and Klehr, *In Denial*, 148; Waller, *Wild Bill Donovan*, 118.

SELECTED BIBLIOGRAPHY

MANUSCRIPT COLLECTIONS

Akiya, Karl Ichirō. Papers. Tamiment Library, New York University, New York.
Bentley Historical Library, University of Michigan. Ann Arbor, Michigan.
Center for Japanese Studies. Papers
Gale, Esson M. Papers
Hayden, Joseph Ralston. Papers
Carter, Robert Jr. Papers. Catalina Island Museum Records Center. Avalon, California.
Charles E. Young University Research Library, University of California, Los Angeles, California.
Fowler, Josephine. Papers
Ichioka, Yuji. Papers
Japanese American Research Project. Papers
Korean American Research Project. Papers
Miyakawa, T. Scott Miyakawa. Papers
Sakai, Yoneo. Papers
Spencer, Joseph Earle. Papers
Fahs, Charles B. Papers. Rockefeller Archives Center, Sleepy Hallow, New York.
Hoover Institution for War and Peace, Stanford University, Stanford, California.
Allman, Norwood F. Papers
Boynton, Charles Luther. Papers
Duff, James Arthur. Papers
Eifler, Carl Frederick. Papers
Goodfellow, Millard Preston. Papers
Hornbeck, Stanley K. Papers
Kohlberg, Alfred. Papers
Price, Ernest Batson. Papers
Remer, Charles Frederick. Papers
Smith, Richard H. Papers
Wedemeyer, Albert Coady. Papers
Willoughby, Charles Andrew. Papers
Kan, Betty F. Lincoln Kan Papers. Chapel Hill, North Carolina
Korean American Digital Archives, Digital Library, University of Southern California. Los Angeles, California.
Lai, Him Mark. Papers. Ethnic Studies Library, University of California, Berkeley.
Library of Congress. Washington, DC.
Farrell, Frank. Papers
Vassiliev, Alexander. Papers

Venona decrypted transcripts

Lockwood, William Willard. Papers. Seeley-Mudd Library, Princeton University

National Archives. Kew, London, England.

Records of the Special Operations Executive

National Archives and Records Administration II, College Park, Maryland

Department of Justice, Record Group (RG) 60

Federal Bureau of Investigation, Record Group (RG) 65

Office of the Assistant Chief of Staff, G-2, Record Group (RG) 319

Office of Cable Censorship, Record Group (RG) 216

Office of the Chief of Naval Operations, Record Group (RG) 38

Office of Strategic Services, Record Group (RG) 226

Office of War Information, Record Group (RG) 208

Shanghai Municipal Police Records. Central Intelligence Agency.

Record Group (RG) 263

Western Defense Command, Record Group (RG) 338

National Archives and Records Administration, New York

Immigration and Naturalization Services, Record Group (RG) 85

National Archives and Records Administration, San Bruno, California

Immigration and Naturalization Services, Record Group (RG) 85

Pusey Library, Harvard University, Cambridge, Massachusetts.

Fairbank, John King. Papers

Langer, William Leonard. Papers

Regenstein Library, University of Chicago.

Redfield, Robert. Papers

Steed, Gitel. Papers

Roosevelt, Franklin Delano. Personal Secretary Files. Franklin Delano Roosevelt
     Library, Hyde Park, New York.

Shanghai Evening Post and Mercury Papers. Xujiahui Library, Shanghai.

Syngman Rhee. Presidential Papers. Yonsei University, Seoul, Korea.

Tsukiyama, Ted. Papers. Japanese American Veterans Collection. Archives and
     Manuscript Department. University of Hawaii at Manoa, Honolulu.

GOVERNMENT PUBLICATIONS

US Census Bureau, Reports on Population, Sixteenth Census of the United States: 1940,
     for Alaska, Hawaii, Guam, and Samoa; and the Statistical Abstracts of the United
     States for the Philippiness at http://1940census.archives.gov.

INTERVIEWS AND MEMOIRS OF OSS MEMBERS

Akiya, Karl. *Jiyūhe no Michi Taiheiyō wo Koete: Aru Kibei Nisei no Jiden* [The Road
     to Freedom (by) Crossing the Pacific: A Kibei Nisei's Autobiography].
     Kyōto: Gyōjisha, 1996.

Chun-Ming, Shirley [daughter of Archie Chung-Ming]. Interview by Brian Masaru
     Hayashi, May 2, 2008, at her home in Maui, HI.

Davies, John Paton Jr. *China Hand: An Autobiography.* Philadelphia: University of
     Pennsylvania Press, 2021.

Dunlop, Richard. *Behind Japanese Lines: With the OSS in Burma.* Chicago: Rand McNally
     & Co., 1979.

Emmerson, John K. *The Japanese Thread: A Life in the U.S. Foreign Service.* New York: Holt,
     Rinehart and Winston, 1978.

Fairbank, John King. *Chinabound: A Fifty-year Memoir.* New York: Harper & Row, 1986.

Fenn, Charles. *At the Dragon's Gate: With the OSS in the Far East.* Annapolis, MD: Naval Institute Press, 2004.

Fenn, Charles. "Remembering Frank Tan," Indochina News Summer 2002, http://www.ffrd.org/indochina/summer02news.html.

Fujiwara, Iwaichi. *F. Kikan: Japanese Army Intelligence Operations in Southeast Asia during World War II.* Translated by Yōji Akashi. Hong Kong: Heinemann Asia, 1983.

Furumoto, Howard. Interview by Brian Masaru Hayashi, April 26, 2008, at his home in Honolulu.

Gale, Esson M. *Salt for the Dragon: A Personal History.* East Lansing: Michigan State College Press, 1953.

Haga, Takeshi. "Nyū Iku Rapusode: Aru Nihonjin Bei Kyōsantoin no Kaisō." [New York Rhapsody: The Recollections of US Communist Party Member]. In *Nihon Heiwaron Taike* [Outline of Pacifism in Japan], Vol. 20, edited by Saburō Ienaga, 6–311. Tokyo: Nihon Tosho Senta, 1994.

Hamada, Dick. Interview by Brian Masaru Hayashi, April 26, 2008, at the Ala Moana Center, Honolulu.

Hamada, Dick. The Dick Hamada Story, 2006–07, The Hawai'i Nisei Project, "The Hawai'i Nisei Story: Americans of Japanese Ancestry During World War II," University of Hawai'i, Manoa. Nisei.hawaii.edu/page/dick.

Hilsman, Roger. *American Guerrilla: My War Behind Japanese Lines.* London: Brassey's, 1990.

Hoppes, Jonna Doolittle. *Just Doing My Job: Stories of Service from World War II.* Santa Monica, CA: Santa Monica Press, 2009.

Ikeda, Maggie [spouse of Chiyoki Ikeda]. Interview by Brian Masaru Hayashi, April 26, 2008, at her residence in Honolulu.

Kan, Betty F. Kan [spouse of Lincoln Kan]. Telephone interview by Brian Masaru Hayashi, February 21, 2011, Chapel Hill, North Carolina.

Kido, Fumio. Interview by Ted Tsukiyama and Jim Tanabe, September 18, 2002. MIS Oral History Project Collection. World War II Nisei Veterans Archives, University of Hawai'i-Manoa.

Komada, Shinji. *Watakushi no Chūgoku Horyo Taiken* [My Experience as a Prisoner in China]. Tokyo: Iwanami Bukkuretto No. 214, 1991.

Koide, Joe. *Aru Zaibei Nihonjin no Kiroku: Renin Gakkō kara Nichibei Kaisen made Jō* [Recollections of a Japanese in America, Vol. 1: From the Lenin School to the Beginnings of the US-Japan War] and *Aru Zaibei Nihonjin no Kiroku Ge: Nichibei Kaisen kara Shūsen made* [Recollections of a Japanese in American, Vol. 2: From the Beginnings of the US-Japan War until Its End]. Tokyo: Yushindo, 1970.

Koide, Joe. Interview by Joe Masaoka and Robert Wilson, April 18 and 25, 1967. Oral History Japanese American Research Project, Reels 33, 34, Box 381, Charles E. Young Research Library, University of California, Los Angeles.

Langer, William L. Langer. *In and Out of the Ivory Tower: The Autobiography of William L. Langer.* New York: Neale Watson Academic Publications, 1977.

Lee, Jongsoo. *Paekpŏm Ilchi: The Autobiography of Kim Ku.* Translated by Jongsoo Lee. Lanham, MD: University Press of America. 2000.

McIntosh, Elizabeth P. *Sisterhood of Spies: The Women of the OSS.* Annapolis, MD: Naval Institute Press, 1998.

MacDonald, Elizabeth P. *Undercover Girl.* New York: Macmillan, 1947.

Moon, Thomas N., and Carl F. Eifler. *The Deadliest Colonel.* Springfield, MA: Vantage Press, 1975.

New, Ilhan. *When I Was a Boy in Korea.* Boston: Lothrop, Lee & Shepard, 1928.

Peers, William, and Dean Brelis. *Behind the Burma Road: The Story of America's Most Successful Guerrilla Force.* Boston: Little, Brown, and Co., 1963.

Soga, Yasutarō. *Life Behind the Barbed Wire: The World War II Internment Memoirs of a Hawai'i Issei.* Honolulu: University of Hawai'i Press, 2008.

Yasutake, Michael Shigeo. Interview with Gail Yamada, nd, ca. 2033. Go For Broke Museum, Torrance, CA. National Education Center. http://www.goforbroke. org/learn/archives/oral_histories_archives.php. Accessed December 28, 2011 and interview by Ron Ikejiri, May 13, 2004. The Virtual Oral/Aural History Archive, California State University Long Beach, CA. http://www.csulb.edu/ voaha, accessed December 29, 2011.

Yempuku, Ralph. Interview by Franklin Odo, March 28, 1985. MIS Oral History Project Collection. World War II Nisei Veterans Archives, University of Hawai'i-Manoa.

UNPUBLISHED SOURCES

Chambers II, John Whiteclay. *"OSS Training in the National Parks and Service Abroad in World War II."* Washington, DC: U.S. National Park Service, 2008.

Choi, Anne Soon. "Border Crossings: The Politics of Korean Nationalism in the United States, 1919–1945." PhD diss., University of Southern California, 2004.

Eubank, Lauriel E. "The Effects of the First Six Months of World War II on the Attitudes of Koreans and Filipinos toward the Japanese in Hawaii." MA thesis, University of Hawai'i, 1943.

Kim, Bernice B. H. "The Koreans in Hawaii." MA thesis, University of Hawai'i-Manoa, 1937.

Kim, Lili M. "The Pursuit of Imperfect Justice: The Predicament of Koreans and Korean Americans." PhD diss., University of Rochester, 2001.

McAuliff, John. "Transcript of the OSS-Viet Minh 1995 Meeting." Southampton, NY: The Fund for Reconciliation, 1997.

Naka, Harry Maxwell. "The Naturalization of the Japanese Veterans of the American World War Forces." MA thesis, University of California Berkeley, 1935.

Suzuki, Masao. "Occupational Mobility of Japanese Immigrants to the U.S.: Evidence from War Relocation Authority Records (1942) and the Immigration and Naturalization Service." Report, Department of Economics, Stanford University, May 1992.

Tottori, Calvin. *The OSS Niseis in the China-Burma-India Theater.* Privately printed, Honolulu, ca. 1997.

Wing, Eugenia "Beah" Chen. "My Family History Record: A Genealogical Record compiled by Eugenia 'Beah' Chen Wing." Jolly Young King, Honolulu, February 1981.

Writing Services Company. *Cornelius Vander Starr, 1892-1968.* New York: Starr Foundation, 1970.

Yamato, Alexander Yoshikazu. "Socioeconomic Change among Japanese Americans in the San Francisco Bay Area." PhD diss., University of California Berkeley, 1986.

Yoneyama, Hiroshi. "Rafu Nihonjinkai Yakuin Senkyō to Zairosuanzerusu Nihonjin Shakai no Henyō: Senkyūhyakujūgonen kara Senkyūhyakunijūichi [Los Angeles Japanese Association Board Members Election and the Change in Japanese Society in Los Angeles: From 1915 to 1921]." Report, Ritsumeikan University, Kyoto, Japan, 2000.

Yu, Shen. "SACO: An Ambivalent Experience of Sino-American Cooperation during World War II." PhD diss., University of Illinois-Urbana Champaign, 1996.

Zheng, Mei. "Chinese Americans in San Francisco and New York City During the Anti-Japanese War: 1937–1945." MA thesis, University of California Los Angeles, 1990.

PUBLISHED SOURCES

Adams, Geoffrey Pharaoh, with Hugh Popham. *No Time For Geishas.* London: Corgi Books, 1974.

Adams, Romanzo. *The Peoples of Hawaii.* New York: American Council, Institute of Pacific Relations, 1933.

Aldrich, Richard J. *Intelligence and the War against Japan: Britain, America and the Politics of Secret Service.* Cambridge: Cambridge University Press, 2000.

Allen, Louis. *Burma: The Longest War, 1941–45.* London: J. M. Dent & Sons, 1986.

Anderson, Benedict. *Imagined Communities: Reflections on the Origin and Spread of Nationalism.* London: Verso, 1983.

Antony, Robert J. "We are Not Pirates." *Journal of World History.* 28, no.2 (June 2017): 249-76.

Archer, Bernice. *The Internment of Western Civilians under the Japanese, 1941–1945: A Patchwork of Internment.* London: Routledge Curzon, 2004.

Asato, Noriko. *Teaching Mikadoism: The Attack on Japanese Language Schools in Hawaii, California, and Washington, 1919–1927.* Honolulu: University of Hawai'i Press, 2006.

Azuma, Eiichirō, *Between Two Empires: Race, History, and Transnationalism in Japanese America.* New York: Oxford University Press, 2005.

Bartholomew-Feis, Dixee. *The OSS And Ho Chi Minh: Unexpected Allies in the War Against Japan.* Lawrence: University Press of Kansas, 2006.

Benedict, Carol. *Golden-Silk Smoke: A History of Tobacco in China, 1550–2010.* Berkeley: University of California Press, 2011.

Bickers, Robert. "The Business of Secret War: Operation 'Remorse' and SOE Salesmanship in Wartime China." *Intelligence and National Security* 16, no. 4 (Winter 2001): 11–36.

Bickers, Robert, and Christian Henriot (eds.). *New frontiers: Imperialism's New Communities in East Asia, 1842–1953.* Manchester, UK: Manchester University Press, 2000.

Birnbaum, Phyllis. *Manchu Princess, Japanese Spy: The Story of Kawashima Yoshiko, the Cross-Dressing Spy Who Commanded Her Own Army.* New York: Columbia University Press, 2015.

Bodnar, John. *Bonds of Affection: Americans Define Their Patriotism.* Princeton, NJ: Princeton University Press, 1996.

Bradley, Mark A. *A Very Principled Boy: The Life of Duncan Lee, Red Spy and Cold Warrior.* New York: Basic Books, 2014.

Brook, Timothy. *Collaboration: Japanese Agents and Local Elites in Wartime China.* Cambridge, MA: Harvard University Press, 2005.

Brooks, Charlotte. *Between Mao and McCarthy: Chinese American Politics in the Cold War Years.* Chicago: University of Chicago Press, 2015.

Brown, Anthony Cave. *The Last Hero: Wild Bill Donovan.* New York: Times Books, 1982.

Buchanan, Daniel Crump. *Japanese Proverbs and Sayings.* Norman: University of Oklahoma Press, 1965.

Camacho, Keith L. *Sacred Men: Law, Torture, and Retribution in Guam.* Durham, NC: Duke University Press, 2019.

Campbell, D'Ann. "Women in Combat: The World War II Experience in the United States, Great Britain, Germany, and the Soviet Union." *Journal of Military History* 57, no. 2 (April 1993): 301–23.

Carter, Carolle J. *Mission to Yenan: American Liaison with the Chinese Communists, 1944–1947.* Lexington: University Press of Kentucky, 1997.

Chalou, George C. (ed.). *The Secrets War: The Office of Strategic Services in World War II.* Washington, DC: National Archives and Records Administration, 1992.

Chambers, Whittaker. *Witness.* New York: Random House, 1952.

Chang, Edward Taehan. "Korean Kaleidoscope: An Overview of Korean Immigration to the U.S." *Korean and Korean American Bulletin* 11, no. 22 (2000): U6–U17.

Ch'oe, Yŏng-ho (ed.). *From the Land of Hibiscus: Koreans in Hawaii, 1903–1950.* Honolulu: University of Hawai'i Press, 2007.

Chen, Yong. *Chinese San Francisco, 1850–1943: A Trans-Pacific Community.* Stanford, CA: Stanford University Press, 2000.

Chieu, Vu Ngu. "The Other Side of the 1945 Vietnamese Revolution: The Empire of Viet-Nam March-August 1945." *Journal of Asian Studies* XLV, no. 2 (February 1986): 293–328.

Chun, Gloria H. "'Go West . . . to China': Chinese American Identity in the 1930s." In *Claiming America: Constructing Chinese American Identities During the Exclusion Era,* edited by K. Scott Wong and Sucheng Chan, 165–90. Philadelphia: Temple University Press, 1998.

Close, Frederick P. *Tokyo Rose/An American Patriot: A Dual Biography.* Lanham, MD: Scarecrow Press, 2010.

Cochran, Sherman. *Big Business in China: Sino-Foreign Rivalry in the Cigarette Industry, 1890–1930.* Cambridge, MA: Harvard University Press, 1980.

Coffman, Tom. *The Island Edge of America: A Political History of Hawai'i.* Honolulu: University of Hawai'i Press, 2003.

Cohen, Paul A., and Merle Goldman (eds.). *Fairbank Remembered.* Cambridge, MA: John K. Fairbank Center for East Asian Research and Harvard University Press, 1992.

Coleman, Craig S. *American Images of Korea: Korea and Koreans as Portrayed in Books, Magazines, Television, News Media, and Film.* Elizabeth, NJ: Hollym, 1990.

Connor, James. *The Sociology of Loyalty.* Canberra: Springer, 2010.

Crost, Lyn. *Honor by Fire: Japanese Americans at War in Europe and the Pacific.* Novato, CA: Presidio Press, 1994.

Daniels, Roger. *Asian America: Chinese and Japanese in the United States since 1850.* Seattle: University of Washington Press, 1988.

Daws, Gavan. *Prisoners of the Japanese: POWs of World War II in the Pacific.* New York: Quill William Morrow, 1994.

Dong, Stella. *Shanghai, 1842–1949: The Rise and Fall of a Decadent City.* New York: Harper Collins, 2000.

Dower, John W. *War without Mercy: Race and Power in the Pacific War.* New York: Pantheon Books, 1986.

Drea, Edward J. *Japan's Imperial Army: Its Rise and Fall, 1853–1945.* Lawrence: University Press of Kansas, 2009.

Druicker, William J. *Ho Chi Minh: A Life.* New York: Thenia, 2000.

Duus, Masayo. *Tokyo Rose: Orphan of the Pacific.* New York: Kodansha International/ USA, 1979.

Eckert, Carter J. et al. *Korea, Old and New: A History* (Cambridge, MA: Korea Institute, Harvard University, 1990.

Eckert, Carter J. et al. *Offspring of Empire: The Koch'ang Kims and the Colonial Origins of Korean Capitalism, 1876–1945.* Seattle: University of Washington Press, 1991.

Edwards, Louise. *Women Warriors and Wartime Spies of China.* Cambridge: Cambridge University Press, 2016.

Fletcher, George P. *Loyalty: An Essay on the Morality of Relationships.* New York: Oxford University Press, 1993.

Fogel, Joshua A. "'Shanghai-Japan': The Japanese Residents' Association of Shanghai." *Journal of Asian Studies* 59, no. 44 (November 2000): 927–45.

Fowler, Josephine. *Japanese and Chinese Immigrant Activists: Organizing in American and International Communist Movements, 1919–1933.* New Brunswick, NJ: Rutgers University Press, 2007.

Fuch, Lawrence. *Hawaii Pono: An Ethnic and Political History.* Honolulu: The Bess Press, 1961.

Fujioka, Shirō. *Ayumi no Ato: Hokubei Tairiku Nihonjin Kaitaku Monogatari* [Traces of Footsteps: The Story of the Japanese Pioneering on the North American Continent]. Los Angeles: Rafu Shimpō, 1957.

Fujitani, Takashi. "Right to Kill, Right to Make Live: Koreans as Japanese and Japanese as Americans During World War II." *Representations* 99 (Summer 2007): 13–39.

Glick, Clarence E. *Sojourners and Settlers: Chinese Migrants in Hawaii.* Honolulu: University of Hawai'i Press, 1980.

Gould, Randall. *Chungking Today.* Shanghai: The Mercury Press, 1941.

Haruna, Mikio. *Himitsu no Fairu: CIA no Tainichi Kōsaku* [Secret Files: CIA Operations against Japan]. Tokyo: Shinchō Bunko, 2004.

Hayashi, Brian Masaru. *Democratizing the Enemy: The Japanese American Internment.* Princeton, NJ: Princeton University Press, 2004.

Haynes, John Earl and Harvey Klehr. *In Denial: Historians, Communism & Espionage.* San Francisco: Encounter Books, 2003.

Horne, Gerald. *Race War!: White Supremacy and the Japanese Attack on the British Empire.* New York: New York University Press, 2004.

Hosokawa, Bill. *JACL in Quest of Justice: History of the Japanese American Citizens League.* New York: William Morrow and Company, 1982.

Howard, J. Woodford Jr. "Advocacy in Constitutional Choice: The Cramer Treason Case, 1942–1945." *American Bar Foundation Research Journal* 11, no. 3 (Summer 1986): 375–413.

Hsu, Madeline Y. *Dreaming of Gold, Dreaming of Home.* Stanford, CA: Stanford University Press, 2000.

Ichioka, Yuji. *The Issei: The World of the First-Generation Japanese Immigrants, 1885–1924.* New York: The Free Press, 1988.

Ichioka, Yuji. "The Meaning of Loyalty: The Case of Kazumaro Buddy Uno." *Amerasia Journal* 23, no. 3 (Winter 1997–1998): 44–71.

Jeffery, Keith. *MI6: The History of the Secret Intelligence Service, 1909–1949.* London: Bloomsbury, 2010.

Jeffrey-Jones, Rhodri. *The FBI: A History.* New Haven, CT: Yale University Press, 2007.

Kashima, Tetsuden. *Judgment without Trial: Japanese American Imprisonment during World War II.* Seattle: University of Washington Press, 2003.

Katō, Katsuji. *The Psychology of Oriental Religious Experience: A Study of Some Typical Experiences of Japanese Converts to Christianity.* Menasha, WI: George Banta Publishing Company, 1915.

Katz, Barry M. *Foreign Intelligence: Research and Analysis in the Office of Strategic Services, 1942–1945.* Cambridge, MA: Harvard University Press, 1989.

Keller, Simon. *The Limits of Loyalty.* Cambridge: Cambridge University Press, 2007.

Kim, Richard S. *The Quest for Statehood: Korean Immigrant Nationalism and U.S. Sovereignty, 1905–1945.* New York: Oxford University Press, 2011.

Kimura, Yukiko. *Issei: Japanese Immigrants in Hawaii.* Honolulu: University of Hawai'i Press, 1988.

Klehr, Harvey, and John Haynes. "Comintern's Open Secrets." In *The Cold War Vol. 4: Cold War Espionage and Spying,* edited by Lori Lyn Bogle, 295–301. New York: Routledge, 2001.

Knaefler, Tomi Kaizawa. *Our House Divided: Seven Japanese American Families in World War II.* Honolulu: University of Hawai'i Press, 1991.

Ko, Swan Sik (ed.). *Nationality and Internationality Law in Asian Perspective.* Dordrecht: Martinus Nijhoff Publishers, 1990.

Kotani, Ken. *Japanese Intelligence in World War II.* Translated by Chiharu Kotani. Oxford: Osprey Publishing, 2009.

Kuboshima, Seiichirō. *Hyōhaku: Nikkei Gakka Noda Hideo no Shōgai* [Bleaching: The Life of Japanese American Artist Hideo Noda]. Tokyo: Shinchōsha, 1990.

Kurashige, Lon. *Two Faces of Exclusion: The Untold History of Anti-Asian Racism in the United States.* Chapel Hill: University of North Carolina Press, 2016.

Kushner, Barak. *The Thought War: Japanese Imperial Propaganda.* Honolulu: University of Hawai'i Press, 2006.

Lai, Him Mark. *Chinese American Transnational Politics.* Urbana: University of Illinois Press, 2010.

Lai, Him Mark. "The Kuomintang in Chinese American Communities before World War II." In *Entry Denied: Exclusion and the Chinese Community in America, 1882–1924,* edited by Sucheng Chan, 170–212. Philadelphia: Temple University Press, 1991.

Lai, Him Mark. "Roles Played by Chinese in America during China's Resistance to Japanese Aggression during World War II." In *Chinese America: History and Perspectives,* edited by the Chinese Historical Society of America, 75-128.San Francisco: Chinese Historical Society of America, 1997.

Larson, Carlton F. W. "The Forgotten Constitutional Law of Treason and the Enemy Combatant Problem." *University of Pennsylvania Law Review* 154, no. 4 (April 2006): 863–926.

Leck, Greg. *Captives of Empire: The Japanese Internment of Allied Civilians in China, 1941–1945.* Bangor, PA: Shandy Press, 2007.

Lee, Chong-Sik. *The Politics of Korean Nationalism.* Berkeley: University of California Press, 1965.

Lee, Douglas W. "The Overseas Chinese Affairs Commission and the Politics of Patriotism in Chinese America in the Nanking Era, 1928–1945." *Annals of the Chinese Historical Society of the Pacific Northwest* (1984): 199–231.

Leek, J. H. "Treason and the Constitution." *Journal of Politics* 13, no. 4 (November 1951): 604–22.

Leith, Hal. *POWs of Japanese Rescued!: General J.M. Wainwright.* Victoria, Canada: Trafford Publishing, 2004.

Liang, Chin-tung. *General Stilwell in China, 1942–1944: The Full Story.* Shanghai: St. John's University Press, 1972.

Loureiro, Pedro A. "The Imperial Japanese Navy and Espionage: The Itaru Tachibana Case," *International Journal of Intelligence and Counterintelligence* 3, no. 1 (Spring 1989): 105-21.

_____. "Japanese Espionage and American Countermeasures in Pre-Pearl Harbor California," *American-East Asian Relations* 3, no. 3 (Fall 1994): 197-210.

Ma, L. Eve Armentrout. *Revolutionaries, Monarchists, and Chinatowns: Chinese Politics in the Americas and the 1911 Revolution.* Honolulu: University of Hawai'i Press, 1990.

Maga, Tim. *Judgment at Tokyo: The Japanese War Crimes Trials.* Lexington: University Press of Kentucky, 2001.

Martin, Thomas. "Silent Partners: SOE's French Indo-China Section, 1943–1945." *Modern Asian Studies* 34, no. 4 (2000): 943–76.

Matsumoto, Valerie J. *City Girls: The Nisei Social World in Los Angeles, 1920–1950.* New York: Oxford University Press, 2014.

McKeown, Adam. *Chinese Migrant Networks and Cultural Change: Peru, Chicago, and Hawaii, 1900–1936.* Chicago: University of Chicago Press, 2001.

McLynn, Frank. *The Burma Campaign: Disaster into Triumph, 1942–45.* London: Vintage Books, 2011.

McNaughton, James C. *Nisei Linguists: Japanese Americans in the Military Intelligence Service during World War II.* Washington, DC: US Department of Army, 2006.

McNaughton, James C., Kristen E. Edwards, and Jay M. Price. "'Incontestable Proof Will Be Exacted': Historians, Asian Americans, and the Medal of Honor." *The Public Historian* 24, no. 4 (Fall 2002): 11–33.

Mills, Francis B., Robert Mills, and John W. Brunner. *OSS Special Operations in China.* Williamstown, NJ: Phillips Publications, 2003.

Miyakawa, T. Scott Miyakawa. "Early New York Issei Founders of Japanese American Trade." In *East Across the Pacific: Historical and Sociological Studies of Japanese Immigration and Assimilation,* edited by Hilary T. Conroy and T. Scott Miyakawa, 156–86. Santa Barbara, CA: ABC Clio, 1972.

Motoe, Kunio. "Hideo Noda or the Unfinished 'Bridge'." In *Amerika ni Mananda Nihon no Gakatachi: Kuniyoshi, Shimizu, Ishigaki, Noda to Amerikan Shin Kaiga* [Japanese Artists Who Studied in America: Kuniyoshi, Shimizu, Ishigaki, and Noda and the American Scene Painting], edited by Kenji Adachi Kenji and Michiaki Kawakita, 187–90. Tokyo: Tokyo Kokuritsu Kindai Bijutsukan, 1982.

Myers, Ramon H., and Mark R. Peattie (eds.). *The Japanese Colonial Empire, 1895–1945.* Princeton, NJ: Princeton University Press, 1984.

Nee, Brett de Bary, and Victor Nee. "The Kuomintang in Chinatown." In *Counterpoint: Perspectives on Asian America,* edited by Emma Gee, 146–51. Los Angeles: Regents of the University of California and the Asian American Studies Center, 1976.

Nitz, Kiyoko Kurusu. "Independence without Nationalists? The Japanese and Vietnamese Nationalism during the Japanese Period, 1940–45." *Journal of Southeast Asian Studies* 15, no. 1 (March 1984): 108–33.

Nunnely, John, and Kazuo Tamayama. *Tales by Japanese Soldiers of the Burma Campaign, 1942–1945.* London: Cassell and Co., 2000.

Obi, Toshihito. *Gendaishi Shiryō: Soruge Jiken* [Modern History Sources: The Sorge Incident]. Vol. 3. Tokyo: Misuzu Shobo, 1962.

Oda, James. *Heroic Struggles of Japanese Americans: Partisan Fighters From America's Concentration Camps.* Anaheim, CA: KNI Inc., 1981.

Oda, James. *Secret Embedded in Magic Cables: The Story of a 101-Year-Old Japanese Communist Leader Who Served Japan, KGB and CIA.* Anaheim, CA: KNI Inc., 1993.

Odo, Franklin. *No Sword to Bury: Japanese Americans in Hawaii during World War II.* Philadelphia: Temple University Press, 2004.

Ogawa, Dennis M., and Evarts C. Fox Jr., "Japanese Internment and Relocation: The Hawaii Experience." In *Japanese Americans: From Relocation to Redress,* edited by Roger Daniels, Sandra C. Taylor, and Harry H. L. Kitano, 135–41. Salt Lake City: University of Utah, 1986.

Ogburn, Charlton Jr., *The Marauders*. New York: Harper & Brothers, 1959.

Ohta, Takashi, and Margaret Sperry. *The Golden Wind*. New York: C. Boni, 1929.

Okihiro, Gary Y. *Cane Fires: The Anti-Japanese Movement in Hawaii, 1865–1945*. Philadelphia: Temple University Press, 1991.

Okinawa Club of America. *History of the Okinawans in North America*. Translated by Ben Kobashigawa. Los Angeles: Resource Development and Publications, Asian American Studies Center, University of California, Los Angeles, and The Okinawa Club of America, 1988.

Oliver, Robert T. *Syngman Rhee and American Involvement in Korea, 1942–1960: A Personal Narrative*. Seoul: Panmun Book Co., 1978.

OSS Assessment Staff. *Assessment of Men: Selection of Personnel for the Office of Strategic Services*. New York: Rinehart & Co. Inc., 1948.

Packard, Captain Wyman H. *A Century of U.S. Naval Intelligence*. Washington, DC: Department of the Navy, 1996.

Pakula, Hannah. *The Last Empress: Madame Chiang Kai-Shek and the Birth of Modern China*. New York: Simon & Schuster, 2009.

Palmer, Brandon. *Fighting for the Enemy: Koreans in Japan's War, 1937–1945*. Seattle: University of Washington Press, 2013.

Patterson, Wayne. *The Ilse: First-Generation Korean Immigrants in Hawaii, 1903–1973*. Honolulu: University of Hawai'i Press, 2000.

Persico, Joseph E. *Roosevelt's Secret War: FDR and World War II Espionage*. New York: Random House Trade Paperbacks, 2002.

Phillips, R. T. "The Japanese Occupation of Hainan." *Modern Asian Studies* 14, no. 1 (1980): 93–109.

Porch, Douglas. *The French Secret Services: A History of French Intelligence from the Dreyfus Affair to the Gulf War*. New York: Farrar, Straus and Giroux, 1995.

Prange, Gordon W. *At Dawn We Slept: The Untold Story of Pearl Harbor*. New York: Penguin Books, 1981.

Prange, Gordon W., with Donald M. Goldstein and Katherine V. Dillon. *Target Tokyo: The Story of the Sorge Spy Ring*. New York: McGraw-Hill Book Co., 1984.

Price, Ernest Batson. *The Russo-Japanese Treaties of 1907–1916 Concerning Manchuria and Mongolia*. Baltimore: Johns Hopkins University Press, 1933.

Robertson, Eric. *The Japanese File: Pre-war Japanese Penetration in Southeast Asia*. Singapore: Heinemann Asia, 1979.

Robinson, Greg. "Nisei in Gotham: The JACD and Japanese Americans in 1940s New York." *Prospects: An Annual Journal of American Cultural Studies* 30 (2005): 581–95.

Romanus, Charles F., and Riley Sunderland. *Time Runs Out in CBI*. Vol. 9. Washington, DC: Office of the Chief of Military History, Department of the Army, 1959.

Roosevelt, Kermit. *The Overseas Target: War Report of the OSS*. New York: Walker and Company, 1976.

Ruoff, Kenneth J. *Imperial Japan at its Zenith: The Wartime Celebration of the Empire's 2,600th Anniversary*. Ithaca, NY: Cornell University Press, 2010.

Sacquety, Troy J. *The OSS in Burma: Jungle War against the Japanese*. Lawrence: University Press of Kansas, 2013.

Sadan, Mandy. *Being and Becoming Kachin: Histories Beyond the State in the Borderworlds of Burma*. New York: Oxford University Press, 2013.

Samuels, Richard J. *Special Duty: A History of the Japanese Intelligence Community*. Ithaca, NY: Cornell University Press, 2019.

Sawada, Mitziko. *Tokyo Life, New York Dreams: Urban Japanese Visions of America, 1890–1924*. Berkeley: University of California Press, 1996.

Schaller, Michael. "SACO! The United States Navy's Secret War in China." *Pacific Historical Review* 44, no. 4 (1975): 527–53.

Schonberger, Howard. "Dilemmas of Loyalty: Japanese Americans and the Psychological Warfare Campaigns of the Office of Strategic Services, 1943–45." *Amerasia Journal* 16, no. 1 (1990): 20–38.

Schonberger, Howard. *Japanizu Konekushon: Kaiunō Kei Sugahara Gaiden* [Japanese Connection: Kay Sugahara the Shipping Magnate]. Translated by Rinjirō Sodei. Tokyo: Bungei Shunjun, 1995.

Seymour, Susan C. *Cora Du Bois: Anthropologist, Diplomat, Agent*. Lincoln: University of Nebraska Press, 2015.

Shelp, Ron, and Al Ehrbar. *Fallen Giant: The Amazing Story of Hank Greenberg and the History of AIG*. Hoboken, NJ: John Wiley & Sons, 2006.

Shibutani, Tamotsu. *The Derelicts of Company K: A Sociological Study of Demoralization*. Berkeley: University of California Press, 1978.

Shin, Gi-Wook. *Ethnic Nationalism in Korea: Genealogy, Politics, and Legacy*. Stanford, CA: Stanford University Press, 2006.

Shin Sekai Asahi Nenkan [The New World Sun Yearbook]. San Francisco: Shin Sekai Shimbunsha, 1941.

Singlaub, John K. Singlaub, with Malcolm McConnell. *Hazardous Duty: An American Soldier in the Twentieth Century*. New York: Summit Books, 1991.

Shklar, Judith N. "Obligation, Loyalty, Exile." *Political Theory* 21, no. 2 (May 1993): 181–97.

Smith, Bradley F. *The Shadow Warriors: O.S.S. and the Origins of the C.I.A.* New York: Basic Books, 1983.

Smith, R. Harris. *OSS: The Secret History of America's First Central Intelligence Agency*. Berkeley: University of California Press, 1972.

Soley, Lawrence C. *Radio Warfare: OSS and CIA Subversive Propaganda*. New York: Praeger, 1989.

Stafford, David. *Camp X*. New York: Dodd, Mead & Co. 1987.

Stephan, John J. *Hawaii under the Rising Sun: Japan's Plans for Conquest after Pearl Harbor*. Honolulu: University of Hawai'i Press, 1984.

Stephan, John J. "Hijacked by Utopia." *Amerasia Journal* 23, no. 3 (Winter 1997–1998): 1–42.

Streifer, Bill. "Operation Cardinal: So You Must Be a Spy." *American Intelligence Journal* 29 (2011): 75–79.

Streifer, Bill. "The OSS in Korea: Operation Eagle." *American Intelligence Journal* 30, no. 1 (2012): 33–38.

Takatsuna, Hirofumi (ed.). *Senji Shanghai, 1937–1945* [Wartime Shanghai, 1937–1945]. Tokyo: Kenbun Shuppan, 2005.

Tamura, Eileen. *Americanization, Acculturation, and Ethnic Identity: The Nisei Generation in Hawaii*. Urbana: University of Illinois Press, 1994.

Tang, James T. H. "From Empire Defence to Imperial Retreat: Britain's Postwar China Policy and the Decolonization of Hong Kong." *Modern Asian Studies* 28, no. 2 (1994): 317–37.

Thai, Philip. "Law, Sovereignty, and the War on Smuggling in Coastal China, 1928–1937." *Law and History Review* 34, no.1 (February 2016): 75–114.

Theoharris, Athan. *Chasing Spies: How the FBI Failed in Counterintelligence But Promoted the Politics of McCarthyism in the Cold War Years.* Chicago: Ivan R. Dee, 2002.

Thomas, Martin. "Silent Partners: SOE's French Indo-China Section, 1943–1945." *Modern Asian Studies* 34, no. 4 (2000): 943–76.

Todd, Ann. *OSS Operation Black Mail: One Woman's Covert War against the Imperial Japanese Army.* Annapolis, MD: Naval Institute Press, 2017.

Troy, Thomas F. *Donovan and the CIA: A History of the Establishment of the Central Intelligence Agency.* Frederick, MD: University Publications of America, 1981.

Tsang, Steve. *A Modern History of Hong Kong.* London: I. B. Tauris & Co. Ltd., 2004.

United Okinawan Association of Hawaii. *Uchinanchu: A History of Okinawans in Hawaii.* Honolulu: Ethnic Studies Program, University of Hawai'i, 1981.

Usami, Shō. *Sayonara Nihon: Ehon Sakka, Yashima Tarō to Mitsuko no Bōmei* [Farewell, Japan: The Political Exile of Picture Book Artist Tarō and Mitsuko Yashima]. Tokyo: Nihon Tosho Senta, 1994.

Wakeman, Frederic Jr. *Spymaster: Dai Li and the Chinese Secret Service.* Berkeley: University of California Press, 2003.

Waller, Douglas. *Wild Bill Donovan: The Spymaster Who Created The OSS and Modern American Espionage.* New York: Free Press, 2011.

Wasserstein, Bernard. *Secret War in Shanghai: An Untold Story of Espionage, Intrigue, and Treason in World War II.* Boston: Houghton Mifflin, 1999.

Watabe, Tomiya. *"Roy" Nosaka Sanzō Setsu ni Ketsugi wo Tsuketa gojūnenme no Jijitsu: Soruge Jiken de Gokushita Gaka Miyagi Yotoku wo Nihon ni Hakkenshita Roi to Yobareru Otoko wa Nikkei Kyōsantoin Kimoto Denichi da!* [The "Roy" Sanzō Nosaka Explanation Resolved in the Fiftieth Year of the Truth: The One Who Sent the Artist Yotoku Miyagi to Prison for the Sorge Affair was the Japanese American Communist Party Member Denichi Kimoto!], 1–24. Tokyo: Shakai Undō Shiryō Senta, 2001.

Webster, Donovan. *The Burma Road: The Epic Story of the Chinese-Burma-India Theater in World War II.* Waterville, ME: Thorndike Press, 2003.

Weinstein, Allen, and Alexander Vassiliev. *The Haunted Wood: Soviet Espionage in America—the Stalin Era.* New York: Random House, 1999.

Winkler, Alan M. *The Politics of Propaganda: The Office of War Information, 1942–1945.* New Haven, CT: Yale University Press, 1978.

Wong, K. Scott. *Americans First: Chinese Americans and the Second World War.* Cambridge, MA: Harvard University Press, 2005.

Wong, K. Scott, and Sucheng Chan (eds.). *Claiming America: Constructing Chinese American Identities during the Exclusion Era.* Philadelphia: Temple University Press, 1998.

Yamamoto, Eriko. "Miya Sannomiya Kikuchi: A Pioneer Nisei Woman's Life and Identity." *Amerasia Journal* 23 no. 3 (Winter 1997): 72–101.

Yamamoto, Taketoshi. *Buraku Puropaganda: Bōraku no Rajio* [Black Propaganda: Strategic Radio]. Tokyo: Iwanami Shoten, 2002.

Yasutake, Rumi. *Transnational Women's Activism: The United States, Japan, and Japanese Immigrant Communities in California, 1859–1920.* New York: New York University Press, 2004.

Yeh, Wen-hsin (ed.). *Wartime Shanghai.* New York: Routledge, 1998.

Yim, Sun Bin. "The Social Structure of Korean Communities in California, 1903–1920." In *Labor Immigration under Capitalism: Asian Workers in the United States Before World War II,* edited by Lucie Cheng and Edna Bonacich, 515–48. Berkeley: University of California Press, 1984.

Yoo, David K. *Contentious Spirits: Religion in Korean American History, 1903–1945.* Stanford, CA: Stanford University Press, 2010.

Yu, Henry. *Thinking Orientals: Migration, Contact, and Exoticism in Modern America.* New York: Oxford University Press, 2001.

Yu, Maochun. *OSS in China: Prelude to Cold War.* New Haven, CT: Yale University Press, 1996.

Yu, Renqiu. *To Save China, To Save Ourselves: The Chinese Hand Laundry Alliance of New York.* Philadelphia: Temple University Press, 1992.

Yung, Judy. *Unbound Feet: A Social History of Chinese Women in San Francisco.* Berkeley: University of California Press, 1995.

Zaibei Nihonjinkai. *Zaibei Nihonjinshi* [History of the Japanese in America]. San Francisco: Zaibei Nihonjinkai, 1940.

Zhong guo Kexue yuan Shanghai Jing ji Yan jiu suo [Chinese Academy of Sciences, Shanghai Institute of Economics], ed. *Nan Yang Xiong Di Gong Si Shi Liao* [Nanyang Brothers Tobacco Company Historical materials]. Shanghai: Shanghai Ren Min Chu Ban She, 1958.

INDEX

For the benefit of digital users, indexed terms that span two pages (e.g., 52–53) may, on occasion, appear on only one of those pages.